I Meant To Be A Lawyer is not only a personal memoir but also a fascinating history of the social and business behaviour of the second half of the twentieth century. The education of talented women mimicked that provided in male public schools, but women's educational choices were restricted because only three out of twenty-one colleges at Cambridge admitted women and the position at Oxford was only marginally better. After reading law at Newnham College, Janet Neel was turned down on the specific grounds of her sex by the four largest City law firms and needed help to get her training to qualify as a solicitor. She entered a Civil Service where only about 3% of women reached the career grade often because the Service in the 1970s was only prepared to offer limited flexible or part time employment to the top Administrative Grade - though Janet helped to change that, pushed as she says by better women. In the 1980s when she moved to work in the City, Janet routinely found herself the only woman on any private sector Board.

In addition to careers in the Civil Service and merchant banking, Janet Neel founded and financed two successful London restaurants, served as a Governor of the BBC and became a successful novelist. Her debut crime novel *Death's Bright Angel* won the Crime Writers' Association's John Creasey Award in 1988.

In 2000 she was made Baroness Cohen of Pimlico and sits in the House of Lords as a Labour peer with a particular interest in education and industry.

I Meant To Be A Lawyer:
A Family Memoir

JANET COHEN

Ostara Publishing

Ostara Publishing 2019

Copyright © Janet Cohen 2019

Cased edition ISBN 9781909619586

Paperback edition ISBN 9781909619616

A CIP reference is available from the British Library

Ostara Publishing
13 King Coel Road
Colchester
CO3 9AG
www.ostarapublishing.co.uk

CONTENTS

ACKNOWLEDGEMENT

This memoir would not have seen the light of day without the assistance of Rosemary Smith, who typed it several times, deciphering my handwriting, and also did the job usually done by a copy editor, preventing repetition in the text and pointing out internal contradictions. She postponed her own retirement to finish the job and I owe her most grateful thanks.

FOREWORD

I had the Law in my sights from about sixteen years old, and I intended to be a barrister. I qualified as a solicitor when I was twenty-five, meaning to work in one of the big commercial law firms for a large salary, in the first of many deviations from the path on which my feet had been set.

I have written the story for my own family, but also in the hope and expectation that other women who have changed direction several times will find it familiar and comforting. I hope also that younger women will understand that they too may have to deviate but that it will all come right in the end.

Chapter 1

MY FAMILY: PARENTS AND GRANDPARENTS

I was born in the early hours of July 4 1940 in Oxford, my parents' first child and the first grandchild of both families. My mother was in Oxford because all the London hospital beds were being kept for emergencies and the victims of bombing raids. The skies were full of fighter aeroplanes, but my mother said that she was too busy to notice the life and death struggle for the country taking place over the South Coast. My father had appeared after work on July 3, irritable from the journey from London, and, meeting my mother padding down a corridor, groaning, had asked why she had not managed to have that baby yet. She had responded to this graceless enquiry by bursting into tears and I arrived several hours later. My father wasn't at the birth – men weren't then – but I have his letter to his mother, my grandmother, written the next morning, saying that I was Janet, Jinty for short, and that I had the Neel cleft in my chin. The letter made no reference to the aeroplanes either. That is history for you, people too busy having babies and writing to their mothers to mention little things like a World War and their country being in danger of invasion.

My father, George Edric Neel, 'Bin' for short, was born on November 5 1914, the eldest son of George Henry Neel, who must have been born in 1885 because I remember his 90th birthday in 1975, at which he spoke for one and a half hours about his life and times. His elder sister, my great-aunt Phillida, an immensely capable woman, snorted, audibly, with impatience and exasperation throughout. George Henry Neel, apart from the fierce Phillida, had another older sibling, Charles (Charlie) Neel.

Of the three Neels, Phillida was childless, and Charles, who was sent to Canada to try and recover from alcoholism, fathered two children, Nairn and Lawrence. Nairn I knew; she kindly had

George Henry Neel ('Gratapa') aged 90 in 1982.

me to stay in my gap year, part of which I spent in Montreal, but she had no children. Lawrence, who grew irises and had his own nursery garden both here and in Canada, had two children, Iris and Myrtle, but the line ends there; neither of them has children. George Henry had three children, my father George Edric Neel born in 1914, my uncle Stephen John Clairvaux Neel born in 1915 and my aunt Jocelyn, always called Jill. She was the youngest, born in 1920 and the only girl.

The history of these three siblings is a tragedy. Two of them, my father and Jill, had their lives blighted by illness; my father died aged 37 of Hodgkin's Lymphoma in 1952, and Jill, following crippling rheumatoid arthritis which fell on her in her twenties, died of kidney failure in 1972 aged 52. Stephen was killed in Hong Kong in 1960, aged 45, in a riding accident. Dad and Stephen both died before their mother, my grandmother Grandy, as we all

2

called her, who died in 1962, and all three died before my grandfather Gratapa, who died in the late 1970s. It is, even at this distance of time, unimaginable, and writing it down doesn't make it any better.

My Neel grandfather as a matter of record never worked at all. He was diagnosed with a heart murmur at 20, but lived to 94. Throughout much of his married life, there was only a small income from a family trust and Grandy took in lodgers to make ends meet. My mother was deeply critical of her father-in-law, she thought (correctly) that the heart murmur was not a problem and that he could have worked and saved Grandy, whom she loved, from quite such hard work. But his children loved him. My father always said it had been a continuing pleasure to have a kindly father who read to him and his siblings and played games with them. I was of my mother's opinion in this as in much else and thought Gratapa could have had a proper job. Now that I have a daughter in her thirties with children and a husband who is making a career as a composer I have understood that this pattern – repeated in many thirty-plus households with children – in which the young men take an equal share in child-raising and are not out all and every day earning a lot of money in return for long hours at an office has huge advantages for the children. They see a lot of their fathers, who become imaginative friends and role models, and they have two parents rather than a mother and a hard-pressed father who arrives home too exhausted to be bothered with them.

Whatever the benefit he felt he derived from having a male parent at home my own father did not follow that model. He did insist on teaching us all to read, at the earliest possible age, on the grounds that no child was civilised until it could read. I was reading at three, although the boys were slower, as boys tend to be. But we saw very little of Dad when we were small, and his focus was on building a successful business.

He must always have been a difficult child. He was educated at The Hall and then at Westminster School but he left home for several months at sixteen to live with a married woman neighbour in Thurlow Road who encouraged him to paint. He could draw, he did lots of woodcuts, often of the Fen churches. He went to Germany *en famille* at seventeen and spoke fluent German. Only a few years ago I met a German woman whose face lit up at his name and called him 'Der Bin' and openly examined me to see how the glamorous Bin had produced this hard-driven, middle-aged person who looked so like him. He was musical, he played the piano, badly but enthusiastically, and sang to himself – the German woman remembered him doing it, as I do.

He went up to Magdalene, Cambridge, in 1933, read architecture and got Firsts all the way through. He always said his maths was poor and it is a matter of family record that he had to take the professional finals twice (in 1938), a disgrace for one so clever.

In 1938, he volunteered for the Army, wanting to find a commission in the upcoming war, rather than sweating it out as a private soldier. He had met my mother by then and they knew they wanted to marry. He was rejected out of hand and told he could never be too far from an X-ray machine. My mother said that a precise diagnosis was neither offered nor did they ask for one, yet Hodgkin's Lymphoma was known and presumably could have been diagnosed. When I was adult I pressed my mother as to what they had both known and she said that no one's life looked very secure with a war coming and at least she knew Dad would not be called up. I believe they knew the truth and so did Grandy. My Budge grandmother, my mother's mother, always maintained that she had asked Mrs Neel – as she called her always – about Dad's health and that she implied that all was well. What would I have done in my Neel grandmother's place with a war in prospect and a son I loved? I don't know, but it was a decision with far-reaching consequences, and Muttie, as we called my Budge grandmother, had some right to the grudge she bore Grandy.

Beyond Grandfather Neel's generation it is a blank. My Neel great-grandparents must have been well enough off to buy a lease for my grandfather on a Hampstead house, to export great-uncle Charlie to Canada and to educate great-aunt Phillida, whom I knew well. She was a beauty but the young man she was to marry died in 1910 of consumption and left her all his money. After the First World War, in which several young men whom she might have married died, she married General Hobbs, much older than she, and became stepmother to Carleton Hobbs, the first radio Sherlock Holmes, not much her junior and deeply fond of her, as were his children. She rather disliked both her brothers and in the middle of my grandfather's ninetieth birthday speech in 1975 she observed to me that she had always considered brothers extremely tiresome, did I not agree? She ended her life living alone but with a devoted woman friend whom she met every day.

4

She lived in a Kensington mansion flat and the rules of engagement were that her friend rang up every day, and if she did not get an answer she let herself in with her own key. This arrangement worked perfectly; Aunt Phil was ninety-odd when she fell and broke a hip one evening and could not reach the phone. She arranged herself as best she might and waited in perfect tranquillity for her friend to turn up the next day, which she did. Aunt Phil, hip repaired (not replaced), died at home, still living in the flat, some years later. I think about that a lot; it would have been easy to turn her face to the wall but she would never have done that.

I remember her in cameo from the funeral of Aunt Jill, my aunt and her niece, in 1972. I stood beside Aunt Phil, and at the grim moment when the coffin was lowered into the grave, she coughed, put a handkerchief to her mouth and took a step forward towards the grave. I was on one side of her and brother Alexander on the other, and both of us started forward, but she checked herself, stepped back, put away the handkerchief and stood solidly on her heels, the handsome, lined face moving as she swallowed. Just for a moment there it had got too much for her as well it might; the last of her brother's children gone. Ally supported her gently away; whatever her views on boys, and tiresomeness thereof, she was fond of him. She had had him to stay four nights a week for a whole term when he was sixteen, with a shattered kneecap, so that he could limp down to a bus to get to the Lycée Française and not need unaffordable taxis to get him back to Hampstead every day. They remained friends, and he loved her.

They were a good-looking lot, my Neel forebears, with the high Norman brow arch and the long Norman nose. The family tradition has it that an ancestor came with the Conqueror in 1066 and, sure enough, a Neel de St Servin is listed in his train, one of the anonymous straight-nosed knights under a helmet on the Bayeux Tapestry.

Dad's mother, my grandmother Gladys Fenwick, came of another dysfunctional family. She was born in about 1891 and she was an only child. Of her mother, my great-grandmother, I know only the single fact that she managed to divorce my great-grandfather – who was an alcoholic – in the 1880s. She married again, a widower, and it was a success; there were older children who were always kind to Grandy. My great-grandmother or my alcoholic great-grandfather must have been a redhead because Grandy was Titian red until her death in her early seventies. She was tiny, standing at under 4 foot 10 with brittle chicken-bones, but she gave birth to my father who was 6 foot 2, Stephen 6 foot or just under, and Jill at 5 foot 6, so it was clear that she herself had starved as a child, like many children of alcoholic parents.

She went up to Newnham in 1909, encouraged by her stepfather, and counted the year she had there as one of the happiest of her life. The family version is that her health failed, that the climate of the Fens brought on bronchitis and rheumatism. In 1913 like my mother she chose to marry a man who would not be called up, a father for her children who did not drink and would not be asked to fight in a war.

It is possible that the terrible ill health in my father's generation may be a result of having a mother who had been starved as a child. Grandy herself always put it down to having made them travel right across London to school, and she and my own mother were to support my decision to stay at a school no more than two miles from home, accessible by bicycle.

Grandy was much loved; she had five boys as grandchildren and me, the eldest and the only girl, and she had highly individual relationships with us all. Her sons and daughter were also devoted but it was a hard life. She died early and we believe meant to go when she did. It was 1962, I was working at summer camp in the USA, and Mum, alerted by some instinct, went round for tea and found her in bed with pneumonia, semi-delirious, being read to by Gratapa, who thought she had a minor cold. Mum called an ambulance, and Grandy opened her eyes and said, in terrible reproach: 'Mary. Don't take the nails out of my coffin.' The 17-year-old Alexander came over to help, and Grandy thought he was his father, one of her lost sons, asked him where he had been, and died holding his hand.

She had seen her second son Stephen die as well as my father. In his early forties, having made a lot of money as secretary to the Green Island Cement Company in Hong Kong he had decided to become a doctor, presumably as a reaction to his two sick siblings, and had started his training. He left a small fortune, divided orthodoxly between his surviving sister and his dead brother's family (Grandy had organised *that* too).

Grandy looked after us when Mum was ill in 1944/45 during

6

the war. She lived with us in Thurlow Road, in a house she knew well, with an ancient nanny summoned from retirement during the week. It is the only serious mistake I knew that admirable woman make – and it was deeply damaging – but neither she nor the retired nanny paid attention to the new baby Alexander, who lay neglected in his cot, while she confined her efforts to me, then aged four and a half, and Giles, just under two. When I look at what else was going on, I have to remember that Gratapa would have been helpless without her, across London in Albany, and that her treasured daughter Jill, crippled by rheumatoid arthritis, had just had a second child, my cousin Hugh, and, with the baby and an elder child, must have been as desperate as we were. None of it bears thinking about, the strain, the difficulty, the sheer shortage of help and food, and a war all around them.

My mother was born Mary Isabel Budge in Wales on September 1 1914, second child of Douglas Budge and Alexandra Jeanette Macdonald. I know more about this side of the family; it is less dysfunctional, more yeoman prosperous, and more dynamic than the Neel/Fenwick side. And there are many more of them.

My grandmother 'Muttie' Macdonald was born in 1884. Her father, my great-grandfather James Macdonald, was a Writer to the Signet, a prosperous partner in Morton Smart Macdonald and Prosser. He and his wife had eleven children in fifteen years from 1872 to 1887; five boys and six girls, and of the girls Maribel, the third youngest, died in her teens. My grandmother looked after her, and this early death can only have added to a naturally depressive temperament.

They were a long-lived lot but she was the only one of the remaining five girls to marry. My guess is that Great-grandfather Macdonald in his prime was an Edinburgh patriarch for whose daughters no one was good enough. He was only outfaced by my Budge great-grandfather, a stiff-necked Highland farmer, who went to see him when he sought to reject my grandfather as a suitor and came home with agreement to the marriage. My Budge grandfather would have been 28 and a qualified mining engineer with a good job at this point in 1911. And Muttie was one of the youngest and, no doubt, even a patriarchal will was losing its force, or Great-grandfather may belatedly have come to realise that five grown daughters at home might not be altogether comfortable, or reflect well on his position in society. So Muttie escaped to marriage in Wales in 1912, and the youngest, Auntie Muriel, escaped even further, after the Great War, to London and a job as secretary to the editor of *Punch* for many years in the 1920s and 1930s, but she did not marry, being of the generation where the men she might have married died in France and Belgium. Aunt Flora had wanted to go and drive an ambulance in France in 1914, but family legend has it that Great-grandfather Macdonald, arm thrown dramatically over the mantelpiece of the principal fireplace, tears pouring down his cheeks into the patriarchal beard, enquired 'Have ye not been happy at home, Flora?', and there the matter rested. Great-grandfather died in 1914, his coffin carried to the grave by five sons and his son-in-law, my grandfather G. D. Budge.

In 1954, when Mum took us all up to Edinburgh with our bicycles for a youth hostelling trip, the three eldest Macdonald women were all alive in their seventies and early eighties, all rather stout, all living together in a grand Edinburgh house with a maid, on the Macdonald Trust monies, waiting their turn to be 'Miss Macdonald', the courtesy title of the eldest daughter; the younger siblings would be Misses Jean, Flora ... and so on until another death brought them the coveted title of Miss Macdonald. I remember Uncle Eric and I know his only daughter my cousin Ann Fraser well. We also met Uncle Ralph and Uncle John on a visit but the other uncles were gone, as are all my grandmother's generation.

There are no Macdonald boys to carry on the name. Ken and Don Macdonald, two out of the three boys among the children of the five sons, were killed within a month of each other in August and September 1940 flying Spitfires, having had the minimum training which was about nine weeks at that time. They were in their early twenties. There are several female descendants here, in Scotland and the USA, all of whom I know, plus some in New Zealand, daughters and granddaughter of Ralph Macdonald, who was seriously injured in World War I and sent to recover in the pure air. One of Ralph's grandchildren is Sir Paul Beresford MP, who came to the UK and ended up in Parliament. I joined him rather later and we both sit on the Joint Audit Committee of both Houses.

My Budge grandparents had four daughters and eleven grandchildren. My mother and Hope both had two sons and a daughter but Hope's son Rory died of encephalitis as a four-year-old in 1950 en route for India where his father was posted. Grizel had three daughters, one of whom, Lucinda, died as a baby in Uganda, and Jane, the oldest, was unable to have her own children and adopted two, David and Alexandra (named for Muttie, as is my brother Alexander). So in this generation, while there are no Macdonald boys, I have four boy and five girl first cousins, all of us now in our sixties and seventies, plus a raft of second cousins. In 2018 I gave an excellent party at the House of Lords for my own generation and the next one down, now in their 30s, 40s and 50s. Forty people came and there would have been 80 if everyone had been able to join us, and that is without counting the generation beyond them.

The other successful, upwardly mobile family in this history turns out to be the Budges, my mother's father's family. They were Orcadians, and the Budge name lives on in Hoy and the south Orcadian islands. Some of them left in the early nineteenth century for the easier lands of Caithness, on the east coast of mainland Scotland, and six brothers called Budge are recorded in 1848 as living in the flat farming country of Sutherland, with the usual names used in Scots families, two generations before anyone I had access to. But a son of one of them came further down the coast to Easter Rairichie, near Nigg on the north side of the Firth of Forth, and took on two small hill farms bordered by the sea cliffs on one side. He arrived there in the 1860s in time to father five sons, among them my grandfather George Douglas Budge, who was the second son, an older boy called Jock, who died in the First World War, and Joseph Budge, who inherited the farm.

My grandparents married in 1912 and produced four daughters: Jane, b. 1913 (d. 1964); my mother, b. September 1 1914 (d. 2003); Hope, b. 1918 (d. 2009); and Grizel, b. 1921 (d. 2017). My grandmother desperately wanted a son and I daresay my grandfather did too, because the Budges ran to boys and he was a Scot. Muttie was said to have been ill and bedridden, 'womb held in with a ring', over the whole of her pregnancy with Grizel. She was in faraway South Wales, where my Budge grandfather was working as a mining engineer for the Marquess of Bute. He detested the easy-going, deceitful Welsh (as he saw them) with a passion, reserving particular hatred for Lloyd George and all his works.

A true exile, he died in his late seventies in 1956 from lung cancer like the miners he managed. He had never lived in Scotland since his twenties, but his Will asserts that he died domiciled in Scotland and that it was to be interpreted in accordance with the laws of that country. He went for his holidays every year to Dornoch for six weeks, and, apart from an expedition to France to bring back his elder brother's body in 1915, he had never been abroad.

Both these grandparents had the Scots' respect for education and considered any that might be available in rural Wales (the tiny village of Rhiwderin, six miles from Newport and ten from Cardiff) hopelessly inadequate and probably dangerous. So they hired a Froebel governess for their daughters, to add to the four indoor staff, two men for the Home Farm and the driver for my grandfather. They were living on one man's professional salary and a tiny allowance for Muttie from the Macdonalds, but in rural Wales it apparently financed a big household and my mother and her sisters considered themselves to have been extremely privileged. Aunt Grizel told me recently however that the finances were always a bit precarious until the death of childless Uncle Wheems, one of my grandfather's brothers, which enabled a good deal of needed investment.

But here again, illness and separation combined to cause distress down the generations. Muttie as an adult was a depressive and probably always had been. A clever woman, she had a poor education, culminating in a domestic science course at Atholl Crescent, the well-known Edinburgh finishing school. She did well there, only failing one cookery examination because she had used nineteen spoons to make one dish (and in this I am her true inheritor). She was also asthmatic, from her teens, and was regularly incapacitated by the disease, so there was physical illness there as well as the depression. My mother (the beautiful Jane died in 1964 from cancer of the ovaries, so she is not here to ask) said that the elder daughters were oppressed by Muttie's depression from early childhood. I do know for myself that Muttie guarded against depression and the isolation from family and friends and society (she didn't find the Welsh congenial either) by engaging in obsessive/compulsive activity. She bought and labelled things madly – I had until very recently a linen tea towel labelled in her hand 'Fruit Room – one of 4'. I have difficulty imagining a fruit room, never mind buying and labelling linen for it, and ultimately I threw it away because the very idea was depressing me.

She did war work like every other woman of her age and class from 1914 to 1918 and again from 1939 to 1945. And, like my own mother and most unlike many other mothers of that period, she had her husband with her. Mining engineer was a reserved occupation, vitally needed to get the coal cut and keep the wheels of industry turning. My grandfather managed Cardiff Collieries for the Bute estate (the Marquess of Bute owned much of South Wales) through two wars, ending his career sorting out pensions for the National Coal Board in 1949.

He was a lively chap, my grandfather, with his full share of the Budge brains. They are Celts, with bulging foreheads and bright blue eyes and of course the red hair that pops up on one in every generation. He was, my mother said, timid, like my grandmother; neither of them knew how to ask for what they wanted but both, being proud people, fumed with distress when their deserts were not recognised, as how could they be in rural, hostile, deceitful South Wales? A sad place to be, too, in the depression of the 1920s and 1930s, when all the coal anyone was going to buy could be hacked out of the deep narrow mines by early afternoon, leaving my grandfather and his labour force free by 4 p.m. and, in the case of the manual labour force, much less well paid than they would be during the Second World War, or had been in the First World War.

Life went further wrong for Muttie over children. She had a bad pregnancy with her third daughter, but they decided to soldier on in the hope of producing the longed-for Budge son. As a precaution she decided that the two eldest, active, demanding children must go away to school. Not just any school, or one close enough to visit easily, but back to Edinburgh, to be boarders – at seven and eight years old – at St George's, loosely cared for by her elder sisters who did not want the responsibility for two little girls, even though they were blood kin. It was, I think, then that the depression from which she suffered fell on my own mother. She did not give way or, as she would have put it, *wallow* in it; she was a competent small girl and she fought, but all her life she hated and felt terribly threatened by depression and by people suffering from it. Mum tried to tell me what it was like; she and Jane felt exiled, rejected, dismissed from their warm home to cold Edinburgh for some reason she could not understand. The

11

exile went on, past any time when it could have been necessary, long past the time when my Aunt Grizel was born in 1921 and it must have become plain that my grandmother would not be able to sustain another pregnancy. I would guess that my grandfather would have rested content but that Muttie felt a failure if she could not produce a boy.

Finally however, four years later, the two older girls got home, back with their parents, in 1924. They were sent to the junior part of Malvern Girls' School, some three hours' drive away, as boarders, but at least it wasn't distant, cold, aunt-ridden Edinburgh.

Mary Budge (Mum), left, born 1ˢᵗ September 1914
and Jane Budge, born 1913.

My mother was bullied at Malvern in the junior forms by the daughters of Birmingham, the confident strident daughters of the steel magnates who persecuted prissy Scottish children. But as she worked her way up the school she was happier; she was really clever, a brilliant linguist, and flourished with good teaching. They had an inspired dance teacher and Mum became a strong dancer, a talent which bypassed me but appears again in our daughter Isobel. Jane and she both got into university easily, Jane to Girton College, Cambridge, and Mum to Somerville College, Oxford. Mum told me that she decided that there was no way she was going to join the dazzling Jane at Cambridge, particularly since they would have been in the same year because Jane, although eighteen months older, had lost a year to scarlet fever as a sixteen-year-old.

But their lives were still made a misery by their mother's depression. They knew, Mum told me, all the time that there was an unhappy mother at home waiting to pounce. And it was an active, aggressive depression, not a quiet, timid, resigned illness, bravely borne. Mum described going back to Wales to escort her mother to the school prize-giving for one of her two equally clever younger sisters, and having to force Muttie out of bed at the hotel near the school. She got her mother up and to the prizegiving – Mum would perhaps herself have been twenty-one – but spent the day and the week after choked with rage. And guilt.

Mum reached Oxford in October 1933, aged 19. It must have been a great moment; unlike me she had no exemplar, but she and her sister Jane were home free, or so they must have felt. I know a bit about Mum's career at Oxford; she was so excited by being there, so overwhelmed with joy at having finally, definitely left behind her depressed mother, that she neither wrote nor communicated in any way with her worried parents for four weeks. Unable to bear it any more, Muttie braved the difficulties of the long-distance telephone (you had to go through the operator) and got through to the austere, scholarly Principal of Somerville who wearily summoned my mother and said: 'Miss Budge, your family seem to be concerned that they have not heard from you and have *telephoned me*. Will you please be in touch with them at once.' One feels that a modern Principal might have enquired whether my mother was all right, was she well, was she happy, was she managing? As it happens she didn't need to; Mum was chagrined that her mother had bothered The Principal, but she was wildly, utterly happy, having found the life she wanted and needed. She had started to go out with John Peck – a clever, smart, attractive undergraduate, son of an Oxford academic family – and fallen in love with him, and his academic mother, whom she called Tante, a widow who liked girls and had just the one gifted boy chick. Tante was not depressed, she was independent and her house was a great centre for the young. My mother had moved, in one step, from a restricted, quiet, country existence with three sisters and parents who felt themselves exiles to a protected environment presided over by a clever woman who was

13

absolutely secure in her background – no exile anxiety there – in a house where there were brothers and lovers as well as sisters.

She had been superbly taught at Malvern and her male colleagues were in the main not up to her weight intellectually. The clever and the stupid products of the public school system alike reached Oxford or Cambridge because there were only a few places for clever girls and competition from grammar school boys was still limited, and that did not change until well after the Second World War. Mum told us, when we reached years of discretion, that she had done no work at all for the first two and a half years of her degree course (Oxford examines only once in the three years). In terror, she worked flat out for the last six months and got a Second Class degree, creditable enough, but to the end of her life she had a recurring nightmare of taking her Oxford finals and not being able to answer any of the questions.

The affair with John Peck ended somewhere in Mum's second year, and she was very unhappy, pined and lost weight. John went on after his degree to join the Foreign Office, to be one of Winston Churchill's wartime private secretaries, and end a distinguished career as our Ambassador to Ireland in the 1960s. Not long after splitting up with him, Mum journeyed over to Cambridge to see Aunt Jane. She was escorted by Stephen Neel, who was going over to see his brother Edric, then reading architecture, well on his way to a good First Class degree at Magdalene. It was after that meeting that my father told his brother Stephen that he had met the girl he expected to marry. My mother did not immediately feel the same but she was glad to be courted and they took it in turns to travel between the two universities for the rest of their joint university careers.

Mum came down from Oxford in 1936, with the aforesaid Second Class degree, and crashed to earth. In those far-off days, the Civil Service, then one of the very few providers of proper graduate-level jobs for women, did not need to recruit every year, and there was no intake in 1936. My mother could not get a graduate-level job anywhere else, so fell back, sadly, on a secretarial course funded by her long-suffering father. Aunt Jane, coming down from a dazzlingly successful social career at Cambridge in the same year, also found herself on the secretarial course. The sisters lived in a dim residential hotel in Bina Gardens, South Kensington, also paid for by Grandpa Budge, while my father, reading for the Diploma in architecture he needed, perforce lived in the family house in Hampstead. Grandpa Budge had a proper managerial job that enabled him to support four expensive daughters, whereas my Neel grandfather could only offer the family roof over the heads of his three children. My Budge grandfather not unnaturally disapproved of my Neel grandfather and did not want my mother to marry into what he saw as an unsatisfactory family.

My mother had her doubts too. She told me that Dad, although she loved him, was really quite uncivilised; rude, arrogant, less than clean. She had bravely to insist he changed the sheets before she would consider going to bed with him, and she shared Grandpa Budge's view of Gratapa, nor ever changed her mind about him. But she was infinitely reassured by Grandy, whose quality she recognised immediately and who was another of the women, like Tante Peck, who provided her with the mothering she needed.

They married on September 16 1939, shortly after war was declared, and produced three children, me on July 4 1940, Giles on April 13 1943 and Alexander on October 5 1944. My father died on April 7 1952, my mother on October 30 2003, aged 89, fifty-one years after my father.

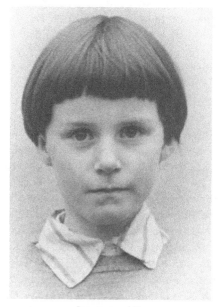

Janet, aged 7.

15

Chapter 2

CHILDHOOD 1940–1952

Mum and I came home to the large draughty Victorian terrace house at 11 Thurlow Road, very close to Hampstead Heath, that my Neel grandparents had ceded to my father and mother, moving away to a grand flat in the Albany belonging to a friend of Uncle Stephen's, both he and the friend being away fighting the war.

It was a huge house, four storeys high, and the basement was let to another family. Accommodation was in short supply during the war, but it was easier in North London; mass evacuation had hollowed out the city while families were huddled together in overcrowded houses in the Home Counties. My mother, pregnant with me, had been briefly evacuated to somewhere like Amersham (when pressed she could never remember exactly where, she had hated it so much) but after three months had insisted on going back to the London house, where she might be bombed but she could live with Dad and did not have to share a kitchen with another woman. Her description of whichever pleasant country town it was, how deadly quiet it was with just the women and children during the week, and how it was all cocktail parties and smart clothes and the children put to bed early when the men came at weekends still resonates with me. My father once shared with her his occasional dream of retiring to the Neel cottage in Sussex to make furniture, and she told him he would have to do that without her, or his children. Brought up in deep Welsh countryside she was never leaving a town again.

We lived, with a lodger upstairs, a sweet, gay architect friend of Dad's, in a state of unusual privilege for those wartime years. Most people's fathers were away at the War, losing years of their lives and seeing little of their wives and families. My father came home to us every night from his office in Piccadilly which was itself close enough to the Albany to visit his mother and father.

16

He was working to get his career established and conscious that he was lucky to be able to do so. I was fortunate too, the darling of three resident adults, despite being bald and covered with infantile eczema until I was a year old. All babies in those far-off days were routinely vaccinated at two days old, and those who, like 40 per cent of us, carry the gene, got infantile eczema or some other form of autoimmune reaction. This went on for years after the war, so enchanted was the medical profession with their ability to magic away the terrible childhood killers of diphtheria and scarlet fever.

I was, I know, precocious. Despite my Budge grandmother's fears, no bombs dropped on our part of Hampstead until October 1943 when I was just over three. One fell onto the sub-post office just beyond our one acre of garden and we, for once, all went and huddled in the basement. Everyone refused to believe this childhood memory when I dredged it up a few years later, but I was able to prove it. Uncle Stephen, my father's brother, who spent the war flying the very slow aeroplanes of Coastal Command (he told my parents he could have neither outrun nor credibly pursued any fighter or bomber being flown by the Germans, but he could, at least, tell Command where and what they were) was staying with us. I remembered the scratchy feel of his uniform as he picked me up to go to the shelter and that I had dribbled a bit of precious egg on the gold crown above his pocket. (One egg a week was the ration, but we did a bit better because we kept unreliable and frightening chickens, as did anyone who had the space.) Uncle Stephen confirmed that I was right, adding sadly that the egg had dried and proved difficult to shift. Similarly, I remember precisely the feel of the table leg (I was sitting under the table defending my space from Giles) in 1944 when the Normandy invasion was happening and no one in the country turned the radio off for a week.

My brother Giles was born in April 1943, two years and nine months my junior. My parents were in a hurry, they had intended to have four children, and my mother once told me that they started trying again for another baby the minute I was able to stand. She went to the GP when she did not get pregnant again immediately, arranged a D and C, and, as she said proudly if tastelessly, next shot, there was Giles on the way.

I was at the Sussex cottage where my grandparents tried to spend their summers even in wartime and I remember the car bearing my parents and the baby turning into the gate. The descent to the cottage was down a precipitous, bumpy, ill-maintained drive which needed a good driver; my grandmother, a terrible driver with no nerves at all, drove sitting up on a cushion, peering over the steering wheel. I welcomed the baby kindly, but if you are nearly three there does not seem a lot to do with a tiny sleeping object that just lies there and does not seem to want to play.

I had by then taken a huge step outside my domestic surroundings and out into the world. My mother had been, once again, sent to Oxford, to produce Giles, well in advance this time. Grandy moved to Hampstead during the week to look after Dad and me and went back to Albany or the Sussex cottage at weekends. My mother feared that entertaining me all day might be too much for Grandy, so six weeks before Giles was born she went round to the local nursery school, Miss Watson's, and pleaded for a place for me for the mornings. Miss Watson explained that she would not normally take a child under three and a half years old, but relented, seeing my mother's distress, and said leave her here now and we will see how she gets on. When Mum came back an hour later I was instructing a boy bigger than myself on how to place the bits of an interlocking toy, and Miss Watson was watching, laughing inwardly. 'Janet will be my contribution to the War Effort,' she said solemnly, and I was enrolled. I loved it; the order, the peace, the Gold Stars for achievement (no modern view that you got one for trying hard ever entered Miss Watson's universe) and I was there until I was old enough to start at primary school in 1945.

My mother, as always, could not wait to leave the cottage, whereas I and my busy father would have been content to stay longer, pumping water for baths, emptying the lavatory buckets, cleaning the septic tank (there was neither the company's water supply nor proper drainage at the cottage). Fortunately for Mum my father was by then setting up a brand-new business, so I returned to the arms of Miss Watson and Giles grew up quietly in the nursery on the second floor and played in the sandpit and flapped at the chickens. The next year, in 1944, Mum was pregnant again and Giles and I waited, with no particular interest, for the new baby, who was to have been number three of four.

And there it all goes dark, and I lose nearly a year of memory. Factually my brother Alexander (actually Geoffrey William Alexander but always called Alexander) was born on October 5

1944. My mother had managed to persuade the authorities that to send her to Oxford again for a month, leaving two children under five in London, was not practicable, so by special permission Alexander was born in a London hospital. My father was working every hour of the day, Giles was too small to be foisted on Miss Watson, Muttie was struggling in distant Wales and Grandy was preoccupied with another grandchild, Hugh Pagan, son of her crippled daughter Jill.

Mum and Alexander came home after a few days, apparently in good order. Giles was walking by then; Christmas was on the horizon, when at the beginning of November Mum was taken back into hospital with a high fever. She emerged after six months weighing five stone rather than her usual nine and a half and had to go into a convalescent home for another four months. Aunt Grizel, the last of the four sisters, recently threw some light on this period and she credits Muttie with saving Mum's life. Over several weeks at the beginning of the crisis Grizel, aged 19, had been visiting Mum, who was twisted with pain and visibly fading away. She rang her parents, which brought Muttie, depression and asthma cast aside on the long difficult wartime journey from South Wales. Muttie listened disbelieving to the hospital's provisional diagnosis of rheumatoid arthritis, and via a network of her distinguished Edinburgh connections persuaded Lord Horder, famous as George V's doctor but actually a world expert on rheumatoid arthritis as his day job, to visit. Lord Horder came and reportedly said at once it was most definitely not rheumatoid arthritis, and recommended they try one of the new May and Baker antibiotic drugs. They did, and although it was a long slow convalescence Mum recovered. The final medical verdict was that she had an ovarian infection, or rather two separate infections, caught from what she had recognised at the time as a very dirty scrub nurse. All London hospitals had worked without stopping since 1940, with too few staff and not enough material, and it is not surprising that accidents happened.

Mum was away from us for nearly a year. The problems of children separated from their parents were not understood and none of us was taken to see Mum more than once. Having children visiting her, they told us, had upset her and it had undoubtedly distressed us. And she was so ill, it was thought for a long time that she was going to die. I find it difficult however (and Giles still finds it impossible) to forgive the lack of imagination that kept three children – aged four, not quite two and the baby Ally – from her for six months. It distorted Giles's childhood and haunted him thereafter, and it didn't do me a lot of good, but then I had had years as everyone's favourite thing which gave me a lot of inbuilt resilience. Alexander had very little of the sustaining attention that babies need – no one from the superannuated nanny brought out from retirement to my overstretched grandmother had had time to do more than attend to his physical needs – and he was showing all the symptoms of severe emotional deprivation.

In August 1945, however, when my mother came back to us, we apparently recovered instantly; the sun came out again; I stopped wetting the bed nightly, and Giles blossomed. Ally, aged ten months, was walking, unsteadily, but walking, sleepless, inexhaustible, demanding, but healthy.

I started primary school in September, transplanted from the competitive middle-class world of Miss Watson's nursery school in Thurlow Road to a very different establishment, propelled by my father's uncompromising view that nothing in England would come right unless and until we were all educated together, and the private schools which had done such a good job of educating himself, his siblings and his wife were abolished. So I was enrolled at Holy Trinity school, just off the Finchley Road. It was not a rough school and not untypical for those times, having six classes, one for each year from five to ten, all with about fifty children, 25 per cent of whom in each year were from Displaced Persons' Camps, mostly Polish, being resettled in cosmopolitan Hampstead, which had been a place of settlement for clever Jewish families since the early 1930s. I was the only child in the school who could have been described as middle class until I was joined by Giles. The Headmaster, a dedicated man, did not think he was there to teach the privileged, even represented by a fierce female child in boys' shorts and scabbed knees and a plump soft-hearted male child, both of whom promptly got nits like everyone else. He was too good a man to be more than faintly discouraging; and it would have taken more than that to worry me at that stage but I remember how the deep warmth of his attention cooled when faced with my privileged middle-class accomplishments like reading and writing fluently.

We painted on old newspapers, there being no other materials to hand, and used more newspaper instead of lavatory paper.

Everything was old, battered and in short supply. I found the lavatories particularly alarming, arranged as they were in a row at one side of the playground with doors with gaps at the bottom, no locks and very primitive plumbing. I took my father to see them one day, and he was bracing about my fears but I could see he was shaken.

There were far too many of us for the teachers to cope with and all of them resorted to simple methods of crowd control, rendered more difficult by shortage of materials. For a year I alternately hemmed and unpicked a handkerchief with the other female six-year-olds while the boys nailed pieces of wood to each other and then reversed the process. For a lot of the day we chanted or sang so that to this day I can multiply up to 13 by 13 effortlessly and I have still an extensive repertoire of hymns by heart.

I flourished, as a confident eldest child, miles ahead academically of my contemporaries. I was even allowed to join a Gang as a very junior member and ended up at eight as second in command to a wild boy of eleven who did twenty years in gaol before he was forty. Early reading, and mature ability had carried me to the top of a school in which many nine-year-olds could not read with any fluency (I was reading *Jane Eyre* by then and frightening myself silly), so late in 1948 I was transferred, against my father's principles, to the private South Hampstead Junior School. He would not have me held back and had also been rattled by having to come and fetch me from the local police station when I and my gang had broken the leg of a rival juvenile gang member in a fight on wasteland in which we were heaving bits of brick at each other. A version of this story appears in *Children of a Harsh Winter*.

I had always been intended for the Senior School at South Hampstead, which was a Direct Grant school and as such acceptable to my father, but the private junior school was a serious shock to my system. I ran into a wall of self-possessed children of privileged families, turned out immaculately by their mothers. In shock and desire to conform I became tidy, insisted on washing my Wellingtons, cleaned my shoes and ironed my uniform shirts. At Holy Trinity all such sartorial niceties had been rigorously ignored, since many children had barely enough clothes, never mind clean ones. And I was for the first time in my life behind in class; I struggled with the mysteries of French, grammar, embroidery, country dance and maths, against competition from

21

the capable early-maturing Jewish girls, who made up a lot of the school population and were good at everything.

From this darkness I was rescued after half a term by an invitation from Barbara Brend, a plump, square, utterly self-possessed child, to join her very desirable gang. There were five of them, Barbara herself, Sue Burn, a child of an academic family, Jenny Meddings, daughter of older parents who had been Communists in the 1930s, Frances Roberson, daughter of schoolteachers, and Margaret Edwards, a daughter of another academic family. The group lived in an innocent fantasy world, an invented family based on the Orlando the Cat books which I still read with pleasure. But Barbara had decided she could not be Orlando, so she became Jet, a cousin of the family and a Prince of Backland, and I became Jamie her younger brother, achieving at one stroke emancipation from my over-responsible position as eldest daughter and becoming a younger son, which felt just right. Jet was a few months my senior, the only child of a rich, eccentric family. Her father Gavin was a solicitor who always came home early to take a great deal of trouble with us girls – I have written of him with love in *Children of a Harsh Winter*, where he appears as a country GP. The real Gavin was a great bear of a man, full of minor accomplishments and wild enthusiasms, a good piano player who could sight-read anything or play by ear. He ran the Sherlock Holmes Society and also founded the White Boar Society, which is dedicated to proving Richard III innocent of the murder of his nephews and generally rehabilitating his reputation; all this, of course, was enchanting to a child of my hard-pressed family. Jet's mum Phyllis we also adored; she called us all 'Laddie', ran the Guides, and had an explosive, uninhibited, enormous laugh when one of us amused her, which I can hear to this day. Her brief appearance in my first novel *Death's Bright Angel*, complete with characteristic 'Laddie' as addressed to the heroine, was greeted with delighted recognition round a wide circle, many of whom wrote to me, warmed by her memory. We all envied Jet, who shared her parents with unthinking generosity. She was, as the loved and only child of gifted parents, much more grown-up than the rest of us, detached, kindly sardonic, even at nine years old, and wonderfully restful to be with for an anxious, competitive hard-driven child like me.

One of the school's other charms was that it was an all-girls' school and I was freed of responsibility for my brothers. I was happy, despite my struggles with the work and the fact that I encountered, for the first time, girls obviously cleverer than I. There was Jet, of course, and there was Lucy Gaster, who would achieve stunning eleven-plus results which put her top of all the London eleven-year-olds, with an IQ soaring off the top of the scale. (No one told us this of course but it seeped out, and all of us noticed the awe with which the unassuming and graceful Lucy was treated for weeks after the exams.) Lucy's father Christopher Gaster was the secretary of the Communist Party of Great Britain, unfashionable even in 1949. Her mother was a Laski, daughter of Harold, sister to the writer Marghanita, and both Lucy and her cousin Lydia Howard, Marghanita's daughter, were beauties as well as clever. We all used to rest our eyes on them at Prayers which they both attended, being in the process, like many academic Jewish families, of renouncing the faith of their grandfathers.

From the end of the war to 1949, Dad was building a very small house on a magnificent site in Hampstead. In that period, such were post-war shortages that planning consent was only forthcoming for very small houses, and then you had to find the materials. That ought to have been a happy time, but I must have known that my father was ill again because I was shoplifting to an extent that was asking for trouble. Trouble indeed came my way when I was challenged by the young manager of Woolworths. I talked my way out of the immediate consequences by emptying my pockets and promising, tearfully, never again to come into that Woolworths in Hampstead High Street. Nor did I until I was eighteen, resorting to desperate, anxiety-producing shifts to avoid going into the shop which was a key part of our domestic economy. I told my mother perhaps twenty years later and she was appalled that she had never noticed that when she sent me shopping, Woolworths had always been closed, or had run out of lavatory paper or bread or flour on that particular day. It is an object lesson in what parents can fail to notice. My father was a shoplifter too, I found out years later, but at eleven or twelve, and wrote in his memoirs that he felt it was a result of being kept too short of pocket money at home, and that he had regulated his behaviour towards his own children accordingly. He didn't observe us carefully enough and he had three shoplifters – the boys were more persistent, more blatant and less competent than

Dad, Edric Neel, about 1949.

I, and unlike me became the subject of anxious parent–teacher conferences.

By the autumn of 1949 Dad, we all knew, was seriously ill again. A lump came up in one of the glands in his throat, and a surgeon at Westminster Hospital decided to operate rather than use deep X-ray which had always worked before. This time it failed and Dad was never properly well again. In the summer of 1949 we had moved into the new house and I remember all that summer, so he must have been briefly alright. I remember helping sow and rake the new lawn, and how the rake broke just as we were in the last stages. Dad swore, cast a baleful look at the darkening sky, stuffed us children into the car and bought a new rake, a real event in our cash-strapped existence.

We never bought things. My mother was invariably overspent on the housekeeping money, because my gifted, deeply frugal father, brought up dirt-poor, never gave her enough of it. Even if I had not been so much my father's daughter, I would have wanted to be a worldly success with my own spending-money, having seen my well-educated mother reduced to tears of misery, trying to manage the housekeeping money and being accountable to her husband. The late Peggy Jay, daughter of another Hampstead family and a friend of both my father and my mother, also notes in her Memoir how much she hated Accounts Day and not having any money of her own, so it wasn't just my mother who suffered.

1950 was my last year in junior school. My Budge grandfather suddenly offered to pay for me to go to Malvern Girls' School, the boarding school at which my mother and her three sisters had been educated. I could not imagine why he thought I would want to leave home but he knew of course that my father's health was degenerating fast. In the spring of 1951 I obligingly took the entrance exams for North London Collegiate, St Paul's and Francis Holland, and passed them all. Dad was in Australia, selling the Arcon houses which he and his team had designed and sold in their thousands as temporary housing for the hundreds of thousands bombed out of their houses during the war. He had gone there by ship in order to get enough rest; he was ill, losing weight, but it was hoped a sea voyage might set him up. He rang from Australia and I boasted to him of my successes. 'Yes,' he said, wearily, 'very good. Can I speak to your mother?' I remember being crushed. I had laid everything I had at his feet, but he only wanted my mother.

He needed to speak to her because she was ill too. She had just had an emergency hysterectomy at only thirty-six. I don't remember her being away for long. I cannot remember how we managed with me going to four different entrance exams but surely someone must have taken me. Nor do I remember most of the schools, except waiting in the dark entrance hall of St Paul's and glancing up at the Honours Board recording the award of a scholarship to Newnham to Jocelyn Neel, my father's sister, in 1939. I think I must already have decided I wasn't actually going to go to any of these schools, that I was staying at South Hampstead with Jet, so none of this was quite real. I was just being efficient, and automatically exerting myself to get all the glittering offers I could, in the hope that it would make everyone feel better. It did briefly cheer me up – the sensation of being wanted, of having power in the world and the ability to open up new horizons for myself is a lasting pleasure and a lasting difficulty; to this day I have difficulty turning things down, when someone offers me some job or honour which I do not, viewed calmly, need, want or have time to do.

I must also have understood my mother's distress over the hysterectomy and how ill my father was and known I could not leave home. Not, indeed, that I would have wanted to; I needed to be involved and important. Even at ten years old I knew *that.*

My mother came back, not ill but a bit feeble, with a huge scar down the tummy, which I don't believe we thought was ugly, but she did.

In the summer of 1951 before I was to go to the Senior School we rented a farmhouse in Cornwall and we all had a marvellous time. Both my parents were with us and the sun seemed to shine throughout except on the day of the Helston Fair, held in what was then a small Cornish market town at the head of an estuary. Like all those places it was mudflats with a narrow stream running down the middle at low tide, but at high tide it filled and looked totally different. On a day when the grown-ups were casting anxious looks at the black clouds above we waited all afternoon for the tide to be high enough for the swimming races. I was a good swimmer and was entered for the under-sixteens – but Dad was getting cold (he was always cold because the cancer was stripping weight off him, as the pictures of that last summer mercilessly reveal) and wanted to get back to the farmhouse. Finally, the tide got there and I was second in the under-sixteens (I was just eleven but fast and trained in the way the children of fishing families who lived by the sea were not) and I won the unheard-of sum of five shillings. I wanted desperately to wait and enter the over-sixteens race where I thought I might come third or fourth and win a whole £1 but my parents insisted on taking us back. That afternoon the tide kept on rising, covering the site of the fair to a depth of three feet and causing the senior race and the rest of the fair to be cancelled but I still found it difficult to forgive them.

We came back from Cornwall and my father went back to work. I went to Guide camp, which was anti-climactic after a joyous family holiday. And *I* came back not feeling well, but I would not yield or slow up, going obsessively to the public swimming baths every day.

I slipped on the edge of the pool one morning and cracked the base of my spine and a week later showed Mum the really bad bruise which would not heal. My mother took me to the doctor. Dr Drew, an older woman (fifty perhaps), examined me and went straight for the telephone – I remember that her hands trembled

– and I was in Great Ormond Street Hospital that night. She thought that I had leukaemia, then almost always fatal; she knew my father was dying of Hodgkin's Lymphoma, and she had just seen my mother through a hysterectomy. It is to everyone's credit that I do not remember real alarm or distress at all, for what must she and my parents have felt?

Great Ormond Street was a difficult experience however. I was a tall eleven, almost too long for the ugly beds, and desperately self-conscious; and I was the display case with an array of bruises all over my arms and legs and this vast bruise at the base of my spine. I had five blood tests every day, I remember, which were always painful. Great Ormond Street must have realised very early that it was not a galloping leukaemia but a (then) rare case of idiopathic purpura (ITP), the disease which has recurred at extended intervals in my life. I understood that what I had was rare and special, but not life-threatening, although every visiting specialist bore down on me. I remember particularly an African doctor, because I had hardly seen a black person (this was 1951) and felt shy, then, remembering my consciously liberal upbringing, I offered to show him the worst bruise at the base of my spine. It was my first contact with children who were seriously ill. I remember a nurse who was patiently thumping a small asthmatic child screaming for breath and frightened silly, and that same child, having been discharged, coming back again only a few days later. I had a moment of appalled empathy with the thin, undersized boy, so small and defeated, his parents looking wretched putting a suitcase down on his bed with cheerful words.

Visiting hours were restricted to the afternoon and Mum came every day except the last day, when it was Dad, looking tired and thin. I could hardly contain my disappointment – I was feeling anxious and I wanted my Mum, and Dad could not summon much energy to deal with me. We sat together on the balcony, not talking much, and he kept worrying about whether I was warm enough, then he reached forward to pull the ugly brown cardigan that had accompanied me into hospital more closely around me. I can see him now, unsmiling, hunched, the full under lip – like my brother Ally's, not like mine which is straight and thin like a baby bird's – in the long serious face, waiting for the time to pass, not knowing what to do with me. When I think back to that scene it is one of Victorian pathos, a man who must already have

27

know his illness was going to incapacitate him – as it did less than three months later – visiting his treasured eldest child in a gloomy hospital, very like the Westminster where he was such a frequent visitor. Moreover, he knew, he must have known, that he would not be able to run his business or to protect his family for much longer. He died on April 7 1952, so the shadow was on him.

The memory of Dad and that ugly brown cardigan – a sort of dark mud and badly made – which did nothing for a pale, fair-skinned, blue-eyed child, reminds me how plain I felt. I had awful clothes and no one cut my hair properly. Clothes were still rationed in 1951, and everything I owned – with the exception of school uniform – had to be capable of being passed down to two younger brothers. So I clumped around in huge boys' shoes, with a raincoat that did up on the wrong side and my straight difficult hair kept out of my eyes with Kirby grips. When I was perhaps seven or eight, all three Neel children and my cousins David and Alexandra, adopted children of my beautiful Aunt Jane, were together staying in Wales with Muttie. In the photographs taken that afternoon are apparently four sullen boys, one of whom was actually me, and our cousin Alexandra, three years younger than I, lint blonde, got up by her cunning mother in a dazzling frilly white party dress (where my aunt got such a garment in 1947 or 1948 one does not like to ask, but she had been a sub-editor at *Vogue* and would always have taken that kind of trouble). In the photographs Alixdra, as she is always abbreviated, looks innocently, ravishingly pleased with herself, a flower among the four thorny children in hideous grey shorts. It is fair to say that everyone's clothes were dreadful, in a way it is difficult to imagine today. Dad had five suits, one for each day of the week, bought from the long-vanished Fifty Shilling Tailors, made of poor material and badly fitting even on Dad who was long and thin. There wasn't anything better to buy.

For six months from September 1951 to April 1952 I don't remember very much. I know as a matter of record that Mum and Dad left for a nursing-home in Bournemouth in November, and that she came back by herself for Christmas and went away again after that. We children were left in the charge of a housekeeper whose name I cannot remember, a fat disagreeable woman. Someone else must have been there some of the time, as she must have had days off, but I recall only trying to defend Giles, to whom she had taken a violent dislike, and praying for my atheist father, offering God anything including my lettuce crop if he would recover, so I must have known that he was ill unto death. I remember the winter going on forever, and the boys clinging to me – they were seven and eight respectively, and we were orphans for all we knew. Mum wrote to us, and we wrote to her and to Dad, and she answered. She told me long afterwards that he could not bear either to read our letters or to have them read to him, or to write to us, it was more than he could stand, the sense of loss. He was in pain, of course, all the time, and no one knew how to control it as they do now. I have a copy of a letter he wrote to my grandmother dated January 21 1952, about ten weeks before he died. It was written at a time when he was briefly out of pain and two paragraphs have always resonated with me:

> 'I have not, of course, the slightest wish to die. I love my life, but in the moments when pain clutches me with its iron fingers I see death as desirable, much in the same way as a powerful narcotic. The fact that one can return to life after a narcotic and that death is final does not register. It's freedom from pain that is sought and life itself does not seem too high a price.
>
> 'I do not think of death in any morbid or gloomy fashion. When the time comes, it seems that I will embrace it as a lover and there find peace. Nor am I very sorry for myself. It's young to die at 37 but so many have died, both younger and older, who have not packed so much of living into the years allowed them. I have had a very full life and have achieved all my dearest aims, wife, children, home, and profession ... My tears and sorrow are for Mary whom I love more dearly every day, she it is who suffers, not I.'

King George VI died in February 1952 while my father was in the nursing home and the BBC broadcast only funeral music and hushed tributes for about six weeks. Mum told me afterwards she felt she would go mad, with Dad dying and his great solace ordinarily being the radio.

In early March 1952 arrangements were made for the three of us to spend Easter, separately, with cousins or grandparents. At some point, the housekeeper left a letter lying about – in Mum's familiar handwriting. 'I am afraid my poor husband is very near the end,' it said, without preamble, and I understood that her poor husband was Dad, and that sentence was unequivocal. Unbelievably, I just buried the information and I did not tell my brothers. We all went off on our separate holidays, I to my loving maternal grandparents, now retired to Worthing. I had only been there two days, in the gloomy first-floor flat, stuffed with the sort of heavy, worthy, built-to-last furniture that had been popular in Edinburgh at the turn of the century, and we had eaten supper, when they said they had bad news for me: my father had been very ill, as I knew. 'My father's dead,' I said, the buried knowledge surfacing suddenly, so the news seemed unsurprising. Muttie tried to explain that he was with Jesus, but my father was an atheist and would have been appalled by this view of the world. I insisted on helping with the washing-up, with my grandfather, who must then have been in his late sixties, hovering anxiously, wanting to hug me but not knowing how to. I did not cry until I was by myself, under the blankets. Giles and Ally were being told simultaneously by the aunts they were staying with. I expect they wept openly. I remember only the complex of emotions, some dim understanding of a towering loss, a sense of some permanent diminution, that life could never be the same again, coupled with huge relief that my mother would be coming back, that we were not orphans, that life would start again. And the whole thing mixed with a shaming excitement at the thought of the drama of it. But the pain of loss was the prevailing emotion, the knowledge that my father was gone, that I would never see him again and that he had not said goodbye. It made him seem very distant; he had vanished, he had gone; months ago I had in some sense already half-forgotten him and now he really was gone.

At his own request, his body was cremated in a grim ceremony in Bournemouth, attended only by Mum and Grandy. What about *his* father, who was alive and indeed lived on another twenty years after this, his eldest son's death? His siblings, his children, his partners? I cannot even after all these years understand why he excluded them and Mum's explanation that he wanted just to go does not help.

I wanted to go home and join Mum and the boys immediately, but I had to stay another few days, while the funeral took place without us and while Muttie took me for walks, bought me a decent grey coat and skirt and presented me with a book showing me how to make clothes for my brothers.

I arrived home on a bright spring day in April, dressed in grey, including a grey felt hat, the whole perfectly suitable for a princess mourning the king, her father, which was probably the model Muttie had in mind. My mother, clad in bright coloured trousers, took one look at me and to my huge relief removed the hat, banished the grey clothing, threw away, with oaths, the good book on overalls for boys, and told me trenchantly that my only job was to go back to school. Muttie also worried the over-serious, over-conscientious obsessive eight-year-old Giles by telling him he had to be the man of the family, and another of the highlights of that period is the memory of my mother roundly assuring Giles that if she required a man in the family she would import one, thank you.

I see this time in 1952 when I was eleven as the end of my childhood, and despite losing my father this was not a tragedy but a blessed relief. A Sword of Damocles – my father's illness – had hung over us all for years and the worst had happened and we could all move on. I had troubles as a teenager but by the time I was twelve I felt that I was on my way, I was an autonomous being, I had influence over my life and I knew where I was going. I was not an orphan, my mother was back in action, we lived in a house I liked with my own room, I liked school and I had good friends and the whole world was safe and stable as it never was during my childhood. Out of darkness into light was how I felt and I knew the boys did too.

And in the end I had and have the security of knowing that my dead father had not left us voluntarily and that the man we mourned was truly the real deal, a star untimely taken. He had, by the age of thirty-seven, and despite a continual battle with a deadly cancer, set up one of the most innovative post-war businesses. He knew that the most urgent need after the war would be housing and so he set up a group of four architects, called Arcon, and then made an alliance with a good small contractor Taylor Woodrow, which would grow to be one of the biggest, Crittall Windows, Pilkington Steel and a major plumbing supplier. He got the companies to put up cash; he and his architect partners designed the masterly Arcon houses and Dad sold them like hot cakes everywhere, here and overseas. They were manufactured from steel, with the kitchens and bathrooms

31

pressed out so that all the fitments came as part of the walls, as did all the plumbing and the lights. The house arrived on a lorry, was erected in four hours on a prepared site, connected to pipes and wires on the site, and the site foreman would make a cup of tea on the stove in the house to complete the job. People loved them; they were intended to last six years but over twenty years later I met two little sites of them in North Kensington when I was hunting for my first house. They were a key exhibit in the 1951 Exhibition and in the early 1980s I was overjoyed to find the kitchen and bathroom from the Arcon Mark V in the Science Museum, billed as outstanding examples of the first time that proper design had been applied to working-class housing.

The obituary from the *Architects' Journal* for May 1 1952 makes the point:

Dad and the Arcon partners about 1948

'Edric Neel, who died last month at 37, was the Golden Boy of architecture. Put him in a room with a collection of business men representing different facets of the building industry, give him the floor, and within twenty minutes to half an hour, he would have their eyes popping out of the heads and their hands reaching for their cheque books to subscribe to the development and design of the particular idea he was putting across. This was his real brilliance. He had also a genius for detail, and a great knack of assessing a manufacturer's plant and pointing out, after only a brief survey, how such plants could be adopted to the particular needs of the project he had in mind. It was these last two faculties which enabled him to build up what must have been one of the most powerful groups of industrialists ever brought together in the building industry ... Edric Neel was perhaps the first to realise the futility of designing in the abstract without carrying those people, whose job it would ultimately be to manufacture the project, along with him at the same time. No major development was ever attempted amongst the Arcon Group without at least two or three manufacturers expressing their willingness to co-operate and their capacity to produce, should the experimental stages of the development prove that the article was both practicable and saleable.'

I can tell that this is a fair description: it was written by one of his partners, and many years after his death people's faces lit up when talking about him. His partners understood that he was the cement and the leader which held them together, and, when he was dying, they agreed that the business should be sold to Taylor Woodrow, and all of them, men of substantial talent, went on to fine careers in other places. All this had to be negotiated five weeks before Dad died; Mum told me he asked his doctor for something to hold him together for a day, so he could talk to his shocked partners, awkwardly gathered in the Bournemouth nursing home, none of them having understood how ill he was.

It would have been better for all of us to have dealt with a man in pain, fading before our eyes. And fade he did; the photograph accompanying the obituary in the *Architects' Journal*, the last one taken when he was still working, shows a man skeletally thin, hair close-cropped as always, the heavy bones, which Alexander has inherited, prominent in a fleshless face.

Like all untimely deaths, his cast a long shadow. Giles confessed years later that he had not believed Dad was dead, thinking that he had been spirited away and was in an asylum or, worse, that he had left us all and Mum could not bring herself to tell us. Alexander turned out not to be able to remember anything at all of this period, and retains no memory of Dad at all. My mother's views are simply expressed; despite various kind offers she never remarried, preferring loneliness to trying to put another man in place of the difficult genius she had married.

Alexander, Janet and Giles Neel, 1950.

Chapter 3

ADOLESCENCE 1952–1959

By late April Mum and Giles and Alexander and I were back home in the new house in Hampstead, surrounded by concrete paths. We loved the house but it was flawed. My father, like many young architects at that time, got his first job in 1938 with the Cement & Concrete Association. So did his great friend Denys Lasdun, architect of the National Theatre and much else, and that first job deeply influenced their designs. I have always thought concrete a horrible material, it streaks, dankly, in the rain (consider the National Theatre on a wet day, the heart sinks), but everyone of my father's generation designed in it. They all believed that The Brick was a ridiculously fiddly unit and no way to build large buildings, and that makes sense but concrete is not the answer.

Our little house, 1500 square feet, had five bedrooms, three for us children, since Dad, unusually for those times, believed that every child needed and deserved its own room, however small, a barely adequate double bedroom for our parents, and a tiny spare bed-cum-dressing room. It also had two bathrooms, both tiny, fitted end to end, because Dad did not want to share a bathroom with his three children and their toys. The Cement & Concrete Association's influence remained strong; although the house was built in the despised Brick to conform to the planning authorities, all the floors were reinforced concrete, as were the foundations of the built-in cupboards in the bedrooms and in the kitchen. It had double glazing and hot air central heating and instantaneous water heating, all well in advance of their time. And even before Dad died, none of it worked; the double glazing seal was too narrow so the windows fogged up relentlessly, and had to be replaced. The heating chamber for the hot air system was too big so that, rather than warm zephyrs wafting through the house, a freezing draught met you at every corner. So the concept of warm air central heating – rare in England in 1949 –

35

was abandoned, and seven years later in 1956 men installing a conventional radiator-based system blistered their hands and broke their drills getting the necessary pipe work through the reinforced concrete floors. Getting hot water out of the instantaneous water heating system involved sitting on the edge of the bath, hand on the tap, gauging the exact water flow which the Ascot could heat. A moment's inattention and it went cold. I remember vowing through gritted teeth that when I was grown-up I would have a house where you turned on a tap and hot water came out without any other intervention being required.

But the house was still a haven and we all relaxed. Dad was dead, but Mum was there. We liked the house, and much attention was paid to us by the rest of the wider family, all shocked by the tragedy that had overtaken us. Rationing was almost over and the first coffee bars opened in Hampstead in 1952; impossible to overstate the importance of the Coffee Bar and the freedom it opened up of association with other teenagers. Our coffee bar was called 'El Serrano' and was neatly positioned in Hampstead High Street with a magnificent glittering espresso machine with six jets. I got to know that machine very well; I worked shifts there from 1955 onwards, when I was fifteen and old enough to be legally employable, joined in 1956 by Alexander, then twelve but as tall as me and assumed to be my twin, and we laid the groundwork for a partnership in catering that lasted into the 1990s. Alexander was fired later in 1956 for eating the whole bowl of fruit salad painstakingly prepared by Chef. I pointed out indignantly that he was only twelve and a growing boy, which confirmed our horror-stricken boss in his decision: not only was this an employee who would upset Chef, but an illegal employee to boot.

None of the three of us however was to escape lightly. Trouble came to me first in 1953, the year after Dad died and the year that Princess Elizabeth was crowned Queen of England in June 1953, over a year after her father had died.

We were invited to my father's old offices in Piccadilly to watch the bit of the procession that could be seen from the corner of a window and the rest of it on television. Like virtually all middle-class families we did not have a television; it was assumed that its presence would prevent any child from doing its homework.

I was not yet thirteen, but hoping to attract one of my father's partner Raglan Squire's big teenage boys. What I got was awkward and unwanted attention from one of my father's employees, a middle-aged married man with a dumpy wife and a taste for the pre-pubertal female child (as a matter of record I did not reach puberty until I was fifteen and worried silly about whether my periods would ever arrive since everyone else in my year was already in the club). He was very friendly, a bit too touchy/feely, and set out to groom me for under-age sex, talking to me as a grown-up, telling me that I was a beauty in the making. I felt threatened and attached myself to Mum, who did not take me seriously. The man would write to me – very funny letters – and would drop by to see me (the family lived three streets away in Hampstead) until I found the determination to say to Mum that I found him creepy and would, if he were not stopped, take pains instantly to leave the house on an errand should he come round. Mum was, incredibly, annoyed with me because the man was a neighbour. I was furious with her too – it had ruined the Coronation for me and I had had to summon more determination than I felt reasonable to stop a threatening nuisance. That resentment I note still echoes, both at the man and at my mother, but I took from it at the time the realisation that, had my father been there, the man would never have dared try anything on with me, at any age, never mind at twelve. The position of widow and orphan was therefore dangerous; men could take advantage and I knew then that I would have either to have power myself so that these things did not happen, or to ensure that I had a powerful male guard. My mother was equally unhelpful in offering protection when a year or so later I found myself being groped every time we met by a much more powerful and more determined man, one of my father's old associates. She could hardly refuse to believe me since the man had done the same to her but she suggested I should be able to deal with it. I was at the time fourteen and really not able to deal with an older man on whose kindness we partially depended, although I did manage to keep it to a grope. I did deal with it finally, aged eighteen, with the pent-up rage you can develop over four years of intermittent trouble, and lost a friend and potential ally. The difficulty with some of these oppressing men who cannot keep their hands off under-age girls is that they often truly like and admire the girls as well and have useful non-sexual things to teach them if they could only skip the sex. Yes, I know, it's like suggesting that tigers would be perfectly all right if they didn't bite. I used the experience in *Children of a Harsh Winter* – the abuse in the book was more severe because the book needed that, and the man in the book was (as it more usually is) a stepfather, not a removed family friend.

But apart from these two wilful pieces of denial, I felt myself lucky to have the mother I had, and so did Giles and Alexander. There was not enough money but she instantly calculated that the house would support us at a basic level. Thanks to my father's foresight in squeezing in five bedrooms and two bathrooms, we had three lodgers from 1953 to well into the 1960s. Giles and Alexander were put into the double bedroom and Mum moved into the small dressing room. Three lodgers occupied the single rooms – and shared one of the tiny bathrooms – and I moved downstairs into the house's other great amenity, the study, which of course I had to share during the day with Giles and Alexander. I cannot remember minding that much. I loved sleeping on the ground floor and being able to walk out into the garden.

The lodgers stayed for years and now I wonder how. They had tiny bedrooms with only a single chair to sit on in the evenings. I do not remember that any of them had a television since all three of us children would have been in there with them if they had. They were all single people with weekend homes to go to but I still wonder how they bore the weeks. Mum cooked for them twice a week, on Mondays and Thursdays (stew invariably on Mondays, fish pie, equally invariably, on Thursdays) and I was not expected to help with any of it. I was welcomed home by a smiling parent always pleased to see me, given a good tea, and allowed to get on with my homework. As I got older, and played (or swam) for every school team, I would find homework a burden because often I would not be home till 6 p.m. with what the school thought of as three hours' work, but I was always fast and by then I had also found a method of eating lunch in five minutes flat and getting at least one prep done and finished before I got home.

Trouble came next to Alexander. By the time Dad died Ally was effectively not in school; from five onwards he had been so disruptive that five different schools would not keep him. Since he was about three he had made a career of injuring himself in new and different ways, capping it after Dad's death by setting fire to our garage and escaping with another disturbed small boy through a tiny window. They both fell into the arms of a local fireman who recognised Alexander immediately as the little boy whom his wife, the head casualty nurse at New End Hospital, had seen six times in the last year. In these escapades I nearly always ended up picking up the pieces; Alexander, significantly, injured himself only when neither parent was present. This incident was not the final straw; that followed a few months later, when my mother opened the door to a woman she had not seen for some years, invited her in and gave her tea only to discover, twenty embarrassing minutes later, that she was an emissary from Social Services, alerted by several different administrative sources, about the out-of-control, distressed, dangerous eight-year-old that was Alexander.

A conference of uncles was called and six months later Ally was on his way to Tormore, a small boarding prep school in Kent, where he was bullied for what must have been an endless first term. He was used to that; violently disturbed, he used to push and provoke until someone broke, either my father, who would beat him, or one of his siblings. I tried to kill him myself – we were probably nine and five respectively – when I found myself banging his head on a concrete slab in full sight of my horrified mother and Giles remembers to this day that he had also tried to kill him and resented me very much for preventing murder.

I am ashamed to say I cried with relief when Alexander was sent away to school; I had always had a lot of the responsibility for this destructive, distressed creature thrust upon me, both by the grown-ups and by the panic-stricken, lonely, furious boy himself. But after this first terrible term the story gets better. Alexander found a father-substitute in his prep school headmaster, settled down, learned to read and to play, and four years later to get a creditable entrance to public school. It was a staggering recovery, so much so that we all forgot quickly what he had been like and what trouble he must have been in.

Then it was Giles, aged eleven in 1954 but only nine years old when Dad died, who had a crashing nervous breakdown; for two months he wept and wailed and washed his hands obsessively, and clung to me, threatening suicide. I was fourteen and on the edge of puberty, beginning to be a success at school in the junior teams for everything from netball to spelling. I was simultaneously agonised for and deeply ashamed and contemptuous of him; I stayed on my feet no matter what, Ally was in pain, but surviving at school, why could Giles not, too, endure? An attitude copied straight from my mother who was always threatened and made miserable by anyone putting down their end of the plank. After two months of this however, Mum understood that her rod and staff, her eldest child, was crumbling, white-faced, unresponsive and increasingly sleepless (I have a dim memory of wetting the bed again) and took Giles to see a child psychiatrist. Alarming though his condition was, it did seem to have had an explanation; guilt and anxiety over the death of our father plus the onset of puberty seemed sufficient. If the excellent child psychiatrist thought otherwise he did not say so. He did tell my mother that when he had first seen Giles – nearly at his full height at eleven and a half years old, having suddenly grown five inches in one year, he had thought this was going to be a long, slow cure, probably necessitating a very quiet and constrained educational career. Giles, however, had confounded expectations by instantly making a strong personal relationship with him which enabled them both to work together and to get Giles successfully and cheerfully through Common Entrance just over a year later and into Lancing College, as planned. Giles also managed to make a strong personal relationship with the psychiatrist's beautiful blonde daughter, an adolescent a year older than Giles and so blatantly a disturbed child that my mother's observations about Cobblers' Children seemed totally justified. Underage sex does not seem to have been something people worried about; I guess my mother managed to tell herself it was not happening, as I did. Denial was the default option for both of us.

Despite all this by 1955 or so we children were happy. We were very popular, being friendly, gregarious, presentable and a good-looking gang which is of huge importance as teenagers. The age distance between me and the boys shrank during those years; both of them were taller than me by the time I was fifteen and both or either made credible dancing partners. Indeed I learned ballroom dancing by going to classes held at The Hall, when Giles was twelve and I fifteen. Alexander despised the whole idea but *he* learned to jive – from a master at his prep school, he said when asked, and I expect Mum and I went into denial mode about that too. He taught me and he and I could still cut into an efficient 1950s Buddy Holly routine when I was sixty-one and he fifty-seven. He also learned, enviably, to play the guitar, getting a lot of mileage out of the four chords he ultimately mastered, this despite the fact that unlike Giles and me he could not carry a tune.

Giles went to public school, apparently cured and happy, in 1956. He was a very grown-up not to say bumptious prep school boy, in the way that the big confident sons of Hampstead were; the Medawars, the Soskices, and other children of the fashionable middle-class right-wing Hampstead Labour Party. Mum had hoped that being in the lowest form of a public school might dent him a little, but it didn't. I went down with her for his first half term – in those days you went to boarding school and stayed there and your parents visited you. It was a perfect late October day and my brother sauntered over the lawn to greet Mum and Muttie (recently widowed and overjoyed to have a grandson close at hand) and invited us all cordially to come and have sherry with Roger. This turned out to be his history tutor Roger Lockyer, one of those gifted bachelor teachers on whom all good public schools depended absolutely, not just to teach, but to be there, and look after the boys through the long weekends. Giles became a historian because of Roger, who is famous among the schoolmasters of that period. He taught Giles and his contemporaries superbly. Giles got an Exhibition to Magdalene College, Cambridge, and, had a depression not been boiling up, would I think have got a First; he was always more academic than I but lacked the rock-solid confidence in his own intellectual abilities that I had, and anxiety scrambled his brains.

By 1956 Alexander was coming to the end at his prep school. He was the subject of some close and careful deal-making among schoolmasters of the sort that went on at good schools at the time and probably still does. My father had been at Westminster, but Mum had been told that both boys needed to live away from home, with male role models, to avoid further damage. My guess is that Mum did not want Ally at home to disturb our peaceful alliance, and I don't think I did either. We got on much better as we got older but he could still rouse me to uncontrollable fury – I remember flying at him, intent on beating him up, or killing him for preference, and stopping, dismayed, in the tiny hall because my well-directed punch caught him in the chest and he was effortlessly holding me at arm's length, he being twelve to my sixteen and over six feet tall and solid from all those years of compulsory games. So Alexander went to Canford, in Dorset, and we all thought that would be him settled for five years.

Through all of this I went stolidly to school at South Hampstead High School and enjoyed it, at least from my second year there.

The first year was a shock. The thirty girls from the junior school were joined by another thirty recruited in cutthroat competition for the eleven-plus entry, so there were two parallel forms. I found the school had deliberately split up our tight group, separating me from Jet and leaving me and Sue Burn in the other stream, so that although we all foregathered after school we were separated during the day. I daresay it did us all good but two years later it was necessary to even up the two streams and Sue and I had our hands up to join the other stream and be reunited with Jet and Jenny and Margaret before our form mistress had finished the sentence asking for volunteers to transfer, so we got back together again.

I had missed Jet particularly in the first year of senior school because my father was dying and I had not much idea of what was going on. I remember only that both of the incoming streams had Froebel-trained teachers as form mistresses which cheered my mother who had had a Froebel-trained governess in her youth. I also remember that it was an extraordinarily quarrelsome year – feuds everywhere and people taking sides. The Headmistress, an admirable and graceful woman, Miss Potter, sister of the humorist Stephen Potter, told my mother that the first year was always difficult; the privileged children who came up from the Junior School without doing the entrance examination had to move over for the newcomers. The girls who came from outside had, without exception, been far and away the brightest at their elementary schools, treated as princesses, and were meeting, often for the first time, other girls as able, and it was a painful adjustment. (The fact that I had had to make that adjustment two years earlier did not make me any nicer or more sympathetic.) And we who came up from the Junior School were not being stretched academically. I think I spent the year drawing Achilles' shield, painstakingly described in the Iliad, and drawing is a field where I have no pretensions even to ordinary competence.

By the second year life was easier; my father was gone but my mother was back and we had settled into a routine. There wasn't enough money, of course, but we had three lodgers and my mother had a job so we didn't feel poor. School became more demanding in the third year; we all started Latin and I started Greek with Lucy Gaster, the only other person in my year who wanted to do it. I think I took Greek because it was known to be well taught and I admired Lucy and thought that being taught with one so clever would improve me. My friend Jet started German instead, a more practical choice. And of course we all went on doing French.

I was a natural athlete, always an asset at school, and was in all the school teams including the swimming team. South Hampstead is a city school and had no sports facilities then, outside of a gymnasium, on the school site. There were two small playgrounds, both asphalted and on a slope, which doubled as netball courts. Both required adjustable legs; I can only wonder how we managed to snatch a ball out of the air and land on desperately uneven ground without injuring ourselves more severely. We played hockey in Regent's Park, which was a twenty-minute journey. I wore straps on one knee whenever I played games and by the time we reached the Sixth Form the school teams sported bandages and straps on every limb and were a sight to strike terror into the hearts of our opposition. For matches we played either smaller, more delicate schools like Channing and Henrietta Barnett, or found ourselves travelling painfully to South London to play one of our companion schools of the Girls' Public Day School Trust (now simply the Girls' Day School Trust). They were all much bigger schools, and their girls were all larger too so that my 5 foot 8 inches no longer seemed a commanding height and I was being bumped off the ball by 6-foot identical twins at Putney High School. And Jet got her front teeth knocked out playing hockey.

In the summer I swam. This is not a social sport; success in swim races depends on establishing a good technique and then grimly building up strength by doing length after length in the water. In modern times competition swimmers do other, varied exercises, many of them on dry land, but the core of the training remains length swimming. The school aimed only to teach us all to swim – an excellent system required house captains (I was one of those) to ensure that all eleven-year-olds in their houses could swim, and I discovered a real talent as a swimming teacher. But if you wanted to swim for the school – and in my case later for the County – you joined the Mermaids and the Hampstead Ladies' clubs in order to get two nights a week of higher training, which is what I did, on top of school work, until I was sixteen.

I came late to puberty and did not menstruate till I was fifteen, well behind my group. I do not know whether it was this late development that triggered a fall into depression. It manifested itself as a profound, deadening sadness, firmly ignored by all around me, although I just noticed my mother's anxious irritation. It was triggered by the untimely death of a Hollywood star called Robert Francis, one of those big, blond, tanned Californians, almost certainly gay, I see with hindsight, like Tab Hunter, that other icon of my teenage years, or Dirk Bogarde or James Dean. However improbably, the world darkened and I hardly knew where to put myself, although I knew, even then, that the death of a far-away young man whom I did not know could not be causing this sadness. I finally managed to put the sorrow where it belonged, with the death of my father, truly felt for the first time, and with *that* recognition I took in other unwelcome facts. The children of the dead have very little protection; their fathers, as Homer says, are not feasting with the chieftains, there are no crumbs falling from the table for them, and that went in spades for the wives and daughters of the dead. My mother was struggling by then, there wasn't enough money, even with three lodgers, and she had taken on not one but two part-time jobs. I understood that, at that time and place, without a man, my mother was a second-class citizen, no longer the respected wife of one of London's most interesting and successful businessmen, but a hard-pressed widow, with lodgers, doing two boring, low-status and ill-paid jobs.

I was engaged in delayed grieving not just for my own father but for Jet's. Gavin had died suddenly that spring from a heart attack and it was terrible for all of us. A light went out, and the survivors in his family diminished. It was then that I decided that the Law was the way to go; only men seemed to be lawyers in 1956 and they all made the kind of money that meant they could support wives and children in style. Exemplars were to hand: Gavin himself, Frank Soskice, the Attorney General, father of one of Giles's best friends, and Dudley Perkins, General Counsel for the PLA whose wife had been at Somerville with Mum. And lots of others, in and out of the Hampstead Labour Party.

This perception was a key part of that summer and it is one of the reasons why I am as I am. Unusually for my generation I saw, at sixteen, that Men's Jobs paid and women's didn't, on the whole. This remained true until maybe the mid-1980s, and still has resonance today. Pick a job that men do, I always advise young women.

Just before my sixteenth birthday I did my O-levels, getting high marks effortlessly; I had a photographic memory, I was a hard, competent worker and I had by then even managed to get a grip on maths. I had given everyone a fright by getting 27 per cent in the maths Mock examination in February. I was in the top set for maths as well as for everything else and no one had noticed that I had ceased to understand algebra. I was (and am) good at arithmetic and geometry, but the minute the subject moved from hard numbers to concept – where arithmetic becomes mathematics – I was lost. Calculus, now confined to A-level, was required by the London O-level boards and I had no idea what I was doing. Again, Jet saved me; she taught me algebra, or rather she taught me all I am ever going to be able to do of it. Teaching me calculus defeated even her, but the O-level exam contained a question from a ten-year-old paper, and, ever diligent, I had worked through ten years back and in the exam reproduced, photographically without any intervention by the brain, the worked answer provided. I passed with distinction but I was not fooled. I do wonder how many more there are like me out there, who look like competent mathematicians but actually are working at the level of arithmetic. I know one at least, my own daughter, one of whose eleven A* grades at GCSE was in maths, but she can't manage algebra either.

Sad or not, I was off to France that summer, for seven weeks. I was to have four weeks in Nontron in the South and three weeks on the Brittany coast, *en famille* but not *au pair*. Someone must have paid the costs: Giles's education was paid for by Uncle Stephen, and Alexander's by my grandfather. I was a scholarship child throughout except for two years in the junior school while my father was still alive and earning – a matter of fierce pride for me, but extras must I think have been paid for by Uncle Stephen.

I can't say the whole French experience was a success; both at Nontron and in Brittany all my fellow boarders were English and we all preferred to speak English. '*Vous aviez pu plus faire, Janette*' was the justified verdict of Marie de Nontron, the 23-year-old daughter of the ancient house of Nontron, a truly academic teacher, wasted on the gang of idle teenagers that we were. But to this day I speak French with a far better accent than most and, despite a marked shortage of vocabulary, can hold my own.

I came back to a ghost house; Giles had gone to Lancing, and

Alexander, at twelve, was in his last year at Tormore. So I had the house to myself, save only for three, blessedly grown-up lodgers. In those distant days there was a marked change of gear between O-level and A-level, which was of a much higher standard, and I can prove it. At A-level in both Latin and Greek we were required to translate into English out of Greek and Latin prose and also to do it the other way round. I could, and did, render longish passages from Jane Austen into Classical Greek, and while I was never much good at lyric poetry I certainly stumbled through getting 'Ode to a Nightingale' into Latin. The Greek set still consisted of me and Lucy Gaster. With hindsight, it was a strange thing for Lucy to be doing as the daughter of a Laski and of the secretary to the Communist Party of Great Britain. We were taught by two distinguished teachers, Miss Phillips and Miss Kitto, and spent a happy two years, huddled over a radiator in the school hall because there were no spare classrooms, reading Aeschylus and Plato and Homer and Virgil, and writing Latin and Greek verse. I like to think of clever Lucy, writing superbly elegant Greek, weeping like me over Homer, while at home her household was being torn apart by the outcry over the brutal Russian invasion of Hungary, and British members of the Communist Party were tearing up their party cards and abusing Lucy's father and anyone who stayed with the party.

In the end neither Lucy nor I had a smooth passage to university. Both of us were confidently expected to get three distinctions at A-level, but we both got distinctions in the subjects we were not intending to read at university, I in Mediaeval History, Lucy in Geography, and we both got B grades in Latin and Cs in Greek. The news hit both families in August; our Classics teachers in tears on the phone to our parents. This was a tragedy for the school and for the Classics department; they had dared to hope not just for two places at Oxbridge but possibly two scholarships, as I understood much later.

Lucy decided, then and there, to switch subjects and do her Oxford and Cambridge entrance in Geography. I was too devastated to make a decision at all but Mum rose to the occasion. She decided, coolly, that it was possible that the perceived excellence of the teaching at South Hampstead High School was a mirage and that perhaps, just perhaps, the B and C grades at A-level reflected an objective truth. She herself was a linguist (doing Russian A-level at the time, I recall) and she had listened with understanding to my distraught explanation, that, somehow, by the time I reached the two three-hour papers of Greek Prose (English into Greek) and Latin ditto, I had got tired and found myself thinking in Latin while trying to write Greek and the same with the Latin paper. She sent me to a crammer, Davies Laing and Dick – may their shadow never grow less – where for three weeks I wrote three Greek Prose and three Latin Prose a week and raced through first-year university set books. The honest men and women of DLD reported at the end of the three weeks that I had, indeed, been superbly taught, should get into Oxford or Cambridge readily and had better go back to school and do so. Infinitely reassuring for me and Mum and a credit to DLD; how easy it would have been to hint that perhaps I had outgrown school and would do better with them.

My sixth form years were not all solid work and team games and swimming. I had met my first real boyfriend, Don Macleod, in 1957 at the Fellowship of Youth, a club for 17- to 35-year-olds run by St Andrew's Presbyterian Church. I knew about the Fellowship because I had been a Guide and 18th Hampstead met in the church hall every Friday night. Don waited a bit before asking me out, perhaps to gather his courage. He was twenty to my seventeen but he was the eldest of three boys, educated in the unremittingly male atmosphere of Haileybury School and probably hadn't met any girls. I had very little real life experience of men, come to that, and was in the throes of experimentation with a perm to bend my uncompromisingly straight hair into a glamorous beehive style. It had also turned my hair slightly orange. Don was very good-looking with dark blond hair, bright blue eyes and the neat contained way of moving which singles out the natural athlete. He was six foot, a comfortable four inches taller than me, as well as being three years older and employed. A real grown-up and I was delighted with him.

It was a very demure affair, however. We both lived with our parents, I was studying for A-levels and Don for his chartered accountancy examinations. These two facts would anyway have cramped our style but we were both additionally burdened by needing to provide exemplars for our younger siblings. We had two younger brothers each, all four of whom wanted to sit watching us, trying to learn how to be grown-up. On cold winter Saturdays I would loyally follow to watch him play rugby for the Old Hayleyburians and to help with tea and we would then go to a party or a film. On Sundays we would end up at the Fellowship of Youth after the Church of Scotland evening service.

We stopped well short of the extremes of physical affection. None of my friends actually went to bed with their boyfriends. We all longed to but everything about the mood of the times and our situation as students living at home combined to discourage us, especially the fear of pregnancy. The Pill was still in development, and as for the barrier methods of contraception everyone had a story about a friend who had used one but it had burst or fallen off and then of course they had had to get married. The late fifties seem a very long time ago.

This gentle idyll lasted just over a year until August 1958 when the twin snakes of ambition and anxiety slithered into our undemanding Eden. After my failure to achieve the glittering A-level results for which I had hoped, I was terrified and unfairly held Don partly responsible for my failure. All my plans for Cambridge and a career were under threat, and I told Don I could not go on seeing him, and plunged into a solid four months of hard work to get into Cambridge in the foolish expectation of being able to pick up with him where I had left off.

I went back to school in September, where we Oxbridge candidates came and went as we pleased, detached from the life of the school, wearing our Own Clothes. And just in time. Uniform was compulsory in those days: navy skirt, length no more and no less than three inches above the knee when you knelt on the ground; a navy tunic, ditto; navy sweater with gold stripe; white shirt with long sleeves for day wear; navy blazer with badge ('Knowledge is Now No More a Fountain Sealed' running round a golden shield). Plus of course the navy raincoat and a dreadful navy beret which did nothing for anyone however worn. The lot of us, as my mother said, looked like housemaids on our day out, a patrician observation that rang oddly in the grim fifties. (She was not, however, the only South Hampstead mother who had grown up knowing what a housemaid on her day out looked like; the wife of any professional man would have had live-in help before the war.) Nor was I alone in wearing the same skirt, blazer and sweater from the day I arrived in senior school, aged just eleven, to the day after A-levels finished. The blazer and the raincoat, being expensive, had been bought to leave room for growth, but I never quite grew into them, and the sleeves of both still hung to the end of my knuckles when I was sixteen. The sweater and the skirt shrank and the collars of the shirts frayed but I stuck with them; only my shoes changed because they had to. I looked terrible, but then we all did, and none of us cared, at least none of us in the academic sets. Nor were our non-uniform clothes much better. It is difficult for anyone born after about 1950 to understand that you could not buy decent clothes in the 1950s – properly made clothes that fitted – because they didn't exist. Everyone made their own clothes using paper patterns and a limited choice of fabric. If you bought anything it was poorly made; I was interviewed at Oxford and Cambridge in a coat and skirt that fitted only where they touched and where the skirt bulged out of shape within a month.

Redecoration of Prefects Room, 1957. Janet as Head Girl on mantelpiece; Barbara Brend (Jet) reclining; Lucy Gaster holding ladder; Jenny Meddings holding the plans on sofa.

Scholarship candidates for Oxbridge did a week of three-hour-long scholarship examinations for Oxford in November, then the next week the same for Cambridge. In those days in the acute competition for the small number of female places only those who tackled the scholarship exams had a chance of getting into a college. South Hampstead High School, like all girls' schools, selected ruthlessly the candidates they were prepared even to enter, and I remember knowing that one of us was considered a doubtful, and one of us who was doing the exams in her fourth rather than seventh term even more doubtful. I was not much troubled by the exams; I had stopped working a full week before, knowing, suddenly, that I needed a break and had gone – unbelievably – by myself to hitchhike round East Anglia, looking at the Fen churches. I met with nothing but kindness, stayed in Youth Hostels and came home much refreshed with brass rubbings that accompanied me to Cambridge a year later. What can Mum have been thinking, I wonder now. Why did neither of us see anything risky in the idea of a lone eighteen-year-old girl hitchhiking round East Anglian churches? It was a different world.

But my truly academic, truly original friend Jet was overcome by nerves. Day after day she would arrive to sit an exam, white-faced, having slept for only the odd two or three hours in the past twenty-four, escorted by her equally pallid mother. 'It's desperate, Laddie,' Phyllis said to me when I sneaked up to her to ask how the last night had gone, too alarmed by my friend's white face and twitching eyelids to ask the victim herself. But Jet was made of stern stuff and every day, ashen-faced, she wrote papers for three hours in the morning and three hours in the afternoon, and was taken away to the school nurse's room to get what sleep she could in the two-hour lunch break. And then, on the very last day of the Cambridge exams, as I struggled to produce a passable three-hour essay on something like 'To err is human; to forgive divine; discuss', I looked up to see friend Jet, still pallid but laughing silently as she pushed her hair away from her face, pen racing, utterly concentrated, utterly happy, and my heart lifted. We fell on her, all five of us, afterwards and asked what she had been doing. 'The Goon Show question,' she said, surprised, and we five, who had avoided that one like the plague, as we had been trained to do, gazed at her in wild surmise. Of course, and as I should have understood at the time, we were looking at the real scholarship candidate. So it proved. Newnham offered her a scholarship, and Somerville did too. I got an Exhibition to Newnham, a Clothworkers Award which also entitled me to a full State Scholarship, and the other four – whatever the school's views – got places, including the brilliant Lucy who, had she not changed subjects, would, I am sure, have got a Scholarship too.

So we were in, and the two fatherless families gathered to celebrate before Christmas. Both families had kept a bottle of champagne from the good days when our fathers had been alive to buy them – but the Neel bottle had got too old, my father having been dead six and a half years, and the cork would not pop but came out with a sigh. The Brend bottle popped; we drank that first and polished off the Neel bottle, flat as it was, with undiminished pleasure. The only sadness was that my boyfriend Don, properly offended by my behaviour to him, had found another girl so, while he was genuinely pleased for my success, that affair was over.

Apart from the triumph, the feeling of doors opening, there are other sharp memories of that period. Letters poured in from far-flung friends and all the cousinhood to my mother, congratulating her on this triumph. She passed them all to me; universally they praised *her* steadiness and the support she had given me, and I rather resented them, feeling that I had done the work after all. That was monumentally ungenerous. Not everyone's mother would have steadily refused all help in the house so I could work undisturbed, and no one else's mother at that time, desperate for her daughter, would have managed to keep her cool, send me off to a crammer, thereby providing another possible route through, and popped me back into school with encouraging words.

My success was wholly beneficial for my brothers. My triumph gave them confidence; if their big sister could do it, you could see them think, so could they. Giles, always clever, and by then in the Sixth, started to work in earnest and he too got an Exhibition, to read history, so he was up with me in my third year, which we both enjoyed. Alexander meanwhile had decided unequivocally against Canford. He felt he had been away long enough and there would be space at home. He had passed seven O-levels at fourteen and he persuaded Mum to let him leave. At fifteen he went to a German school in Freiburg im Breisgau through the good offices of one of our neighbours, from where he returned speaking very good German, and in September 1960 he started in the sixth form of the Lycée Française, where he was taught in French and did four A-levels, running second only to a clever girl just older than him. He did not get into Magdalene, presumably because he had explained to the modern languages tutor that while he loved languages and found them easy he couldn't be doing with Literature. He had to take the Scholarship examination at Fitzwilliam House, then very small and not even a proper college of the University, in a hurry, but they took him, and he arrived in Cambridge in Giles's third year to read architecture like our father. He passed his first year living in lodgings by the railway station but spending every day with Giles in his beautiful rooms by the river at Magdalene Bridge. To this day I glance sideways as I cross that bridge half expecting to see Giles or Alexander lying on the grass or in a punt, hopelessly sideways on to the current, with one or other of them clinging to a pole. They were both good athletes but neither ever learned to deal with a punt.

I accepted my Award and its matching State Scholarship in December 1958 but none of us was going to start until the next university year in October 1959. Characteristically of that era, Jet's mother Phyllis and mine were united in wanting us to learn shorthand and typing because that might be the only way we would ever get a job. So off we both went to secretarial college, despite our Awards, working side by side with young women who had never expected to go to university or do other than work in an office. My brilliant supervision partner at Cambridge, Cherry, had a mother like ours and she too did a secretarial course. No man of my generation would have considered learning either shorthand or typing.

After the course I went to Montreal in March 1959 where my father's first cousin Nairn Casgrain lived. Nairn, daughter of great-uncle Charlie Neel, the alcoholic brother of my Neel grandfather, had stayed in Canada and married a French Canadian, Johnnie Casgrain, who had died young, also a victim of alcoholism, so I knew her not at all, but she hospitably offered to look after me for three months. I went to Montreal on a small freighter which carried perhaps a hundred cars. Four hours out of the Port of London I started to be appallingly sick and ten days later in the calm waters of the St Lawrence seaway I was still being sick every time I lifted my head from the pillow. I remember almost nothing of that dreadful voyage except the agonising slowness of the trip, exacerbated by gaining an hour on an already interminable day every night as we ploughed and pitched westwards. I also remember the increasing, kindly, desperation of the freighter's captain – they didn't carry a doctor – who radioed all round the Atlantic for a remedy that would work. There wasn't one and there isn't one now. I was advised later that it is a defect of the middle ear and that I would always suffer from motion sickness after a few hours on a boat. I arrived in late March, several pounds lighter, still suffering from sickness, at the end of the hardest winter Montreal had had in a decade, and I remember that the people of the city all looked slightly mad, desperately tired and somehow yellow.

Cousin Nairn was probably fifty when she found herself with an eighteen-year-old as a houseguest in her flat for three months, and it was more than good of her to have me, used as she was to living by herself. She had another, unexpected houseguest at the time too, a woman friend in her late thirties coming out of the ruins of a second marriage, attached to a married man who she hoped would be her third husband. She was staying with Nairn to further this objective and Nairn offered me bits of the story by way of embarrassed explanation. The campaign to attach the married man, a big, dark, dull banker from Toronto, was not going smoothly and one morning a phone call from him cancelling some arrangement caused Jean to weep and swear while critically studying her make-up. 'Don't look like that, Janet,' she said savagely – I suppose I must have been gawping. 'You think you'll feel different and do different when you're my age, don't you? It never changes. I feel just like I did when I was eighteen.'

Well, I thought primly, I expect if you are wicked enough to have had two husbands and are trying to detach a third from his present wife, that might be true, but surely not for the educated girl like me. The words however stuck; Jean was right. I am 78 years old and still often react like a teenager and see others old enough to know better unable to avoid the rush of teenage emotion.

It was an uneasy three months. I was working as an accounts clerk in a bilingual office and my prissy European French was not quite good enough; in fact I was 'let go' two weeks before I would have needed to leave anyway, much to my chagrin. What I chiefly remember is the surging throng of immigrants from Europe. In 1959 Canada needed people and made it easy for them to come and settle and almost none of my friends and acquaintances was

Canadian born. Most seemed to be German, fleeing their history, wanting a clean, guilt-free start in a country where they were not hated as they were in Europe. One forgets, but as late as 1969 my husband Jim was being totally ignored in a Yugoslav restaurant until he asked for something in English and they were all over him, apologetically explaining they had thought him German.

Lots of English immigrants had come too, poorly educated, seeking to get away from the English class structure, the rotten schools and the dull country, and a fair admixture of other nationalities, so that I, on one evening, was propositioned by the Japanese boyfriend of an English girl and also by the German boyfriend of a native Canadian who was finding her heavy going. This was more than fifty years ago and I imagine all the immigrants are now Canadian, with Canadian children and grandchildren and with their home countries a distant memory.

I went on from that protected environment to work in one of the summer camps for New York children. I had applied to the camps for deprived city children run by the *New York Herald Tribune* Fresh Air Fund. I thought I knew what it would be like; my mother was after all a social worker on a voluntary basis for the Children's Moral Welfare Fund, dealing with the kind of families that were too difficult for the statutory authorities; the US could have nothing frightening to show me.

I arrived, at nearly nineteen, in Poughkeepsie in upstate New York, a few days before the first batch of teenagers, and was shown the camp – beside a large lake, surrounded by trees. I was to be a bunk counsellor, jointly responsible, with a seventeen-year-old colleague Pamela, from a liberal middle-class Jewish family, who had never been a counsellor either, for looking after twelve teenagers. It did not occur to the Americans running the camp to tell me that at least 60 per cent of our teenagers would be black and most of the rest Puerto Rican, because they were New Yorkers and they knew that.

Pamela and I met our allocated twelve, mostly black, thirteen-year-olds as they arrived, frazzled and scowling, at six o'clock on a hot August Saturday. I was not at my best; that morning I had said casually to one of the senior staff that I had never been vaccinated against poliomyelitis and found myself driven to the camp doctor and given a polio shot which had disagreed with me. The Americans were shocked by my explanation that eighteen-year-olds in England were not eligible for vaccination because the vaccine was in short supply and priority was given to younger children with fewer immunities; they had not understood how infinitely more prosperous the USA was at that stage than any European country. So I had a sore arm and a headache and probably a fever when our twelve arrived and I was barely on my feet when we got the raging, quarrelsome, tearful pack of them into bed at 2 a.m.

They ran us ragged over the next two days and when one girl produced a knife Pamela collapsed and had to be taken to the camp infirmary. I had the advantage not only of eighteen months in age but of having a mother in the social work business, and had realised that the knife-wielder was not merely delinquent but mentally ill, hearing voices urging her to terrifying random violence. I persuaded the tough middle-aged camp leader who was in charge of all 144 kids, twenty-four bunk counsellors and twenty assorted specialist staff and senior staff to get the relevant New York social worker out of bed and get her to read the files on the knife-wielder, remembering my mother's strictures about social workers' inability to use data available to them. It was my nineteenth birthday and I was exhausted but something must have carried conviction. The telephone rang red hot all afternoon and the knife-wielder was removed from the hospital tent later that day; she turned out to be a known schizophrenic, put on the list at the last moment by a social worker who indeed had not read the files but thought the mother needed a break. We were lucky no one got killed. Without her the other eleven settled down and Pamela refused bravely to go home to her mother and weighed in at my side. It was the second week when, flushed with success, we two innocents decided to wash everyone's hair but our campers being mostly black the result was chaos. All our poor kids looked like the terrible warnings about what happens when a home perm goes wrong and neither of us knew what to do. We had to be rescued by the only black counsellor at the camp who, worn out herself, stayed up to all hours, plaiting up the hair on our panicked kids. Pamela and I, scions of white liberal families, were deeply ashamed of our incompetence and lack of sensitivity.

We waved goodbye to the first group, and all rushed to celebrate our day off which we spent in a bar in Poughkeepsie, eating pizza and drinking beer and falling asleep. It was an extraordinarily hard life for young women of seventeen, eighteen and nineteen, and I am reminded as I write of how tough and capable teenagers actually can be.

Several of my colleagues fell by the wayside that summer and I found myself in charge of thirty-six kids and six counsellors, but then I was nineteen and an ex-Head Girl, so I started with all the advantages. And we got cleverer; we learned to look critically at the kids who got off the buses and to watch out for the ones who should never have been sent to camp. The level of mental illness among those groups was startling; back in 1959 in New York the social workers must have been as harried and overloaded and incompetent as London social workers have become, and probably for the same reasons. We had to send one in ten back to the city, usually within the first two days.

At the end of these nine weeks, the reward was to go on a tour of the South – the camps gave us Europeans pocket money and the rest of our salaries went to the organisation that had arranged our camp placements and our visas, who used the cash to organise the tour. There were fifty of us on this particular tour, including ten young Germans from a church group, who were agonised about their lives and Germany's past. They apologised, as a group, to the British contingent and it is I think to our credit that we just gaped at them in astonishment, rousing ourselves to point out that no, really, they couldn't have done of these terrible things because, like us, they had been babies in the war. And anyway, we Brits agreed afterwards, they had *lost*, hadn't they, and we had won, why did they need to apologise?

The tour was fine, hugely enjoyable, staying with overwhelmingly kindly and hospitable American families, until we got to New Orleans, where we were in a student hostel and due to move on after three days. On day four, no bus arrived, and the hostel turned out not to have been paid. Agitated phone calls to the New York headquarters received only a confused response and promises of transport that never materialised. The organisation – the predecessor to the well-organised Camp America of today – had gone bust, and we waited three long days in hostile New Orleans, our limited cash running out, all of us getting dirtier and more harassed, until a bail-out was arranged which enabled a bus to be sent to pick us up and take us back to New York, missing out only one of the stops on the way back. I have never been back to New Orleans, whatever the inducements, and I have never been able to eat cheap hamburgers since. We were frightened and I know exactly how it must feel to be a refugee.

I collapsed on the way back with a recurrence of the tonsillitis which plagued me through my teens, and had to be looked after for a week by a kind American family. I got back to New York with a raging penicillin allergy to find that somehow Mum had found the cash to fly me home via Gander in Newfoundland, which was the only way in those days when aeroplanes could not get across the Atlantic with a full load. The plane never landed at Gander, and I assumed this was just part of air travel, until we were all woken up as we approached Ireland. The pilot explained that we had overflown Gander because, while he could get the wheels down, the light that told him they were locked would not come on, so would we please, now, remove shoes, and assume the brace position, while he flew round Shannon airport to use up the last drop of fuel. We landed, safely, it was the light bulb not the locking device which had failed, but we had fire engines and hoses all around us as we peered out of the windows. I can't think why it didn't put me off flying but it didn't.

Chapter 4

CAMBRIDGE AND THE AFTERMATH

I came up to Newnham College, Cambridge, in 1959; then as now an all-female college, in the little village of Newnham, now part of the city itself. It was founded by Henry Sidgwick and the poet Arthur Hugh Clough. Both were inspired by their sisters, with whose academic ambitions they were fully in sympathy, to buy the land and build the college. That's what the brochure says; seeing those stern, commanding female faces in the portraits in Clough Hall some of us wondered whether their brothers' generosity might have been partly inspired by the need to find their sisters a place outside their own household circles. It is a spacious well-appointed place with fine confident nineteenth-century buildings in the East Anglian style, which has strong Dutch elements. I never looked at it properly when I was up because I was then fixated on the late medieval beauty of King's Chapel or Trinity Great Court, but I regret what I missed.

I had an Exhibition to read Classics, but about three weeks before the start of term I wrote to the Principal saying I wanted to read Law instead. I had thought long in the nine months since I had been accepted, and decided that if I wanted a Man's Career I needed to spring from university with two-thirds of a qualification, and why I waited until three weeks before I was due to arrive, I do not know. The Principal and tutors at Newnham neither then nor afterwards tried to dissuade me, or even commented on the difficulties that this belated decision caused them. Had I read Classics I would have been supervised by excellent women in my own college, who needed every pupil they could get; because I wanted to read Law, and Newnham had no lawyers to supervise me, complex swap arrangements with three men's colleges had to be made for my teaching. I can only be grateful, then and nearly sixty years later, for the automatic acceptance of the right of a nineteen-year-old girl to pick her own destiny, regardless of what inconvenience it caused them.

I arrived with a huge trunk which had been sent by train. The trunk rested at the college in some ground-floor fastness as long as its owner was resident in college; a far cry from the modern practice whereby parents, bent under the weight of CD players, books and duvets, bring their offspring and all their possessions at the beginning of term, and reverse the process eight weeks later so that the college can let every room in the college for a conference. In that post-war era when only ten per cent of the eligible age group was expected to go on to tertiary education, universities were generously funded and so were students. As the child of a widow with a low income I was entitled to the full State Scholarship which covered all my university fees and college fees and left plenty over, including a substantial allowance for books. The young women from professional families or those with private money like my friend Jet were alright, but the daughters of shopkeepers or clerks were often pressed for money, because their grants assumed a Parental Contribution that in many cases said parent was unable or unwilling to make.

I was also encumbered by itching spots on my scalp and face as a result of the penicillin allergy but, realising I could not hide away, unpacked and spread my possessions around a large single room in Peile Hall and went down, wearing my newly acquired second-hand gown, its warmth useful on a cold October evening. We all milled around sizing each other up, and I sat down with a group of three other young women who became my closest friends for the next three years. My experience was not unique; others who came up at the same time also found themselves sitting, on the first day, with people from whom they would be inseparable thereafter. Years later I read about the work done by a group of psychologists who had put a random collection of volunteers together and asked them each to find, without speaking to each other, one other person with whom they felt an affinity. Each pair was then asked to find another pair on a similar basis, and in all these self-selected groups the participants turned out to have vital dominant characteristics in common.

So it was with the four of us; we were all middle-class, all good-looking and all apparently confident, capable people. Jenny, Heather and Anne had been privately educated, but it was tacitly agreed that my school, South Hampstead High, as part of the Girls' Public Day School Trust, was as near private education as made no difference. There were plenty with similar characteristics in Peile Hall, Newnham, and it was not until later that the essential psychological similarity between us emerged. Three of us were first-born children, Heather and I both had two younger brothers, and Anne was the eldest of six. Our most important common denominator was the lack of an effective father. Mine was dead, Heather's died, dramatically, in our second year; he had not lived with the family for some years, being said to be working abroad, but there was no money when he died and many rumours. Anne's father, as she found out in our first year, had been having a serious affair for years. And Jenny had a fractured relationship with both parents; she was a changeling in that solid business family, and but for a strong physical resemblance to her father one might have concluded that the hospital had sent home the wrong baby.

That first night each of us felt a bit outgunned by the other three. I was intimidated by their travelled sophistication. Anne was a daughter of the diplomatic service, brought up and educated in Geneva, bilingual in French and English, with dramatic black hair and startling blue eyes, an exotic, at least to me. Heather was a striking redhead, Roedean-educated, bilingual in Spanish and English, whose parents had lived abroad for years, and Jenny, ex-Wycombe Abbey, very dark-haired with olive skin, hardly looked like a daughter of Birmingham. The other three were a bit daunted by me, because I was reading Law and was an Exhibitioner. I was alarmed by them because they were all sexually experienced. Jenny had been having an affair with a much older married man. Anne had been loosely engaged to the son of one of her father's colleagues, and Heather with a young man in the Merchant Navy. I had never slept with anyone and indeed would not have known at that stage how to avoid pregnancy. I felt distinctly inferior to all three of them until I managed to find an older man in whom I felt enough confidence to give it a go in the Easter term of my first year. Naturally, the morning after I rushed to tell my three friends whose relieved congratulations I can still hear.

The four of us all had an uneasy passage through Newnham and caused the college authorities a good deal of worry. Anne's and Heather's worlds were disrupted by the defections of their idolised fathers, who had both turned out to be very far from the men they had thought them to be. Anne's boyfriend for the whole of the first year was a brilliant, arrogant young man who none of the rest of us could stand. He ended the relationship and it was a confidence-sapping experience even for a clever attractive woman. She recovered of course and went out with a series of much nicer men. She also decided to change to reading Law which turned out to be a mistake. It did not suit her mind, and once again, at the end of our second year, I saw a clever, capable young woman fight her way, white-faced and sleepless, through a week of exams. There were only three women in the hall for the Law exams but we sat a long way from each other in the massive examination rooms in the Senate House, since Anne's surname began with an E and mine with an N. My supervision partner, Cherry Busbridge, the best female lawyer Cambridge has ever had, was writing her way serenely to her second Starred First. I was, as usual, scrambling to finish on my way to my second good 2:1, but I was desperately conscious of poor Anne. Heather made a mess of her exams in French and Spanish and embroiled herself in a non-stop series of rows with the college. She was involved with a young man just older than us, who was living in London, and in her general state of distress she fled to his side whenever possible, openly breaching the rules about staying in college for every night of full term.

Jenny, whose father was still present, was always in trouble sexually; a *femme fatale*. Men were always attracted and she was never without one, usually someone who fatally distracted her from her work or from a course she had intended to pursue. I wrote about her, with much affection, in *The Highest Bidder*, where she appears as the wife of a solid Midlands businessman, which she later was for many years.

I was in trouble too, though not so obviously. My life was also disrupted, at the beginning of my second year, by a family upheaval, slow to arrive, but seismic in its effects. My father's only brother, Uncle Stephen, whom we hardly knew because he had lived in Hong Kong since the late 1940s, died at forty-five, ridden onto the rails by a Chinese jockey. No one could imagine why Stephen had taken up racing in middle age, exposing himself to the perils of a notoriously corrupt sport, rendered so by the Chinese passion for gambling. It must have been part of a mid-life rethink; he was also retraining as a doctor and was two years into the course, and had acquired a Chinese mistress and her three children.

He left a small fortune; he said to Grandy that you would have had to be a fool not to make money in post-war Hong Kong and he parlayed a couple of legacies and a professional man's salary into enough money to enrich his sister and her boys and to rescue his sister-in-law and her children. He left something of the order of £280,000 to each family, worth perhaps £3m in today's money. He left half outright to his sister and the other half in trust for my mother for her life and for my brothers and me thereafter. My mother, who had seen money ebb away in Trusts in her Macdonald family, declared her intention of breaking the Trust as soon as legally possible and advanced what cash she could immediately to us children so that I knew in my second year that the need to earn money from the moment I left university had evaporated. It is to my mother's credit that I had never believed I would need to support her or the brothers but I had operated on the basis that I would have to find every penny I needed for myself.

It was something else that went wrong for me, very early. Part of the Cambridge experience lies in the solidity of the teaching and the close relationship with your college. Apart from lectures, all students are tutored (called 'supervised') in small groups in their colleges with their college contemporaries, and learning and living together is a key part of the course and distinguishes Oxbridge. In my case Newnham had no one to teach me, I was at least for the first year the only Newnham undergraduate reading Law. My supervision partner, the brilliant Cherry, was in the same position at Girton, so that our two supervisions a week were conducted by male supervisors with groups of young men at three different colleges. Nor could I work effectively in college; the Newnham Library did not keep law textbooks, not for just one of me, so I always worked in the Squire Law Library, next to the Senate House, and drank my coffee and ate my lunch and spent most of the day with the young men of my year reading law. I could not savour the experience as friends could, who loved living and being taught all in one place. I often write now in the old Newnham Library, which I like and appreciate and prowl round picking up books, but I entered it perhaps twice in my undergraduate career. I hardly ever sat in the beautiful Newnham gardens because in those days I was always hurtling downtown on a bicycle.

I was also handicapped by family history. My father was a Magdalene alumnus, and my grandmother was a Newnham alumna, so was my Aunt Jocelyn, her daughter. My mother went to Oxford, Aunt Jane, my mother's sister, to Girton, and another

62

sister, Grizel, to Oxford. All that inheritance made Oxbridge a standard rite of passage for the women of my family rather than the all-encompassing liberating experience that other women found. On top of all this the requirement to do National Service had been withdrawn, abruptly, for young men born, like me, in 1940. I had expected to be at university where the men would all be at least twenty to my nineteen and instead I came up with eighteen-year-old men who looked and acted very much like my brothers, then seventeen and fifteen, and as such were beneath my notice sexually or socially. I missed out on many a young man who later in life might have suited me, either as a lover or a good friend. My husband Jim was up when I was and, since the then Principal of Newnham, Ruth Cohen, was his father's first cousin, we might easily have met, but it is a blessing that we did not. I would not have been able to fancy (or possibly even *see*) him, because he is eighteen months my junior and would have looked exactly like one of the younger brothers I had left at home.

So I never did find a man at Cambridge, though I longed to. I very much wanted to act and auditioned successfully for both the Mummers and the ADC, thereby joining a long list of former undergraduates who have faded photographs of themselves in saggy tights or ill-fitting all-purpose peasant dresses as part of the crowd supporting the real stars. I appear as a Court Lady (in crinoline) with Liz Proud prominent in the title role of Ondine, or downstage, dressed as Peasant (baggy bodice, long skirt) with Derek Jacobi and Ian McKellen in the principal parts of something by Shakespeare. Richard Wilson, who I got to know later in the Board of Trade and who became Cabinet Secretary, had a similar theatrical career – he appeared as Second Porter in Macbeth, sporting the compulsory wrinkled tights, and both of us hide the pictures.

After getting a look at the talent available on the stage – I was in the same year as Derek Jacobi, Ian McKellen, Roddy Dewar and Liz Proud, and two years down from Margaret Drabble and Eleanor Bron – I decided I might be a director rather than a performer. Then I met Trevor Nunn from my own year and saw, immediately, that I was an amateur and a dabbler compared with a man who had been directing plays since he was about eight. I did however join the backstage crew for the Footlights Review. I am glad I did; how else could I have known Peter Cook, in his third year to my first, or John Bird (in his fourth year), or David

Frost – or John Fortune, then called by his real name of John Wood? I longed for John Fortune, who was away with what my daughter calls the Cool People, the university glitterati, among whom I never quite moved; too serious, too insecure beneath the confident exterior, or too prissy for that set. Perhaps also there was something wrong with my year; Peter Cook used to maintain that there should be a public enquiry as to how the whole of the 1959 year had been recruited, given that there was not a single decent light entertainment talent among them. None of us was able to retort that the 1959 year contained three Nobel Prize winners and ten top politicians, because that is the sort of thing that only emerges years later when the Cool People are dead, or working for the BBC.

In the end, I channelled both my theatrical and sexual ambitions into a playwright called Keith Johnstone, eight years older than me, who came up to direct a student play, Arnold Wesker's *The Kitchen*, in which I was, as usual, a serf, with barely a speaking part. I did what serfs do, I knocked off the director. I did fancy him but it was what he did that drew me; he was an Assistant Director at the Royal Court Theatre, he was old enough and kind enough for me to be able to tell him I was still a virgin, and he knew all the cool London people. It was a great era at the Royal Court, George Devine was still working there, as were Bill Gaskell and Ann Jellicoe and Tony Richardson. Keith was also a playwright, with *Brixham Harbour* having just been performed.

My affair with Keith, which went on for about nine months, took me away from Cambridge. He had a room in London; indeed he had the room made famous by Ann Jellicoe's play *The Knack* about three men sharing a house and the girl who disrupts their arrangements. Keith's – and mine for a bit – was the room painted black, with spare chairs hung on the walls and a mattress on the floor. He shared the house with Roger Mayne, an almost speechlessly shy, brilliant photographer. What no one had told me – and I was too self-obsessed to notice – was that Keith had been having a long affair with Ann Jellicoe. Ann came up to Cambridge to see the play and for supper afterwards, and I, whom she was ignoring, leaned over Keith proprietorially to reach a glass. Ann got the situation at once and, impressively, told me to go away and do something else while she talked to Keith. I did as I was asked and watched, thrilled and appalled, out of the corner of an eye, as Ann remonstrated with Keith and finally

64

slammed out of the room, leaving him pinned against the wall by a flooded table. I used that in a book later (*Death of a Partner*). At the time I just felt triumphant and grown up; I was not yet twenty; teenagers are capable of horrible behaviour and I was no exception.

Ann naturally did not forgive me and was never other than superficially, contemptuously civil to me. But *The Knack* is a very good play in which Keith and Roger Mayne – who became her husband – are completely recognisable. I would have been honoured if the girl had been modelled on me, but I did not recognise much of myself in Rita Tushingham, who played her on the London stage. I thought the play brilliant, both funny and true on several levels. It was a lesson to me about creative writing; that you can get a wonderful result out of rage and pain, that you need not make up dialogue if you can get it from real life, and if you know two of your major characters really well you can make the others up.

The affair with Keith, while exciting and interesting, simply didn't suit me. He was working-class, talented, difficult, and had no aspirations to be other. He was quite content to starve to work in the theatre; coming from where I did that was my idea of a nightmare. I was looking for a husband with prospects, so I managed to ruin the affair. I still have his eloquent reproach to me, written on the back of a picture of me in bed in a nightdress, taken by Roger Mayne, in which he argues that I never gave the affair a chance and always held back. True. And sad. I should have gone with it while I was young and had time.

While I still nursed hope of being a director, I did a couple of stints as an Assistant Stage Manager at the Royal Court in the Long Vacation, including two one-night Sunday shows, and it was then I realised that this was a track I was not going to follow. No one was paid; every actor was overwhelmingly hopeful, desperate to please, all had their mothers, fathers, agents, sisters, cousins and aunts to swell the audience for the one-off experimental Sunday show, and the whole thing smelt hopeless. No one qualified in a conventional profession would ever have to be that anxious, that hopeful, that eager to please, and I decided then and there to defect to the ranks of the business professionals. I was, of course, rejecting Keith's world, months before I rejected him.

The break-up happened however because I met another man, just before Christmas in my second year. I was getting very high marks on International Law papers, which caused mine and Cherry's supervisor to suggest that both of us entered for Gray's Inn and started eating Dinners – then as now part of the qualification for a barrister – as soon as possible so we could do the Bar exams as soon as we had finished our degrees, and join the Foreign Office. I planned to be a barrister at that stage, preferably in International Law, and to swank around impounding Iranian oil ships, like our mentor Professor Lauterpacht.

We were arranged in different 'messes', namely groups of four, at Gray's and greeted in Latin. The other three members of my mess were men, as was nearly everyone else in the huge hall in which we dined, and I was happy; this was where I was meant to be, this was the road to a Man's Job, and to prove it I was surrounded by men. And one in particular, a very good-looking older man –five years older, as we rapidly established, an Etonian, who had done his National Service and had just left Oxford. I could hardly believe my luck, I remember, we talked solidly through the whole of the dinner and it was only over coffee when he asked me out for a nightcap that I recalled that I was staying the night with Keith in Notting Hill and struggled for an excuse. Michael was sufficiently experienced to see what my difficulty was, and invited me to lunch the next day instead. Jettisoning a supervision without any hesitation, I accepted, and so began an affair which ended seven years later, after a short-lived marriage. I left Keith immediately and brutally, but I don't remember feeling guilty; meeting Michael seemed to confirm the rightness of the path on which I was set.

At Cambridge, therefore, I was in a situation where the key part of my emotional life was being conducted in London. As usual, I was trying to do too many things at once; conduct an affair in London, do enough work to get a good degree and live a full social life in Cambridge. It wouldn't all go in, and it meant that I had trouble being fully present in any one place, a pattern in which I have continued. I did try to stay with the Cambridge experience. I had a good friend, Chris Widnell, and I took an unashamed loan of him, knowing that at that stage he would have liked to be my man. He was a gifted biochemist, he taught me to cook, we spent a lot of time together and we liked each other. *He* was good husband material and, although I treated him badly, he forgave me; he was one of the ushers at my grand and doomed wedding to Michael, where he and Anne, my dear friend, who was a bridesmaid, decided to get together. I was typically utterly blind to this affair and was found months later incredulously asking Anne if she was sure, pointing that they had known each other *forever*. I cannot think how either of them tolerated me. They were married for nearly fifty years. Chris went on to a successful academic career in the USA and Anne took a PhD in French and Russian, regretting bitterly the time wasted at Cambridge on all those men (I quote her). Chris died in 2015 and I miss him still.

Our second year brought changes to my friends too. Heather, still distressed by the unexpected and unexplained death of her father, and her mother's demands, effectively had a breakdown, wilfully ignored what the college was patiently saying to her about keeping term and not spending four nights a week in London with her lover, and found herself being sent down without a degree. She raged against her sentence, saying that this was utterly unreasonable and inhumane. To my shame I did not acknowledge that she was right and the institution wrong; she should have been helped and supported and sent for psychiatric help, and ten years later all that would have happened. But this was 1961 and a harsh era; it was assumed that all of us could, when warned clearly, avoid doing what we had been told not to do, and that if we did transgress, well, then that was wilful and would attract condign punishment.

Jenny, who was also struggling, having lost a man she really loved, was saved by her tutor who suggested, forcefully, that she should live out of college for her last year. Jenny changed her subject from History to History of Art, about which the college was helpful and accommodating, as always in academic matters, and was invited to live as a lodger in the household of Francis and Odile Crick. Francis had won the Nobel Prize for his and James Watson's work on DNA just before we all came up, and was a major Lion, his household legendary for its parties. The Cricks kindly offered for me as well but I knew I was too uptight for a house in which the host might open the door to guests wearing only his socks, and I declined. Another opportunity lost, I now think.

The college also made known its views to Anne and me. They persuaded Anne, who was more willing to be told, that she should stay in college, abandon Law and go back to reading French, being quite clever enough to do Part II in one year. They told me I should stay in college too and do some work, on the basis that I was a safe 2:1 but might do better. So we did that. I got the 2:1, Anne and Jenny got 2:2s, and Heather, once over the shock, walked into UCL and got a First.

And then it was over and we felt no desire to prolong the experience. I was offered a fourth year, to do an LLB, and remember being incredulous with horror at the idea; I wanted real life to begin and so did the other three.

I retain another good male friend from that time, Patrick Holden, who was indeed one of the older men I had hoped to meet, three years my senior and having done National Service, who was at St Catharine's College. He was part of a gang, several of whom were members of the Union and of the Cambridge University Association and many of whom turned up as members of Mrs Thatcher's last Cabinet in the late 1980s. He married one of my best friends from school, Jenny Meddings, five years after we all left university and, although they divorced after about thirty years of marriage, stayed close to her and kept in touch with me and Jet. Pat, not particularly successful at Cambridge or in a corporate career, took to property development in his forties, buying and converting for sale or letting very small units of commercial property in what he cheerfully described as the tertiary sector, servicing the lets himself, allowing no repair to wait and ending up with a substantial portfolio which enabled him to endow his old college generously. I was and am full of admiration for this pragmatic and hard-working solution to finding a conventional career did not suit him.

And I also kept a very large acquaintance of young men from the Law School. I was one of a tiny minority of women in the 700-strong school, and it turned out the men all remembered us. Years later in the City I would be greeted as I walked into a meeting by warm embraces from rising stars in the banking and legal professions, people whose faces I just remembered. And it was comforting arriving in new places; when I arrived in the House of Lords, there was Gareth Williams, who had sat next to me on the bench reserved for regular attenders at lectures, as Leader of the House. I noticed the same phenomenon with young men who had been to Eton; they had a network of people they had hardly known at school but who were none the less part of their hinterland.

I have kept fewer women friends outside the four, Jet of course, and Anne Campbell, who became the Labour MP for Cambridge in the 1992 election. We sang together in the Parliament Choir many years later, and after she lost her seat in the aftermath of the introduction of student fees she took on many community jobs like Chairman of the Cambridgeshire and Peterborough NHS Foundation Trust and Chairman of a Cambridge multi-academy trust which now has five schools under its care. In retirement I have joined another gang, the old Newnhamites, women I knew only very slightly when I was up, from which I gain a lot of pleasure and interest.

So in 1962 I waited to find that I had indeed got a 2:1 and had been accepted on the professional course which would be my last law course, then Anne and I found a basement flat in North End Road. I had more money than she did so we did what she could afford which was a shared bedroom and a small living-room with a kitchen and lavatory. The bathroom was two floors above, shared by the whole household. The place was darkly squalid but we expected to redeem it with the traditional painting of all the rooms while we stayed at my family's house in Hampstead so the squalor was postponed for a couple of weeks.

I had abandoned my original desire to be a barrister. Michael already was and I thought two of us in a notoriously uncertain trade would be difficult, so I was studying for the examinations of the Solicitors' Law Society that would lead me into the less fashionable but more secure side of the profession. As I had a good law degree and a photographic memory, it should have been easy, but there was a paper on Solicitors' Accounts and I could not grasp the concept of double-entry bookkeeping, and spent increasing amounts of the very short time the course allowed on it. I did the exams in February 1963 in the middle of the paralysing cold winter of that year, walking across the park to the College of Law in five layers of clothing, which I would tear off as I struggled to finish. Six of the seven papers were straightforward, but Solicitors' Accounts nearly did for me. After one and a half hours of a three-hour examination I had managed to do bits of five questions, but could not find a sixth that I could even tackle. I had always found examinations both predictable and easy, and I knew, beyond doubt, that what I had on paper would guarantee failure; I would have to retake the paper and delay by at least six months the time when I could qualify. I was by then fighting panicky tears but I blew my nose and realised that I could either go and weep into a coffee or I could put together something that might enable me to scrape through, so I stayed where I was.

Somehow I passed but God help any solicitor who had me doing their accounts at that point. Extraordinarily, three weeks after the finals, the whole structure of double-entry bookkeeping slid smoothly into place in my mind.

Meanwhile, in that bitter winter, my friend Anne was labouring through a secretarial course, death in her heart. She knew she was in the wrong place and on the wrong track. We were both unhappy; my relationship with Michael was spluttering and Anne could not find a boyfriend to suit her. I think it must have been that time when we foregathered with Heather and with Jenny and the four of us, all just twenty-three, agreed that we should aim to marry before we were twenty-four, because otherwise no one would want us, a conversation more credible in the era of Jane Austen, but we held it in all seriousness and with a good deal of anxiety.

While I had been doing the exams I had also been looking for my Articles, or what is now called a Training Contract. These days, a girl with a good law degree from Cambridge would have a choice of the Magic Circle Firms; back in 1962 I was rejected by Linklaters, Allen and Overy, Slaughter and May and Freshfields on the specific, stated grounds that I was female. Anyone who wonders about the value of compulsion should think about that; had the Equality legislation been in place one of those four, however grudgingly, would have had to accept me and my life would have been different.

It had never occurred to me that I might need help in getting training, but Mum, resourceful as ever, talked to Dudley Perkins, then President of the Law Society, an old friend of hers from her days at Oxford. He held, as I heard later, a meeting at which six decent second-row London firms were made to volunteer to take me. He pushed me gently towards Frere Cholmeley and Nicholsons, based in Lincoln's Inn Fields, which had had a recent female Articled Clerk, herself daughter of a previous President. I was by now sufficiently intimidated by the world to accept guidance and gratefully took their offer. They didn't want me until June, when the next batch of Articled Clerks would come in. I had three months between exam and employment, and as a native Improver I turned my attention to my own skill set. Michael and I still expected to marry, and the deficiencies in my education for the wife of a successful barrister with a background of Eton, Oxford and the Brigade of Guards were becoming clear. I could not cook anything beyond a boiled egg or toast, except sauce Béarnaise which Chris had taught me. I had spent much of my time at Cambridge dressed in Army surplus and while I had bought some respectable skirts and jumpers in order to fit into Michael's world, I knew that more was going to be required. So I signed up to a three-month course at the Lucy Clayton School of Modelling for the mornings and a part-time Cordon Bleu course for the afternoons. It was my first encounter with Training rather than Education, and I noted immediately that Training was much better done than most Education I had met.

The Lucy Clayton modelling and grooming course was a revelation. Most of the pupils were being trained, quickly, to enable them to model, either for catwalk or more probably as catalogue models. It was a different trade back in 1963; all the girls were sixteen or over and none was a beauty but all were, critically, the right shape to fit into the clothes; this meant then being over 5 foot 6 inches but not being more than a size 8, which was smaller in those days. I was 5 foot 8 inches, a well-built size 12, not fat but a different animal from the slight young women whose trade this would be.

The school was run by steely, middle-aged, beautifully turned-out women and by a cheery middle-aged Jewish gentleman who wasn't Mr Clayton but was demonstrably the boss. He turned up at seemingly random intervals to critique our efforts to float down a catwalk or pose for a photograph, and we all sought to impress him. I thought I was doing well one day as I managed to get down the catwalk without wobbling or letting go of the smile that was required of all of us until I saw his expression of embarrassed horror, and faltered. 'Listen, dear,' he said, in an urgent whisper, beckoning me to him. 'We didn't admit you for modelling, did we?' Surely I had not been that inadequate, I thought, as I explained, haughtily, my academic credentials and future intentions. 'Thank God for that,' he said fervently, placing a fatherly arm around my shoulders. 'You're a good-looking girl, don't get me wrong, but for Our Work you'd need to lose twenty pounds, and even then ... well, you're not going to be right for catalogues.' I laughed, and the whole group, who had been waiting, breath indrawn, for me to burst into a flood of disappointed, heartbroken tears, like one of the younger girls last week, laughed with me. The man who wasn't Mr Clayton smiled, in pure relief that he had not made an embarrassing mistake which would have meant humiliating a customer; a lesson about the care you need to take with your customers in a service industry which has stayed with me.

We were taught how to buy and put on catwalk make-up, with the result that we burst out into Bond Street at lunchtime looking like ladies of the night. It does however mean that I know how to do it. Like many another middle-class young woman in that era I had never looked at my face with a view to enhancing it or said to myself that I had good cheekbones but very deep-set eyes so I needed a light eye make-up, or even that I had a square face. Any teenage girl these days would have worked all that out years before.

The staff made us work through every outfit we had at home, and critiqued the results without pulling any punches. We learnt that hemline length was critical, and so was Maintenance. No stain or spot, no sagging hemline or sat-out skirt escaped our instructor's eye because a prospective model could not afford any weakness. After the first week the instructors increasingly left us to peer review and we all turned into fashion police, observing in chorus that the hemline on one outfit, or the cut, or the colour was all wrong.

When sufficient damage had been done to our wardrobes and morale, the ladies in charge told us how to do better. Another dictum which still lives in my head is that you should always buy either a dress or a suit to go to work. A lot of money could be wasted on separates, the ladies said severely, without getting much of a result to show for it. How true, and while I invariably wear a suit for work, I also spend a lot on separates for the weekend without achieving an altogether satisfactory result. But back then, having enough money for clothes thanks to Uncle Stephen and with technical support for my judgement, I bought two suits and two dresses – and several pairs of shoes – in which I felt confident and looked a lot more like a prospective lawyer and prospective wife of another lawyer than I could have achieved without guidance.

The afternoons at the Cordon Bleu were quite different. A dozen people, mostly women in their thirties, turned up at the school, then in Marylebone Lane, wearing flat-heeled shoes and carrying substantial aprons, pens and huge files in our enormous handbags. Our instructors here had the same steely uncompromising style as the Lucy Clayton team, but made no attempt at glamour and after a few sidelong looks I took to scrubbing off the make-up in which I attended the morning classes.

My mother had never taught me to cook, insisting that I needed all the time for academic work, and I would have been baffled by any meat outside of fillet steak which I could deal with – you put it under a red-hot grill for four minutes each side and then put Béarnaise sauce on it. I could see that this would not do every day and was pleased – and liberated – to learn how to make a decent casserole out of much less glorious ingredients which even incorporated vegetables. British cooking had just recovered from the 1950s and we used herbs liberally and glasses full of red and white wine, and you can get some very tasty results that way. We took home what we had made – Michael could hardly believe his luck – and I felt myself the domestic equal of the smart young women he had been brought up with who were now cooking for merchant banks or well-off husbands. Fashions in food, as in clothes, change but I learned a lot. My sauces and gravies do not go into lumps because one of my instructors always, invariably, told us only to add flour 'off the fire', and if you do that your gravy will be smooth. And I make double quantities when I cook casseroles or sauces and put one in the freezer. Practical women, my mentors there, and I still have and use the Constance Spry cookbook, 1234 pages long and with space at the back for Additional Recipes. A far cry from the modern cookbook which has about five per cent of the information for the money. No pictures in Constance Spry, not even a tasteful line drawing so you have to know what you are doing. I console myself with that book when I fail to understand the instructions on the mobile phone.

Janet, aged 20, in all-purpose classical costume at Cambridge.

Chapter 5

A WORKING LIFE; FINDING A PLACE TO BE

This peaceful interlude came to an end, of course, and in May 1963 I reported for duty at Frere Cholmeley and Nicholsons in Lincoln's Inn Fields. I was one of twelve Articled Clerks and the only woman. I had been given to understand that all my colleagues would have first-class degrees from Oxbridge and Blues but my 2:1 was the best degree among the group. There were two half-Blues in unusual sports and one rower who had just missed a Blue from Oxford, Stewart Douglas Mann, one of the large and distinguished Douglas Mann clan who cropped up in the ranks of the judiciary, in the leading staff of several public schools and also in politics. Stewart had never had a problem getting Articles and knew he was entitled to his place and promptly threw his protective cloak about me.

In my day we didn't do work experience. There were lots of jobs and young people like me entering the professions were assumed to know what they were and how those worlds worked. It took me three weeks to understand what life as a solicitor dealing with conveyance (and Trusts and Wills) was going to be like, and to realise that it didn't suit me. I was held in place by a combination of factors; I had been massively helped to get where I was and would have been embarrassed to confess failure. I had also understood how difficult it was for a young woman to get her training and knew that I would be better to finish my two years and make a change then. I was also reconciled by having found a gang of brothers in my fellow Articled Clerks with whom I bonded instantly. So I settled down and helped them to negotiate a pay rise, from £6 to £8 a week, nowhere near a living wage, but in 1963 Articled Clerks had only just started to be paid at all. These days a graduate trainee gets £40,000–£60,000 a year at the age of twenty-three and is worked to death. We were paid badly and on

74

that basis were only reasonably conscientious, but that was all that was expected of us, and we worked a peaceful ten to six.

Anne and I lived in the basement flat till the autumn and I then went to live at home with Mum because she was going to travel and someone needed to look after the house. She had decided to go on a trip round the Far East, staying mostly with friends from the Women's Council but spending a couple of weeks with Michael's father, then Lt General Sir Rodney Moore, the C in C for the Far East, and Michael's stepmother, Boo, in Kuala Lumpur. They had invited Mum to stay with them on her tour; she and I packed three evening dresses on the entirely correct assumption that she would need them. She was due to leave in December 1963, but her sister Jane was whisked into hospital with suspected ovarian cancer, recognised then as now as the 'silent disease'. Jane's husband Dougal Martin was a distinguished surgeon but of course did not operate on her. The colleague who did appeared white-faced after an hour to report that the cancer was everywhere and he had been able to do nothing. It was not then customary to tell people that their days were numbered, and Jane was told only that she would have to rest.

Agonised discussions raged in our household, and finally it was decided that Mum should go on her long-planned trip because to cancel it would have told Jane how ill she really was. She left in December and early in March Jane collapsed and was rushed into Dougal's hospital, St Richard's of Chichester. When she came round she insisted on being told what was wrong and so I was able to call Mum home from Dakar where she was staying with Pauline and Roland Hunt in the Embassy, old family connections because Pauline was one of the six children of Maxwell Garnett, who had lived next door to my Neel grandparents, and sister to Peggy Jay, who had been a girlfriend of Dad's.

Michael, supportive and sympathetic throughout, drove me to meet Mum off the plane, and we took her straight to St Richard's because we all feared we might be too late. I left the sisters – Jane, the family beauty, a small, shrunken, yellowish little body, with the bones of the skull very prominent – and sat in a café with Michael while Mum worked out what to do, and then we drove her to Jane's house where she took over a stricken household. Dougal had died of a heart attack shortly before, no doubt from the strain of coping with a dying wife and keeping secret from her how ill she was, leaving two children, Alixdra and

David, of 19 and 23. I have never admired Mum more; she had travelled for thirty-six hours and was shattered by Jane's appearance but at the hospital you would not have known that she was other than overwhelmed with joy to see a loved sister again. She cried in the car and told us how appalled she was, but she was smiling for my cousin Alix ten minutes later and she spent ten days running a strange household and spending long hours in hospital as Jane grew weaker and died.

The whole episode had drawn Michael and me together, and we announced our engagement a few days after Jane's funeral in March, intending a June marriage which would give my mother just time to reorder the garden and hire the marquee and buy me a wedding dress. Only just time; there is a photograph of Mum, taken by Michael who looked out of a window early one morning and saw her surveying the garden, in her dressing-gown, surrounded by piles of earth and a wheelbarrow, two days before the wedding.

We married on a hot June day in 1964, me in a Balmain copy made for me and a tiara lent by my prospective stepmother-in-law Boo, pinned with many kirbigrips to my short slippery straight hair. I was given away by Giles, just twenty-one, in a morning

Janet and Giles on day of her first wedding, June 11ᵗʰ1964.

suit which he loyally had made for the occasion – he too had got a chunk of Uncle Stephen's inheritance by then. My old friend Chris Widnell was Chief Usher, also well-suited, assisted by Alexander, aged nineteen, in rented morning-dress which fitted him nowhere. Mum was in a pretty silk suit. The other side were giving a display of upper-middle-class awkwardness. Divorce was not common in those days but Michael's mother had left her second husband, and Michael's father, contentedly remarried, was finding the whole situation very difficult. Michael's stepmother suggested that she herself would not come to the wedding, but Michael threw a useful tantrum and she came after all. So the wedding photographs feature Mum, Rodney and Olive, Michael's mother, looking strained, and Boo nowhere. My bridesmaids, three of them, in blue-grey silk which suited them all, were Anne and Jet and an old girlfriend of Michael's. My mother had corralled an old school friend who had married a bishop so that Robert Stopford, Lord Bishop of London, whom I very much liked, officiated at the service.

The Best Man – in a curious footnote to history – was Michael's flatmate Simon Blunt, nephew to Sir Anthony Blunt, who sent us an umbrella stand which I still have. Sir Anthony had been discovered to be a spy earlier that year, though no public disclosure was made until the 1970s. My father-in-law was by then Chief of the General Staff, the head of the Army. I now suppose he must have known about Sir Anthony and been terrified of meeting him at his son's wedding, on top of all other embarrassments.

We left, orthodoxly, for Brown's Hotel in Dover Street from where we were going to Morocco on honeymoon, which was Michael's idea; I would not have been as enterprising. As we left, there was a clap of thunder and shortly afterwards the weather broke with a vengeance and rain poured down and all our guests had to run for cover.

Morocco was under military government and the advice to visitors was to look as much like tourists as possible and to go everywhere hung about with cameras, dark glasses, sun hats and brightly coloured bags. Michael was the obstacle; he looked like the conventional son of a military family that he was; wearing a panama; armed with a very expensive Leica and driving a hired Mercedes, he was viewed with unease and suspicion anywhere in the cities. I was dazzled by Islamic architecture. I was and am deeply attached to high, cold, pale Gothic churches, but the colour and style of the Islamic buildings knocked me over.

When we came back, we were almost immediately to be separated. As if our marriage was not going to be difficult enough – not that either of us acknowledged this key fact – we doomed it from the outset by making a plan which involved Michael going to the Harvard Business School to do the first year of the MBA while I finished my Articles as a solicitor. I supported his plans but could not give up my own training in order to go with him. Michael was wretched in the first year at Harvard; it was he who had changed careers and he knew that it would have been unreasonable to expect me not to finish a hard-fought-for qualification; he never suggested I should give it up, but it turned out that he never forgave me for not doing so.

I had a lonely year, living with Mum and waiting only for Michael to come home at Christmas and at Easter, but I was helpfully distracted by the social life of the young at Frere Cholmeley. The oldest of the Articled Clerks, apparently a Grown-up who had, like Michael, done National Service and who was going out steadily with the young woman who was to become his wife, suddenly fell like a truckload of bricks for a close friend of mine who was a trainee barrister. Everyone was taken aback; she had done nothing to provoke this interest and had a young man of her own. The rest of us, accustomed to treating him as an uncle figure, were appalled but fascinated. For about four weeks the office was paralysed – we would rush up the stone steps of 28 Lincoln's Inn Fields desperate to know what today would bring. It was like watching a car crash in slow motion, but after six weeks it was over and our friend and colleague resumed his engagement, plainly bewildered by the experience. I used the whole thing in *The Highest Bidder* including the bit where my fellow articled clerk Geoff Knight and I late at night had somehow to scramble together two important drafts which our admired mentor had totally failed to attempt. We exchanged, Geoff and I, the incredulous looks of people with no experience of hopeless passion or unrequited love, but they were lying in wait for both of us.

I became a solicitor in June 1965. Michael and I had a peaceful two months together, then got on a plane to Boston, he to do the second year of the MBA and me to get what work I could.

At that point I must have seemed like one of the most motivated, well-organised and successful young women of my generation. I had a good university education and I had qualified as a lawyer, and I should have been starting on a successful and well-directed career. In fact I had thrown up the whole thing. I was on my way to a country which did not recognise my hard-won legal qualification, committed to getting any job I could in order to support a man, albeit my husband, in his career. I must still have thought that in real life I was going to be looked after by a good husband who would live into old age and be faithful to me throughout, that everything that had happened to my family of origin was an aberration and that, lucky me, I had found a husband to support me and carry me with him. I cannot, as the children say, imagine what I was smoking.

After three weeks in Boston, with cash pouring out and finding myself in competition for every job with hundreds of well-qualified women trying to put husbands through graduate school, I was rescued by Giles who was in the second year of his Masters at the Fletcher School of Law and Diplomacy, part of Tufts University. He had just spent the summer in Brazil, making a film about the military junta there, with, unusually, the full co-operation of the regime. Alexander had joined him and learned enough Portuguese inside a week to be a real help, reading James Bond books in Portuguese nonstop until he had the language. They had smuggled the film out of Brazil and arrived, triumphant, in Boston, just in time to descend on our tiny flat, annoying Michael dreadfully but reuniting me with the gang I was missing.

Alexander with water ski, 1964.

Giles sent me off to take part in a game or, more accurately, a simulation exercise set in Latin America being run by a small consultancy in Cambridge, which had been advertised at his graduate school. I was allocated the role of rich repressive land owner from which unpromising position I ended up as President of the country at the end of a four-hour game. The Americans were just not as used to hard negotiation and knew even less about Latin America than I did.

Drinking beer afterwards the head of the firm, Clark Abt, said he was having trouble finding people who could write scenarios for games and would I like to have a try on a part-time, two weeks' notice basis. I had retained enough confidence to say yes. As it turned out, I could do it; whole, fictional Latin American countries complete with fake histories flowed from my pen, so authentic that at one point Abt Associates was visited by three CIA men who wanted to know where I was getting my information. My explanation of the logic of history fell on very stony ground and for some time we all feared for the security clearance I needed just to work in the firm.

My Latin American countries also owed something to a middle-class British upbringing. Clark Abt was heard to observe that all my countries seemed to postulate a privileged caste, all of whom, from left-wing revolutionary through right-wing landlord and the whole of the political class, had been to the same school, and did this reflect reality? 'Damn right,' I and my fellow Brit in the group said in unison; brought up in post-Second World War Britain we had both recognised Latin America immediately while Clark, child of Jewish East Coast academics, an outsider in the WASP community, had no means of doing so.

It was a lively place, was Abt Associates. I was a permanent employee after two weeks, joining only twenty-three others, twenty-two American and one other English person, a star economist, John Blaxall, who went on to have a distinguished career with the World Bank. He had the sort of student visa that required you to return to your deprived country of origin for two years before applying for a proper US visa, and John did not want to go back to the UK, so he was doing time at Abt. The company also sheltered a few young male graduates from being conscripted to serve in the Vietnam war. The USA, unlike the UK, had not abandoned compulsory military service after the Korean war and by 1965 was calling up its young to serve in Vietnam where the war was moving against the USA and requiring huge increases in manpower. Some of the best and brightest working at Abt Associates would otherwise have been on the ground in Vietnam.

We were also working on a strategy for Vietnam. The major Abt contribution was a very clever game, a fifteen-player interactive simulation which it was hoped could be developed into a predictive model and was, even in its early stages, a powerful training and learning tool. It postulated three villages with three players in each, which were visited in alternating twenty-minute periods (simulating day and night) by government forces (three players) and the Vietcong (three players). Villagers, government forces and Vietcong all had chips and counters to achieve their objectives. Our customers played for three hours at a time, with three umpire/observers placed in the 'villages'. Some of them were better at it than others. We went to Fort Gordon, Georgia, where (in 1965) black troops were strictly segregated from white in different barracks, and played the game with the black troops, many of them refugees from the streets who understood it immediately and extended its parameters, while we umpire developers huddled in anxious groups between rounds, making quick changes to the rules where the clever streetwise young black men were taking us closer to the reality we were trying to simulate. John Blaxall and I, the two Brits, turned out to be among the best in the group at both umpiring and the delicate tinkering that was needed.

We also played it with people back from the front, most of whom were rendered silent, thoughtful and anxious by their session. 'It turns out,' an Air Force General said grimly, 'the things you do to win the war militarily tend to lose you it politically.' Indeed, and indeed. Our Vietnam game made that point more eloquently than I; no matter who played it the government forces achieved a stalemate at best and mostly lost, although US policy never changed. Nothing could have been less popular – or less successful – than the US efforts to win in Vietnam and as all know it ended sadly and abruptly in 1973. The Air Force General who had so disliked our game died there, as did many of the gifted black soldiers from Fort Gordon. Hundreds of thousands of the villagers in Vietnam died also at the hands of both sides and Vietnam forces and the Vietcong lost thousands of young men. I was in Vietnam last year and, in the museum commemorating the American War, read the words of Ho Chi

Minh. He said, about the war with the French in the 1960s, that it mattered not at all if the Vietminh lost ten for every one that the invaders lost. The invaders would be politically unable to sustain their losses, small though these were compared with the losses they were inflicting. I don't remember anyone quoting this speech or thinking in these terms but it came to pass in the war against the Americans, as in the war with the French.

The trouble with Abt Associates was that it was all-absorbing. The twenty-four of us became each other's family, working all hours, writing bids for new work far into the night. John and I were useful there too. 'The Brits are really good at bullshit,' Clark Abt said admiringly, but John and I would point out that we were trained to the Essay, the one in good clear English with a beginning, a middle and an end, which the more liberal American education seemed not to have included.

John was far cleverer than I, another in the list of people like Lucy and Cherry. It was like being in a Rolls Royce, all you heard was a faint click as their minds went into another gear. He taught me classical economic theory, without patronage, with drawings, so that 'savers' will for me forever be represented by little old ladies in tennis shoes with frizzy perms.

I met Management Science at Abt too. One morning Clark came to a staff meeting looking both restless and furtive, and his gang of twenty-somethings urged him to unburden himself. 'Well,' he said. 'I've got a few questions for you all.' He looked down at the piece of paper in his lap. 'Erm, how many of you are only children?' Twelve people out of the twenty-four there present put up their hands. 'Eldest children?' Six of us stuck hands up. 'The only child of your sex in the family?' Four, including John Blaxall, who had three sisters, two older than he, raised their hands, and all eyes turned to the remaining two, Luis and Steve, both mathematicians and both by now sitting with arms folded, scowling. Clark, under pressure, explained that he had found a piece of research that said if you wanted tough self-starters willing to tackle any task, you hired only children, eldest children or children who were the only one of their sex in the family because they would routinely have had more parental attention than other children, would have absorbed more of the parental values and would all have become eager-to-please self-starters. If you wanted divergent geniuses, he added hastily to the stone-faced Luis and Steve, you went for a middle child. They were both the meat in a sandwich of three brothers, and also acknowledged stars, so we were able to stop them storming out of the room.

The Abt experience came to an abrupt end after a year. Again, I had not thought my way forward – I suppose I hoped to go on working there but I was married. Or thought I was. Michael had been having a successful second year at the Harvard Business School following a very unhappy first year; he was highly intelligent with a first-class analytic mind but not robust and the first year had been brutally difficult; by the second he had found his feet and was using the brains and his analytic ability. He had also attracted a good deal of attention from the young women who graded the papers for the MBA, and I had not seen them coming; I was working all hours leaving Michael without a wife to come home to. A very good-looking man of thirty, he had plenty of time on campus to get to know these young women. I had assumed that they were not more than a half step up on the young women then cooking lunches for bankers in my home town, and believed he had outgrown all that. He hadn't, I was neglectful (though I observe, in my defence, that I was working to support both of us), the inevitable happened and one of them had managed to detach him from me and from a marriage in which we had both invested a lot. Michael didn't tell me about the girl but I understood long afterwards that it was already an established affair by the end of his second year. He complained that I had neglected him and that he was unhappy and I was too inexperienced to spot the familiar male tactic of going on the attack when you have much to defend, and tried to make amends. I resigned my treasured job at Abt and we had a long and gloomy holiday touring the western USA, and I went with him as he reported for work at Hill Samuel in New York. After two months in a small serviced flat in New York, with no work of my own and an increasingly hostile man, my nerve broke. I got on a plane for London, on the face-saving basis that I was going home to get us organised. But I had been successfully frozen out, the marriage was at an end, and I felt as if I had driven into a brick wall.

I swung between blaming myself and, more reasonably, being furiously angry with Michael. What I needed and did not find was someone to say, look, he's seeing someone else, he means to freeze you out, stop blaming yourself. My father was long dead, my brothers were miserable for me, as inexperienced as I, shocked, and very censorious of Michael, which was not actually helpful. My mother was panicked – she had relied on me to be a success, she had put a great deal of support into Michael and she felt betrayed and wretched and resentful of the weeping, incompetent mess that was what seemed to be left of the capable, successful, well-married daughter she thought she had reared. Curiously it was Michael's stepmother Boo who had, Michael told me, put up with Rodney's various affairs for years, who came closest to helping. I complained to her, bitterly, and she said look, the crux in all this is, do you love him and do you want him back, or not. It stopped me in my tracks because I realised that indeed love had died and I did not want him back; I could never cope with someone who was going to go off with other women, even if he always came back. Boo could and did, but I would never have been able to, given my childhood experience of loss and desertion. And indeed I thought, refreshingly, why should I or anyone else have to put with that? I viewed Boo with genuine and I believe reciprocated affection, both of us tacitly acknowledging that she could do what I could not and wouldn't even have wanted to try. It gave me strength, did that encounter, and even though I was still very unhappy there was no going back from that revelation.

It was a very bad time however. I couldn't do anything or even decide what job to apply for and had finally to acknowledge I needed help. I started in classical Freudian analysis and felt better but not well enough for me to feel safe in a proper job. In any case I had put myself in a position where there was no proper job to go to. I was only just qualified as a solicitor and had never practised and my skills as a games designer were hardly marketable in the conservative UK.

Alarmed by my own incompetence and not at all comfortable living with my mother because it all felt like failure, I moved out of her house into a flat and set myself to write a crime novel (unpublished) which restored me sufficiently to start me looking for work, because the creative process is energising of itself. I recovered some of my natural bounce. I took the entrance exam for the Civil Service, got in but decided not to go because I would be in the same position as people three years my junior and (I thought) all the struggle to get a legal qualification would be wasted. I used up lots of other people's time as well as my own being interviewed for jobs I realised I wasn't going to do but confidence slowly returned. The one place I didn't try and go to was a solicitor's office. I knew I didn't want a career in Trusts and Conveyancing and by then I understood how difficult getting into commercial law would be, and how hard and long everyone in that field worked and how little time *that* would leave me to get my social life back on track. Abt Associates had nurtured me, so I looked to try and replicate something of that experience.

I found a consultancy that seemed to be doing interesting work (PEP – Political and Economic Planning) and went to see them. Barbara Shenfield, one of the senior people there, was examining an important hypothesis, namely that the large industrial groups who had an expressed social ethos as part of their culture did well because enacting the ethos also improved the business as a whole; in short what looked like an ethical social policy might also be a sound business practice. She had just finished working with Marks and Spencer, where she had taken each plank of their policy on the social welfare of their employees and examined it for its effect on the Group's business success and found that the Group's then practice of giving free hair care, free uniforms and a good free canteen had resulted in a very low turnover among their predominantly female workforce. An unsurprising conclusion like much social science work but a useful one, for the first time properly statistically analysed and laid against employee turnover, and a real guide to the Group on what was worth paying for. This was my second encounter with Behavioural Science, following on the research that Clark Abt had uncovered, and it seemed both interesting and important – the application of science to business management and development was very new in the 1960s.

PEP wanted to look at John Laing Construction who had a long-standing policy of offering steady lifelong employment rather than the industry practice (in 1967) of taking on labour only for the duration of a particular building contract. You'll have to ask the employees, I said helpfully, and she said she had been looking for a young man to do that on a selection of sites. I assured her that the men on the sites would tell a woman more than any young man, adducing the shade of my architect/builder father and somewhat exaggerating the time I had spent on sites with him. Barbara was convinced, and introduced me to Laings who, once recovered from the shock, were supportive and indeed enthusiastic.

John Laing was an old-established Northern company with a firm moral stance, and they believed that stable employment was a must in social terms. They also believed that it benefited the group, providing them with experienced workers who would feel loyalty to the company and who would move round to the different sites as required. The Group understood that a lot of their employees would spurn this offer, but they needed to know who was likely to accept and whether they would provide them with the useful stable labour force. So I spent a happy year, much of it on their sites, sitting in huts, interviewing a series of men, some bewildered and some belligerent – I learned much about body language from men of all shapes and sizes reluctantly easing themselves into a chair, leaning back and folding their arms. They melted, virtually all of them, talking for the first time about their jobs and their lives, answering a string of questions designed to test the interaction between money, the convenience of the site, and the benefits of stable employment. I don't think anyone had asked them what they thought about their lives before.

The sites varied. A big house building site in Croydon turned out to be staffed entirely by Indian labour from the Punjab. The supply was organised by gang masters, as the site management very fairly warned me, and there we had to break the rule of random selection and interview only those who were prepared to be interviewed. A substantial percentage refused to talk, citing inability to speak English, but from those that would, and could, a picture of immigrant settlement in the late 1960s rose before my eyes; this one came ten years ago, Miss, and yes, Miss, had always worked for Laings. He had lived at first in a room belonging to an uncle, shared with two other cousins, and now he and the cousins owned their own houses and let rooms to other younger cousins. They worked all hours, as did their wives whom they had subsequently brought over to join them. A story with which we are all familiar in 2017 but in 1968 it was truly new, except to Mum, who as a social worker in Camden was dealing with a similar pattern. British Rail in the 1950s and 1960s had brought 300 single men from Jamaica into a hostel in Camden Town with, as Mum put it primly, a catastrophic effect on the morals of the native-born young women. Then the Jamaicans brought in wives, sensible, god-fearing women, who made them buy houses and have children and educate them, in the teeth of local prejudice. 'No Blacks, no Irish' was a familiar notice in the windows of the Camden Town lodging houses until the legislation of the 1970s outlawed it.

I was moved on to the civil engineering side to look at the huge Western Avenue site, then in its third year. Western Avenue was driven through five miles of some of the worst slums in London, and a haunt of criminals, where even I, a confident Londoner, did not go after dark. The criminals, along with whole neighbourhoods, were transplanted or disrupted, and everyone was rehoused into the sort of tower blocks no one builds for public housing these days because they rapidly turn into hells of non-working lifts, urine-redolent public spaces and lawless teenagers.

In 1968 the whole neighbourhood was noisy and dust-covered. The site's boundaries were six feet away from houses in which people were trying to live, and on site the conditions were more cramped than would now be permitted. It sprawled from just outside Paddington down to White City, an elongated factory, divided administratively into six sections. Health and Safety was then much less in evidence, though Laings as a good employer insisted – on pain of instant dismissal – on proper safety boots and a hard hat. I wore them too, as accessories to the short skirts all women were wearing that summer.

Western Avenue was staffed as to about sixty per cent by 'travelling men' as they were known in the trade, almost all Irish. They lived in caravans on a site specially set aside, or in cheap lodging houses, and they worked seven days a week rather than sitting in their temporary homes drinking at weekends. They got home to Ireland perhaps once every six weeks and were men to whom the offer of stable employment with the company meant nothing since their objective was entirely to earn as much money as possible. These were skilled men; scaffolders and shuttering joiners who built all the framework for the many thousands of tons of concrete that go into a motorway. They worked ferociously hard, displaying real project management skills, and a wise management would ensure there was neither let nor hindrance to their progress.

They did not all spend the substantial sums of money they earned rationally. For the first three days all my interviewees were hard-working sons of Ireland sending every penny home to aged mothers to buy a farm, but I had been taken by one of the Laings managers to the huge pubs that sprang up surrounding the site and watched a scaffolding gang getting in eight pints a man immediately after their shift, then going off to visit their bookmaker, and understood that I was being misled. As everyone got to know me better – I found that everything about me, from the safety boots to every detail of my background was relayed from one end of the site to another in hours – they started to tell me how their lives really were. Some at least of these hard-working men did save their money, usually in the form of property, which was in the bones of every Irish expatriate coming from a situation where five or six sons would be disputing a farm barely large enough to support one of them. Two of the shuttering joiners I met were in the process of building substantial property companies in the UK, now quoted on the stock market, an example of what a man could do who had started 'on the tools'. But others spent the money in the betting shops, or, indeed on actually owning the horses they bet on.

It was here that I met another man who taught me a lot and turned into a lifelong friend: Gerry Donnelly, a serious, careful Dublin-born and -trained civil engineer who was running the casting yard on Western Avenue, supervising the immensely difficult business of building the non-standard concrete forms that would support the motorway. I was interviewing one day in a hot site hut when suddenly a grateful shade fell on us; Gerry had caused the big crane to be moved to give me shelter, a gesture akin in its extravagance to placing his cloak in the mud for me to walk on. He taught me, just by doing it, how to look at a site, how to see if a group was not working well, to notice at a glance any stupid or hazardous or lazy practice and how to get men to work to time. His son Ruaidhri is my godson and is much like his father in his careful study of what he does, with all his father's beautiful manners.

I did two stints on Western Avenue, the first while I was collecting material and the second after the project had finished and we had produced a preliminary report for the Board of John Laing. The Board were depressed by my key finding, which was that the employees who wanted stable employment above all else were, predominantly, unskilled, black or brown, and over forty, but the Board had rallied to say that surely they were right in harvesting a stable force who could be deployed to the most difficult sites. I knew my sites very well by then – so I rang up the Croydon site agent who reminded me that anyone who had served three years was a 'Laings Man', and as such a protected species. He had been allocated dozens of them to help start a difficult site, all of whom had asked to be transferred somewhere easier within a week. No busy site agent was going to go through the wearying process of firing them and tangling with Head Office; he just moved them on, didn't he? Why did I think his site was organised by Punjabi gang masters if he could have got English labour? A simple desk exercise on transfers of Laings Men in the first six months of the Croydon site confirmed the point and left the Laings Board further depressed but a lot better informed.

For a young woman suffering from rejection a building site is a good place to be. I got a good deal of uncritical male admiration and this gave me the strength to sit down and look at what had once seemed the ruins of a life. I accepted that I had been irrevocably deflected from my chosen path and that I had to find a new route to a Man's Job in stable employment which – unlike the Laings travelling men – I knew I needed. John Laing Construction offered me a permanent job but I thought I had only a very slim chance of getting to the top in an organisation where everyone else was male and a qualified engineer. I was exhausted, I decided, fighting the good fight all by myself and perhaps a more structured and female-friendly organisation might suit me better.

So I looked again at the Civil Service and found that there was a window of opportunity, a small experimental programme which would admit a limited number of people aged twenty-eight to thirty-five directly into the top Administrative stream on level terms with the people who had been in the service since they left university. It looked like redemption, something that would validate my casual abandonment of the law and allow me, despite my wanderings, back into a mainstream career.

So I applied and was taken into the meticulous two-day assessment procedure. I enjoyed it; the statistics exercise was easy for someone who had designed and executed a big behavioural study as I had, and the other exercises seemed pretty straightforward. Towards the end I was interviewed by the Intellectual Assessor, Robin Mountfield, only a year older than me. He asked me about one exercise which had involved writing a letter to dismiss tactfully a man who had been a distinguished help on some Commission but whose services were no longer required, and to do this without making an enemy. 'You dismissed him in the first paragraph of your excellent letter,' Robin said, 'and everyone else fired him in the last paragraph.' Relaxed, I told him about my mother who had agonised over a three-page letter to an employer when she was resigning her job in order to marry at the outbreak of World War Two. Dad read it and pointed out that she had not, in three pages, actually told the employer she was leaving. And I had in my time made the Principal of Newnham read two pages before reaching the key fact which was that I no longer wanted to read Classics. 'So you always state the purpose of your letter in paragraph one,' Robin said, delighted, and plainly longing to entertain his fellow adjudicators with this thought. 'But you really can't go to the Home Office,' he said, consulting another bit of paper on which we had been asked to produce a list of Departments we would like to go to. 'Full of men and they all address each other as "Mr". You won't like it.'

No, I wouldn't, I agreed, but where should I go? Robin suggested his own Department of Economic Affairs but warned me with characteristic detachment that it might not be long for this world, and after ten minutes' hard discussion we agreed on the Board of Trade, with the DEA second and any of the big economic departments after that.

This was not quite the end of the road; the Final Selection Board was waiting for me, a formal interview by a dozen senior civil servants chaired by Sir John Wolfenden. The interview itself was alarming but I thought I was doing all right until a woman in her fifties, wearing a brown cardigan over an unremarkable blouse, leaned forward to ask me why, with my background as a lawyer and experience of two behavioural consultancies I was not applying for one of the departments that dealt with Social Affairs. I was struck dumb but found the truth. 'The thing is,' I said apologetically, 'my mother is a social worker and ...' 'Thank you. No more questions.' The woman sat back and I was out, trying to shut the door quietly while hearing gales of laughter breaking out behind me. What had I done? Ten years later, when Martina, widow of Sir John Wolfenden's eldest son, living with us while she qualified as a social worker, brought Sir John to dinner, he told me. 'We had spent the *entire morning*,' he said with relish, 'interviewing pleasant young people whose sole desire was to help people. How refreshing to meet you, whom we all thought a very good candidate, so plainly appalled by the very thought. We agreed we *must* take you but we should assume you might not stay for ever.' Prescient and shrewd, the lot of them, as it turned out.

Safely into the Civil Service, I found myself back on Western

Avenue for the summer; Laings were engaged in a claim against the Department of Transport because late decisions from the Department had held up the site the summer before, just when I was there interviewing, and I was in a position to substantiate their statements and work through the site turnover figures to prove the claim. Ah well, I thought, at least I'm going to be working for the Board of Trade not the Department of Transport, and settled down to help bring an action against the Government.

I was put in the site office this time so that I could get at all the staff records. Gerry had moved on but I was adopted by the new site agent, Jimmy Baxter, a very senior Laing employee. He took me out for lunch so I could see where the work was done, as he put it, to one of the huge pubs just off the site. We sat down with a drink and the tables around us filled immediately with men, all greeting Jimmy who explained to me that these were all his subcontractors. The nearest man glanced at our half-full glasses and raised a finger to a barman and, a minute later, second glasses stood beside our drinks – out of nervousness I had accepted the offer of a glass of white wine. The work did indeed get done, problems were sorted, and, at regular intervals, another man would do the finger-raising bit. I ended up with eleven glasses of white wine, nine undrunk – it was a matter of honour to buy your round, and the barman naturally did as he was asked. Jimmy didn't take notes because he didn't need to, and he drank on even terms with his subbies because he always had. A Scot, a stocky hard man from a poor family in Musselburgh, he had found his way to a degree in civil engineering and had turned round several of the really big London sites, where problems like high labour turnover, uncontrollable subcontractors and engineering complexity were common.

He always took me with him after that first lunch even though I stuck to tonic water and he taught me a lot about running a site and about the Metropolitan Police. I was at his side while he courteously but bluntly told a big policeman – sweating under the pub lights, jacket off, radio sitting in the pool of drink in front of him – that no special site security would be needed at this stage, thanking you just the same. 'Can't do that,' Jimmy said to me afterwards, assuming I had understood what I had heard. 'Means you could never control a London site again.' 'And if you don't accept the kind offer?' I asked as we reached the car. 'Nae bother, they'd just know what you are.' Indeed. Jimmy's stance reflected Laing policy but it was also part of him. You did not put yourself in the power of others. I have often and often thought of him and that policeman. I used a lot of this in *Death on Site* years later.

I had been there for about a month when the site's human relations man disappeared without explanation. I asked Jimmy, who said irritably that the man couldnae hold his drink, which turned out to be a euphemism for a nasty case of the DTs. Jimmy suggested that I might temporarily fill his post .

The first part of the job happened every morning when I scanned the list of people required on all six sections – usually scribbles saying things like 'Four shuttering joiners, one banksman. No more black chippies.' This was not entirely racial prejudice; the Jamaican carpenters were not trained to the same level as the Irish tradesmen so I was driven to hoping that the two Irishmen loitering just outside my office were the usual combination of useful man being introduced by brother/cousin/uncle already working on the site. Like many London sites of that period our other principal recruitment tool was to send a van down the Kilburn High Road at 7 a.m. on a Monday where burly men would crawl into the back of it, sweating drink. I also took on the role of conciliation between management and men on pay and rations, particularly in relation to bonus schemes. A misjudged or over-complicated scheme could halt a site while the scaffolding gangs or groups of shuttering joiners would trickle off the site. I found an ability to explain how a scheme would work out to men who were often functionally illiterate but could grasp numbers in a flash. It brought back the days of finding brilliant intuitive games players among the depressed black soldiers at Fort Gordon, Georgia.

It came to an end of course, that happy summer, but not without a wonderful day out at Ascot for the races with Jimmy, some of the subbies and the leaders of two shuttering gangs, one of whom was the owner of the three year old Ribofilio, son of the all-conquering Ribot. My associates, who routinely bet in units of £1000, did not know you could get into the enclosure at Ascot by paying; they had assumed you had to be posh and when they came in with me they had some difficulty finding their usual bookies, who were on the main course and everyone had to lean over the wire to place their bets. My views on form were courteously sought and equally courteously ignored, but they put, alongside their own bets, a fiver for me on whatever they were on. Just before the last race Jimmy told me I was £200 to the good, which they proposed to put on an Irish horse who hadn't come all the way to Ascot to lose, had he? '£200?' I said, aghast, visions of washing machines for the little house I had just bought rising before my eyes, and wouldn't let them, and was reluctantly congratulated on my prescience when the horse in question came fourth. Jimmy, deeply amused, said I would never make a gambler, any more than he would; you couldn't do it if you saw washing machines instead of gambling chips. Another thing I have not forgotten.

Jimmy remained a friend; he rose further in Laings and was a director by the time somewhere in the 1970s when my husband, also Jim, a rising star in the Civil Service, was leaving a party at the Dorchester, engaged in sedate discussion with the senior partner in a surveyor's whose guest he was. 'Wheesht,' he heard, 'Jimmy,' and found himself irresistibly summoned to the group of senior site men, similarly dinner-jacketed, of which the centre was Jimmy Baxter. I had expected husband Jim home by midnight but it was 4 a.m. when he arrived. 'I fell among thieves,' he said just before he fell face first into bed, and I was so charmed by hearing Jimmy Baxter's standard explanation for being inveigled into a night out that I got up ungrudgingly, got my Jim out of his clothes and lied to his boss for him the next morning.

Chapter 6

THE CIVIL SERVICE 1969–1979

I arrived at the Board of Trade in 1969 and found myself with Establishment Division (Civil Service for Personnel or Human Resources) in the person of an older man in a good suit who regarded me with bright-eyed interest.

He greeted me warmly, asked about my past and said kindly he was so sorry to hear that I had been through a divorce but he was sure I would find myself a nice new husband in the Board of Trade. It sounds dreadfully patronising and politically incorrect but it cheered me; I was close to admitting to myself that a husband was what I truly wanted and it was encouraging that E Division thought there was one to hand.

I was posted to the Agricultural Imports division of the Board of Trade, whose raison d'être was to negotiate quotas for various imported foodstuffs. I was concerned with imports of butter, cheese and bacon. This was four years before our entry to the EEC, but when and if we got in we would be subject to the EEC's rules, which would preclude the favourable access arrangements for Australian butter and New Zealand lamb and Danish bacon, and the dairy and farming industries of all three countries were scrambling to adjust and trying to negotiate large protected quotas in a secure market. Negotiations were a stately process; all teams were led by an Under Secretary, two grades above me, and my team consisted of my immediate boss, Kate Boyes, twenty-five years my senior, who had done all this before. Given the acute international importance of these and related negotiations about sugar (New Zealand in particular faced being set back for many years had they gone wrong, as did the economies of the whole of the Caribbean and Ireland), it was not possible to give a new recruit much autonomy. I knew this wasn't going to work for me but just had the sense to decide the Board of Trade was a big place, there were other jobs, and I could sit quiet and learn how the whole organisation worked before agitating for a change.

I liked the Service from the first; clever, cultured people, many deeply eccentric, a bit like Cambridge. Kate Boyes I admired very much, and the difficulties she had had to face put my own in context. After a distinguished Civil Service career, Kate had been required to resign when she decided to marry, and to start all over again, a rule only abandoned in the early 1960s. Unlike other doughty Board of Trade women who had hidden their wedding rings and concealed their real relationship with that nice man in the next Division, Kate had insisted on marrying Cyril Saunders, an Under Secretary by the time I met him. The Board of Trade did not go in for fashion icons but the brilliant Cyril was beyond scruffy; there was a legend that a foreign visitor encountering Cyril on the steps of Horse Guards had given him a fiver with the suggestion that he should get himself a good meal. Had he not been introduced to me as Kate's husband I might have done the same. Kate didn't give a damn for clothes either; faced with a Foreign Office edict that all women were to wear hats and gloves for a Lunch, she appeared in an ancient straw gardening hat and long green evening gloves. Another distinguished female colleague, Mary Lackey, appeared with her fine hair falling out of its usual bun with an embryo fascinator sliding off the top, and what can only be described as motoring gauntlets. I felt I had let our side down by wearing what brother Alexander memorably called the three piece suite left over from another life, expensive hat, short white gloves and matching handbag.

The 1970 General Election brought about one of the periodic upheavals in the Civil Service, eliminating the DEA – as Robin Mountfield had forecast – and combining the Board of Trade with Industrial Sponsorship to create the Department of Trade and Industry (DTI). It brought with it Sir Antony Part as the leader of the combined operation whom I met at a party to welcome our new colleagues. I was doubly of interest to him, being Female and an Experiment. He agreed that I would be better in a more managerial role and, in the teeth of the nice man in E Division who believed you never moved anyone until they had at least eighteen months in post, I was placed in the division that had responsibility for Airports.

We did not of course actually *run* any airports – a task I would happily have taken on – but we oversaw the people who did run Heathrow, Gatwick, Stansted, Edinburgh and Prestwick, all five then publicly owned. We were the hinge between Ministers, the newly constituted British Airports Authority and the public. The BAA were then in their first full year of operation with the Department's wise guidance – usually transmitted by me – available to them. It was intrinsically an uneasy relationship, inasmuch as on any occasion it was not clear whether it was for the DTI to intervene or whether it was properly and entirely the business of the new Authority. For example: in one week planes coming in from Los Angeles were forced to land, five days out of seven, at Prestwick in Scotland rather than Heathrow because of fog, and there were many furious letters to the Secretary of State from passengers who had had to struggle with a seven-hour rail trip on top of a long transatlantic journey. Did we, the DTI, put up a draft reply for the Secretary of State to consider? After much deliberation it was decided the BAA could answer this batch, but if the problem were to persist into the next week the Secretary of State would have to take the load.

I knew that I was working a couple of steps away from where the real decisions were being taken but after having had to invent my own jobs I found the firm structure of the Service attractive. The debate was always of high quality and my colleagues were a treat; clever, careful thinkers, even the really eccentric ones. I enjoyed the process of producing, on two sides of a sheet of paper, the arguments for and against a particular course of action so that several people could discuss the issue in the critical but uncensorious manner of a university supervision, with the crucial difference that everyone had done the homework. It was like being with Cherry or Lucy or John again, discussing an essay or a presentation, only this time Action This Day would be required.

I had to learn a lot. The Civil Service had no plans to train their Experiments, hoping that clever people with administrative experience would pick it up as they went along. Up to a point, Lord Copper, I used to mutter to myself, staring at yet another mysterious file requiring Action. I found a friend, Jim, on the other end of a telephone, who had the same job as I did in a different division; he was responsible, in the same hazy way, for the newly constituted British Overseas Airways Corporation (BOAC) and British European Airways (BEA). The difference was that he knew how to do it, having joined the Service at the age of twenty-three and done all the things the high-flying graduate trainees did, culminating in a spell in the Secretary of State's office as a private secretary. He was generous with his time; he got a call from me nearly every morning with pathetic questions like 'What is a Parliamentary Question and why is it in a yellow file? And why do I have it?' Slowly I grasped that it was my duty to ensure my Ministers (as in 'my children', it was clear) were able to reply in Parliament on every facet of a Question (always with the capital Q). It was Jim who guided me through writing a Cabinet paper (never in those days more than two sides of a sheet of paper) and exactly who should receive copies (more people than you would think possible).

I met him face to face after eight months of this, at a party given by another of the Experiments, Neville Abraham, and was stunned to discover that my respected mentor was a tall bespectacled person with uncontrollable red curly hair sticking out at all angles, jeans held up with a tie, and blatantly younger than me. He asked me out after the first half hour of conversation. I made a mess of the response; as when I met my first husband, the truth was that I had someone else around, and Jim, thinking I meant no, withdrew pleasantly, saying he was just off for a holiday. By the time he got back I had gathered the sense to dispose of the someone else (married, and older). I rang Jim up – as usual – but this time I invited him out. We became a couple, enduring many a Civil Service joke based on the theme that Jim was looking after Aeroplanes while I did Airports, hur, hur. Brought the house down every time.

He turned out to be an exotic, rather than the familiar son of a Hampstead civil servant that I had assumed. Jim comes of a Jewish family that arrived here from Holland in the eighteenth century, having been respected Burgomasters in Amersfoort, not fleeing persecution like the parents of my Jewish friends at school. His father was born into the Cousinhood, the intertwined network of Cohens, Waleys, Rothschilds and Sebag Montefiores, and Jim's great- grandfather was the first Jew to be elected to Parliament. His grandfather was on the mad side of eccentric, the principal protagonist 'Mr M' in C.P. Snow's book *The Conscience of the Rich*. Charles Snow and Jim's father Dick Cohen met at Cambridge. Dick took Snow home to the big family house in Paddington where he, a brilliant boy from nowhere, spent most of his undergraduate career with the Cohens. He had a good ear, and in *The Conscience of the Rich* I can hear all the Cohens that ever spoke. Jim's grandfather, Mr C in real life, died long before

97

I met Jim but two of his sons, my father-in-law (who is Charles March in the book) and Uncle Harold, I knew well. In real life, as well as in the book, my father-in-law insisted on becoming a doctor, to his father's infinite distress ('a practitioner', he would moan, reportedly wringing his hands). This honourable profession, the height of many a Jewish family's ambitions, was not smart enough, and Dick had been destined for the law or a bank or Parliament or all three. As in the book, Dick became a doctor and married out – Jim's mother was the brilliant daughter of a United Free minister from Hamilton, who got the top First from Edinburgh University in English and met Dick while doing a PhD at Cambridge.

While we were courting, Jim decided he needed a more immediately useful piece of education than his good Cambridge degree in classics and got himself sent to the University of York to do a one-year Masters degree in Economics, normally only open to people whose first degree was in Economics. Its distinguished Professor, Alan Peacock, could not resist taking someone who was actually practising economics in government service. I shied at the thought that once again I would support a husband through graduate school only to have him leave me, so we agreed not to think of marriage for the time being and Jim went off to York, while I came up to join him at the weekends.

It wasn't at all the same as my experience in the USA. Jim was settled in a working life and on full pay from the Civil Service and not dependent on me, which made for a much better relationship. And of course he was the same stable capable warm man I knew and that did not change. Halfway through his first term we decided to marry and did so at Christmas 1971, following a large party at the DTI where, in keeping with the family atmosphere, both our Deputy Secretaries, very senior civil servants, made speeches giving us away; mine, Robbie Burns, was at Oxford with my mother, and Jim's, David Hubback, was an old friend of Jim's father who had also been at school with my father. We spent our honeymoon in a cottage owned by Jim's family on the northwest coast of Scotland where there were about six hours' daylight every day. The very long winter evenings were spent not as colleagues and local friends assumed but in Jim painfully learning calculus: a victim of early specialisation at Westminster, he had been taught virtually nothing other than Latin and Greek since he was fifteen, and he needed calculus to get through econometrics. The day he left the University late in May the next year, having passed top of a group in which everyone but he had read Economics for their first degrees and qualifying himself to do a PhD if he wanted, we got the night train to Inverness again to the cottage and, as it turned out, conceived Henry, our first child.

Dr R.H.L. Cohen CB, Janet, Jim Cohen, Margaret Cohen, Mary Neel at Jim and Janet's wedding, December 18ᵗʰ 1971.

As I joined the Civil Service and found myself a man I was also involved in starting a restaurant. I did not plan to go into business, but as often a brother, Alexander this time, led me into something new. He had left university after six years reading architecture with his plans in disarray. He had intended to go into a four-man partnership with three friends, Bernard and John, and Richard, then Prince Richard of Gloucester, but the death of Richard's elder brother William in a flying accident changed that plan. Richard knew he would have to take his brother's place as the Duke of Gloucester with all the commitments that entailed, and the other three could not find a new basis for a partnership. Alexander was casting about for what to do when he met an old friend with an empty shop on the Fulham Road and no money who wanted to start a restaurant. He threw himself at this project with his characteristic demoniac energy and three months after I had joined the Civil Service he arrived, filthy dirty, in the middle of a dinner party, to explain that the hearing for the drinks licence was next week, and the magistrates would not entertain an application for a licence unless lavatories, washrooms and kitchen were completely finished. He couldn't get tilers for love or money, and in any case money was running short. By the next day I had become a 20 per cent shareholder and a Laings subcontractor had provided a crew of tilers but of course the work didn't stop there and I spent time and energy helping him get a very successful and fashionable restaurant off the ground.

I had also become involved with the Notting Hill Neighbourhood Law Centre, set up and financed by the local authority to provide the poor with the kind of legal advice available to the middle class. It was operating with only two qualified solicitors, headed by Peter Kandler, and one Articled Clerk, James Saunders, and it was trying to provide a free twenty-four-hour service in an area where lawyers were only just less rare than giraffes. I was qualified so I volunteered to cover a shift so that everyone could have a night off. I did the evening session when we received clients with appointments from 6 p.m. to 9 p.m. on Fridays, then remained on call for those of our clients who found themselves guests of the Metropolitan Police, and would represent these when necessary in a magistrate's court on a Saturday morning. I had lots of energy then. I was happy and Jim approved but it was appallingly strenuous and I only lasted nine months, which was long enough to learn a lot about the condition of the local citizenry. It reminded me of the descriptions of the first days of the NHS when doctors were overwhelmed with patients suffering from lifetimes of neglect. Our clients had suffered for ever from appalling landlords, cynically poor treatment by every supplier of goods, and behaviour from their husbands that was endangering life and health. At first I was confident in the power of a lawyer's letter but it was James Saunders the Articled Clerk who looked over my shoulder one night as I struggled with the office typewriter and snarled: 'Janet. Don't fuck around, put in a writ.' He was of course right; these people had been ignoring letters for years but a writ got their attention and I was reminded that one of the reasons why I became a lawyer was that I want justice. I had to stop rather abruptly; advancing pregnancy with Henry rusted the brain and impaired the ability to get up, fully alert and ready to take on the police, in the middle of the night.

What with a new marriage and Parsons Restaurant as well I was not putting enough time and energy into the day job, and, unusually, my probationary period in the Civil Service was extended so that I would have longer to prove myself eligible for Lifetime Employment and the Pension at sixty, which was the offer in those vanished days. I was deeply offended but Jim told me bluntly that I would be mad to flounce out of the Service, my CV already suggested a distressing volatility, and I needed to settle down. I was in the habit of doing what he advised, so I swallowed hurt pride and worked very hard so that by the time I had to break it to E Division that not only had I found a good husband, just like they said, but a nice baby was on its way the Civil Service had confirmed my probation and I was one of their own.

I was superbly looked after on the medical front. My father-in-law, by then Deputy Director of the Health Service, had been both overjoyed and panicked by the news that I was pregnant. His own experience had been traumatic; their oldest child, a girl, who would have been Jim's elder sister, was stillborn after three days' hard labour and Margaret damaged in the scramble to get the baby out once the hospital realised the problem. The next pregnancy had ended in miscarriage, but finally in 1942 when Margaret was 38 Jim was born, after a long labour but healthy, under the charge of a female gynaecologist. The photographs of him and them in the early days show a very cheerful baby and two parents plainly incredulous with relief.

Dick approached Jim to plead with him to let me go to a top gynaecologist, privately if need be. I agreed instantly, specifying only that I wanted a female person, and Dick produced, shyly, the CV of Dame Josephine Barnes, then in her sixties, a person of such appalling distinction that I could only hope she would actually take me on. She did, and I would run into her Holland Park house, ten minutes from ours, with a urine sample, we would have a nice chat and on I would go to work. After a trouble-free pregnancy I endured fourteen hours in labour during which I had made no discernible progress. I abandoned all plans to give birth naturally and had an epidural and slept the night propped up in the operating theatre of the old Elizabeth Garrett Anderson hospital. I woke once to find Alexander, clad in a fashionable goatskin coat, explaining anxiously and untruthfully that he had come to see that Jim was all right, and a second time to find an air of suppressed alarm. Alexander had gone, Jim was awake and on his feet and Dame Josephine was explaining that the baby had turned round and was now presenting as a breech birth, and if she could not reverse his position she would have to do a caesarean. She told Jim, out of my hearing, that she might have to push and tug a bit so was he sure he wanted to be present? Yes, he said, as he had promised. Then he would please stay at the head end.

Dame Josephine was tiny and fine boned but sure enough, just as I had assumed, she turned the baby round and pulled him out, presenting us with Henry, with the forceps marks on his forehead that would fade within a day or so. That skill I am told is now almost lost, and this loss accounts in part for the increase in deliveries by caesarean section.

I fell asleep again while Jim went to ring everyone up (his father had been awake all night) and I woke ravenously hungry to the smell of bacon. I waited hopefully (Henry was in the hospital nursery) but nothing happened so I shyly asked. Horrified faces all round and I wondered what I had done until a senior nurse appeared. 'Mrs Cohen. We assumed you'd not want the bacon.' I considered explaining my High Church upbringing and Jim's atheism but in the end said that we were Reform and I ate everything.

Henry was not an easy baby; like his future brother and sister he suffered from colic for the first three months and infantile eczema for years. Jim and I both have Scots mothers and red hair runs in both families, a genetic mix which tends to produce pale, irritable skin, and all three have that. If colic did not wake him, the eczema did every time he wet his nappy, so even after seven months I was always tired. Additionally we had unwisely moved house when he was six months old, doing a wholesale conversion, so I was overstretched. The answer seemed to be to go back on a part-time basis, a privilege extended readily to women in the Administrative grade, and I counted myself fortunate.

Virtually all policy jobs in the Service were then uncompromisingly full time, structured to support Ministers at all times, and the only way to deal with a part-timer was to tuck them away in a bit of Establishment division tidying up a piece of administration, in my case the recommendations of the Fulton Committee. Brutally summarised, the Committee had decided that lots of functions undertaken by Government could be entrusted to other bodies. And, while we were at it, some bodies already nominally independent could be detached altogether, like the National Physical Laboratory. David Durie, a capable full-timer, and I were there to sort out which of the Department of Trade and Industry's functions could be detached and separately financed. We were both under the charge of Dennis Church, who had gone blind at the age of twelve but had got his way through school and university and into the Service. He had to have all his papers read to him by a clerk reader; a slow, hard way to work that meant Dennis had to listen to stuff that David and I and the rest of the Service were speed-reading. He explained to us both that since he had been able to see until he was twelve we could usefully describe to him anything that a man who had been blind since 1932 would have seen. Dennis's arm crooked in mine, surrounded by senior scientists, I stood in front of the National Physical Laboratory's pride and joy, an advanced gasometer, and explained to Dennis that we had before us something that looked like a typewriter with a giant balloon attached to the back. Scientists around us rolled their eyes but the truth was that although, typically of the Administrative grade, neither of us were scientists and one of us couldn't see, we were seeking to answer a strictly commercial question, namely, if Government stopped funding and controlling this activity, would the private sector do it? The answer was clearly yes, and when finally that recommendation was accepted, the private sector did indeed do it better. Years later Johnny Lynn and Antony Jay got the general attitude to science down pat in *Yes Minister* when Sir Humphrey, Jim Hacker and Bernard are discussing the siting of a chemical cracker. 'Doesn't *anyone* know any chemistry?' Jim Hacker enquires. 'Oh *no*, Minister, I was in the *scholarship* stream,' Sir Humphrey replies, triumphantly. We had all been in the scholarship stream and at that time none of us was a scientist. It seems now like another country.

Our second son Richard was born (in March 1975) almost two years to the day after Henry. He was also delivered by Dame Josephine Barnes, and his birth was attended by every nurse and midwife not immediately employed elsewhere. This time it was a straightforward birth. Dame Josephine's contribution was to stand at the business end, gloved hands held up encouraging me to push, until the last minute when she moved like lightning to make the quick cut that let Richard out into the world without leaving me with a jagged tear. 'Another boy,' she said, picking up a very long baby and placing him on my tummy. 'Ah well. Easier for clothes.' Four Jamaican midwives looked at her appalled, and one snatched Richard up exclaiming indignantly that this was a lovely, lovely boy, look at dem big eyes, he gonna have all de girls after him. I *had* hoped for a girl but, in common with all mothers I found the minute the baby was there it seemed impossible that they could have been other than they were.

Richard wasn't much easier than Henry because he too had the colic and the eczema but we had a maternity nurse this time and a nanny who loved him immediately as she loved Henry and would take him from my exhausted arms at breakfast time so I could fall into bed, and I recovered more quickly. I decided to go back to full-time work because it was then the only way to get one of the good policy jobs, and I had a fully staffed and expensive household behind me (live-in nanny, cleaner three days a week, Mum in reserve). Jan, our nanny, was only twenty-one at the time and badly needed to know that she would be off duty most days after 6.30, so all would be well provided I could leave the office at 6 p.m. I found that this absolute constraint made me grittily efficient. No leisurely cups of tea with colleagues: I learned when my energies flagged to drink coffee and get right on with the next task because otherwise it would be 6 p.m. I couldn't finish any work at home because the children would not let me and by the time they went to bed I could only manage to eat and watch a bit of TV.

The Department had available a job that was right up my street (career management for mothers in the Department was (and is) constrained by what posts need filling at the moment the returning mother pops up again). The Industry Act 1975 had just been passed, empowering Government to put financial assistance into failing industrial companies in areas of high unemployment where jobs were at risk. A new unit had been set up consisting entirely of secondees from the private sector, four very senior men plus a dozen clever twenty-eight- to thirty-five-year-olds, mostly accountants from the big firms. I was to be the hinge between the unit and Ministers for companies in the regions of high unemployment.

While I had been away the Government had changed and it was Labour in charge. Everyone was new; Eric Varley was Secretary of State, and happily Alan Williams, whom I knew, was the Minister responsible for my bit.

The day I arrived I went to a ministerial meeting to find among those present Sir Kenneth Cork and his son Roger, the most senior partners in Cork Gully, accountants specialising in receivership. A cosy discussion was taking place with the Corks assuring the Minister they would do everything to help the Department by saving which jobs they could, but it was going to cost, ooh, £100,000 a week to keep the business ticking over and they were so glad there were departmental funds. The next day, by agreement with my new colleagues, who had been trying to persuade Ministers not to be too eager to step in, I read Alan Williams the relevant passage of the Companies Act which provides that a Receiver is responsible entirely to the bank who appoints him and has no responsibility to any other creditor other than to avoid kicking them in the teeth. Into a silence, Alan said heavily, 'So what you are telling me, Janet, is that a Receiver is not a good man entirely concerned for the welfare of the workforce?' Over a general murmur of well, I'm afraid so, Minister, we collectively managed to say that the bank might not give a toss for the workforce but they were interested in getting the best price for the assets, which was usually achieved by keeping the saleable bits running. 'So they can damn well put up some of the money, then? We don't have to do it all?' Alan was always quick, and to cries of Yes, Minister, all round, the tone of negotiations with Cork Gully and the other specialist firms usefully changed. It reminded me why I had originally gone into the law; if you can produce the written word, you can ensure that reason and justice prevail.

I had a very happy three years; I had a huge caseload but (unlike the modern day) colleagues and I did our best without having to consult the layers of private sector experts who are now attached to every public policy decision. We were cheap, and we were smart. Some colleagues were engaged in enormous potential rescue jobs, like Alfred Herbert and Kearney Trecker Marwin, huge engineering firms who were being destroyed in the dying throes of the British shipbuilding industry and the decline of British car manufacturing. Where I was in the regions we were usually dealing with smaller companies, with the signal exception of Brentford Nylons, a business set up by Lithuanian immigrants based in Northumberland which manufactured very cheap sheets and bed linen and sold the factory's output in many little shops all over the UK. In those distant days the Bank of England thought it had a responsibility to ensure financial stability and kept a check on bank indebtedness for companies in serious trouble, and Brentford Nylons was on their list. The local MP had also come in, accompanied by constituents, to plead for the company to be kept going.

We were old hands by then, so we put in the Industrial Development Unit to have a look, and concluded that there was no point financing the existing management who had run the business into the ground. The bank put in Cork Gully, who decided that the shops had to go unless the Department would provide the cash to keep them going. We decided not to; the shops were barely profitable and mostly outside the areas of worst unemployment, so the Cork Gully troops in dark suits went round three hundred shops on Friday, slapping tapes on the doors and notices which declared the business was in liquidation. In virtually every case shop managers, seeing a suit on a Friday, handed them an envelope full of cash; the 'skim' which had not gone through a till and would not be reported to the Inland Revenue. It taught me that fraud and a failing business often go together; the fraud is sometimes a cause, but quite often an effect, of the failure, as the owners of the firm resort to sequestering cash in order to keep the enterprise – and the owners' lifestyle – going. I turned this experience into my first crime novel *Death's Bright Angel*.

The factory, and principal source of jobs, was preserved by the Department offering a £6m loan to Lonrho which would enable them to take over and modernise the machinery and upgrade the nylon sheets and to use their existing textile business to sell the products. That negotiation brought me into direct contact with 'Tiny' Rowlands, then the Lonrho chairman. It was Maundy Thursday and I was the most senior person available when the Lonrho Board – all eight of them – asked for a meeting. I assembled somehow a meeting room and three junior colleagues so that we were not so visibly outgunned, and twelve, unmatching, coffee mugs plus some broken biscuits. The Lonrho team arrived, expensively besuited, eyeing our preparations disbelievingly, and proceeded to explain that the whole plan would be very much helped if we could suppress a hostile report, due to be published shortly, into Lonrho's other activities. We had by then found John Lippitt, not my direct boss but two grades up on me, who said primly that the Report was the business of a different Department over whom we had no control, a sound pawn to Q3 delaying move. When John left, to ring a Minister, I told Tiny and his board what I believed, which was that no one was going to be able to make that deal (this was a Labour government after all) and (sigh) we would just have to find someone else for Brentford Nylons. They left, the Department's Nescafé and powdered milk mostly undrunk, and we settled to the task of Getting the Minutes right, and thankfully John, arriving to see affronted Lonrho backs vanishing out of the door, reported that Ministers had taken the same line. No harm had been done; in practice, Lonrho were prepared for business reasons to take on Brentford Nylons even though the very critical report was published. Tiny cultivated me thereafter – I liked him and never found it necessary to equivocate with him. He knew a fact – or at least an honestly delivered opinion – when he heard one, but the relationship was destroyed when he wrote to Ministers to say he felt I was the only person in the Department who really understood him. My senior colleagues, alarmed, forbade me, absolutely, to have lunch again with him by myself. Tiny had a reputation for getting his way with the judicious use of incentives like a handful of emeralds but I am here to say he never offered me anything other than a good lunch and I was sorry to be deprived of his company. It was some consolation to deal thereafter always with Alan Smith, an excellent experienced manager who made a good job of Brentford Nylons for many years.

So my time in Rescue ended well but not without another scene typical of the Department at that time. The final loan documents were the subject of a meeting between the Department – represented by me and a senior member of the Department's legal service, Lonrho and their lawyer, head of a very small firm whose principal client was Lonrho, and the bank represented by a partner in Freshfields. We settled down with the Nescafé and the unmatching mugs and Freshfields called for a list of documents – a reasonable, lawyerly request – but the Department's lawyer had gone to sleep. Cautiously, I nudged him, his eyes opened, he stared wildly around him and threw out an arm which pushed his file off the table. It flew apart, scattering the contents. My staff and I had to recover the papers and spread them out all over a long table, securing enough documents to complete the deal, under the incredulous stare of the Freshfields people. I thought I had covered everything but I had not thought to worry about our own lawyer; a good man on his day but, like a few senior civil servants of that era, a heavy drinker and not reliable after lunch.

Jim had not fared as well meanwhile. He was still in the Department of Energy where Tony Wedgwood Benn was Secretary of State. Jim was the youngest of his grade in the whole Civil Service, and had, in his previous job, been secretary to the Nuclear Power Advisory Board which had concluded, under a Conservative Government, that new nuclear power stations were essential and should be built using the PWC design rather than the gas-cooled or water-cooled reactors. Wedgwood Benn as Minister decided that this was a mistake, and that what was essentially the Betamax design of nuclear power stations should be selected instead. The Department, as was their practice, moved Jim; the view was there were limits to Civil Service impartiality, and you did not ask a civil servant who had worked for two years to arrive at one conclusion to spend the next two doing the opposite.

He had ended up, bored rigid, in a leisurely bit of electricity division and decided he could not stand it. He was offered a secondment by GEC, then headed by the triumvirate of Arnold Weinstock, Kenneth Bond and David Lewis, with whom he had enjoyed working on the NPAB and who were as frustrated as he with Wedgwood Benn's decision. Under the Civil Service rules Jim could not go to GEC and do Power, so he was taken into GEC Transportation which did railways. In his first week there in 1977 he contracted pneumonia, both viral and bacterial, and for three days his fever of 103° would not abate. He was off work for two months altogether before he could even cross the threshold of GEC Transportation, and he tired easily for a long time after that.

I also arrived at Christmas 1977 exhausted and on Christmas Eve noticed funny lumps all round my jawline. Mumps, my GP said, dangerous in an adult, and warned me that I was highly infectious and would be in serious pain quite soon. I went home and rushed to get the final work done for Christmas lunch for ten, being confident that all parties including the children had

had mumps and I could not infect them. In the event I was never ill enough to go to bed, although over the next three weeks I had three separate crops of lumps. I worried that hard-pressed colleagues were carrying my caseload, but my colleagues were young men, yet to start or complete their families, none of whom had had the disease, and they were unanimous in preferring overwork to the (limited) risk of orchitis and sterility. In the end I had three weeks off, precluded even from going to the shops by my doctor father-in-law for fear of spreading infection.

It was around this time that I found myself invited to join the Women's Forum, set up by Barbara Hodgson, Mary Baker (wife of Kenneth Baker MP), the journalist Katharine Whitehorn and Heather Brigstocke, then High Mistress of St Paul's Girls School. They wanted to found a network to encourage and support women in executive careers. Scratching around to find such women (as you had to in the mid-1970s), they arrived at me, largely on the basis that I was chairing Parsons Restaurant as well as being a senior civil servant. I accepted at once before they could change their minds, and the whole, increasingly distinguished, gang stayed together for years. We gave up the Forum title when we felt the group was getting too large and that younger women needed it more, and turned ourselves into a smaller powerful dining club called Links, which was the greatest support to all of us for (in my case) forty years.

I got back to work late in January 1978 to find I was promoted to the career grade of Assistant Secretary. It was a triumph – I had started late but had managed at thirty-seven to catch up with all but the very best (Jim had achieved the same grade at thirty-four). I was to lead a second team negotiating compensation for the newly nationalised aircraft and shipbuilding companies. I shared an accountant adviser with Team 1, Alistair Catto, a fellow civil servant but a refugee from one of the national accountancy firms, and I had a very good female Principal, Virginia Novarra, and an excellent female graduate trainee. We were up against negotiating teams headed by senior merchant bankers and QCs supported by expensive lawyers and accountants, but I was always better briefed than they. Both teams managed to dispose of the shipbuilding compensation cases quickly for the simple reason that the legislation – passed after a three-year battle – gave those companies far too much money for useless assets. Both teams got stuck on the aviation cases, where the legislation, with fine impartiality, gave the aircraft builders sums well below the value of their assets. I got on with the easy stuff but reached impasse with the lead negotiator for the British Aircraft Corporation and a couple of other aircraft builders.

I was just wondering how many years would have to elapse before we could settle the aircraft builder cases and I could change jobs when I discovered that some higher authority had settled my personal fate. I was pregnant again. Henry was nearly six and Richard nearly four, and they both slept reliably through the night. After a few weeks of worrying about everything Jim and I realised we were both delighted but the news was received coldly by the Department. 'You *really* didn't need to do this, Janet,' my man in E Division said, plaintively. 'I was going to move you soon, anyway.' I did not dispute this reductive view but went serenely on, getting bigger by the minute, polishing off what negotiations I could. I discovered that a twitch plus a fidget as of one suffering the advance pangs of childbirth encouraged people into reaching a deal with me, for fear they might have to start all over again with someone new.

At this point, as if there was not enough going on, I was recruited to a group led by Virginia. She and a couple of her other single colleagues bought me lunch and pointed out that I was a privileged species; I could look forward to as much maternity leave as Jim and I could afford and a good job, part-time if I wanted it, on return. Other women in the Executive and Clerical grades had no such rights and above all no attempt would be made to find them part-time work. This was not only morally wrong but inefficient; did I know what percentage of the high-flyers recruited from university at 22 were women? Thirty per cent, that I did know. And did I know how many of *them* got to my grade? Fifteen per cent, I hazarded, but the answer was just over three per cent. I had always liked the service and found it user-friendly but for the first time I had to acknowledge that privileged treatment at work, a London house fully staffed and a supportive husband might account for my comparative success. We need someone pregnant and a mother, Virginia said bluntly in answer to my feeble attempts not to get involved; we cannot have three single women heading up this crusade. What they wanted, and what logic and fairness and economic common sense demanded, was equal rights for all Civil Service women of whatever grade and an absolute right for all Civil Service women to part-time employment.

I suggested we go and talk to my friend in E Division but Virginia and her team, like James Saunders in the Notting Hill Law Centre, said that we needed to stop using conventional methods. We needed to put in the equivalent of a writ. So we developed a plan for inviting all the Civil Service women we collectively knew and a lot we didn't to a meeting in a month's time, at which our ideas would be explained, and modified as necessary in discussion. The meeting would be chaired by me, five months pregnant but looking as if I were going to give birth at any moment.

The day of the meeting in January 1979 didn't so much dawn as turn, slowly, to a paler shade of grey. A mixture of sleet and snow was falling miserably and heavily but an audience of 250 including some of the Service's most senior women was there and loud in support. I did my bit with conviction and a sense of duty well done, and then sat down, heavily, beside the legendary June Bridgeman, mother of five and two grades up on me, and asked how she did it. She answered my unspoken question by telling me that the last three children were largely the result of finding herself in postings she didn't like or was finding stressful. It was clear that she also loved children and babies but for women like the two of us the only way to get off the train seemed to be to have another baby. Was I going to end up with five too? Not if I could find another way of getting some time off, and the answer ought to be a responsible and interesting part-time job, instead of one involving oversight for paper clips (procurement and stocking) or near offer. It was the moment when belatedly I understood that women with children or other dependents need the world of work rearranged for them, this conviction reinforced by dozens of women at the meeting with aged parents or mentally ill siblings who were up against problems fully as difficult as those facing the mothers of children.

It is a bit late to wait until thirty-eight years old to question the whole concept of the world of work. I was never a queen bee – I am naturally a team player and co-operator – but like many women I saw my route through via assimilation to the dominant class, namely Men. The answer should always have been to improve women's lot with every weapon at my disposal and to reform how work was undertaken rather than seeking to join the men. Mea culpa, but I did then help to launch a movement that after a few years of steady Civil Service resistance ('That *really* wasn't necessary, Janet. Why can't we deal with it case by case?')

resulted in equal treatment for all female civil servants, and, critically, the absolute right to part-time work. It took a variety of forms, from the job share to the policy job reconfigured just enough so that able women could do it in four days rather than five and get one day in the working week when they didn't have to travel and were not chained to a desk. There are, gratifyingly, senior women ten years my junior who were enabled to get to the very top on a part-time basis. Alice Perkins, wife of Jack Straw, who worked under the additional handicap of being moved every time Jack's career even in opposition took him into her area, is a shining example, having made a hugely successful career on the basis of four days a week, and there are many others. I didn't do the real heavy lifting but at least I provided the initial figurehead and stayed with the programme.

Chapter 7

FAMILY, TRANSITION and MRS THATCHER 1979–1982

Dame Josephine Barnes said that what with being President of the BMA she could not guarantee attendance at the birth of a baby and had referred me to UCH. It meant long waits in clinics instead of a blood test and a quick chat with Dame Josephine, and I found it exhausting, to the point where my mother insisted on coming with me in case I turned faint. I was as always glad of Mum's company but UCH was in the heart of the area where she had been a social worker for thirty years and there were a lot of teenage mothers in the clinics, children of her various difficult families. I was introduced to a lot of incredulous pregnant fourteen-year-olds all too clearly wondering what someone of my age was doing there. I was by many years the oldest mother there, and one of the few accompanied by her own mother.

I had the tests for Down's syndrome and spina bifida. Up to age thirty-seven all women have about the same risk of producing a baby with either of these abnormalities, but at thirty-eight the risk goes up tenfold, and the conclusion was inescapable; the tests had to be done. In 1979 the only definitive test was amniocentesis which meant taking a sample of the amniotic fluid in which the baby was floating and culturing it, an unpleasant procedure which also carried a 1 per cent risk of miscarriage. I promised my anxious father-in-law I would have the test and in the event it had to be done twice, but never for one moment did I think there would be anything wrong with the baby. That's hormones for you, I am a worrier but I was protected from all cares about the baby and I do understand how some women manage to go through pregnancy ignoring or discounting every warning sign of trouble.

I had understood that the test would also reveal the sex of the baby and asked whether I was expecting a boy or a girl. The hospital demurred, making it clear that they would tell me if I insisted but that it was not policy, experience having taught them that, if anything else went wrong and you knew what you were expecting, the grieving process was worse. I thought they might be right and I did not insist.

Isobel arrived at four in the morning of June 6 1979, on a night when there were no students on and the maternity staff were heavily occupied with mothers having a far worse time than I was. They greeted her arrival as a delightful surprise ('Oh it's a little *girl*') when a cursory glance at the notes would have told them exactly what I was having, and I was grateful for their enthusiasm. We *were* overjoyed to have a daughter but so surprised that it took us a week to reach the obvious solution of naming her for both her grandmothers. We had taken her home by then, to be received by her brothers, who rushed to the cradle only to retreat after a few minutes, disappointed by this creature who would not get up and play with them.

Her arrival also meant we lost Jan, who had been with us for six years, since Henry's birth. She had decided she needed to train as a State Enrolled Nurse. In 1979 you needed two O-levels to get into the SEN course and Jan only had Art. She had tried very hard and we had finally sent her off to be expensively coached for English but she failed O-level yet again. My father-in-law wrote to the local hospital explaining Jan's relationship with the family and offering his view that she would undoubtedly make a nurse despite her puzzling inability to pass exams. The Royal Free accepted her and two years later she passed out third in the hospital. The answer was that she learned through her hands; show her how to do something and she could not only do it perfectly but could then tell you about it in writing and could pass an exam. There are lots of girls like Jan, and even more boys, who go backwards at school and turn into capable professionals as soon as they meet a practical training. My interest in vocational training stems from this revelation.

The hunt for Jan's successor was turning into a nightmare – there seemed to be no qualified nannies anywhere – when Kim rang us up. Eighteen years old, she said briskly, and had just passed the Nursery Nurses diploma. I was doubtful and said so. 'You're very young and you've never lived away from home, no, no, I don't think that would work.'

'Why not?'

Well, I said, taken aback by this self-possession, well, I dunno, come and see us.

She did, a plump pretty girl, twelve years older than our Henry, twenty years younger than me, and settled down for a cuddle with both our boys. We all loved her, daughter of a crowded Mablethorpe house, with three brothers and desperately hard-working parents. Dad was a carpenter and Mum ran a shop and I always felt I was robbing Kim's mother of her right hand. She stayed with us for five years and only left because the man she wanted to marry decreed that she should not marry straight from our house; she had gone from her mother to me and he felt she needed to live on her own before marriage. Kim interpreted this in her own way and got a job as the administrator with our builder, a hundred yards up the road – everyone who ever met her offered Kim a job – which came with a flat.

As all will remember, the Conservatives under Mrs Thatcher had won a landslide victory in May 1979. The winter of 1978/79 had largely passed me by because I was pregnant but I remember vignettes of large thick-necked men explaining proudly that it was for the good of the general public that they were not driving trains, not doing the laundry in hospitals and not burying the dead. Everything I had found unacceptable in the party of my allegiance was displayed, in colour, right where the public could see it and decide they wouldn't be having it.

1978 and 1979 were not a good time for left-of-centre politicians. We had all watched, gaping, as the leader of the Liberal Party, Jeremy Thorpe, was charged, along with others, with conspiring to murder his erstwhile lover Norman Scott. JT, as he seemed to be known, had had to resign as Leader in 1978 but unbelievably he had persuaded his constituency party to select him as its candidate for the 1979 election, and the police to postpone his trial until a few days after the election. To no one's surprise except his he lost his seat to a Conservative rival and to most people's amazement was found not guilty of attempted murder or conspiracy to murder a few days later.

I had no one in the family to share my disbelief and indeed guilty pleasure at the turn of events – my party might have troubles but not quite like this. Jim's parents were lifelong members of the Liberal Party and Margaret had been a distinguished speaker for them before the war. The whole thing was so embarrassing the only possibility was to avoid the subject of politics altogether, until Dick came back from a lunch at the National Liberal Club still giggling to himself. He had been approached by a very senior party member who was taking up a collection for JT's legal expenses. Dick, always sympathetic to people in a complete mess, had indicated willingness to contribute, and the man (alas that Dick would not tell me who it was) had thanked him gratefully, observing with dreadful earnestness that it was the sort of thing that could happen to *anyone*. My father-in-law had been too stunned to reply at the time but wiping his glasses, choking back laughter several hours later, he conceded that it really wasn't, was it. Margaret laughed too and it became possible to commiserate and talk about politics again.

In September 1979 I went in to see what my friend in E Division had pulled out of the bran tub this time. I refused a job involving Regulation which my old friend professed to think I would like, and accepted the one he probably wanted me to take – I was always several steps behind that cunning man. Steel Division, he said gloomily. Responsibility for British Steel. Your rescue experience might be useful. I leapt at it.

The British steel industry as a whole was indeed a basket case, and the nationalised British Steel the worst piece of it. Post-war governments had planned an industry capable of generating 40 million tonnes of steel a year, while in 1978/79 we needed about 9 million. The collapse of our civil shipbuilding industry (we still built for the Navy) and the rapid decline of the UK car manufacturers meant that the demand projected in the confident early 1960s was gone and wasn't coming back. The incoming Conservative government had told the managers of British Steel that they would not fund them to make losses, leaving the managers with no option but to close several plants, make a lot of the workforce redundant and hold down pay. The Labour Party should have done the same in government; the facts of the situation were before them, but I did understand why they had not felt able to make the Winter of Discontent any worse.

I joined in September 1979 when impasse was being reached and the Union headed by Bill Sirs was threatening a strike. I wasn't welcome; my predecessor had been a stolid, calm man some years my senior who had what was described to me as an excellent working relationship with British Steel, which I understood to mean that he was a victim of agency capture, the phenomenon so brilliantly described in *Yes Minister* as a system wherein the Department of Transport works for the hauliers and the road builders, the Department of Education for the teachers and the Foreign Office for foreigners. And much of the DTI was working for the nationalised industries – it came off like a smell from some divisions. Starting from where I did it was inevitable that the Chief Executive of British Steel, Bob Scholey, and I were not going to get on as well. In addition, Chris Beauman, a fellow parent with a son at school with our Henry, was working as right-hand man to the chairman of British Steel, Sir Charles Villiers, so I needed no other channel to the top. Bob, a Yorkshireman, also didn't *do* working with women; in his world you told them what to do and took the ferret out for a walk while they did it, a grim reminder of what life outside the liberal Civil Service was still like. He was also running a huge, well-funded group inefficiently; as my new boss Solly Gross pointed out, they simply were not getting the throughput in the factories or the steel out of the gates.

As the strike got underway in December that year, it became plain that the real challenge for the Civil Service lay in the relationship with Mrs Thatcher. No one had anticipated that the Prime Minister would want to take personal charge of everything to do with a strike in a nationalised industry, or that she would have such a staggering command of detail, or that she would concentrate on every twist and turn. No one thought that at my grade I would have much contact with the Prime Minister; there were at least three experienced and senior men whose task that would have been but then we didn't know Mrs Thatcher.

The first warning came our way when I was doing some wearying bit of briefing on the supply situation in the early stages of the strike, building bricks from straw and rumours (later proved true) of salesmen for the big German steel plants, speaking perfect English, appearing in the boardrooms of the British Steel customers offering them steel in exactly the kind and quantities and delivery dates they hadn't been getting from British Steel. I was summoned to a meeting, now, this minute, which turned out to consist of everyone in Steel Division above the rank of Principal, called by the Deputy Secretary, John Steele, responsible for us and four other divisions. He was issuing confused instructions as I arrived. I tried to take notes, failed and just sat and watched this normally cool and competent man.

He stopped after five minutes, looked across the bent heads of our colleagues, and said – I know because I wrote it down an hour later: 'Quite right, Janet. You see before you a broken man.' We all gaped at him, but he explained he had been summoned by the Prime Minister for a discussion about the strike in the course of which she had asked him what a boilermaker earned (they belonged to a different union). John had replied that he didn't know, sorry, PM, but he would get Mrs Cohen to get her the answer forthwith. A perfectly reasonable response as we all assured him. The PM had fixed him with a glacial blue look and said that *she* knew what a boilermaker was paid, why didn't he, and indicated the audience was over. John had walked back from Number 10, death in his heart, made a few phone calls, and a month later resigned from the Civil Service for a top job in the European Commission looking after shipping.

So when my immediate boss, my Under-Secretary Solly Gross, was called to Number 10 he took me with him, armed with all the facts about the industry we could think of, and I met the PM. The blue gaze slid over me, she didn't reckon women, as I had known from other sources, but I was too interested to summon up any proper outrage. The Foreign Office was there too, explaining, as usual, that given the huge over-supply of steel in Europe someone was going to have to close a plant and it ought to be us, not the efficient Germans. The DTI view had always been that the Foreign Office was so named because they were working for the other side, so we listened, resigned. As he reached the end the Prime Minister asked him to repeat the whole. Voice failing, he repeated his argument awkwardly, sounding less convincing by the minute. There was a pause. 'I never heard worse nonsense in my life,' she said roundly. I think the Foreign Office melted into the carpet but any proposal that we should yield up one of our plants in the interest of efficient Germans never reared its head again.

Over the course of the four-month strike I spent quite a lot of time in 10 Downing Street. I found her both refreshing and impossible. She had a perfect ear for Received Nonsense, formidable powers of concentration and was full of confidence, scornfully demolishing poor arguments. She was also a lopsided personality and a warning to all women. Somewhere along the line she had assimilated herself entirely to the dominant male species. Her father was often mentioned but she never spoke of her mother or her sister, indeed I assumed for years both to be dead. She had no understanding of privilege; she saw herself as someone born in penury and obscurity with none of life's advantages who had risen to the very top, a view of the world which ignored entirely the love and support she received from a powerful father, the stability of her upbringing, her own considerable intellect and an Oxford degree. It was a useful experience for me; I might have been found ignoring the advantages conveyed on me by parental effort and native brains, had I not seen her do it. Her judgement of people was flawed by who she was; she never promoted two excellent women, Lynda Chalker and Angela Rumbold, to Cabinet where they deserved to be, and installed two men, very much less competent than Lynda or Angela. She would have been better served if she had been able to see us, and women everywhere could have been unequivocally inspired by her.

The strike ended in complete defeat for the ISTC and its leader Bill Sirs. It was a stupid strike to call; the facts were against them, those jobs could not survive, and Union attempts ought to have been concentrated on alleviating the consequences for the people who would be out of work. The unions however had been frightened silly by Mrs Thatcher and saw their only hope in resistance to the death, and they had a point. When the strike was beginning to wane my immediate boss Solly, himself within months of retirement, made a quiet effort to bring it to an end. The PM got wind of this, and, in total ignorance of Solly's efforts, I was rung up at midnight and told that I would be taking his place at a European steel conference the next morning. No more awkward fixture could have been devised; it was the second day of the conference, all the key participants in the strike were present and it was glaringly obvious that Solly had been recalled. I arrived in Paris at lunchtime, still not knowing what had happened to Solly or why, to find myself seated between Sir Charles Villiers and Bill Sirs with our Ambassador to the EEC, pale with anxiety, beyond Bill. Anything I said could be a disaster, but I remembered Nancy Mitford, whose heroine Fanny in *Don't Tell Alfred* found that one simple opening would get her out of trouble. 'You must be very tired, Bill,' I said, and listened for ten minutes while Bill Sirs complained about everything, and we all settled to lunch. Our Ambassador, who must also have read Nancy Mitford, did the nose trick with his soup, and was still coughing and mopping up minutes later.

I had one more encounter with Mrs Thatcher, after the strike was over. My new boss Ken Binning had moved me within the Division to look after private sector steel firms rather than the nationalised British Steel – I was tired, out of sympathy with them, and Bob Scholey and I didn't like each other any better after the strike than before. The private sector steel firms had mostly done well during the strike because their people had gone on working while the British Steel plants lay idle, but when the strike was over world over-supply, coupled with big, efficient, English-speaking German steel firms, bore down inexorably on the smaller steel firms. The directors of one of her most admired firms, who had kept going all through the strike, came in to tell us they were bust without government support. We put up a submission to Ministers advising that substantial subsidy would be required to keep this particular firm going, even on a short-term basis, and that it didn't seem sensible in the current and foreseeable economic conditions. Sir Keith Joseph, my Secretary of State, agreed but of course we advised that it be put up to the PM. One of her private secretaries called me to say she agreed that assistance should be refused. Grittily we asked to have the submission back signed; the PM had spoken warmly of this firm who had kept going in the teeth of picket lines and Ken Binning, Solly's successor, and I wanted to be sure she had absorbed the consequences.

The private secretary was irritated and said so, but the submission came back with a scrawled signature, so as was my duty I asked to see the directors and gave them the bad news, and reminded them that they should consider, with their lawyers, whether they were legally able to go on trading in these circumstances. At 7 a.m. the next morning I was summoned; the firm's directors had got in to see the PM and now assistance was to be given after all. 'She *signed* it,' I said, and Ken said yes, well, that was yesterday and we were due a debate on the steel industry today. In the medium term some jobs were saved when the company combined with another so it wasn't an economically stupid decision. It was still a volte face brought on by political pressure which none of us thought Mrs Thatcher did.

The incident however brought to the surface an enduring problem for a Conservative government. As the law stood they had no alternative but to go on funding a nationalised industry competing on a taxpayer-subsidised basis with private sector companies which were struggling and dying. Something had to be done so we devised a policy which meant that where British Steel and the private sector were in competition, the assets of both would be put into new, jointly owned companies, reduced in size as necessary to be capable of holding their own in the new world, with government funding fed in via British Steel to help them to viability. It fell to Sir Keith to introduce the new policy to two senior GKN directors who had come in to explain that the GKN wire rod companies in South Wales would have to close, largely because of competition with British Steel. Sir Keith – a very nice man – had not fully assimilated the brief and the GKN directors rose to go, having assumed they had been told there was nothing to be done. I reminded the Secretary of State that there was this New Policy. Ah yes, he said enthusiastically to GKN, well, why don't you sit down with Janet here who will explain. They looked at me in wild surmise – we had not met before that day – but a room was found and coffee in Ministerial matching coffee cups, and they and I knocked out an outline plan to combine British Steel and GKN's wire plants (steel wire is a key component of reinforced concrete as well as much else) in Cardiff. The project was called Phoenix 1 until it became a joint company, Allied Steel and Wire, in 1981.

I was, once again, in my element, patiently pulling together one new joint company in Wales, and doing the spadework on two more, one in Sheffield and a much more complicated group in the Midlands. We were more constrained this time; City lawyers and a merchant bank, Hill Samuel, had been pulled in to advise, so that the foundations of the present practice, which sees lots of expensive private sector advisers doing the negotiations rather than the Civil Service, was being set. At the time I didn't mind, Hill Samuel were a new breed to me, we knew much more about the industry than they did, and I found it restful to watch their struggle with Sir Keith's hazy grasp of things financial.

In the middle of all this in 1981 family complications arose; our Henry was miserable at his local authority school in Islington which we had taken some trouble to choose. I went to see the headmistress only to be told that the eight-year-old Henry, who could by then neither read nor write, was the victim of stupid middle-class parental pressure and would learn when he was ready. I wasn't having any, knowing as I did that there is no such thing as a privately educated child of eight who cannot read, but Jim was very reluctant to move – Richard was also at the school and flourishing. I took Jim to see the headmistress, and she said the same to him, even more patronisingly. Jim, always slow to anger, always reasonable, actually walked out, towing me by the hand, and we faced the task of getting Henry either into Jim's old prep school Arnold House, or The Hall where my brothers and father had been. Both schools were full but in the summer of 1981 the headmaster of Arnold House rang to say a boy had moved unexpectedly and there was a place.

The new school provided us with some new friends among the parents, notably a couple of writers, Ian Kennedy Martin, father of one of Henry's contemporaries, who wrote *The Sweeney*. He came of a family of writers, his brother Troy also wrote for TV. Another of Henry's contemporaries was Edward Lynn whose father is Johnny Lynn, actor, director and writer who had devised *Yes Minister* with Antony Jay, and, after its huge success, was seeking further material. Johnny and Antony both knew that comedy came from a sound analysis of what was actually going on, which they worked on with the assistance of Bernard Donoughue. I am a good observer and while I am not the only model for the female Mandarin ('Satsuma perhaps, Minister') who, exasperated, left the Civil Service for the City, I gave them one or two of the ideas and crawled through the odd script to check for accuracy. I loved Johnny's wife Rita too, a psychotherapist working with the great Robin Skynner, who explained to me that she was of the Dynorod school of psychotherapy; she worked fast, and expected her patients to cooperate and if they didn't like it they could have their blockage back.

I had been two and a half years in Steel Division – the average posting for my grade – when an old friend from Frere Cholmeley, Stewart Douglas Mann, popped up. He too had left the Law and was a director of Charterhouse Japhet, a small merchant bank in the City. Would I like to come and work for them, he asked, they needed someone who understood about the Government's programme to privatise state assets, and would lead them into those putatively green pastures. Like my father I was opposed to the old Clause 4 proposition that governments should own the commanding heights of economy; they don't do it well and the assets devalue in government ownership, see British Steel indeed. I could see that privatisation needed people who could act as a translator between Government and the people with the money to buy the assets. I had been very attracted by the City when I had done a course in it, influenced perhaps by the fact that I do not think we drew a wholly sober breath in three days. I was also fed up with the right wing rhetoric, led and lived by the PM, which suggested everyone working for the public sector was an overpaid drone acting as a drag on the economy.

At this point however the children were still very young and Jim was in a travelling job working for GEC Transportation selling railways in distant countries. It was also clear that we would have to move house. Henry was doing well at Arnold House, but the logistics of getting him there and back were impossible. Jim dropped him in the morning by dint of going out of his way to work, but Kim at the other end of the day was putting Richard and a very small Isobel into a car and driving forty minutes across London to collect him, and the stress was showing.

I suggested I might come on secondment from the Department so that we could all find out whether this was going to work. Charterhouse were comfortable with the idea and so it turned out was E Division. It was part of Conservative policy to cut down Civil Service numbers, so that fewer of us did the same work, so E Division had for the moment too many people for the jobs available. My world-weary friend there said in his experience in the first year all new governments wanted to cut the Civil Service, but then discovered that if they wanted to pass their legislation and make it work they needed every experienced hand they could get. He expected this process to repeat itself just in time to welcome me back.

The process of seconding me was halted abruptly by the then Permanent Secretary, Sir Peter Carey, legendary still for his wartime service with the Resistance in Croatia when the Croats were German allies. He was a smallish, bright-eyed, slight round figure, who didn't look at all like a famous guerrilla fighter. He had wanted, he said crossly, to set up an Industrial Strategy Unit with me at its head, and had then found I was off to the City. Why was I doing this? I considered the point quite seriously; why was I leaving a secure home where I was a success for a place where no such success or progress could be guaranteed, and found myself stumbling on the truth.

'I don't think I am going to make it to Permanent Secretary, Sir Peter.'

Not a muscle moved while he considered the point.

'No. Probably not. You started a bit late. But you are certainly going to be promoted further.'

'So I thought I might go off and see something else.'

He laughed and wished me well and said he expected our paths would cross again. At least, I thought, I had negotiated a desperately needed, unpaid, break between leaving the Civil Service and joining Charterhouse, in which we had to move into a house full of builders, and move Richard into Arnold House as well, and settle us all into a new neighbourhood.

My current Secretary of State Patrick Jenkin, who had replaced Keith Joseph, was even crosser. I only had three months working to him but I thought we had got on well.

'It's outrageous,' he said crossly as I and his Private Secretary rode with him in a Government car screaming round Parliament Square on our way to a Debate. 'Civil servants taking good City jobs and allowed to go out on secondment so they can come back if they don't like it.'

Cross myself, I suggested that it ill behoved a government advocating a smaller Civil Service to object when a civil servant took the hint and headed for the private sector. The Private Secretary sucked in his breath and gazed rigidly out of the window, but Patrick Jenkin laughed and said fair enough and we were friends from that time on.

I left the week we were meant to move into our new house on the borders of St John's Wood, minutes from Henry's new school. The day of the Royal Wedding in 1981 I sat packing and supervising a gang of four men while I watched, rapt, the whole thing on TV. All four men had denied any interest in The Wedding; all four of them sat with me and the children and Kim and the packing crates, wrapping stuff without looking away from the screen. We moved into St John's Wood a day later, wedging our possessions into the rooms that were roughly habitable, and moved out again because there was still no kitchen. We have never been efficient about moving house; our fatal desire always to convert and change any house we buy and the inability of the building trade to work to time mean we always move in with the builders no matter how much time we leave or how carefully we plan.

We went off on holiday to Scotland with my parents-in-law,

seven of us in our small three-bedroom cottage, for a couple of weeks, but when we came back there was still no kitchen. We sent Kim home, with one of the boys, to lighten the load, and I begged a few days with old friends in Brightlingsea. Still no kitchen, so my mother moved out of her flat into a bedsit so I and two children could move in, a low moment for all of us. Then it was the beginning of term for the boys. We had two gas rings and no master bedroom so we shared a small room with Isobel and the boys had to share another small room. The living room had loose wires all over it and only Kim's room was truly habitable because without her nothing else was going to work. For months I would depart for work with the boys – Jim was in South Korea negotiating the Seoul Metro contract – leaving behind a party of Kim and several builders drinking tea round the table, with Isobel being passed from knee to knee.

As Christmas neared I hoped we could get rid of the builders and move the boys into separate rooms. Brother Giles however was in trouble. He had been sent as Head of Station for the BBC to Toronto the winter before and the whole posting had been a nightmare; he was sent straight from Paris where he and Elisabeth, my French sister-in-law, and the children had been very happy, to Toronto and one of the worst winters ever, during which Elisabeth's father had died. Giles was struggling with a deep fit of depression and a hostile BBC office which had languished undisturbed for years. Elisabeth, worn by everything, the climate, Giles's illness and her father's death, had left, taking the children with her. The BBC called Giles back to HQ and tried to fire him, unfairly we all felt, and Jim had spent weeks of the summer helping him to write a defence document; beautifully argued, written in the dry clear Civil Service prose that I never quite mastered. It was a formidable piece of work, and the BBC had had to withdraw and find Giles a London job, but he was miserable. Elisabeth would not come back from Paris and Giles could not bear the house where once they had all been happy. Kim told me firmly that we must take him in while he recovered and decided what to do next, so we added him to our chaotic household, persuading the boys to go on sharing a room by simple bribery.

Jim got home for Christmas, then went off again and in February 1982 I realised I could not cope and for once managed to say so, in a three-page letter with the conclusion in the first paragraph. Whatever my superficial resemblance to Superwoman, I could not cope with a new job, three small children, my in-laws, my own dear mother, a desperate brother and an absentee husband, Something would have to give. Jim, characteristically, agreed immediately that his career as a gifted negotiator who liked travel would have to be heavily modified, and that my career should not be subordinated to his. It was the first time he had had to adjust to enable us both to work but it was not to be the last.

Chapter 8

THE CITY AND THE FAMILY
1982–1988

Charterhouse Japhet's offices were in an undistinguished sixties block overlooking the north side of St Paul's Cathedral in Paternoster Row. Demolished in 2000, it was neither a thing of beauty nor particularly comfortable – there was limited air conditioning so the third and fourth floors boiled in the summer, and the Cathedral bell practice rendered thought impossible for two hours on Tuesday evenings from 5 pm, but I was very fond of it.

I had gone into the City with high but ill-defined hopes, one of which was to make money. I was on a Civil Service salary (Charterhouse reimbursed the Civil Service with a levy on top to cover the cost of my pension) but I wanted to share some of the City goodies like rich holidays and designer clothes rather than damp cottages on the far north-western coasts of the UK and M & S. Plain cash was welcome too, because the move from Highbury to St John's Wood had left us heavily mortgaged.

I was kindly welcomed at Charterhouse and given an office and a share of a secretary and that was it. No in-tray, no comforting stream of documents to be dealt with. No one cared whether I put in my expenses on time or attended the course on fire safety. I was back in the situation where I had to invent my own job and sell myself to other people rather than inhabiting a cosy existing structure.

I had burnt boats behind me so I decided to have lunch with everybody I knew in the City. I spent as much time as they had with my new colleagues, and attached myself particularly to Tom Bartlam and David Parish as well as to old friend Stewart. I had hoped to find Philip Ralph, the Head of Corporate Finance, who had recruited me, but he had gone to GEC and been replaced by Victor Blank, a brilliant high-flying corporate lawyer who had been the youngest-ever partner in Clifford Chance. On close examination indeed virtually the whole of the corporate finance department including Victor was younger than me. At forty-one I was back again in an all-male group, this time younger even than Alexander.

I arrived three years before Deregulation, the Thatcherite reform which removed the regulations by which the City had lived. In those distant days corporate finance advisers, stockbrokers and stock jobbers existed next to each other in watertight compartments. The City was British and everyone spoke English. The famed City culture of long alcohol-filled lunches still existed; when I arrived I was always offered a couple of gin and tonics before lunch and wine with and brandy or port after. The City was not exceptional in its habits in the early 1980s; offices in the most serious organisations were a boys' playground, and the Department of Industry had half a dozen men at its top whose judgement was known to be unreliable any time after lunch and from whom a swift grope in the lift was just part of Life's Rich Tapestry. All that vanished not just because we all awoke to the deleterious effects of heavy drinking; they were always obvious. The advancement of women helped because none of us had time to drink ourselves stupid at work. The routine of excessive drinking and bullying younger men into doing the same also disappeared, except on the trading floors. Life just got harder and the chroniclers of the joys of male-dominated society and alcohol, like Kingsley Amis, were beginning to record in sad but brilliant books like *The Old Devils* what happened in old age to the men who had lived like that.

My efforts to bring in business paid off inside six months when I got the job of advising the Department of Transport for the bank. They wanted to explore financing road building by the private sector, an early version of the Private Finance Initiative which would be used to restore some of the UK's battered infrastructure under the Labour Government many years later.

The Department had three roads ready to go; planning consent done, outline specification ready and rather than getting contractors to do the job on the usual basis (stage payments from government, lots of measurement, huge arguments about what was an Extra) were seeking bids that would give them a fixed price not only for the construction of said roads but for their maintenance over thirty years. This was and is the dream of everyone, that you could hold a contractor to a fixed price and make him guarantee the job for thirty years. In addition the government wanted to find a way of risk-free financing where no cash would be required up front. Their favoured method was to remunerate the contractor by shadow tolls, a payment of X (to be determined) for every vehicle that went down the road for the next thirty years. The contractor in essence would own the road and use all their ingenuity and experience to build it well and keep it in good condition.

I shared the problem with David Parish, the finance director of Charterhouse. I am a careful logical A-B-C thinker, and I looked hopefully at David, who had left school twenty years before at fifteen and gone into the City, for an innovative solution.

'It'll cost Government an arm and a leg,' he said, kicking his chair. 'And the banking charges on top will put another load on. If we can find anyone to do it. Tell them to change a bit of the M1 to a toll road and use the cash to build these new roads.' He looked at me over the glasses I suspected of being wholly unnecessary but worn to add gravitas. 'Be an easy fee, that.'

Sighing, I enumerated the policy objections, explaining that it was hoped that huge efficiency gains could be secured from the contractor, that cooperation rather than conflict would be achieved, along with major savings to the public purse.

'That's how Government thinks, is it?'

I reminded myself that I was there to get banks and the government to understand each other, and slowly got David to take the Department's views seriously. We met many contractors – all of whom confirmed in various circumlocutions that it would indeed cost Government an arm and a leg, the more creative among them pointing out that it might be only an arm and half a leg if the Government would carry the risk on the groundwork because that was where the worst risks lay; you never knew what you were going to find when you advanced on the earth with a bulldozer. The banks adduced the unfamiliar risks they would be taking, both on the construction work and on thirty years' maintenance. And anyway they never lent for thirty years – seven was more like it. It became clear that they would want someone to put up a slab of equity behind which they would lend a limited amount at a rate well above the usual commercial level.

It took us six months to arrive at the point David had seen immediately. The Treasury was discouraged by the very high costs envisaged by all participants. Nor was David's clever alternative of turning the M1 into a toll road and raising cash to build new roads acceptable on policy grounds. The contractors were disappointed, but ten years later in 1993 Jim, then working for Balfour Beatty, found himself appointed to head up the process of making the UK's largest civil engineering contractor work in this new way under a fully-fledged Private Finance Initiative. It was expensive, as we had foretold in 1982, but major efficiencies in contracting were also realised as contractors had to take responsibility for their own mistakes or failures in planning rather than claiming in the traditional manner that that would be an extra, guv. Huge projects, including major hospitals, got built on time because the banks would not stand for uncertainty or deviation. In 1998 Jim was the central coordinating point for the fifty-nine different parties involved in getting the Edinburgh Memorial hospital rebuilt, when a week before Donald Dewar, then Secretary of State, was due to put spade in ground some consultants wanted minor changes made in some of the operating theatres. Jim explained that all things were possible but the banking arrangements were in place, and paid for, and a week's delay would mean redoing all this, at an increase in rates and fees. The project went ahead unaltered, and completed on time and to the price, as did other hospitals, schools and major roads. The PFI programme was introduced by a Conservative government but was developed extensively by Labour governments from 1997 onwards and the public got a better deal on the actual buildings themselves and they got it when they needed it. The programme is now unpopular but compare and contrast the hideous overspend and waste that keeps on coming to light in the Ministry of Defence, to which experienced people (including me, many years later) failed utterly to introduce the discipline offered by PFI schemes.

Back in 1982 our fee was paid, and despite the fact the Department had not got what it wanted, we were felt to have been honest and useful. This modest success was overwhelmed by a brilliant coup masterminded by Victor Blank who had managed to persuade the American Woolworths to sell off their UK stores and had turned the UK business into a new and interesting company, rejuvenated under new management. It was a difficult deal, only rendered possible by the fact that Victor knew everyone on all sides of the project and by his staggering gifts as a negotiator. It changed us, in the words of a sardonic observer, from a third-rank bank to a good second-rank in one step.

I had always been interested in the financing of small companies and decided to find out whether this would be a useful source of business. I knew conventional lenders were cautious and I did not blame them. A risky loan is one for which you can charge perhaps 4 per cent above the rate at which the bank can borrow. Let something go wrong with the company and that margin will disappear like snow in July, leaving you looking at a nasty career-destroying loss. The real risks do have to be taken by equity investors who spread their bets, accepting losses on some projects and expecting large profits on others.

There was a persisting belief in government – shared by me at the time – that there is a pool of money waiting to be invested in new businesses. I started on my own doorstep with Charterhouse which had a small company that did invest in small businesses, Charterhouse Development Capital (CDC). They were conservative investors; they would not look at a company unless it could produce a three years' profit record and was doing something the Directors could all understand. Even so, out of every ten investments roughly four went well and made money, three failed and the remaining three mouldered along in the ranks of the living dead. I noted this but I was interested in *starting* new businesses and thought I knew how to do it, too, having by then started one successful restaurant and being in the process of starting another. Tom Bartlam, a rising star, was also interested in start-up and prepared to be responsible for me so we embarked on a tour of the investment institutions of the City to see if we could find people interested in putting up true venture capital which would be invested in new businesses, preferably in high-tech industry. CDC feared that we would contaminate their staid and carefully cultivated brand, so Tom and I had to agree that the new fund would not use the Charterhouse name and its offices would be hidden at the other end of the City; a classic skunk works, in the American term. What we found was that *no one* wanted to put up other than very small amounts; they believed the failure rate in new businesses to be too high and were prepared only to commit tiny percentages of their funds and wanted a fee for doing even that. (The key to success in banking is to get as much of your money back as you can in the first ten minutes via a fee.) Tom and I got the fund going in the end; it never made much money and ironically one of its most profitable investments was a restaurant, hardly an example of the cutting-edge new business we had hoped for. I understood then that if government wanted to get investment in start-ups it would either have to do it by way of grants, or give investors huge tax breaks which would enable them to recover a lot of their money in the very early stages. The Business Expansion Scheme (BES) introduced a few years later enabled top-rate tax-payers to get 60 per cent of their investment back immediately and was very popular but it was instantly subverted into things for which it was not designed. It was used (by me) to start a second restaurant and (by Newnham College and many others) to finance new buildings. Give private people a substantial tax break and they will invest in new small companies, but it comes at a price to the public purse of course. There is *no* pile of institutional money waiting to finance start-ups, and the funds from any source available to new small companies are strictly limited.

Tom, being interested in making money rather than the public policy implications, went a different route after this. He saw the need for another sort of money, somewhere between Equity and Lending, called mezzanine finance, which has elements both of lending and of equity. As a loan, it rates after plain vanilla bank loans but ahead of equity if the enterprise founders. If the enterprise prospers the mezzanine lenders usually have the right to warrants enabling them to buy shares cheap and can share in the growth of their value. Several years later Tom and four friends from the banking industry were to set up Intermediate Capital for Companies (ICC) which specialises in this useful and now ubiquitous form of finance and has grown into a substantial quoted company, making him a millionaire several times over and enabling many companies to grow who would not otherwise have been successful.

In 1983 Victor, still riding high after the success of the Woolworths deal, and our Chairman John Hyde, a Yorkshireman, were putting together a deal which allied us with Mark Weinberg's well-run and well-organised insurance company and (Lord) Jacob Rothschild's Rothschild Investment Management (RIT). The businesses were radically different and so were the management. Mark Weinberg was a charismatic manager of a large successful business, but nobody could have been less charismatic or communicative or interested in the management of people than

RIT. Crucially the market didn't understand the rationale for the merger and took against it so that Mark Weinberg's share price, along with RIT's, proceeded to drop like stones, until the deal had to be hastily unwound.

Upheavals are not uncommon in the Civil Service and, at a stroke, you could end up in another Department with different Ministers and strange new policies, but mostly civil servants moan a bit and return within the day to their desks and in-trays and their secure contracts of employment and the inexorable machinery of government. In the City there is no machine to carry you forward so no one did any serious work for six months, many-tongued rumour flourished and senior people either went into a sulk or made arrangements to go to other jobs. I was sufficiently alarmed to go back to my friend in E Division and ask if he would have me back, on promotion. Of course he would have me back, he said, but under a Conservative government no one was ever going to be promoted, darkness lay over the earth, and if I could stay where I was I should, so I looked for another job and found the ANZ bank. I do not know whether I would have been any use, or enjoyed it, because my plan was aborted by a piece of paternalism worthy of the Civil Service. John Hyde summoned me to tell me that ANZ had asked for a reference on me. 'Don't go, Janet,' he said. 'I think we have done a deal – I can't tell you about it but it will see us into a much better place for you. The ANZ are in almost as much of a mess as we are.'

A week later the announcement came that the Royal Bank of Scotland had bought Charterhouse and all its works, our jobs were safe and new opportunities were opening up. Charterhouse people would have access to the RBS balance sheet and would be able to take on larger deals and larger clients and would run the RBS capital markets business. We all settled down instantly and I thought about what John Hyde had done for me; I was not yet of proven use and he need not have made an effort to keep me. It was a truly kind and protective act.

Two days after the announcement of the RBS takeover John died of a massive heart attack, a result of the strain of saving his enterprise. Victor, the obvious successor, was told while he was having a battery of medical tests because he too had been heavily and stressfully involved in the complex negotiations. John was much mourned; Victor, ambitious and capable man as he is, took over his job, and said to me that John had become one of his best friends and he missed him every day. We all did.

Not long afterwards, in consultation with my supporters in the bank, we agreed reluctantly that Charterhouse was too small credibly to bid for the big government advisory jobs. Unlike the Rothschilds or the Lazards, we did not have the manpower (and I do mean manpower; I was the only woman of executive rank in the organisation) to provide a team of ten or the market power to be able to place millions of pounds in investment, so if I wanted to stay, I could either learn, from scratch, how to be a corporate financier, a stupid abandonment of comparative advantage, I thought, believing there must be a place for a well-trained well-networked civil servant who also knew a lot about banking.

I found it in the small but highly regarded investment arm, CDC, specialising in management buy-outs. The government had by then produced a list of state-owned industries or parts of them which should be sold to the private sector and could well work as management buy-outs. All I had to do was match up the list and CDC's desires. At this point I met John Neill, the MD of Unipart Ltd, the aftermarket wing of Austin Rover, at a City party. Unipart's problems were familiar to anyone who had worked in the DTI and I had not been surprised to see them on the official list as a possible subject for privatisation. I told John my background and he asked me if I could organise a management buy-out, I said indeed CDC and I could.

It was to take up over three years to get the deal done. It wasn't easy to arrive at an outline valuation for Unipart based on Companies House figures – bankers want to talk to management and think about forecasts, but Austin Rover, who didn't want to sell Unipart, interdicted John from telling us anything. We decided from published figures that we would need £5m in equity funding and some imaginative lending. CDC had never put more than £1m into a deal and weren't going to start now, particularly with a company owned by government which they assumed would have all sorts of nasties buried in the accounts. I went to David Hardy, Chairman of the mighty Globe Investment Trust, the only other person in the investment community who I knew both commanded funds and understood government. 'We'll do it, Janet,' he said, over lunch; he knew Unipart as a brand and he knew about the List. So that was the financing done – in outline and in theory only, but it was loosely agreed that Charterhouse would do £1m, Globe £1m and Electra (brought in by Globe) £3m, and they were all still there in 1987 when we managed finally to complete the deal. The difficulty lay in getting Austin Rover to do what the government had decreed and sell Unipart.

I had help: I found Peter Warry, of the Number 10 Policy Unit, and he and his seniors agreed that a credible bidder should be helped to carry out this bit of government policy. A large and powerful nationalised industry, however, even one bleeding cash and market share like Austin Rover, had a wide variety of weapons and a lot of expensive hired help to enable them to resist Government and for more than two years nothing moved. I was close to giving up, when everything changed, with the Westland scandal. Two senior cabinet ministers, Michael Heseltine and Leon Brittan, committed a mutual act of hara kiri and the Prime Minister was seriously weakened. In the aftermath the newly appointed Secretary of State at DTI decided to replace the Chairman of Austin Rover and recalled Sir Graham Day to the colours, an immensely capable Canadian who had made his name in shipbuilding. Graham, whom I had met at the DTI years before, did his background reading over one long weekend and on a Monday in July called his senior management team together, and in a general speech covered Austin Rover's future including the sale of Unipart, observing that although there were arguments for keeping it the politics were impossible. John rang me the minute he could get out of the meeting. I thought, Graham's abilities notwithstanding, it was clear that Austin Rover was going to fail whoever was in charge, and that the Government was right to extract Unipart. Austin Rover indeed was to die in the 1990s, together with a shed load of public money, while Unipart survived and was able to diversify.

The deal made my name, along with some useful money for CDC and the two other powerful investors. At the time however it was overshadowed by the much larger investment led by CDC in MFI, a large company in the cheaper end of kitchen unit manufacture. The corporate finance wing of Charterhouse (whose deal it wasn't) took a reserved view, believing the field overcrowded and the economics doubtful. In October 1987 the stock market fell by almost a third, overnight, the disaster heralded by a mighty storm that brought tall trees and power lines crashing to the ground all over the south of England. CDC did not renegotiate the price for MFI, fearing to lose the deal, and so, in the disdainful corporate finance department view,

135

compounded error by paying too much. In the event MFI traded poorly, lost value, the plan to place it on the public market proved impossible to execute, and everyone lost money, leaving us in corporate finance to indulge in bouts of group *schadenfreude* over CDC's misfortune. (The City response to a disaster overtaking another investment bank or a unit of your own bank on whom your bonus does not depend is the use of the words 'oh *dear*, what bad luck' accompanied by a smile running from ear to ear of the speaker.)

The negotiations to buy Unipart from Austin Rover and to structure it as the management team wanted had been difficult and Charterhouse insisted on handcuffing me to a young assistant director, Paul Baines, and a manager, Lawrence Guthrie. Paul was a solicitor, like me, and Lawrence a gifted mathematician who could do financial modelling – a rare skill in 1987 – and they have both gone on to important City careers. Paul rose to head of corporate finance at Charterhouse, leaving in 2000 to join Hawkpoint where his patience, negotiating skills and all-round unflashy ability (I don't think Paul has ever lost a client) took him to Managing Director then Chairman, and Lawrence to a senior directorship. Both have moved again since but both have had solidly successful City careers.

Between us the job got done and the innovative Unipart employee share scheme which saw employees and management own 20 per cent of the shares was launched with a spectacular stage show – John's idea, marketing man to his eyebrows as he is. This was not encouraged by Paul and me who sat dourly through the first night of the show, grimly conscious that Lawrence and the team were still struggling to button up the detail of the buy-out.

The deal took three and a half years start to finish and no real corporate financier would have put in the time. The demands of ambition would have meant it was put into what the Civil Service used to call the Too Difficult box. I hung on because of the huge upside I could see and my affection and admiration for the Unipart team. John and his head of strategy Muir Moffat and I were closer than brothers throughout those years – as usual my relationships followed a familial model – and also assimilated Tony Mourgue who came in as Finance Director late in the process when the original FD *did* give up and went off to a large corporate job. I got a book out of that years later, a novel called *The Highest Bidder*, which is the Unipart story translated into the construction trade.

It is worth noting that a Conservative government, despite a clear public mandate for action in 1983, had not been able to make a nationalised industry do as it was told. Huge amounts of Austin Rover senior time were deployed working out how *not* to do what its sole shareholder wanted. I had this experience in mind when Alan Cox, CEO of Allied Steel and Wire, the company I had helped to set up in 1981 in my last year at the DTI, came to see me later in 1987. GKN wanted to sell their shares, and British Steel, then still in public ownership, wanted to buy them. Public policy was clear; the government's intention remained to sell ASW into the private sector; and once again a nationalised industry was straining every sinew to frustrate the public policy aim. GKN had insisted that Alan Cox, himself originally a GKN man, should be allowed to talk to City investors about financing a management buy-out and he had already secured Warburgs and 3i as core investors. He had watched me extract Unipart from Austin Rover's grasp and had insisted on me being brought in to help on the assumption that matters might not be as straightforward as they looked. Space was therefore made for CDC to be the third lead investor and Charterhouse allocated Tom Bartlam, by then a director, as well as me, to ensure their interests were looked after.

Alan had been right to worry; the politics surrounding the deal were savage. Peter Warry, still in the Number 10 Policy Unit, told me, shaken, that he had been tipped off that both of us had been watched for some weeks by private detectives in the hope that British Steel would find us sexually entangled and thereby dent our credibility. The detectives must have had a very boring time; Peter and I worked almost exclusively on the phone, meeting occasionally for hurried lunches in very public places. *The Highest Bidder* has a junior Minister with whom the heroine is indeed having a raging affair but in real life a romantic involvement of any of the participants would probably wreck any deal. We were both serious people, dedicated to our jobs and happily married – I suppose this has never deterred anyone from an illicit affair but it seemed to both of us bewilderingly unlikely. Peter reported the tip-off to the head of the Unit, as was his duty, and from there it went to the Prime Minister, who told BSC this had to stop. I know only that she had expressed herself forcibly and the last time I saw her do *that* a Foreign Office man had melted into the carpet before our eyes.

Warburgs were doing much of the heavy lifting, producing the financial models in hundreds of sheets of printout – this was 1987, well before the days of small laptop computers – all of which Tom and I received with scepticism. Tom demanded a room at Warburgs in which to confer with his distinguished colleague, the usual arrangement whereby colleagues wishing a private discussion would retire to the gentlemen's lavatories not being available to our mixed-sex team. We spread out the bits of paper and gathered together the key figures from the cash flow projections on the back of the traditional envelope. We chopped 30 per cent off the projected inflow and added 20 per cent to the projected costs. Tom presented our view to the investor group with great charm; I did the bad cop part, responding to pleas for more optimism by repeating, dourly, 'It's a *steel* company', meaning that it was – and always would be – highly cyclical and up against cutthroat competition from the Far East.

We had one blip; GKN, either hoping for a much better price or more likely for fear of offending British Steel – with whom they were involved in many different ways and places – sought to resile at the last minute and keep their shares. We very slightly improved our offer with the reluctant agreement of our fellow investors who were by then reminding us that it was a *steel* company, Janet. My other contribution was to arrange for GKN to be reminded that there was no question, ever, of British Steel being allowed to use public money to buy the GKN stake.

This second successful buy-out solidified mine and Charterhouse's reputation in the difficult Government buy-out field and the third deal came through the door unprompted. I was asked to see Malcolm Williamson, then Chief Executive of National Girobank (Girobank), which was wholly owned by the Post Office but on the list earmarked for privatisation. Malcolm told he came with the full agreement of his Chairman, Sir Ron Dearing, whom I had worked for at the DTI and who would not be prepared to put himself in opposition to the view of an elected government. He and I and Malcolm arranged to have lunch at which Malcolm would be formally authorised to commission us to produce an outline proposal for a management buy-out of Girobank. Just before Christmas 1988 Ron's office rang me in some embarrassment to say they couldn't get a table anywhere at a reasonable price – so would it be possible for me to find a table at Café Pelican, which I had helped set up. Inevitably this key meal took place with the three of us hunched round a tiny table between several large noisy office parties. Crackers exploded around us at surrounding tables as we shouted at each other to set out the rules of engagement. Ron was a truly good man, as his later success in the difficult field of vocational education attests. I was delighted to see him again, virtually unchanged from the day of his appointment as Chairman of the Post Office when I and colleagues at the DTI had insisted that before taking up his duties he must, must, get rid of the threadbare duffle coat he had bought at Oxfam in about 1960.

Paul Baines was called in to help again because he knew a lot about retail banking, but we failed to put a buy-out together. Girobank needed a full banking licence to be a free-standing company but there were structural problems. Most banks have customers who do virtually all their banking business with them, including having their salaries paid in to current accounts so the bank can see that there is a regular funded cash flow. More than half Girobank's customers really belonged to big high street banks but kept a small Girobank account for the housekeeping, or the nanny, or for their aged mother, funding these accounts as needed on an ad hoc basis. The lesser numbers of Girobank customers who *were* using it as their sole bank tended to be on small salaries and while they needed efficient transactional services, which are expensive to provide, were not in the market for the lucrative lending, saving and credit products on which high street banks depend for their profits. In short Girobank lay between a bank and a social service and was unattractive to conventional management buy-out financiers. Kenneth Clarke, who was the relevant Minister and the selfsame bruiser and good clear mind he has always been, was in charge. I had known him at Cambridge, got him into lunch to meet some of our larger clients and cornered him on his way down in the lift. 'I'm not going to stand up in Parliament explaining why some impoverished old lady lost all her savings, Janet,' he said, hunting in his pockets for his cigarette case. 'I'm not selling Girobank to anyone who doesn't already have a full banking licence and lots of assets.' Armed with this succinct guidance we went through every sizeable foreign bank who already had a UK banking licence, reasoning that the foreign retail banks might be interested in getting a larger presence in UK retail banking. One after another decided that the Girobank customers were either fugitive or unprofitable or both and dropped out. Then the Alliance and Leicester Building Society swam into the picture. They were used to customers with not much money and they had a full banking licence, but alas they also had their own advisers. So although we got our fee we lost the continuing business to an ex-Treasury colleague Gerry Grimstone at Schroders and said a sad farewell to Malcolm who went on to see Girobank into safe hands before going off to Standard Chartered Bank and rising rapidly to be its CEO.

We never did act for Malcolm again but we never lost touch and on Black Wednesday in September 1992 I was due to have a drink with him. I expected him to cancel as interest rates went up into the stratosphere, but his secretary said to come and as we embraced he explained that if interest rates were really going to stay at 13 per cent, about two-thirds of Standard Chartered's customers were going to default on their loans and the bank would be bust, and he might as well sit and talk to a friend while it happened. So we had several drinks and a lot of sandwiches while rates rose to 15 per cent and it became clear by 9 p.m. that the UK were going to crash out of the ERM and that both of us would still have jobs to go to the next day. That evening with Malcolm told me why you have to have control of your own currency and your interest rates. I would never thereafter have supported any attempt to join the Euro, and usefully Gordon Brown as Chancellor of the Exchequer from 1997 to 2007 felt the same and was in a position to frustrate powerful colleagues tempted to join the club.

Meanwhile of course there were three children growing up, Jim was still travelling but for shorter periods and my brothers were still having difficulties. And I had added to the mix by helping set up the successor to Parsons Restaurant in 1984, a huge place called Café Pelican, in an old gas and electricity showroom in St Martin's Lane. Parsons had run its course for Alexander and me; by 1982 he was on his third marriage and in debt so that he had allocated much of his shareholding to two ex-wives and two people to whom he owed money, and with a shareholder base so dependent on income, further expansion was going to be impossible. We managed to find a solution; a capable friend bought out the rest of Alexander's shares and the restaurant and took responsibility for the other shareholders. Louis, who had worked at Parsons, and his wife Caroline told me they would find a site if I would find the cash. The top rate of income tax was still 60 per cent and under the BES scheme the tax man returned 60 per cent of their cash to investors so we started debt-free, leveraging Alexander's track record (and giving him a carried share) and the place was a success from the day it opened its doors until the early 1990s when we sold out.

Our dear Kim was leaving in 1983 when Isobel was four and we thought to put her into the nursery class of a nearby private school. She could read a bit but her grasp of writing was not secure and I feared that many children of her age had been taught to do both. She was asked to write her name, which was fine, then the date, which neither Kim nor I had felt a necessary accomplishment. I watched her struggle with the figure '8'; she sat back and looked round the classroom walls until she found one and copied it neatly. Oh dear, I thought, but the teacher administering the test was laughing and told me that it was the sign of a high intelligence to use all the resources available to you. I remembered that but in the end we waited another year and sent her to my old school at five.

Henry continued to flourish at Arnold House. He turned out to be a bit dyslexic but with proper teaching caught up with the rest. The easy-going, fast-learning Richard who had never had a problem with school on the other hand started in 1985 aged ten to have terrible nightmares. We took him to Caroline Garland, née Medawar, sister of Giles' schoolfriend Charles. She saw Richard for one long session, then invited us to join her with Richard, who was doing somersaults off her sofa in order not to hear too much of what was going on. He was, she told us, highly intelligent, which we knew, but sensitive and perceptive well beyond his years. Essentially he had a skin too few and was dealing with disturbing adult emotions and concerns with which he was far too young to cope, and he needed reassurance.

We were told to confiscate the Japanese horror comics which another child had lent him. Although he was ten and had read since he was five, we were to read fairy tales to him which explored issues of violence and abandonment, over and over again if need be, so that he could tackle all this from the safe arms of a parent. And we were advised that, moreover, the family relationships needed some examination and family therapy – which Caroline did not herself do – got very quick results. Both of us felt terrible as we went home with our middle child who was, typically, trying to reassure us that he was alright when plainly he wasn't.

For a year or so we ploughed through fairy stories. We went into family therapy with Dr Robin Skynner, famous then for the book he produced with John Cleese, via an introduction by Rita Lynn who was working with him. Family therapy is an immensely powerful tool but it requires much of its practitioners. Children and parents, given a protected environment and a serious therapeutic purpose, will speak truths to each other that they have withheld out of a wish not to upset or distress or sometimes that they did not even know. The practitioner has to log and make sense of it and ensure that the family go home together, however distressed, with new channels of communication open. Robin was a bear of a man, six foot four, uncompromisingly masculine, son of a fisherman, quite unlike the gentle, civilised male therapists in North London at that time. He explained, somewhere near the end of one memorable session, to Jim and to two startled boys of twelve and ten that families worked best when the men led and you were doing women no favours by refusing to state an opinion or using words like 'I'll leave it to you, dear'. (It goes both ways of course; men have a hard time with women who suppress their wishes.)

It was a painful process for Jim and me at times but in the end liberating. The therapy works by all involved feeling free to speak the truth as they see it, which can be devastating, and we had cause to remember the old adage which says that the truth will make you free, but first it will make you miserable. A couple of sessions ended with me and the boys going on to school in a taxi, with me unable to utter a civil word to either son. But we endured. Jim and I had further individual therapy, and we are married still after nearly 50 years and all three children are in successful careers and are happy in their marriages.

The other shoe dropped in 1985. Alexander was giving us all cause for concern. At just forty he was living apart from his third wife and had two children he hardly saw. He was trying to set up another new business and had hired people to help him and I could not think where the money was coming from. Then Mum rang to say that he was in the Priory, having been admitted, talking on two phones at once and high as a kite. We had suspected he was taking drugs but we had no real idea what to look for. Giles and I had both shied away from offers of cannabis or indeed anything stronger at Cambridge, as had Jim. But it wasn't just drugs; early in his stay in the Priory he was diagnosed as a sufferer from bi-polar disorder, then called manic depression. Lots of things suddenly made sense; the periods of intense creative activity, followed by deep depression, the way he ran through any cash that came his way and the instability of his relationships. While Jim and I were still winded by this discovery, the Priory asked to see Giles and he was diagnosed with the same disorder so we all belatedly understood the likely cause of the depressive breakdowns he had suffered, starting from when he was eleven years old.

I refused to be tested. I had always known that my brothers were carrying burdens that I did not. I had never suffered the deadening depressions which I had seen reduce my lively brothers into heaps of gloom, unable even to get out of a chair. And I had never felt the need to buy six phones or a flat in another country or to tell people that I had an idea that would save the world.

The illness was not well known or well understood in the 1980s and the brothers reacted differently to the dismaying news. Giles did not believe the doctor's verdict and would not enter treatment, and it was only many, many years later when he was suffering from yet another black depression in France that he told the French doctors that he had been diagnosed as bi-polar and then they were able to help. Bi-polar sufferers need to be on stabilisers to control the condition and anti-depressants are of very limited use when the black depression strikes.

Alexander accepted the diagnosis and took the pills but inwardly despaired. He had started another business, Videoshuttle, which rented out videotapes to the well-off middle classes, a market he understood, but he owed money everywhere and the business was always heavily burdened. The pills helped however. He settled at a rather lower level, no longer the same sparky energetic creature he had always been, but he started to write and to look inwards and to have therapy and we all hoped for better.

It was a tragic irony that, just as physical illness destroyed my father's life, his sons should have had theirs blighted by less visible mental illness. We know now that bi-polar disorder mostly affects men, but is carried in mitochondrial DNA by their mothers. Inheritance is not inevitable; Giles I think being ill so early may always have been going to suffer but Alexander said later that he had opened the door to the disorder by heavy use of cannabis resin in the 1970s and 1980s. If he had known he wouldn't have done it. And I was spared; I am a bit over-excitable but that is the worst I can say. And, blessedly, neither of my sons shows any signs of bi-polar and nor do Alexander's boys, and nor does Giles's adopted son Nicolas.

Chapter 9

WRITER AND BANKER 1988–1989

February 1988, just after the commercial successes of Unipart and Allied Steel and Wire, saw the publication of my first book *Death's Bright Angel.* I had started to write it during the long wait to get the Unipart deal to work, and it was published by Constable. Miles Huddleston, the commissioning publisher, had bought the book almost two years earlier for an advance of £1000, introduced me to a star editor, Prudence Fay, and indicated that substantial rewriting would be required. It had been painful to wait so long for publication but Miles had been adamant; not only did much of the book need work but no publisher would launch an untried author in the autumn. One of the given facts of an author's life is that most of the public buy only one book a year, at Christmas, written by an author whose name they know. In February 1988 however the book was a critical success. Miles entered it for the John Creasey prize, awarded for the best first crime novel, and it won, delighting both of us although Miles warned me not even to think about giving up the day job. I was up against some stiff competition including the first of Mike Ripley's Angel series. Mike, a journalist and PR man, had managed to talk to Someone Who Knew who had told him that the winning book had 'Angel' in the title so Mike naturally assumed it was his book, until the day the winner – my book with 'Angel' in the title – was announced. He made a good story out of this disappointment but it was decent of him to forgive me.

A series of press interviews and an appearance on *Start the Week* with Melvyn Bragg had been set up for me so I met Melvyn, later to become a colleague in the Lords, and in another radio interview met a gifted fellow panellist Tim Binyon, who wrote crime reviews and a couple of crime novels as T. J. Binyon, and whose second book, *Swan Song*, was on the short list for the senior prize. Tim was a fellow of Wadham College, Oxford, teaching

Russian; like many of the clever young men just older than me he had learned Russian as part of his National Service in order to deal with the cold war.

Tim was a kind man and encouraging to fellow crime writers. He had gone into crime writing – and thence reviewing – because his academic salary would not support a family. When I knew him better, I suggested that finishing the biography of Pushkin, for which he had a publisher and which he was writing very slowly, might be a better investment. This brisk Head Girl approach was no more help than other interventions by well-meaning friends, and it was not until he met his second wife, Ruth Ellis, herself working for a publisher, that he finally wrestled Pushkin to a finish in 2002. I was to have the pleasure of going to the launch party, hosted by the Russian Ambassador of the day. A group of four or five middle-aged Englishwomen, well-dressed and jolly, were being treated with deference and deep bows and much hand-kissing. They turned out to be the lineal descendants of Pushkin himself, although none of them was Russian or showed any sign of mixed blood, while Pushkin was famously the grandson of an African slave. One of them confided to me that in Russia she and her mother could not even pay a taxi, so great was the regard in which her ancestor, who died in 1856, was held.

Tim appears as David in my third book, *Death of a Partner*, published in 1991, the older man brought in from academia to advise Francesca and her colleagues in the DTI. I realised as I wrote the book that he had the same intellectual independence and curiosity and the same kindly, sardonic way of dealing with the quick, impatient, ambitious ones like me as Gavin, long-dead father of my friend Jet. I miss Tim; he died of a heart attack in 2004 but he had by then seen his book on Pushkin received as the definitive biography.

It was Ian Kennedy Martin, who had been so helpful in getting me started with writing at all, who enabled me to write a second book. I had started writing *Death on Site* (published in 1989) while waiting for publication of *Death's Bright Angel*, but was making no progress. Ian and I met up at an Arnold House Sports Day – Richard's last – and he congratulated me courteously on Book 1 and asked after the next book. I confessed that I had just thrown away the first five chapters for the second time. 'Don't ever do that,' Ian advised, urgently seizing me by the arm and steering me round the playing field, ignoring our sons. 'Get them out of the trash can, now get writing and finish it. Once you have a finished script you can do something with it.' He told me the sad story of his brother Troy (writing is the family trade and their mother was in it as well) who had had a brilliant idea for a series and had done all the research only to find it didn't, quite, hold water. 'Now if he had written the script he could have made the idea work somehow, even if he had to change it a bit.' It was the best advice about writing I have ever received and it has application to a lot of fields. Just *finish* the piece, then you can do something with it. So I finished *Death on Site*, which is based on my experience of Western Avenue, and in which a scaffolder is murdered by being doped up with antihistamine so that he falls from the top deck, a hundred feet up, and much of the plot is played out on that giant site where I had spent a year twenty years before. A part-time author doesn't have much time for Research and I write from life, leaving only a decent time after any experience to do so. *Death's Bright Angel*, written in 1985, draws heavily on the work I was doing from 1975 to 1978, and *Death on Site* from my work as a consultant in the 1960s. It was reasonably but not rapturously received, but by then I knew how to write Number 3.

I wrote easily at the rate of about a thousand words an hour on a first draft and I could, in those days, write anywhere and at any time, provided only that I was alone and in silence. I still work in silence but the ability to write without fuss in odd moments has deserted me; it is a ponderous performance these days, necessitating the certainty of half a day clear before I can get going at all.

The publication of *Death's Bright Angel* started me on a media career. The combination of being female and a banker had already secured me spots on TV but my first appearance had not been a success; I was asked by ITV to talk about social security as a foil for Tessa Blackstone, then Chancellor of Brunel University, and Jock Bruce-Gardyne MP as the representative of the Conservative Party. I could hardly get a word in, and when I did the words sounded stupid. I moaned to Jock – another really nice man – afterwards and he told me that any of his constituents who saw him on TV never remembered anything he said but noted immediately whether he had had his hair cut and whether his suit looked new. I did better with *Any Questions*, and in 1988, in the course of doing PR for *Death's Bright Angel*, I found myself invited to do the Budget edition of *Question Time*, then run by Robin Day and with an audience of 5 to 6 million. Charterhouse and I panicked and they put me through two days of television training in the week before my appearance. TV training is merciless, every awkward twitch, every irritating habit or gesture, along with any deficiencies in one's best suit, show up with dreadful clarity. It revealed that given a question requiring thought, I would nod and look away before the questioner had finished speaking, which looked dismissive, disrespectful and generally rude. The truth was that as soon as I had got the point of the question, I would look away to consider my answer but it looked awful on TV. I had to learn to fix my gaze on my interrogator, doing my thinking while they got to the end of their question, *then* nod and answer, without looking away to think. All politicians do this because they have all been TV-trained and I was to be up against three politicians, John Major for the Conservatives, Malcolm Bruce for the Liberal Democrats, and Alistair Darling for Labour. Under television lights my best suit had looked a bit shiny along the seams and didn't quite fit round the front, reminding me of the old days at the Lucy Clayton School where whatever I wore shrank or popped a button when exposed to the critical eyes of my classmates. I bought a new suit in an hour that morning.

It was traditional for the four *Question Time* panellists to have dinner together at the BBC before the programme. I am naturally sociable but had learned from doing *Any Questions* not to waste my best aperçus at the dinner before and not, ever, under any circumstances, to drink anything other than water. The TV trainers re-emphasised both points so I was sober and frightened as I sat, tugging down the skirt of my new suit, between two grey-haired men, both called John. I had been too nervous to listen to the hasty introductions and turned to the John on the right to enquire what it was he did. He replied that he was the Deputy Director General of the BBC and was there to do the audience warm-up. Despite the grey hair, he looked a bit young for the job, but if indeed he *was* the Deputy DG, I asked, why was he required to do the warm-up, traditionally the province of the floor manager. The other John, listening amused on my left, patted my hand and said no, Janet, the man on my right really was the Deputy Director General. He himself was John Major, Chief Secretary to the Treasury, and he knew *all* about me. Charmed, as he had intended, I told him about writing and my life, but I remembered my manners and talked to John Birt for one course as well. He was always a serious man with a mission to inform, but I felt the audience was more respectfully baffled than warmed up when we four panellists filed on to take our places.

My performance was on the good side of competent; I didn't have to compete for air time with three men because Robin Day was careful to give us all a fair crack of the whip. The fact that Nigel Lawson, as Chancellor, had just lowered the rate of income tax from 60 per cent to 40 per cent, the same as capital gains tax, so obviously made economic and practical sense that it was easy for me to say that in the City we welcomed this budget and to offer a couple of anecdotes about the lengths to which City folk had historically gone to turn highly taxed income into much less highly taxed capital. John, Alan Beith and Alistair Darling said what they had been saying to the media all day, and we all returned to the Green Room for drinks. The TV trainers had also warned me about The Room and I was about to make my excuses and go home sober while I was still ahead when I heard a raised female voice berating John Major for his and his party's total disdain for the working classes. It belonged to the producer, who had had a drink, doing her best to confirm the Government's view that the BBC was a bunch of closet Lefties who would stop at nothing to undermine them. John Birt was vainly trying to shut the producer up and John Major was seeking to get a word in edgeways. I hurled myself into the fray, feeling it was wrong that that nice John Major should be treated in this way by a harpy from my party, and discovered after a couple of heated moments that he was deeply amused, entirely unbothered, and assuring all parties that politicians expected to stand their ground and listen to other people's opinions. He waved away a second drink and, taking my hand, said he would give me a lift home and swept me out, leaving trouble and recrimination behind us.

I had a chance to re-assess him in the official car. Younger than I perhaps but neither shy nor defenceless, and how indeed would he have made his way to Chief Secretary in a Conservative government if he had been either? We talked about politics and I reminded him I was a member of the opposition party ('I know that,' he said, laughing). The car dropped me at our house in St John's Wood but there was no one to boast to because Jim was away. And I know now where John went to, because Edwina

Currie's autobiography records that she had watched us on *Question Time* while waiting for him to meet her.

John and I remained friends, even given our different political allegiances. I had seen a formidable personality, which coloured my view of what started to happen inside the Conservative Party. They had scored a huge political success in the 1987 election, and in March 1988 the UK had a budget surplus of £3.9 billion although interest rates were around 8 per cent and starting to rise again. The Government were riding high and we in the Labour Party had good cause to fear that the tide would never turn.

The cracks however quickly became visible. Nigel Lawson had been Chancellor since 1981 and seven years is a long time to hold that job. Mrs Thatcher moreover had come under the influence of Alan Walters, a distinguished economist, British in origin, who had worked largely in the USA. He was an opponent of Nigel Lawson and all his policies, and the tension during 1989 ratcheted up steadily. In July 1989 Mrs Thatcher got tired of another of her long-standing Ministers and Geoffrey Howe was replaced at the Foreign and Commonwealth Office by John, by then perceived as one of the PM's favourites. We met again at the time; John was anxious but excited about this unexpectedly rapid promotion to one of the three great offices of state. He didn't get much chance to grow into the job because in October 1989 Nigel Lawson, who had lost the favour of the PM, gave up the struggle and resigned. John was moved out of the FCO after six weeks, leaving bewilderment and consternation behind him, to become Chancellor of the Exchequer.

Almost the first thing he did was to ring up one of our mates in the Civil Service, Richard Wilson, a friend since Cambridge, newly promoted to Second Permanent Secretary at the Treasury and well known to John from his previous spell there, and to suggest they had lunch together 'at Janet's restaurant', my much loved Café Pelican on St Martin's Lane. Richard warned me they would be honouring the restaurant, so an hour before they were due to arrive, I rang up Gérard, our day manager, who assured me he had noticed the booking and, assuming correctly it was the real John Major, had arranged complimentary champagne, and asked whether he should comp the entire meal. 'No, no,' I shrieked, audible right down the corridor at Charterhouse. 'He has to be treated *exactly* like anyone else, put away the champagne and let him pay the bill.' Gérard could not imagine what the fuss was, evidently in France if a Minister deigned to eat in your restaurant you provided the whole meal and probably free women as well. I reassured my colleagues and rang Richard's office to see if he felt he and John could accept one complimentary glass of something. He did, on consideration, think it would be alright, and told John about the call, which gave them both a good laugh.

John retained his general benevolence towards me, and early in 1990 accepted an invitation to lunch at Charterhouse, knowing full well that he was doing a favour. He brought Richard with him and his own principal private secretary, a job which always went to a Treasury high flyer, in this case John Gieve, who was to become one of the key people involved in dealing with the 2008/9 financial crisis. At Charterhouse we invited a roll call of the bank's biggest clients and a set of industrial stars whom we had not hitherto been able to lure through our doors. I spent the morning trying not to bite my fingernails; Ministerial lunches were always anxious occasions because, in any crisis or if another meeting intervenes, the Minister in question cancels or arrives very late. Just as I was beginning to relax – a phone call from Richard had told me John was running to time – I got a call from Victor Blank's office enquiring anxiously what the arrangements were for John's security people. I knew that at that stage only the Minister for Northern Ireland and the PM travelled with security guards, but I had to make yet another phone call to Richard to check the point. After all that it was a great party; John set himself out to be entertaining, and several of our guests also had useful conversations with the two Treasury stars he had brought with him. 'A triumph, Janet,' people said kindly, but it was John who did it.

As I knew from Richard, John had a difficult time as Chancellor; it is a long step from Chief Secretary, where he had served only just over a year, to Chancellor, particularly when succeeding a long-serving and popular predecessor. He was only, in the event, to introduce one Budget, in March 1990. He and Geoffrey Howe and others persuaded Mrs Thatcher, against her every political instinct, to join the Exchange Rate Mechanism. This linked sterling to what is conventionally described as a basket of currencies but effectively tied sterling to the Deutschmark. In October 1990 at the Party Conference the PM looked weakened and furious. She had been intending to introduce a Poll Tax, which would have replaced the rating system levied on property with an individual tax levied on people; logical, since it is people not property who are the users of local services, but desperately unpopular. Immediately after that Conference, in November 1990, another leadership election was triggered, this time by Michael Heseltine, sidelined since he had walked out of a cabinet meeting in 1986.

It took John a little time to decide to run for leader but I thought I knew the man and the Conservative Party and put £25 on him to make Prime Minister before he even put his name forward. After a frenzied week, during which he was said to be having his wisdom teeth out, he put his name forward and appointed his Treasury colleague Norman Lamont to run his campaign. At this point, as Charterhouse's unofficial political adviser, I told my colleagues that I thought John would win and that my £25 was where my mouth was. My calculation was simple; politics is a hard, zero-sum game in which there is only one grand prize, namely the office of Prime Minister. Those who have acquired real enemies among their fellow MPs – like Michael Heseltine – cannot win unless they are up against someone with even more bitter opponents. John had no serious enemies at that point; he had great charm and took huge trouble with people as I knew for myself. He had been a popular Chief Whip, in itself a contradiction in terms. He had seen service, admittedly briefly, in two great offices of state. He was also thought to be Mrs Thatcher's appointed heir, and most of her party, even if they had begun to fear that she herself was becoming an electoral liability, did not want to abandon her policies or her principles. He won, handsomely, I pocketed £550 from Ladbroke's and John went on to break Labour hearts by winning the 1992 election for the Conservatives.

Another consequence of an increased public profile was an invitation to the Königswinter Conference of 1989. This particular group was set up in 1947 by a combination of Germans who had opposed Hitler and sympathetic British people, many of whom had known Germany well before the Second World War. I was busy and was about to throw the invitation away; but a Charterhouse colleague, seeing the distinguished list of names at the top of the letter, suggested I think again. So I did, though not without checking with Richard Wilson, then at the Foreign Office, that this was not a front for a foreign terrorist group. Richard, trying not to laugh, assured me that it was eminently respectable and effectively run by our and the German Foreign Offices.

The British participants were offered three nights and an introductory programme in Berlin before the conference. I arrived at Heathrow very short of sleep after an early morning funeral ceremony for the latest hamster of the Cohen collection in the back garden of our London house.

I was immediately befriended by Trevor Taylor, a defence materiel specialist, then teaching at Stafford University and working extensively for Chatham House. He understood about the hamster, being a father himself, and he knew Germany well; his wife Petra is German and he swapped his window seat with mine so I could look out of the window at the flat endless plains where the UK trained its tank crews, along with the British Army of the Rhine. We were bussed to our quarters in Berlin, an erstwhile Trade Union hostel (one of the features of the Königswinter Conference was the austerity of the accommodation provided, so that startled grand persons of both nationalities would find themselves tossing uneasily on hard single beds), and rushed out to the first of the dinners and receptions in our honour. Our little group contained distinguished political scientists, defence practitioners and, pleasingly, two rising Labour MPs, Chris Smith and Doug Henderson, as well as a bemused captain of industry. Chris explained gently to us all that he lived with a male partner; he was the first politician of any party who had made clear to everyone including selection committees that he was gay.

Trevor carried off the captain of industry, me, Chris and Doug to a Berlin bar where a great deal too much beer was drunk by all, high as we already were on the exhilarating Berlin air. Chris, Trevor and I made great efforts to persuade our new industrial friend that Labour was business-friendly but our efforts were sabotaged by Doug, MP for a Newcastle seat, who told the man around 2 a.m. that he was a right-wing exploiter of the people. Labour's problem encapsulated, Chris and I sadly agreed; those like Doug who were closest to our people tended to spit in the eye of the people we needed to help them flourish.

The next two days were full of new experiences; my first sight of the Berlin Wall, and going through Checkpoint Charlie for a visit to our Ambassador to East Germany. It is difficult now to remember the tension in the city; the military briefing from our senior man which felt like something from a 1950s film, or the

153

awkwardness of the visit to a sad and beleaguered Embassy in East Berlin. Looming over all was the Wall, and the barrier streets either side of it. The old hands took it for granted as part of the scenery but I found the place and the situation unbelievable and kept asking people when and how they thought it would change. The British military bluntly assumed that it wouldn't and the political scientists we met, British or German, seemed to feel the same, except for one woman, East German in origin, who said that change would come in the end, she could not see quite how, but it had to come from the East.

It did of course, and six months later we were watching – in open disbelief in my case, having believed the disheartened comments from the old hands – as the Wall was swarmed over, kicked down and picked apart by equally disbelieving Easterners. The next year, at the 1990 Königswinter Conference, I met a West Berliner who owned a travel agency in Berlin. He and his staff had looked out at the crowds surging through West Berlin that night in October 1989, stopping to press their noses against the windows of the shops, and decided they must open the agency and offer everyone who came in a coffee and something to eat. The next day they found that every last travel brochure had left in the pockets of the visitors. He went out and snapped up beds in every cheap sunny destination in Europe and matching aeroplane capacity, having understood that the first thing everyone from the old Eastern Europe would want to buy would be a proper holiday in the sun, and that of course it would need to be cheap.

The Königswinter provided several new friends of both nationalities; Patricia Scotland, at thirty-four a staggeringly young QC, as well as David Willetts, then a young Conservative policy adviser looking for a seat to fight for his party. The German contingent included two of the great names of German history, Herr Dr von Moltke, their Ambassador to Britain, and Herr Dr von Richthofen, grandson of the fighter pilot ace who had shot down so many of our aeroplanes in the First World War, as well as Dr Gunther Peise who was head of the Fachhochschule in Münster. We were rushed from place to place, in the manner of conferences everywhere and I found myself scrambling onto a bus, more or less clothed in my best silk dress which featured eighteen buttons down the back rather than a zip. I asked Patricia Scotland to help and we stood swaying together as she painstakingly did me up, barracked by the rest of the busload, and I tried to explain to her and myself why I was travelling with a garment which needed a dresser or a husband. David Willetts handed me off the bus, enquiring smoothly whether I had anything *else* they could help me do up and I marked him then and there for a successful political career.

The 1990 Königswinter was held in East Germany, in Dresden, as a signal that the times were finally a'changing. Delegates were put up in the hotel previously used by the Stasi and their guests in the central square with an arresting view of a huge pile of rubble, once the Frauenkirche, whose ruins had been left there by the Russian invaders, in memoriam and in warning. We all had sniffles and runny noses throughout the three days we were there and an odd taste in our mouths because the city then ran on ancient lignite coal-fired power stations which tainted the air and the beautiful bridges over the Rhine offered a view of a greenish yellow river, smelling heavily of chemicals. We saw some of the city's best things, the museum with its staggering tapestries and jewellery. 'People must have gone blind doing that,' I said to John Monks, the rising star in the TUC, who gave me the look so often bestowed by the left of the party on the middle-class centrists. 'I expect they did not have the representation to which they were entitled,' he said in exaggerated Manchester. Fair point, but things strike you when you see them, not when you are told about them.

That year the Conference ran for three days and on the third was thrown open to East German guests, politicians, political scientists and such businessmen as could be found. I forget the formal subjects we discussed; what stuck in my mind was what individual East Germans told us in the breaks in the official business. There was the representative of the teachers' union who was trying to find alternative employment for fifty-seven teachers of history, in their fifties and too old to retrain to teach the rather different history now revealed. It became clear that here, in the country which had been the showcase of Eastern Europe, a whole generation's skills and training were going to be redundant, people who had worked long and hard and been part of the nomenklatura of one society were going to find themselves in poverty and low status in a new society. We tried to talk to everyone, some of us struggling because unlike West Germany where all our contemporaries had learned English at school, in

East Germany they had learned Russian and very few people had fluent English. I had started German lessons after the 1989 Conference but I wasn't anywhere near fluent. We talked to businessmen whose trade had vanished overnight as the Russians switched their orders to Russian plants, to senior members of university departments which had been devastated as the Russians withdrew funding, and to local administrators left helpless among the ruins of social services, which had been abruptly cut or eliminated altogether. Comparing notes afterwards, we agreed that the most depressing thing was that each speaker would warn us, urgently, not to believe a word the one before had said, 'because, gnädige Frau [or gnädiger Herr], you must know that he/she is Stasi'. We could not imagine how to reconcile and rebuild a society in which, as was then becoming clear, one half of the citizenry had gained advantage by spying on the other. And no good us feeling superior, as John Monks said, it would have happened to us.

We did, however, like our West German colleagues, understand that this was a problem to which a German solution was required so that when we got back to find Mrs Thatcher, as Prime Minister, seeking to put the full weight of her influence against the reunification of Germany, I was incredulous. I had admired her capacity for analysis and her judgement but it seemed she had now lost contact with reality. German law – as UK newspapers were not slow to remind us – entitles anyone of German birth to German citizenship, and Reunification plus refinancing of East Germany was the only option on the table for the West Germans. And even if it wasn't, who did we think we were to tell West Germany what to do? The West Germans were equally incredulous, and I shall long remember a dinner at the Königswinter in Cambridge a year later at which Mrs Thatcher and Chancellor Kohl were seated, not speaking to each other, either side of the British Ambassador to Germany, whose diplomatic skills were more than fully stretched. I was at one of the long tables with a sideways view on to this improbable sight, next to Paddy Ashdown, and, good European as he was, he couldn't believe it either. Now that we know the end of *that* story we know our disbelief was justified and that her blindness to the obvious on this point was one of the things that brought Mrs Thatcher's downfall.

Chapter 10

TRANSITION 1989–1991

The pressures of two working lives, middle age, and the needs of two teenage boys and a daughter rapidly approaching her teens were making themselves felt, despite career success for both of us.

An early sign of trouble came in 1989 as I contracted what turned out to be the first in a series of auto-immune diseases. These are usually not life-threatening – asthma, eczema, rheumatoid arthritis for example – but they sap energy and are all familial; my maternal grandmother and my mother were asthmatic, I had had infantile eczema and had also suffered from a mysterious silvery rash which had arrived when I was pregnant with Henry and showed no signs of going away twenty years later. My distinguished father-in-law diagnosed a psoriasis and I accepted his view. The next auto-immune disease came on me at a time when Michael Besser, Professor of Medicine at Bart's Hospital and a neighbour, was driving me, his teenage son John and our boys to the City of London School, whence I would climb up the steep steps to St Paul's and Mike would drive on to Bart's. One morning, as I was limping towards his car, with the boys well ahead of me, Mike got out. 'Janet,' he said, in the manner of an Old Testament prophet. 'You have viral arthritis and I will take you into my hospital now.' He delivered me to the rheumatology clinic, dismissing my feeble protests. 'They'll tell you it's rheumatoid arthritis but it isn't. I've had it and I know. It's viral arthritis and it goes away in seven weeks. It lasted eight weeks in the event but returned at intervals for the next ten years, just as Mike also said. I was unable to go to work for two months because everything hurt too much but in August Jim and I decided that everyone needed their break and we would carry on with our plans for a two-week family holiday in a Portuguese villa.

We never then flew en famille; Jim as an only child did not feel able to risk us all dying in the same plane leaving devoted parents and grandparents neither chick nor child. We went in three groups: Jim and Richard, Henry and the current au pair Gabrielle, and Isobel and me. She and I were transported through Heathrow in a motorised cart with our luggage, but at Faro airport the whole system broke down. Horror-stricken Portuguese watched and exclaimed as Isobel, aged nine and small for her age, bent under the weight of a substantial rucksack and pulling a suitcase at least half her size, was led through to the taxi rank by her well-built mother, carrying only a small handbag, Ottie, a battered toy otter, and *his* luggage, a pink plastic suitcase measuring six inches by nine. At the villa the driver pointedly gave Isobel Ottie to carry and lugged the rest up a flight of steps himself, no doubt fearing what I would otherwise inflict on the child. The fact was that I could not raise my arms to shoulder level, never mind lift or pull anything, and could only just walk.

I recovered just in time for the menopause which was rendered painless by hormone replacement therapy on the advice of Dame Josephine, still working in her eighties. A blood test, however, revealed that my thyroid level was exceptionally low so I ran to Michael Besser, who looked at my eyes and then with the simple pleasure of the specialist went over me testing my reflexes, then called for further blood tests, which only served to confirm that I was hypothyroid. I might feel fine now, he said, in another six weeks I wouldn't. Yes, of course, it was an auto-immune disease, and it had got me because the immune system was less able to keep these things at bay in people over fifty, particularly those who worked too hard. I tottered out feeling more like a hundred and fifty years old; whatever *next*, I wondered crossly. Two little pills daily did, and continue to do, the job of keeping me in good health.

We were at the time trying to get two teenage boys through their education. Henry, in 1989, had done reassuringly well at GCSE, helped very much by his grandmother, a first-class coach in most subjects. One of her successes was to get him to an equally academic French friend of hers. Somehow she overcame the male teenage horror of making a fool of themselves in a foreign tongue and gave him the confidence to speak another language well. This did not at the time carry over into German, in which he failed, getting a D in GCSE. He had gone on into the sixth form to do three tough sciences with the aim of going to university and after that becoming a vet. Or so we thought, but it turned out we had understood nothing. We found him intermittently intolerable at sixteen but we thought that was probably par for the Teenage Boy, particularly one who was very successful with the girls of the Pony Club. Worryingly, it became clear that our clever Henry was not coping with A-level physics, biology and chemistry. His marks were poor, he was doing some work in the holidays but refusing to do any test questions which his loving and efficient grandparents would have got someone to mark for him. In addition he started to dig his heels in about going to university at all. It was a horrible and worrying period, and, dragging our reluctant boys, we all got ourselves back to see Robin Skynner, three years after we thought we had said goodbye to him.

For forty minutes Jim and I explained how difficult Henry was being and that it seemed likely he would not get more than Cs or Ds when he needed three As and that he had to *change*. Henry put in the odd, sullen contribution and Richard, as always, tried to broker a peace, while Isobel was quiet. 'Mm,' Robin said, pleasantly, into an exhausted silence. 'Well, we've all heard what we think *should* happen with Henry. This is the moment when I'm going to ask what we think is *going* to happen. Isobel?'

Isobel, aged not quite eleven, replied without hesitation that Henry would get Cs or Ds in his A-levels. We all stared at her while we understood that Truth had once again arrived in the room. Jim and I had to accept that our ambitions for this son were not going to be fulfilled because his considerable will was set against us. We trooped home in furious silence but that evening we sat down to make a deal with our eldest son. We would support him to ride semi-professionally for a couple of years since it was the only thing he seemed to want to do but in return for our support he must get decent A-levels and find a way of doing something that would enable him to progress towards earning a living. Jim and I were clear that no one made a proper living out of horses while Henry was equally sure that he could, which did not make this negotiation any easier.

A few days later Henry proposed that he should go to work in Ian Stark's stable for a year after the summer. He had been there for two weeks in the summer of 1989, arranged by my cousin Anne Fraser, Chairman of the BHS in Scotland, and mother of three horsey children. Ian Stark, then European champion in the three-day event, was one of her neighbours in the Borders. We had arrived with Henry and sat down for coffee with Ian, thin and pale, still nursing injuries from a riding accident earlier in the year, his wife Liz and various children and the Head Boy aged all of seventeen. It had been arranged that Henry would stay with the Stark family and pay for his keep at the rate of £25 a week and I had shyly asked Liz if I could give it to her in cash or would she prefer a cheque. She indicated that cash would be fine and the eyes of the whole household followed the transmission of the five £10 notes, which were all too clearly going to have to feed more than our Henry; Cousin Anne said Ian had been having a bad time, European champion or not, and as she turned the car she stopped to let Henry, riding one very large off-white horse and leading another, go past us. 'Ah,' she said with pleasure. 'The Grey brothers', the local term for Ian's two best horses, valued then at around £250,000 each, which were being taken out along a public road to exercise by a sixteen-year-old. We drove back to Hawick and doubled up the insurance for Henry himself and for any damage he might cause to Ian's horses.

When we got him back two weeks later, he had told us that the Head Boy, stopping only to indicate the stable and its principal occupants, had taken the next day off, his first in nearly a year, and had in the second week gratefully accepted Henry's offer to take charge while he got a weekend home. Our son had had a wonderful time and conceived a lasting admiration for Ian and affection for Liz, but it didn't seem to us to be much of a life for a clever child of privilege.

So we refused to consider the idea and negotiations were broken off. Henry however returned to the table within a week to say that if we could get him a place with the World Dressage Champion, who was German, he might think about that and would of course learn German while he was there. I saw this as a deliberately impossible condition but Jim rang around until he found the man lived and worked in Münster in North Germany, not far from the Dutch border. I rang my friend from the 1989 Königswinter Conference, Dr Gunther Peise, saying apologetically that I knew he had absolutely nothing else to do with his time, and put our problem to him. 'I know little of horses,' he said, but he knew a man who did, Peter Wagner, senior partner in A. T. Kearney. Two weeks later as school broke up for the Easter holidays, Henry and I were on a plane to Düsseldorf. We drove, in ill-tempered silence, across the German plains to Münster, where we were met by a selection of German horse persons led by Peter Wagner, a sinewy, fluent English speaker in his fities, who took Henry from me and put him up on an enormously tall horse. A stallion, someone told me, as our Henry disappeared into the mist with a group of riders. He had never ridden a stallion but after an interminable thirty minutes the gang and he appeared again from the fog and various Germans patted me and him and the horse and offered to help us. I knew that Henry rode well and had observed that the stallion was confiding in him as he rubbed its neck but finally understood then that our son had not only a dream but a skill and that we would have to change course.

We were driven the next day to the stables where the World Champion had his base and we watched as beautifully groomed expensive animals went round the immaculate ring under the guidance of the well-dressed young of several nations. This was plainly a rich man's game and was going to be very difficult to finance but I knew we would have to try rather than lose our eldest son. Henry, however, had by then been round the stables and met the World Champion and, blessedly, had taken against him on sight and it would not surprise me if the World Champion had felt the same. I was just drawing breath to talk about What Next when I found that had been settled. Henry was going to live 'wie Sohn' as one of the family at a stud owned by a Münster farmer called Hubert where Peter Wagner's six horses were kept, and he was to ride said horses for Peter, who was away on the business of A. T. Kearney during the week, and work in the stables with Hubert's staff, from September.

I had hoped that since Henry had so comprehensively put us back in our box that he would feel able to do better in his A-levels, but in the event he did indeed get two Cs and a D, hugely beneath his abilities. It was nearly twenty years later when I asked him, casually, why he had done quite so badly; had he been in the wrong subjects for his mind perhaps? 'Oh no,' he said, going very slightly pink. 'I never went to school in the sixth form. I went to the pub instead.' We gaped at him. 'I thought they were all assholes, starting with the headmaster,' he said, sounding like his teenage self. 'And they never noticed whether you were there or not?' 'Well, I went in first thing then bunked off.' We were furious (I still am) that a highly thought-of fee-paying school should have been so casual as not even to notice that some of its pupils were simply not there – Henry was not the only one bunking off to the pub. But I was heartbroken for our son, unable to tell us or his loving and anxious grandparents that he was simply not covering enough of the syllabus in three tough science subjects to write a credible examination. He must have been desperate for quite a lot of the time and no wonder he was so appallingly sullen when we tried to help. It must have been a very lonely two years for him. Henry, grown to man's estate, characteristically dismisses sympathy and says he was a bloody fool, but all he wanted to do was ride. With hindsight he and we should have been able to see much earlier that, for a boy who only wanted to ride, the path to being a high-grade vet was too long and too uncertain. Only the highest grades get you a veterinary training and most vets, as Henry says, spend their lives with their hands up a cat's bottom rather than with horses.

So by Christmas Henry had been in Münster for four months, speaking fluent, ungrammatical German (a D at GCSE not being much of a basis for grammar and syntax) with a horde of friends. He had mellowed greatly in the time away from us. As he got off the plane at Christmas, limping from the broken toe he had not told us or anyone else about, hair in his eyes because there had been no time for a haircut, he said as he kissed me, 'Property development'. I was stumped for a moment then remembered that as we had said goodbye, I had suggested that he kept his eyes and ears open to see where the money was being made because after all (gulp) his father and I might be out of date and it might be possible that new developments like selling sperm for breeding enabled money to be made from horses. He was telling me that the stud did not make money but was kept going by the occasional sale of a field on the edge of prosperous Münster. It was a gracious acknowledgement.

We managed to do a bit better with Richard. Sometime in a crowded 1990 the school had written a report which suggested we were wasting our time dressing him up and sending him there every day. Jim was away and, deciding to try a different tack, I passed the report over to our second son and suggested maybe he should try a different school. When he recovered from his astonishment Richard told me how bored he was and how fed up with all-male environments, and we set out together to look at alternatives. Richard, as teenagers can if given a bit of space, turned into someone sensible and practical and decided to stay at the school to do GCSE, on the basis that it was too late and too difficult to change, but that after *that* we would please find him a mixed Sixth Form College. My childhood friend and neighbour Anne Beament's husband Roger was Deputy Headmaster of one of the best and agreed to take Richard, subject to him getting a reasonable number of B-grades at GCSE, which he managed without noticeably increasing his work rate. So by 1992 Richard was settled, not doing enough work to be sure, but happy and with a girlfriend and a double bedroom (both children were sixteen by 1991 and Clare's parents agreed with us that we would rather have them safe in our house than dangerously finding a corner on Hampstead Heath or in a squat somewhere).

In 1990 I had also managed to take the ten-year-old Isobel to Dallas, Texas, to see Kim, her nanny for the first four years of her life. Kim and husband John Nicholson had left England for a good job in the USA after their third child had died in the womb. Kim with her usual resilience as well as help from an American hospital had managed a successful fourth pregnancy, so she met us, carrying her daughter and accompanied by her two sons, Harri, my godson, and Felix, who thrust a drawing into Isobel's hands. 'What is it, Felix?' 'It's a feeush.' We grasped after only a moment that this was Texas for 'fish' and that Kim's children had assimilated, as children do, to a completely different society. We met Felix's kindergarten teacher who, on being told by Kim that Felix was starting to pick out words when she read with him, replied 'Praise God,' and we knew we were in the South. It was only April and we boiled in the sun; Kim told us that in the summer they all skulked indoors in the air conditioning, occasionally running out through the blistering heat to jump in the lukewarm swimming pool.

We went, of course, to the grassy knoll in the middle of downtown Dallas from which President Kennedy had been shot, and stared at it. We went up to the top of a neighbouring building where there was a small, slightly shabby Museum of JFK and an account of his untimely death, and suddenly it all came back, nearly thirty years later. It is said that everyone knows what they were doing when JFK was shot; I was listening to a BBC radio interview with Denys Lasdun, one of Dad's closest friends, who had just got the commission to do the National Theatre. I have no idea what Denny said because the interview kept being interrupted, the President had been shot, Jackie had been shot, they had been taken to hospital and, incredibly, Jackie was uninjured but the President was dead, all this in the course of the same half-hour interview.

I left Isobel with her other family and went on up to Pittsburgh to see my friends Anne and Chris Widnell. We had seen each other only infrequently since the late 1960s when they had emigrated to the USA. Their two children, Katherine and Nick, weren't there; older than ours they were making their way through the US college system, both at top universities, both doing well, due entirely, I felt sadly, to careful upbringing by a mother who had not worked until both were at boarding school. I would have been cast down but the Widnells were, as always, encouraging and fed me beautiful meals, and were sweet and admiring with Isobel when she arrived to spend the last weekend with all of us before she and I flew home, she to prepare to move into South Hampstead High School senior school and me to have another look at my career.

By 1990 after the two successful buy-outs and one near-miss with National Giro it was difficult to work out what to do next. The problem – that Charterhouse was a bit small credibly to bid for the big privatisations – remained and I was not finding any more buy-outs. CDC had made good money on Unipart and an even better return on their investment in Allied Steel and Wire which had been floated on the market late in 1988, and were content to wait for me to do it all again.

I went on holiday that August with the family to our small cottage in Wester Ross, where the pace of life slowed to a crawl as soon as we had managed to get there off the overnight sleeper train with all three children, and a morning's shopping in Inverness – shopping was and is difficult on the West coast, and the tiny village is serviced by one small shop five miles away and a van that comes once a week from Gairloch with fresh meat and vegetables. I was woken from a peaceful existence of walking and sitting and sleeping and feeding a husband and three children aged from eleven to seventeen, by a summons to meet my colleague Sandy Muirhead and a team in Edinburgh. We had been invited to go and see Scotland's second biggest generating company, the Scottish Hydro, about a potential privatisation. I persuaded Jim that Duty required me to put him on the overnight train to London with the three children on our way back while I caught a different train to Edinburgh and did a meeting, having, somehow, bought a set of garments that weren't jeans and an anorak. And some make-up. And combed my hair. And stopped scratching my midge bites.

The Charterhouse team was led by Sandy, a half-Scot twelve years my junior, a chunky, very clever redhead. Child of an invalid father, he had gone through public school on scholarships and got the top first class degree in chemistry from Oxford, but had refused to consider an academic career; needing the security of a well-paid professional career he had qualified as an accountant and gone from there into investment banking. Our owners, the RBS, who had found this opportunity for us, had urged us to field as many Scots as possible so we had found two more half-Scots to add to me and Sandy and we were all busily explaining our family connections to the management of the Hydro. I scored heavily I thought by having just come from a cottage owned by us on the West coast, but with hindsight I don't think anyone at the Hydro was impressed; years later one of my favourite political colleagues, George Robertson, pointed out that Scots had not much time for the poor weaklings who had fled to the soft South, particularly those who then boasted of their Northern origins. We got the job, however, and settled down to understand the business, being toured around the Hydro plants and the bigger ones owned by the much larger South of Scotland Electricity Board, who very much wanted to take over the Hydro. Distances in Scotland are huge, as we half-Scots forget, and an early crisis was caused when the four of us landed to find we faced a journey in a rented car of forty miles to one plant, then another fifty to the next. Sandy announced he would drive, and I said that since I was carsick I would sit in the front. Our juniors both confessed that they too were carsick and both had either to drive or at least sit in the front. We all eyed each other for a bit but finally a compromise was achieved; Sandy drove, but he had to stop every ten miles to enable the one in the back who was feeling most sick to rotate to the front. This arrangement broke down utterly after the first power plant where we were received with a five-course lunch ('if ye've no petty fowers to follow, Hamish, we'll mebbe look at the site,' our guide said dourly), but the onward journey defeated us. I was white and sweating by the second plant and one of the juniors had been comprehensively sick, and the other had survived by falling into a deep sleep from which he was woken only with difficulty, so he wasn't a whole lot of use either at the next stop. For all subsequent visits no more than two of us travelled in the same car.

At its peak the job took nine people from a small corporate finance department, most of whom had to stay in Edinburgh for weeks at a time. It was a good job culminating in a flotation for Scottish Hydro. I was released early from the team, having done the political job, and sent off to look for more privatisation work in Scotland. We acted for the Government in the disposal of Scottish Transport, though usefully, given that the lead Scottish team was sick at the sight of a ship, Caledonian MacBrayne was excluded from the brief. The simplest of desk-top calculations revealed that no one was going to buy that vital lifeline to Highland communities without even more substantial subsidy than the Government was already providing. We worked on bus privatisation as well.

We also landed the job of advising Scottish Nuclear on their privatisation. The company owned two plants, both nearing the end of their lives, as well as the brand-new state-of-the-art Torness plant on the Fife coast, built pretty much regardless of cost. I discovered that management believed Government had been stingy and over-cautious and that, could Scottish Nuclear but escape into the Private Sector, money for new nuclear power stations would rain down upon them. It was clear that someone was going to have to explain concepts like risk, return on capital employed, and How Markets Work. Translating the rules of one trade to the practitioners of another is my strong suit, so I put together a presentation designed to depress unrealistic expectations. Unless the price of electricity doubled overnight, the return on a new nuclear power station would be too low to interest investors, even if you could get them to contemplate the scientific and political risks involved and the potential client needed to understand that.

I faced my audience with some anxiety and twenty slides. A Charterhouse director would not normally have been allowed out alone to do a presentation; a junior would always be sent with them to gauge the audience reaction and make the kit work. On this occasion half the department had flu so I had offered to go by myself, on the basis that with a room full of nuclear engineers someone would know how to work the overhead projector. Wrong, as it turned out; all the engineers were in the plants, my audience was Management and Finance, and no one could find the right switch or the spare bulb. My presentation got under way twenty-five minutes late with the assistance of a young man from the canteen. It was not a happy occasion; my audience was far too intelligent not to recognise the truth revealed in the numbers, but they were sadly disappointed in the messenger and presented me only grudgingly with a vast bunch of flowers which leaked greenish water over my best suit all the way home in the plane.

It gives me no pleasure to have been right, but only one other nuclear plant – Sizewell B – has been built since Torness, and that construction had already been commissioned well before 1990. Over twenty-five years later, despite huge guaranteed prices for the power to be generated by Hinkley Point, most of us are powered by economic, familiar, reliable, polluting Gas.

Scottish Nuclear, unable to find anyone to invest in it as a stand-alone company, ended up in the arms of the old Central Electricity Generating Board, and our involvement came to an end. Price Waterhouse were advising the CEGB. I would need to find something else to do.

Chapter 11

CHANGE AND TRIBULATION
1992–1993

1992 was a terrible year for any Labour-supporting person. We thought that up against a fourth-term Conservative government – even one under new leadership – which had run out of steam, and was being torn apart on the issue of Europe, we ought to win. To lose was a terrible blow; it was like the death of President Kennedy; all of us remember what we were doing at 11.30 that night when a Conservative MP was returned for Basildon, a key marginal for Labour. The City, even, was braced for a Labour win. I had always invited Labour friends to lunch and for years neither the City nor our clients were interested, but from 1990 onwards I could always get serious City people to meet Gordon Brown, Peter Mandelson, bright young advisers like Ed Balls and Ed Miliband, and in 1991, when John Smith himself came to lunch, we were expanding our biggest table.

Early in 1992 it was possible to feel an uneasy undertow. John Smith's proposed budget made me very uneasy when it was published to show what we would do in office. Delivered in February 1992 in the middle of a recession, it substantially increased pensions and other benefits, financing this by a large rise in income tax. It made economic sense; the extra money would have been spent immediately by needy OAPs and other people living on benefit, delivering a useful boost to consumption, and it might have jolted us out of recession, but the people who were going to be asked to pay the extra taxes were not, I was sure, going to see it that way. I lunched with a Conservative friend, David Mitchell MP (father of Andrew Mitchell MP), then a backbencher who had served for years as a junior Minister, a careful, patient, clever man. He had come on from asking John Major the key arranged Parliamentary Question: 'When will my Right Honourable Friend the Prime Minister call a general election?' and received the expected answer that it would be four weeks hence on April 21 1992. 'We don't deserve to win, Janet,' he said over the soup, 'but we will, you know. When I campaign in my constituency all I have to say is, well, if that is John Smith's *first* budget, what is the *second* going to look like?' It was this fear, not the *Sun* or premature triumphalism at the big rally in Sheffield, wot done it. In elections it is always the economy, stupid, that matters.

A couple of months after the lost election I found myself on a train hopelessly delayed somewhere north of Leeds, with Mo Mowlam MP and Peter Mandelson MP. After the first few hours, when we had exhausted the contents of our own briefcases, Mo, typically, insisted we pool our reading resources and Peter turned out to be carrying the sociological analysis of the election results. The members of social class E – the unemployed, the OAPs living on the basic state pension, the very people who would have been helped by the Smith budget – did not vote, at all, for anyone, and more than half of social class D, whom we also consider Our People, didn't either. It was the numerically small social classes A and B who had voted, mostly for Labour, and the much larger social classes C2 and C1 who had elected to continue with a worn-out Conservative government rather than pay higher taxes.

The 1992 election results led directly to New Labour. We were not going to get elected on policies which would benefit people who were not going to vote. In order to be elected – and to be able to help 'our' non-voting people – we would need policies and language that appealed to the aspiring voting C1 and C2 people, and to hope that enough of the Bs and As would continue to vote Labour anyway. Peter and Mo, I am sure, had already got there, while I was digesting the facts revealed. I have always been in the centrist or Hampstead wing of the party (as our detractors said) and had recognised Tony Blair and the Islington Labour Party as the inheritors of Gaitskell, Soskice, Jay and Greenwood in a way that Gordon and Eds Balls and Miliband were not. (David and Ed Miliband were Hampstead but brought up by a father well to the left of the Hampstead party of the 1940s. My own father indeed disapproved of David and Ed's father Ralph because he had been a member of the Communist Party, along with many others of the Left.) I was reminded of that long train journey later, in 1996, when Tony, addressing a meeting on his home patch of Islington, was moaned at by a female interlocutor who said how sorry she was to see Tony and the party abandoning our most idealistic policies. 'Well, I'm not sorry,' Tony said, looking like Bambi and sounding like the Big Bad Wolf. 'I can do absolutely nothing to help Our People unless I am in power, and we won't get elected on those policies.'

I was on that train in 1992 because I was on my way home from a meeting at the Yorkshire Building Society where I had been appointed as a director in 1991, my first NED job. I had been approached by Simon Russell, a hereditary peer and friend of Jim's who worked for an executive search agency, and I had agreed eagerly to let my name go forward. The Yorkshire was and is a Mutual society, operating on the principle of taking in deposits from Members which are then lent out to other deserving and creditworthy Members to enable them to buy houses. It was then admittedly rigid; if you wanted to borrow money to buy a house you would have to have a substantial deposit in an account with the Society from whom you hoped to borrow, and you would need to be steadily employed, and then you would need to wait as you rose up the queue for funds. Things had changed even by 1991 with deregulation, but well into the 1990s the Yorkshire definition of a cowboy building society was one who would lend to borrowers amounts in excess of those monies which their Members had placed with them. But deregulation was here to stay and the YBS had felt the need to take advice on how to move away from the old governance structure wherein seventeen local businessmen met monthly while the Chief Executive told them what he was doing, then all had an enormous lunch. It had worked because the Board knew and understood their customers very well, but with deregulation and the increasing growth of the business outside Yorkshire change was needed.

The YBS had been advised to reduce the size of the Board, not all at once but over five years so as not to offend good men who had rendered long service and to introduce a Chairman with extensive knowledge of the City, and another non-executive director who had connections to the government and Civil Service and would provide insight into their thinking. Peter Courtney, who had been Finance Director for the mighty Boots plc, got the Chairman spot and I was put up for the government nark position. Simon told me afterwards that he had described my CV and qualifications in enthusiastic detail, reserving till the end the information that this excellent candidate was, well, a Female person. He had urged that after all my sex could be seen as another qualification, another bright new piece of modernisation, and he was helped by being able to point out that the First Commissioner of the Building Societies Commission, the regulatory board for building societies, was a woman, Rosalind Gilmore, a distinguished Treasury insider and a contemporary at Newnham, who had left for the private sector in the 1980s but had been lured back to run the Commission.

Some of the non-executive members never overcame their reservations; eight years later in 1999 when I was retiring with honour as Deputy Chairman and we were interviewing for not one but two women to replace me, I asked a good colleague, an accountant, Jeff Atkinson, what he thought about one of them. No good asking him, he said, he didn't approve of women on this Board. 'But, Jeff,' I protested, 'you have sat next to me for eight years.' 'I didn't vote for you either, lass,' he replied, stuck fast on the rock of principle.

I was an early appointee but by the mid-nineties most building societies had one woman on their board. The list read like a roll call of 'our gang' at Links, Rosalind at the helm, me at the YBS, Prue Leith at the Leeds Building Society, Frances Heaton at the Alliance and Leicester, to name but a few. More radical change came as many Societies decided to become banks in order to swim in the warm seas of the wholesale markets. This move was very popular with the Members because there was cash involved; Members got several thousand pounds of shares in exchange for the loss of their Membership status and most promptly sold these shares as the companies were launched on the Stock Exchange.

The Yorkshire Building Society however considered and rejected demutualisation, indicating to the two southerners in their midst that turning societies into banks was for the weaker brethren and that no good could come of it. They decided that the mutual model was sound, well rooted, and would last their time. Events have proved them right and the 2008 crash took with it most of the societies that had become banks. Northern Rock, with its heavy dependence on the wholesale financial markets and its practice of giving 100 per cent mortgages, was the first casualty in 2007, but two years into the crisis in 2009 the Halifax, the largest of all the societies, had crashed, taking Lloyds Bank with it, and it was the same story all over the sector. The Yorkshire on the other hand has survived with its mutual model and finances intact and has taken over two large failing societies.

My Yorkshiremen were not only shrewd businessmen; they held a principled belief in a society where one citizen helped another; those who had cash lent it for a fair return to those who didn't and wanted to buy houses. A version of a credit union and, as I pointed out to my fellow Board members, a clear statement of Socialist principles. They were dismissive of this interpretation, maintaining that the building society was but a model of common sense as opposed to any Socialist model which would no doubt involve folks with a bit saved being forced to squander it on the feckless and ill-deserving. I was about as successful in explaining Labour policies to Yorkshire as I was trying to persuade New Labour to hang on to the mutual model wherever they saw it. It was a further irony that it was the ultra-conservative building societies that gave many good women their first Board experience.

The disappointment of the 1992 election caused me to think more coherently about my future. I was fifty-two, and in an investment bank anyone who is still there in their fifties is typically the Chief Executive, the Chairman, or at least the Head of Corporate Finance, and I wasn't going to be any of those. There had been several other ex-civil servants serving in investment banks but most seemed to have been forced out, with the distinguished exceptions of Frances Heaton, a director of Lazards, who had converted herself into a proper technically qualified banker, and Gerry Grimstone at Schroders who had steered his bank into some very big privatisations.

Janet with Malcolm Richardson, CEO of Standard Charterered Bank 1991.

Charterhouse had never tried to turn me into a conventional banker, preferring to use me as a frontline business-getter. So banking, per se, would not last me out; I wasn't going to be Chairman despite the fine example of Sir Peter Carey, once the Permanent Secretary of the DTI and the man who had been disappointed when I left to go into the City. Peter took me out to lunch, congratulated me on my success and asked about my experience of joining the City. He told me he had been expensively recruited and effusively welcomed at Morgan Grenfell, given a room and a secretary and an in-tray and then left to work out how he was to earn his corn. Same here, I said, and we had both reacted in the same way; like me, he had lunched with the whole of his address book but, unlike me, he said courteously, he was spinning his wheels until disgrace overtook Morgan Grenfell arising from their involvement in the bid for Guinness Holdings. This bid uncovered a lot of traditional City practices like artificially pushing up the share price of the potential acquirer. In the resulting holocaust, with senior members of Morgan Grenfell falling on their swords under pressure from the Bank of England, Peter had risen overnight to Chairman, keeping the ship under tight control, while working furiously to sort out the future. A dreadful mess is what Permanent Secretaries deal with on a daily basis and they were lucky to have him on the spot.

Charterhouse was also, late in 1992, in some disarray. Our owners the RBS were restive; in times of recession their corporate bankers were looking sideways at the large salaries being paid to Charterhouse people. Corporate bankers are farmers and investment bankers are hunters and in lean years farmers are traditionally unwilling to share their crops with their hunter brethren. Victor Blank, now Chairman of the Group, came to the conclusion that the model which had worked successfully for the last eight years was broken and found a new home for us in a complicated process that left Charterhouse owned jointly by a German corporate finance boutique and a larger French bank, Crédit Commercial de France. At the same time, Sandy Muirhead became Head of Corporate Finance and decided to tidy up the Department. The advisory work in Scotland was coming to an end, and my role as privatiser-in-chief was being eclipsed by a much younger colleague, Geoff Arbuthnott, an employee of our sister operation, Charterhouse Development Capital. Following the success of Unipart and Allied Steel and Wire CDC had finally understood the essential tenet of privatisation buy-outs: they were an enormous struggle to bring off but were very profitable because Government does not, then as now, necessarily demand the best price for an asset if it can get enough of its other objectives. So there were good deals available for those who like me understood this equation. Geoff was put in the same office as me and a pleasant lending specialist, Adam Seymour, in the hope that we would form a team to gain more of the large buy-outs from Government and the (privately expressed) expectation that Adam and I would combine to make Geoff's business behaviour more emollient. This part of the plan failed totally; Adam and I found ourselves assimilating Geoff's incisive brutal Scottish approach, to the point where within weeks all three of us greeted proposals from any part of the bank with the same snarling, scornful brevity, and the same strong Scottish accent as he did. Geoff turned out to be a star, a lightning-quick learner, who made a spectacular success with the purchase of Forth Ports in 1993, followed in 1994 by a buy-out of railway rolling stock (the Porterhouse deal) which he sold onto a bank consortium for a very substantial profit. It was clear that a group led from CDC by Geoff would be the most effective way to use the bank's assets and that my particular skills and expertise could be used on a part-time basis.

I had my own reasons for bowing to this logic. I was, at fifty-two with three teenagers and a travelling husband, beleaguered and tired. I wanted some time off and I had all sorts of ideas about how I was going to use it, including writing a lot more. So Sandy and I made a deal; I would be Redundant in June 1993, thereby lightening the load of fixed expense in the department, and I would return in September on a three-day-a-week consultancy arrangement. The Bank got first call on my expertise but I could take as many non-executive directorships as I wanted and keep the fees. It seemed to me like the promised land and I was happy to trade the limited job security any investment bank offers for an arrangement which gave me a chance to build up a part-time portfolio career and write more books.

Ten years in an investment bank on top of thirteen years in the Civil Service had left me with a decent pension, I still had my good colleagues and half an office, the children were growing up and the sunny uplands beckoned as I approached my fifty-third birthday. Jim too was redundant from his job at GTE where they wanted to sell the bit he managed, but relaxed about it; our mortgage was at a tolerable level and he reckoned to do consultancy work or jobs for old friends, another version of a portfolio career.

I should have remembered the old Spanish observation that, if you want to make God laugh, tell Him your plans. 1993 turned out to be an annus horribilis, to borrow HM the Queen's description, but it started out well. We had, as planned, a fascinating month touring liberated Central Europe, starting in North Germany where the twenty-year-old Henry was working in a big stable, having decided he had found his country as well as his métier. He was exhausted but cheerful, refusing support, working at everything from riding other people's horses for money as well as his own in competitions, to breaking in three-year-olds for another employer. He was as scornful as ever of any form of Higher Education so our attempts to suggest that the Germans were even more demanding than we were about proper Qualifications fell on stony ground.

We drove on down the long main road to Dresden, roughly surfaced, full of grindingly heavy trucks, and decorated every fifty yards with young women in very short skirts lounging against a tree, all from the poor countries of the old East making money as best they could from the flow of truckers from the rich West.

Dresden itself was another shock; I guided us confidently to the main square but we drove round it three times before I realised we were in it. Instead of a grim pile of rubble surrounded by space, it had become a builder's yard in which every brick or piece of stone from the rubble was numbered and placed on steel racking. West German money had decided to rebuild the Frauenkirche from the ground up, using what material could be salvaged, and was getting on with it, with the same speed and ferocity with which they were restoring the hotels and the historic buildings, putting modern offices and interiors behind the newly braced baroque facades. We counted forty-eight cranes from a street near the featureless Stasi hotel. It had been given a coat of paint and a quick refurbishment of the bathrooms since I had stayed there in 1990, but the ambience was as chill as ever.

It was the same in other parts of the old East Germany too; in Weimar we would find a patch of beautiful crumbling buildings, roughly propped up, then within a few yards a slum of dreadful post-war flats. Prague was better; the buildings were beautiful

175

and the people were more cheerful, and everywhere we went there was music; superb trumpeters giving little concerts in churches for the tourists, grateful to us for buying their badly produced, beautifully played CD recordings. We went on to Hungary and great houses and estates, full of ruined splendour. All this, the books told us, had been as nothing compared to grand Vienna where the eighteenth- and nineteenth-century Austrians thought Budapest a boring provincial town and its so-called Hungarian aristocracy only a cut above their peasants. Then home, via Passau and Bomberg because I had wanted to see the magnificent stone Knight, der Ritter von Bomberg, and a final sprint up to the Channel.

Home at first seemed to be in good order; Isobel was delighted to see us, having been kindly looked after by the schoolfriend's family in whose care we left her, and we swept her up to Scotland to the family cottage in Alligin for August. Richard had stayed with friends too, and while he was a bit furtive when asked about his A-level exams he was well and delighted to be out of school. We would have swept him up too but he had other invitations. And, usefully, Jim found that BICC, who had offered him a job in 1990 which he did not take, wanted to see him and he had a good lunch with them just before we went to Scotland.

By September the storm clouds had gathered. The first blow was that Richard had failed just as badly as Henry in his A-levels; one B, one D and a couple of Es. He was always a late developer and at eighteen it was impossible to think he would manage in a crowded labour market, but equally we were not prepared to send him to any university that would take him with those grades. We had been here before with Henry but that didn't help our collective mood. Isobel, who loves her brothers dearly, was cast down by his failure, as was he, and we were all cross and frustrated.

The second blow came from my brother Giles, still living apart from Elisabeth and still hoping for a reunion, who had asked if he could stay in our house while we were away; he was, he said, finding living by himself in a rented flat very gloomy. We had been too busy to take proper account of the warning signal implicit in this request, but we got back to find that Giles was jobless again and in the throes of a black depression. We said, firmly, that we needed our space back but agreed that he could stay a further week after we got back. I was away with Isobel when Jim and Richard found they could not wake Giles up at all on the day he was due to leave and realised they must call an ambulance. We were all unsympathetic, deeply angry and fed up, as often happens in families trying to deal with serious depression. The Royal Free duty psychiatrist however sat down with him patiently and asked what could the hospital do for him? Giles, shocked by how close he had come to the edge, replied that a week in somewhere quiet with someone to talk to would help, and was moved to a rundown mental hospital where he did a bit of basketwork and talked to everyone. Elisabeth, as ever in a crisis, rushed to his side and somewhere in that week she agreed to take him back. 'He will always be fragile,' she said to Mum, 'but neither of us has found anyone else in thirteen years of living apart, so...'

We had been less than kind or helpful but we were desperately busy because Richard had to be helped to get himself in a crammer and retake his two least unpromising A-levels, and Jim had been offered a job with Balfour Beatty, helping Sir Robert Davidson sell their services in mainland China, and was preparing for life on an aeroplane. And as September changed into October it became clear that something had gone wrong for Isobel. She was always slight but she was eating very little and looking very thin although full of energy. The GP dismissed our worries, but three weeks later Isobel and I went swimming together; at fourteen she had been faster than I for a year or so, but this time I overhauled her easily on a couple of lengths, and as she got out I realised with a terrible pang that there were hollows behind the muscles at the top of her legs, her arms were bone thin, her bathing suit was creasing in odd places, and the febrile energy had given way to exhaustion. We overrode any further hesitation by the GP, demanded a specialist reference and turned up at the Charter Nightingale hospital in Marylebone, with the assurance only that A Psychiatrist would see Isobel, hunched and gnawing at her fingernails.

We had the great good fortune to find Dr Michael Best on duty that day, after a black moment when the receptionist denied all knowledge of Isobel, us, or our GP. A large, apparently clumsy, dark blond man in his forties, he sat down beside us – all trying to talk at once – and said that he wanted to talk to Isobel first by herself. Isobel went with him looking very frail and more like eleven than fourteen, wringing our hearts with an anxious backward look. Neither of us found anything to say to each other so we read newspapers assiduously until she and Dr Best returned forty-five minutes later, to a waiting room by then empty of everyone but us. We looked up at him expectantly but he waved a hand to bring Isobel forward and waited while she tearfully told us that she understood she was anorexic and that she needed treatment. We did not realise at the time how crucial and how difficult this painful admission was for Isobel, or the degree of skill and empathy Dr Best had used to get her to that point, in less than an hour on no prior acquaintance. Denial is the most common barrier to treatment with young anorexics, and that was the strategy she had used successfully up to that day.

I went into full protective mother mode and tried to take her home to comfort her, but Dr Best wasn't having any. He told all three of us that this was a serious disease, that the tests showed that our treasured daughter was close to the point where starvation and weight loss would affect the functioning of her brain, and that she needed to come into the clinic as soon as possible. We went home, all three of us shattered, and it took us nearly a week and several consultations with Dr Best to get our collective heads round this verdict, during which Isobel interviewed everyone at the clinic down to the janitor. We were all finally persuaded by the meal lists Isobel brought home after her interview with the clinic's dietician, which set out in detail the three solid meals a day plus three between-meals snacks that she would have to eat to get her weight back to normal, after weeks spent probably not eating more than 500 calories a day.

'I don't think we can get all that down you,' I said, appalled.

'Nor do I,' my daughter said. 'I need the clinic.' We looked at each other, and I realised that she knew what she was doing. It was a huge relief, although I wept afterwards, to deliver her to the clinic and sign the papers agreeing to abide by all their conditions.

She was there for four months, missing a full term and a half at school. We had understood how close we had come to tragedy and did not worry about what she was missing, but, despite the loss of school time, a year later she got nine A* grades and one A at GCSE, equal first with another girl at the highly academic South Hampstead High School. Dr Best was throughout clear, inspiring and uncompromising, teaching us that teenage anorexia starts with a teenage depression but that it then takes on a life of its own, with particular characteristics. He used sometimes to say to us – we and Isobel were required to come for therapy regularly, and he also asked to see the boys, which meant bringing Henry back from Germany for a week – that he could hear the disease speak, rather than her. Jim and I found this way of looking at the problem useful; love and logic have no place in dealing with anorexia in full flow because you are dealing with a malignant and cunning enemy. The strategy that worked – for Isobel and perhaps two of her twelve fellow teenage patients – was uncompromising; she ate three meals a day and three snacks, every bit of all of them, under the eye of a nurse, however sick she felt. She attended therapy every day, including a group which contained all the adult patients as well. Our treasured sheltered daughter found herself in a group with a woman in her forties explaining that her husband had suggested she needed a rest, which was so good of him. We asked Isobel cautiously what her view had been and she said, well, the poor woman was in denial, wasn't she; the husband wasn't coming back any time soon and was probably in the arms of another woman. Jim and I anxiously consulted Dr Best – another rule that he insisted on was that any disagreement between parents and therapist was aired well away from Isobel, because anorexia leaps to exploit the thinnest crack in the parental/therapeutic facade – and he said that teenagers who like Isobel were recovering benefited from the knowledge that adults were also human and got into muddles.

After the first two weeks we were allowed to visit her every evening after dinner and to take her for the walk her teenage energy needed. She was only allowed to go a limited distance and wasn't allowed to go into places of entertainment; we enlivened these restricted evenings by deciding which pub we would all go to when she was allowed out. Her treatment was rigorous and carefully planned; first she was allowed to come home for supper with her allocated social worker for the odd evening, with Jim, Richard and me trying to look sane, calm and sensible, then for a weekend away with us. Jim decided to take the three of us to a hotel near Gatwick which catered for homesick Japanese businessmen, on the basis that a totally different sort of food might give Isobel a break. He was right – we ate two beautiful high protein Japanese meals a day, and watched Isobel eating with real appetite again. Japanese food – as Jim had imaginatively seen – is perfect for a child who has been wearily munching her way through English stodge, being tasty, light, beautifully presented and arriving in lots of small courses, and it marked a turning point.

The Japanese weekend was particularly welcome since Christmas had been difficult. Isobel was allowed out for thirty-six hours, from 9 a.m. on Christmas morning to 4 p.m. on Boxing Day, and Jim had to fetch her and take her back in a tiny sports car, lent to me by Charterhouse to replace the big station wagon that Henry (still a horrible driver at that stage) had crashed on his last visit from Germany. Jim said his head seemed alarmingly to be level with the top of the tyres of the various behemoths he came up with on the A1(M) and he and Isobel both arrived in Cambridge cold and alarmed. My mother, who was with us for Christmas, and Jim's parents were also worried and distressed by their thin withdrawn granddaughter.

But the spring came, and Isobel emerged from the clinic and went back to school. A young woman of eighteen, four years Isobel's senior, Vonda, also emerged and, like Isobel, never went back again. Von had initially been threatened by Isobel's stolid determination to eat and had sought to bully her to the extent that I was about to involve Dr Best, but she had suddenly decided to join Isobel instead, so that they both ate, speedily and without fuss, both stuck to the rules and both managed to get out. They may have been the only two out of the twelve who got away; we know that two very sick young women, both walking with sticks, both with tubes up their noses so that they could be fed at all, died soon thereafter. Michael Best would not tell us but Isobel doubts that any of the other eight escaped entirely and probably the majority would live the half-life of the anorexics who never quite beat the disease, in and out of hospital, always anxious, always threatened by the food we take for granted, descending, often, into alcoholism as mature women. Michael Best himself in the end gave up treating anorexics; our guess is because the success rate was so painfully low.

Charterhouse urged me to come in only when I could, and Balfour Beatty – to whom Jim was new – uncomplainingly paid Isobel's considerable medical bills while giving Jim as much time off as the nature of the job permitted. For six months he alternated flying round China first class with Sir Robert Davidson with visiting a sick teenager in hospital. Like writers everywhere, I chose to write my way through it, producing the first draft of a second novel for Susan Watt at Harper Collins, called *Children of a Harsh Winter*, which we hoped would help me to an alternative career as a bestselling novelist. It is about a group of four children, and strongly autobiographical; the only girl is based on me, and two of the boys have elements of my brothers. The book also contains my own, mortally ill, father, transmuted into a charismatic Labour councillor, and friend Jet's father Gavin, who turns up as a country GP, centre of a devoted group of his daughter's friends, trying desperately to stop them reading the medical magazines he brings home. 'Someone doing it with sheep again, Dad?' I enjoyed writing that book, but, published in 1994, the only national review it attracted (a very good one by Elizabeth Buchan in the *Sunday Times*) appeared at least six weeks after publication, too late to do much for the hardback sales.

I also had the time and space to help Isobel in a practical sense; at an early stage of her recovery she told us that she wanted to change schools and to escape from London and an

Giles Neel, Janet, Professor Trevor Taylor, Muir Moffat (Deputy Chairman Unipart Ltd) at the 1992 launch party for The Highest Bidder.

all-girls school. We decided not to consider any of the boys' schools which took girls only into the Sixth Form, on the basis that they had not thought through the problems of bringing up girls and just wanted to improve their A-level results. As I tentatively produced brochures for Isobel to look at, she cheered up, visibly, so once she was out of the clinic she and I visited schools, usually difficult to find up long leafy lanes, and were escorted around acres of playing fields and theatres and music rooms, all a far cry from the cramped facilities of a central London grammar school. I learned to judge how Isobel felt about a school – she still had difficulty communicating her real needs – by whether she picked her cuticles and bit her nails as we left the building. One famous school, specialising in every known sport including dance, which she wanted to do, had really scared her. She had observed that several of the girls there were anorexic or close to it – you cannot deceive an ex-anorexic and a scandal the next year confirmed her judgement – and that the Headmaster preferred thin blondes. Another famous but very academic school worried her because the Headmaster was sure she should do four A-levels and Oxbridge entrance, and I think she felt she was being interviewed by her mother. Finally, we came to Bedales, a long-established co-educational school with a distinguished tradition of arts and crafts and liberal views. The school had been recommended to me by a brilliant, nonconforming civil service colleague, Jenny Bacon, then right at the top of her department, who still wore a tracksuit to work if that was the first thing she saw when she got up. We arrived late in the winter dusk with Portakabins looming out of the mist and small groups of cheerful young wrapped up in scarves and sweaters against the cold. We were taken round by a Senior Child wearing what appeared to be the uniform of tight jeans and heaped assorted woollen top garments and I found myself crowded out on the narrow paths as Isobel, chattering hard, edged closer to her. As I fell behind them Isobel gave a little skip to keep up and asked about dance classes. By the time we had toured the badly painted Portakabins and the magnificent beamed library it was clear that she had found a home.

They offered her a place before they knew about her dazzling GCSE results. Their only stipulation was to ask for a letter from Dr Best; anorexia was not a barrier to enrolment, they said, stoutly, but they would need to know how to cope if it recurred.

We got a shock when we saw a copy of the letter. Isobel wanted, it said, to be away at a boarding school because she was anxious about being the last child left at home, the only support of her ageing parents. I was fifty-three and Jim fifty-two, and both of us with absorbing lives and virtually full-time jobs. It goes to show how little we know of what goes on in the heads of our teenage children.

Chapter 12

BBC GOVERNOR AND NED 1994–1995

At the same time as Isobel was recovering and finding herself somewhere she wanted to be, both the boys were struggling to do the same. Richard, with two A grades at A-level thanks to first-class coaching, was accepted at UCL and passed the test for his driving licence and felt himself a success. We prepared to send him off for an abbreviated gap year but then he could not get himself out of the house. He had abandoned Clare but was miserable when she found herself another boyfriend and it took him an age to get himself to Cyprus to join his schoolfriend Vijay and work in a bar – despite his easy sociability he was still the same anxious thin-skinned kid.

We were also worrying about the twenty-one-year-old Henry who we thought was beginning to struggle in Münster. Jim and I went over to see him and organised the delivery and installation of a washing machine because Henry was beginning to smell rather strongly of his trade. Later that day I stood, up to the top of my boots in straw, watching our boy consoling a horse with a bad foot, and bravely asked whether we could bribe him to go to university. In any country. 'Yes,' he said. 'You can. I need to stay here but I could try the Fachhochschule.' We helped him enrol with the assistance of Gunther Peise, still head of this important Münster business university, and went home feeling we were at last doing right for this son.

In the summer of 1994 Jim and Sir Robert decided to recommend against Balfour Beatty trying to establish themselves in China, on the basis that any civil engineering contract would involve unacceptable levels of risk. Sir Robert had previously had eight years selling power stations manufactured by GEC but neither he nor Jim believed, despite the respect in which Sir Robert was held in China, that it would be possible to make decent profits if you were only providing the civil engineering expertise to put up plants which had been manufactured in China.

Balfour Beatty management were waiting for both of them to come back and immediately offered Jim the job of working out how to deal with the new Private Finance Initiative, the method of contracting that Charterhouse and I had advised on twelve years before. This time the Government had taken the decision to try this new technique for getting roads and other key infrastructure built and financed by harnessing the private sector. Balfour Beatty were looking at the loss of a large amount of public sector work unless they changed their approach to match the Government's. Jim was put in charge, and a brilliant accountant who had also qualified as a barrister, Anthony Rabin, recruited to help him, and Balfour Beatty Capital Projects was born.

Before Jim's appointment was formally confirmed he was required to do the various personality and IQ tests which were becoming standard at that time. As we knew, he has a very high IQ and a substantial component of loner in the personality, which means he is able to work and think without direction and without approval. Operating PFI meant that it would be necessary to put a substantial part of the BICC, then Balfour Beatty's owners, balance sheet behind Capital Projects so that Jim and the CEO of BICC would need to be fully in agreement. The Personnel Director, the gifted Barry Keates, looked at the test results, which told him that Jim and the CEO were very very like each other and told them both that they might find each other difficult, and why. They always worked easily together. It turns out that, given two intelligent men, you tell them the problem and, consciously or unconsciously, they will deal with it.

In 1994 I was approached to become a Governor of the BBC. I was tapped up for the job early in the year, but not appointed till July, by which time two seats on the twelve-person Board had been empty for some months, one of them vacated by P. D. James. I owe the job to two people, Patricia Hodgson, then Head of Policy at the BBC, who nominated me, and the Prime Minister, John Major, who approved the appointment. Richard Wilson, who had by then become Permanent Secretary of the Department of the Environment, rang to congratulate me and to offer to buy me lunch – at Café Pelican for old times' sake – and to introduce me to Hayden Phillips, the Permanent Secretary of the Department of Culture and the Arts. How kind, I said gratefully, but Richard indicated that the boot was on the other foot; any Permanent

Secretary of that Department would have expected to know any appointee to an organisation as important as the BBC, and Hayden had not met me. The morning of the lunch Richard rang me to say that he was moving, with his Secretary of State Michael Howard, to the Home Office, a promotion which, as we did not need to say to each other, put him a half-step ahead of all his contemporaries on the route to Cabinet Secretary. Hayden and I dealt with any awkwardness that might have been felt by vying with each other to invent examples of catastrophes lying in wait for Richard and Michael Howard – another Cambridge contemporary – at that known disaster area, the Home Office.

My time at the BBC started badly, and it was at least partly my own fault; I had given an interview in support of *Children of a Harsh Winter* in which I had spoken mildly disapprovingly of John Birt, then Director General. I got a three-page handwritten letter of complaint from him, and nothing I could say or do when I met him improved the matter at all. I went to the Chairman, Marmaduke Hussey, whom I did not know, to ask what I could do to put things right. Always discreet, he didn't tell me that I had got myself entangled in the war between Director General and Chairman. It became clear John Birt thought I had declared for the Chairman and was seeking – in a frivolously expressed but minor criticism of his management style – to undermine him and all his works, and our relationship never quite recovered. No one ever told me quite how that situation had come about, and indeed it is not unusual to find a chairman and a CEO at loggerheads.

Sir Marmaduke Hussey, 'Dukey' as he was always called, went everywhere with a stick because he had been critically injured in the war. He had survived only by luck and good nursing and was in pain every day from the bits of metal still in his spine. He retained a military bearing and old-fashioned attitudes like rising whenever a woman entered the room, even women he knew well, who would plead with him not to. He had, aged thirty-six, persuaded the eighteen-year-old Lady Susan Waldegrave to marry him, and when we met in 1994 she had been a lady in waiting to the Queen for many years. Dukey looked like the military grandees I used to meet but had the brains and the acumen and the ability of a first-class businessman. He was ruthlessly capable; when he arrived at the BBC he found a lax culture of high living, drinks cabinet in every office, and uncontrolled expenses, which he dealt with uncompromisingly. The then Director General Alasdair Milne (father of Seumas Milne, adviser to Jeremy Corbyn), who was determined to oppose reforms introduced by Dukey, found himself fired. Michael Checkland, his successor, had not proved successful and had in his turn been replaced by John Birt.

I was much cheered to find Michael Cocks as Deputy Chairman. He had been Callaghan's Chief Whip and had got government business through in the hard years from 1976 to 1979 when the Government had a majority of three and the sick had to be brought in by ambulance and Ministers called back from important missions abroad to vote. (The play *This House* best describes this period.)

The Statutes then governing the BBC Board decreed its membership to be twelve people, three of whom were to be representative of each of the Nations, the Welsh Governor, the Scottish Governor, and the Northern Irish Governor. Someone had to have trade union experience, and someone else business or financial experience, and another someone had to have experience of the arts, and yet another someone had to have educational experience. Suitable representation of minorities, including women, was also required. And of course there were two slots reserved for Chairman and Deputy Chairman, both of whom were political appointees; so since Dukey was Conservative he was balanced by Michael Cocks. Bill Jordan, now Lord Jordan, had the trade union slot and Sir David Scholey, of Warburgs, had the business and finance post, while the distinguished conductor Jane Glover had the arts job. The Welsh Governor then was Gwyn Jones, Welsh-speaking as the Statutes also required, a clever technocrat businessman, the Reverend Norman Drummond was the Scottish Governor, and Northern Ireland was represented by Sir Kenneth Bloomfield, lately Permanent Secretary for the Northern Ireland Office. A capable Indian woman represented both women and other minorities and a headmistress from Bolton, worldly and smart, did education. Lord Nicholas Gordon-Lennox, lately our Ambassador to Madrid, provided the essential sophistication and knowledge of Foreigners. Since I had replaced P. D. James and was myself a published writer I felt I had a share in the arts brief and as a banker also batted for the financial team.

Board meetings came as a serious shock. Mountains of paper were couriered to us all, and while as an erstwhile civil servant I could and did read it all, it was a burden. The meetings were largely a waste of time; we twelve Governors met jointly with the Board of Management and plodded through item after item, during which it was clear that the Management present were either dying of terminal boredom or covertly doing something else. It was Michael Cocks who enlightened me. 'They have the meeting the day before, Janet, to make sure they are ready to defend themselves and get all the business through the Governors.' No commercial enterprise would waste time and effort like this and what it told me was that the BBC senior executives saw themselves as the custodians of the BBC and all its works, and Governors as a transient nuisance requiring careful management. Michael Cocks agreed with this reading, but some of the others were more optimistic. Or nice, as Michael suggested, nice being a synonym for bloody daft in his thinking.

It didn't take long to work out that if I felt strongly about an issue I would have to find allies among my fellow Governors and spring a concerted attack at a Board meeting without even warning the Chairman as would be the normal practice in a private sector company. I got some things through on this basis, but it was unnecessarily effortful. My natural allies turned out to be Bill Jordan, Gwyn Jones and Norman Drummond but Gwyn was in Wales half the week, Norman in Scotland, and Bill in Geneva at the ILO, so rallying them took time, patience and substantial telephone bills.

Roger Jones, BBC Welsh Governor (1998–2003) and Gwyn Jones, BBC Welsh Governor (1994–1999).

Despite the awful meetings I was and am a fan of the product, and watch BBC TV in preference to nearly anything else. (I was one of the few dedicated TV watchers among the Governors, most of whom preferred radio.) While the place was riven with small 'p' politics and backbiting, somewhere somehow superb things were being commissioned and shown, and important artistic events and groups all over the UK supported and encouraged.

The War, unbusinesslike and self-indulgent as it surely was, was prosecuted at a level where Governors could ignore it, until 1995 when it erupted like Vesuvius. Dukey as Chairman had agreed with the Board that Governors, including himself, would never see a programme before it was transmitted so that there could be no issues of censorship. The policy had led on occasion to difficulties but all had agreed that anything was preferable to having Governors involved in decisions about what could and could not be transmitted. In 1995, when the marriage of the Prince and Princess of Wales was known to be on the rocks, John Birt had authorised the purchase and transmission of a TV interview with the Princess of Wales and did not tell his Chairman that the programme existed until just before the schedules had to be published. He justified himself on the grounds of Policy and also that Dukey would have been conflicted because of his close connection to the royal family through his wife. We all instantly perceived this was a key battle; Dukey was going to be gravely embarrassed whatever happened to the programme, but my mates on the Board and I thought he should have been forewarned much earlier and that the Director General should have found a way. The interview – famously revealing the Princess of Wales' take on her marriage – went out on a Wednesday. The day afterwards was celebrated by a concert long organised by the BBC for the 300th anniversary of the untimely death of the composer William Purcell. This was held in Westminster Abbey, attended by much of the royal family, several members of Cabinet and by all Governors, with spouses, all of us seated in close proximity in the North Transept, and all bidden to a buffet supper afterwards at Church House.

It was not, we agreed in anxious conclave, a moment when any of us could desert, pleading grandmothers' funerals, serious illness, or the school play. Nicky Gordon-Lennox, mentally reviewing a long and distinguished career, said, as we walked together between Abbey and dinner, that he had lived through

189

more difficult occasions but not many of them. The only hope, he felt, was Not to Talk about the War, to quote the famous line from *Fawlty Towers*.

We all tried to talk about Purcell but, imperceptibly and inevitably, everyone started to talk about the War. I found myself in a group of four, Virginia Bottomley, then Secretary of State for Heritage, Robert Runcie, recently retired as Archbishop of Canterbury, and Lady Susan Hussey. The Archbishop led off with some harmless statement to Virginia, who, like me, talks too much when she is nervous, and she rapidly floundered into a bog. I tried to help but I heard myself say to the Archbishop that I did not know where he stood on divorce. 'I am professionally against it, of course,' he replied kindly while I prayed for death and Virginia snatched back the batting. When I recovered I realised that the other three had managed to achieve cosy agreement on the horror of people who talked to the TV about their private affairs. I thought their disapproval not wholly merited and suggested that a man of thirty-six marrying a girl of eighteen ought to have looked after and protected her rather than assuming he could go right back to his own pursuits. A snarl of derision from Lady Susan Hussey smothered noises of tentative agreement from Virginia and the Archbishop. '*I* was eighteen and *he* was thirty-six when I married Dukey,' she said. I recalled – far too late – the old adage about holes and the unwiseness of digging. Virginia and the Archbishop were silenced and – again far too late – a small rescue party of my Jim and Virginia's Peter appeared at our sides with offers of drink and refreshment.

The next elegantly named BOG/BOM (Board of Governors/Board of Management) meeting was grim. On the surface normal business was being formally transacted but the atmosphere seethed with hostility. It was plain that several conversations between various different factions had been held before this meeting, which had resolved none of the real problems but that somehow it had been agreed that the Board would not discuss them. It is both difficult and irritating to take part in a meeting where all the real business has been transacted somewhere else but I took my cue from Nicky Gordon-Lennox who was indestructibly looking for points of agreement and oiling the whole proceedings with elaborate Foreign Office courtesy.

I sought out Gwyn Jones afterwards. 'What are we doing here? Is one allowed to resign?' 'Oh no, cariad, goodness me,' he said, wrapping me in a warm Welsh embrace, and sweeping me off to lunch. We agreed that being a Governor was fundamentally a high status position of no influence whatsoever but that we were both lifelong supporters of the BBC, the Governors were interesting people and we would hang in there and do good when and as we could. For the rest we would derive what pleasure we could from the entertainment offered, formal and informal.

The formal entertainment was high quality. We Governors were at that time allowed a box, two nights in the season, at the Prom concerts to entertain people who would be useful to the BBC and we used that privilege to the full. Boxes for the Proms at the Albert Hall were even more difficult to come by than Glyndebourne or Covent Garden tickets and at the beginning of my term we got two for free. Later in my five years' service we were reduced to one box but I used to book and pay for another two through the BBC.

We were also invited to all the BBC celebrations, everything from the Young Musician heats (not the finals) to a private showing of the BBC's *Pride and Prejudice*. I took my Mum, by then in her 80s, who enjoyed it very much, as did I. In the interval she said to Nicky Gordon-Lennox that she kept waiting for everyone to go off to Lyme Regis and for one of the girls to hurt her head, faltering as she realised she had conflated the plots of *Pride and Prejudice* and *Persuasion*. 'I know just what you mean,' Nicky said, warmly. 'I am waiting for one of them to marry Mr Knightley.' No wonder he had been an ambassador.

Dukey, having served ten years, was succeeded by Christopher Bland who had been John Birt's Chairman at London Weekend TV. John was openly glad to get a new Chairman and we Governors just hoped for a less fractious atmosphere. I knew Christopher from his chairmanship of National Freight Corporation and admired him as a sound businessman who knew his own mind and would have no patience with BBC politics in general. The whole place settled down to get on with the transaction of business and, as usual, to Renewing the Charter. This process occupied a policy department of some seventy highly intelligent people, headed in those days by Patricia Hodgson, a friend and another of the Links gang. She had been Secretary to the BBC before becoming Head of Policy and was a BBC insider, and is now Chairman of OFCOM. She has a first-class mind and the analytic capacity that goes with it, and writes beautifully, with spare eloquent clarity. Indeed it was always assumed that she had actually written the various White Papers and submissions to Ministers which achieved the continuing settlement that enabled the BBC to go on being the creature it was: a dominant public sector broadcaster, envy of the world, securely funded and supported.

John Birt as DG did have a clear eye for what he needed to achieve for the business and he had already established his digital policy. He convinced us that the BBC as part of its mission had to be available to everyone, free, by every distribution channel possible. It followed that BBC programmes had to be available on platforms belonging to its major rival, the Murdoch-owned Sky. It also involved starting, from scratch, BBC Online, which was just underway when I arrived in 1994. He was right and we knew it but he had to do it with limited informed cooperation from his Governors. Gwyn Jones was the exception; a computer engineer himself who had made two fortunes from technology-related businesses already, he understood the importance of putting the BBC on to the net. The rest of us were on a scale from Luddite to seriously underinformed. John insisted on kitting us all up with Sky satellites so that any of us who wanted to watch any television, ever, came face to face with what he was trying to do. BBC engineers descended on classic listed houses to install Sky dishes and several of us had to get planning consent for the dish, illustrating neatly the problems of modernising Britain. Gwyn of course had already had satellite dishes in both his houses and his office for some years. I had written my first published book on a green screen Amstrad in 1986, but that was my only effort to come to terms with the digital revolution. Worse, I had prophesied confidently in 1985 that the mobile phone would never achieve general acceptance. My only excuse is that in 1985 mobiles were hideously expensive and the size of two bricks. My formative experience had been when a Charterhouse team had set one up, occupying all the space on the table of a British Rail compartment, and sought to communicate with John Neill of Unipart who was twenty miles away from us in a car, expensively fitted with a car phone. All we could get were occasional cries and curses, snatched away as if by a mighty wind. Armed as we all are nowadays with a machine that fits into one hand, carries a database of 900 contacts and three years' diaries, and receives and sends email as well as a host of other functions, I am reminded daily to keep my mouth shut about the future for any modern technologies that come my way. I was equally hesitant about Online and satellite TV but I did at least embrace them, however gingerly. Not all my fellow Governors did; Nicky Gordon-Lennox never mastered the TV programmer and we all agreed that you really needed Gwyn Jones given away with the kit.

The BBC put up with all this patiently because they regularly had worse to deal with. The engineers who fitted our satellite dish told me that often they would be sent to a radio listener who persistently complained of poor reception and would find an old person in possession of a radio set dating from the 1920s with a battery not much younger. The only realistic answer was to get a new set, but this was not an acceptable response, so highly paid BBC engineers would sneak in a new battery and then spend hours coaxing ancient kit into marginally improved reception. I hope that in my own old age I shall remember those patient engineers and go and buy a new TV or radio forthwith.

(Lord) Michael Cocks, Deputy Chairman of BBC (1990–1999) and (just visible) Dame Stella Rimington, Head of MI5 (1995–1998), at Janet's leaving party, 1999.

Being a Governor helped to bring me a lasting benefit in the shape of a new NED job. I had invited Richard Price, Chairman of BPP, to lunch with John McGregor when he was Secretary of State for Education because BPP was then the only quoted company concerned with the business of training or teaching. Richard and his partners Charlie Prior and Alan Brierley had set themselves up as accountancy tutors, teaching in church halls and hotel dining rooms in the early 1980s. They had understood that the revolution in desk-top publishing would enable them to get ahead of their competitors by writing and printing off their own materials, which could be updated easily with every Finance Act. The business had prospered, they had bought their own building and floated on the Stock Market in 1989, basing their appeal more on the publishing than on the tutoring side.

As soon as my appointment as a Governor was announced I got a phone call from Richard Price. He and Charlie Prior (Alan Brierley had by then retired) bought me lunch and invited me to join their Board as an NED. The Stock Exchange, they explained, had been after them to appoint one and who better than someone who was a merchant banker and would understand corporate finance. And a Governor of the BBC in electronic publishing would also be particularly useful because BPP was in partnership with BBC Engineering to produce accountancy courses, based on material produced by BPP and downloadable overnight when BBC Engineering had bandspace. £500,000 had been committed by BPP to this joint venture which did not seem to be prospering, or indeed happening at all. I had not even been to a Governors' meeting and was very concerned about conflict of interest, but Giles who had worked for the BBC for twenty years saved me from this difficulty. He told me that BBC Engineering was a barony and it seemed likely that if Head Office were not right behind this venture, BPP should forget it. Richard and Charlie nodded in perfect, rueful understanding when I told them, and Charlie went to see his BBC Engineering counterpart the next day, asked the right questions and came back, crossly, to write the venture off. We were able to agree that time and money *not* spent was always worth having and the concept of the Sunk Cost (you've spent it, don't pour good money after bad) was right. So I joined them, BPP prospered, and I was to be on the Board for twelve years, four of them in succession to Richard as Chairman, two years on the Academic Council and finally eleven years as

President then Chancellor of BPP University.

In 1994 we also had family problems. Margaret, hitherto dauntless, a devoted and active grandmother and capable of doing as heavy a day's work as any of us, was beginning to fail. Her blood pressure had always been high but it had gone up and she was getting very tired. Worse, far worse for the true academic that she was, her eyesight was failing badly from macular degeneration and there was not a lot to be done. Suddenly, at nearly 90 and 87 respectively, Jim's parents were no longer the self-sufficient unit they had been. We had been heedlessly fortunate in our older generation – at one point earlier in their 80s both of them had had flu, complete with high temperatures. When they had confessed to us that both of them were in bed, I volunteered to come and stay. They had refused, firmly, on the basis that when one of them was feeling dreadful, the other always felt well enough to get out of bed and get them a cup of tea. But by 1994, if either of them was ill, one of us had to be mobilised immediately. They hated being dependent and disliked having people to stay, and we struggled to achieve a sensible compromise. We persuaded Jim's cousins Lucy and John to rent the other half of the Cambridge house to us and to let us do a swift refurbishment of the ground floor so we had somewhere to stay independently on our forays up to help.

Dick had to have an operation for bowel cancer early in 1995. He had been Deputy Head of the Health Service until 1973 and the first Chief Scientist at the Department from 1973 to his retirement, and he dreaded the operation because back in his day twenty years earlier you ended up with a colostomy bag and at its best you spent weeks in hospital. He had listened incredulously as a handpicked specialist respectfully explained to us both that improvements in surgical technique meant that you removed the piece of bowel containing the cancer, joined up the two ends, and restored normal service within the week. I took Margaret to see him shortly after the operation when he was still surprised at how well he felt – anaesthetics had also got much better since his day – and when I popped in a day later he could still not quite believe that no bag was going to be necessary. He was *so* pleased that he came out rather sooner than the hospital would have wished but he could not bear to be parted from Margaret.

This was the year when the *Sunday Times* first alerted its

readers to the plight of people in their forties and fifties who found themselves stretched between teenagers who needed a lot of attention and cash and ageing parents of whom the same was true. We felt ourselves lucky because while Jim's parents needed help, my own mother was going along nicely despite being severely asthmatic, and our two younger children were settled. Again our best-laid plans fell apart. Richard had started at UCL in October but having parents in London was not eligible for student accommodation. He had chosen to share a flat with his closest friend Vijay and they were housed on the ground floor of a house in Willesden, damp, dark and with very little plumbing, and it was clear that he was depressed, not getting to lectures, and would not last the course. We gathered together all the spare cash we could find and Richard and I set off for Camden Town. Halfway through the day, having seen three or four grim, damp flats and having had to step over supine drugged bodies in the streets, I refused to give Camden Town – or at least the bits of it within our price range – any further consideration. Richard and I packed ourselves into a telephone box – such things still existed in 1995 – and rang Jim, who suggested we try Primrose Hill. I knew it would cost more than Camden Town but we went and Richard fell in love with the third flat we looked at, spread over the third floor of two narrow houses in Chalcot Street, in need of refurbishment, but with two bedrooms, living room and decent eat-in kitchen. We bought it in his name using money given to the children by Jim's parents and all our spare cash to pay the deposit and to redo kitchen and bathroom and wiring. We paid the mortgage while Richard was a student and it saw him through his university career, and Isobel was to have the flat for three more years after that. We finally handed it over to Richard, including responsibility for the mortgage, six years later, by which time the flat had nearly trebled in value. We had, by pure luck, bought at the market's lowest ebb; and as often with the best financial decisions we had not acted primarily for gain and the timing had been forced on us rather than cunningly calculated.

1994 was also the year that John Smith died, in London, of a heart attack. The Bart's Hospital paramedics and a doctor had got there immediately but they could do nothing although they laboured for forty-five minutes. The news reached me via the BBC, announced by Michael Besser, almost unable to speak for tears, who had lost not only a good friend but his hospital. John

Smith had guaranteed privately that Bart's would be the major hospital for East London but his death enabled the advocates for the Royal London to ensure that their hospital was selected for the central role.

John's death threw into stark relief the effect of sixteen years in the wilderness on the party. Roy Hattersley, Neil Kinnock's deputy, had resigned with Neil back in 1992 and there was a shortage of anyone with Ministerial experience. The up-and-coming stars Gordon Brown and Tony Blair were elected in 1983 and had had no opportunity to serve in Government.

I had invited Mo Mowlam to lunch at the bank for the day after John's death. I offered her a chance to cry off but she said no, and I went off in the Charterhouse car, in order to assure her that no one at the lunch would be so lost to all sense of decency as to ask her to speculate on John's successor. She nodded gravely and said that all that sort of discussion must properly wait until after the funeral but it *had* to be Tony, didn't it? Absolutely, I agreed. Tony looked like a leader, and Gordon, sound man and experienced politician though he was, looked more like an academic. I also thought it unlikely that an English electorate who had rejected a Welshman and only just brought themselves round to accepting a Scot were going to extend a welcome to another, less user-friendly, Celt.

Much has been written about the hectic weeks that followed but for me the choice was clear and I still believe that if the Granita dinner had never taken place and Gordon had stood for the leadership, Tony would have won. Even the people who recognised Gordon's greater political experience were desperate for a charismatic articulate English leader and would have voted for Tony despite private regrets. And the story of the Labour Government's historic four terms would have been quite different.

Chapter 13

TOWARDS A LABOUR GOVERNMENT
1995–1997

We took Isobel, complete with trunk and an estate car full of teenage clothes, and a glittering record at GCSE, down to Bedales in September 1995. We unloaded her trunk and within minutes it became clear that we should leave now and allow our daughter to dive into all there was on offer. The look I got on reminding her where her hastily purchased boots had been packed told us to go long before we could advise her to be neither a borrower nor a lender and to her own self be true. We trailed disconsolately to the empty car, passing two young persons who could not have been more than fourteen standing, handfast, gazing into each other's eyes.

Isobel took to Bedales as the proverbial duck to water. She was doing an eclectic mixture of A-levels, history, German and chemistry, which she had chosen in defiance of all experienced advice. The rest of the time she was acting, doing yoga and dance and taking in everything the school had to offer. She came every Saturday afternoon to London for two professional dance classes in Covent Garden but we were never invited to meet her; she wanted no parental interruption to the experience.

The sixth form at Bedales was two thirds female, the girls being almost uniformly fierce, capable women and the boys the gentle sons of liberal North London families. Teenage problems were well understood; Isobel who had to keep her weight up discovered that a regime of toast and starch did not suffice and we organised a supply of steaks which she would eat with the footie team, all huge feet and teenage acne, hanging at her shoulder, offering to help her out. Being brought up with two elder brothers had stiffened her resistance to this behaviour so she managed not to defeat the object of this provision by sharing. She became an advocate of male rights, however; she said both to us and to the headmistress that it was clear that the Bedales girls could all make their own livings at once if need be, but that if they were to find anyone to marry, the Bedales boys would have to be encouraged to be dominant and noisy, and rediscover their historic ability to hunt down food and beat off enemies. She had learned that from Robin Skynner, we realised.

Henry's life was also changing; his teenage career in the horse world, where girls vastly outnumber boys, had featured a series of conquests in which he had behaved as the Teenage Boy does; push like mad for what they think they want at the time and drop it ungracefully afterwards. It was not until he had left for Germany that we understood that several local fathers had only just put their shotguns away. He had continued in this vein in Germany, while working a fourteen-hour day, until the day in 1995 when he saw a tall slim girl with a mass of long curly red hair walk across the stable yard where he had a tiny room with kitchen and bathroom. Silke had entered his life; a slightly older woman, with her own flat and a proper job as a pharmacist, with two degrees. Henry was twenty-two to her twenty-six but she agreed to go out with him, he maintains because he had a washing machine to offer. Silke's widowed mother was very taken aback; she was herself already ill and understandably she did not want her daughter settling for a penniless, unqualified foreigner who did not have a proper job. My sympathies were with her; much though we liked Silke we had all hoped that Henry would, after a bit, come back to England to live, and we had not envisaged him marrying a German girl four years his senior who did not want to leave Germany. Henry had also found he was making no headway at the Fachhochschule. German universities operate on huge classes, mass deference to the teaching staff, leisurely courses and almost no individual attention, which did not suit Henry who wanted to be taught anything efficiently the day before he needed to use it. It was Silke who convinced him that he could not make progress in Germany (or with her) without qualifications above Abitur (their A-level). If a German university did not suit him, she said, why not try an apprenticeship, which counted as two years of a university course. It was Silke who wrote all the applications – Henry's German, while fluent, was at that stage also totally ungrammatical. Even with her help he couldn't get in anywhere, but at the point where it looked as if he would have to come back to the UK the horse-riding fraternity prevailed on a small specialist tiling company, who had never had an apprentice before, to take him on.

The experience left us all with a lasting respect for the German apprenticeship system. Henry worked three and a half days a week in the office and on site and was educated for the other day and a half. His teachers would not put up with his unwillingness to engage with German grammar and made him speak and write correctly, indicating that he could not expect to live and work in Germany unless he took more trouble to assimilate to his adopted country. They taught him the rudiments of economics, and enough business law, finance and accountancy to ensure that he could run a middle-sized business without coming to grief financially or falling foul of bureaucratic requirements. He completed his apprenticeship in two years rather than the usual three, having improved his employer's business by teaching his fellows how to plan and quote for tiling contracts using computer-aided design programmes rather than pen, pencil and a tape. He was top of the Münster apprentices in his examinations; with his usual beady common sense he reminded us that it was not the most academic of his German contemporaries who took the apprenticeship route, but we were very proud of him.

He got a job at once. He had seen a programming position advertised by Hutchison Telecom which he could not then do but he wrote suggesting they should see him anyway. Imaginatively they gave him a start in their call centre dealing with complaints from the general public about their mobile telephones. Customer relations had never struck anyone as Henry's forte but, very clever, and laconic to a fault, he got the point faster than his colleagues and, dealing with more complaints per hour than anyone else, disposed of them more effectively. It turned out that our Henry was a customers' man, ahead of his time in production-dominated Germany. He was promoted into sales support and thence into sales management and upwards from there into Control which covers finance as well.

Jim's parents were much distressed when Henry settled in Germany; he was their favourite grandchild, although they were always even-handed between the three of them. They also found it particularly difficult that it was Germany he had chosen; both of them had spent the 1930s urging rearmament, despairing of appeasement and rescuing Jews from Hitler's Germany, and both had suffered in the Second World War. They never came with us to see Henry in Germany although he came back regularly to see them. By late 1995 Margaret could not travel; not only could she no longer see very much but she was suffering a series of small strokes, or 'incidents' as the medical profession put it. Dick hired part-time carers, then, by the spring of 1996, had to install twenty-four-hour care. Agency personnel were of very variable quality but he found two wonderful nurses, one Belgian, one German, both of whom had originally come to work in our far-famed NHS. Everyone breathed easier and Margaret was much happier when either of them was on a shift; utterly professional and highly trained, they had been distressed by conditions in NHS hospitals and amazed by the limitations of our nursing training. They would routinely and single-handed turn Margaret in bed and make her comfortable, and observed with scorn that in the Cambridge hospitals they had been required to seek assistance from a second nurse. Ruth, the German nurse, was with them through Margaret's last illness and death in 1996 and it was she who reconciled my parents-in-law to Germany, by being who she was, the loved and loving daughter of a big German Catholic family. I came rushing in one day from London and heard what I had never expected, young voices speaking German in my parents-in-law's kitchen; Ruth, Henry, home on a visit, and Isobel, whose German was fluent.

Margaret died in June 1996 and Dick decided he would continue to live in the house, now that we had tenure of the other half. Neither of us wanted to live full time in Cambridge at this stage of our lives but he assured us he could manage if we came at weekends and if we would arrange matters so that there would be someone else in our side of the house. We spruced up the outside student room, which we intended to let very cheaply to a sturdy young man – late twenties we thought, old enough to be responsible – from somewhere like Canada or Newcastle. What we got was a patrician New Englander, the 67-year-old Louis McCagg, who had come in the train of the Vice Chancellor, Alec Broers, to help raise funds for the University. It fell to me to interview Louis; he was dressed in jeans, boots, shirt and sweater, clean but old and shabby, every inch of his 6 feet 5 inches and still thick blond hair radiating Anglo-Saxon Trust Fund. I gave him a drink, explained our situation and doubtfully showed him the room; even spruced up with a coat of paint and a proper desk and shelving fitted, it looked very small. Louis breathed in the smell of paint, took his hand hastily off a hot radiator and professed himself enchanted. He was living, he said, in a huge cold room in the house of a distinguished Cambridge acquaintance and confidently expected to get pneumonia in the oncoming winter. No one, I assured him, gets cold in any house run by me, and soon we were swapping horror stories of our freezing WASP youths. It was a foregone conclusion, Louis became part of the household and was with us for the next five years. His referees – I recovered myself long enough to ask – were the Vice Chancellor, the Master of Emmanuel and the Lord Lieutenant of the county; it turned out that Louis had been a Harkness scholar at Emmanuel in 1952/3 and rowed in the winning Blue Boat in 1953.

We had explained that he was not expected to look after Jim's father but neither of them could resist making a relationship with a neighbour. Dick derived endless entertainment from the flood of visitors that poured in to see Louis, who had the run of our house when we were not there and used it to full advantage. Louis was drawn to Dick's own vast knowledge of English literature (Dick read English at King's before he decided at age twenty-seven to qualify as a doctor) and optimistic personality.

Dick was a capable resilient man, and, despite the loss of Margaret and regretting that his treasured Henry lived in Germany, he had us at weekends, Louis for the week, and good friends in Cambridge including his neighbour and contemporary, another doctor, Peter Dick, and he settled down to have as nice a time as possible. It was not to be; within a year after Margaret's death, in the spring of 1997 he found himself flagging. He had the capacity, uncommon even among doctors, that he always knew whether someone was seriously ill and with what, and he never entertained false hopes. His GP diagnosed mild leukaemia but Dick pushed for further investigation, which revealed that he had liver cancer, undoubtedly a secondary tumour following the bowel cancer of three years before.

He told me without fuss what the diagnosis had been – I rushed to ring Jim but as I came off the phone I heard Dick gently singing to himself. Disbelieving, I loitered on the upper landing to listen. I have thought about that often; he didn't want to die and he knew it was a death sentence, but perhaps there is some relief in knowing the number of your days, and that they would be spent in the company of your son and daughter-in-law and grandchildren.

Margaret had died at a time when at last it looked as if after nineteen years we were going to elect a Labour government. I was only cautiously optimistic; I thought that a hung Parliament was entirely possible. I had too much on my plate to work for victory but I gave money to several election campaigns. It is the patient hard work on the doorstep that gets you votes on the day that is important in elections, but money pays for printing costs, feeds young volunteers and sends exhausted older volunteers home in taxis when they turn faint after ten-hour days on coffee and biscuits.

I was also worried about my own mother, seven years younger than Dick but I feared beginning to flag. She had been settled for many years in a ground-floor flat in Kilburn and had built up a network of neighbours and friends; she looked after herself well and sensibly but she was eighty-three and the flat was starting to look a bit grubby. I prevailed on our treasured Margot to take my Mum on so her flat got really cleaned once a week. She loved Margot and Margot loved her and Mum would turn up to have coffee with Margot at our house whether I was there or not. She had a gift for finding good daughters and Margot was most certainly that to her.

I took Mum to Morocco in February 1997 before we knew Dick was ill, to ensure she got a proper holiday. She was a good traveller, interested, well read and prepared to try anything, but Marrakesh was a bit daunting; we both had good French but all the signs are in Arabic and we were besieged by people, young and old, offering services, as is standard in poor countries with very high unemployment. Mum got worn out on the first expedition we tried but the tour guide, Mohammed, a bright young man and a graduate, suggested quietly to me that we might have him for the afternoon all to ourselves to take us around, with a driver. I asked him how much he and a driver would want for five long mornings and hired him on the spot. It made the holiday; Mum and I decided where we wanted to go, the driver took us all to the steps of mosque or park or souk; our guide whisked us in, dealing with tickets and formalities so we could stop to look and be told the history. Mohammed left us briefly when he needed to fit in one of the periods of prayer required of a good Muslim but he would whistle up an acquaintance to keep an eye on us. He took us to the souks – always obligatory in developing countries – but Mum was familiar with the networks holding life together among the poor and recognised with pleasure a version of the Kilburn market in which she had had a stall on Saturdays. She was treated with the respect due to age and spent a happy time selecting small junk presents to take home, and paid sensible prices. My role as Rich Person was equally well understood and I found myself probably paying too much for a small rug for Jim's birthday and some jewellery, but it was well worth it.

Just before we got the plane home Mum confided that she was producing small amounts of blood from the bowel. I hoped aloud that it was only part of the diverticulitis which had afflicted her for some years. 'I don't think so, darling,' she said. I knew that tone of voice very well; she never fussed but she was frightened. The diagnosis was bowel cancer, as she had feared, and within a few days she had been admitted to the Royal Free and by April 30 1997, the day before the election, I was watching a young Danish anaesthetist do the routine tests, all of which Mum was failing. The surgeon, a bustling cuddly bear of a man, arrived, had a brisk discussion with the pallid, openly worried Dane, and sat down heavily on the bed.

'I must operate, you see,' he said cosily to Mum. 'I can't leave you with an obstruction. But you're asthmatic and your heart's not that good and we're a bit concerned about the anaesthetic.'

'Mum's asthma goes away in a crisis,' I said boldly; we both knew it did and it had been true of my asthmatic grandmother as well. The Dane rolled his eyes, but the surgeon looked interested.

'Does it now, I've met that before. Well, Mrs Neel, what do you think?' My mother said the only thing she feared was being unable to look after herself and she didn't want to be incapacitated. How did *he* feel about operating on that basis? He replied after only a minimal pause that if a patient over eighty died on the table, hospital policy was not to revive.

'Oh good,' Mum said warmly. 'Well, I think we should go ahead.'

'It'll ruin their batting average if you do die, Mum,' I observed, seeking to cheer.

Indeed, the surgeon agreed, which was why they would do their very best. He shook hands with both of us, saying to Mum he would see her tomorrow before the operation and swept his wilting Danish colleague away. Mum and I in perfect accord were able to go on to have a sensible conversation about her estate, to check her Living Will and agree where to find her papers, and I went home to watch the BBC news.

It is part of election folklore that Labour voters huddle at home if it is wet whereas Conservatives pull on their wellies and plastic hoods and force themselves to the polls, so my heart lifted when May 1 1997 dawned sunny and warm. I voted and tried to do some work; Mum was known to be early on the operating list but we had been warned that it could be postponed if there was an emergency. By late afternoon however it was all done. I was at Mum's side in the Royal Free and my brothers were hot on my heels. She was breathing easily and she was indeed to be free of asthma for a week while she recovered.

I went off to get some supper before the BBC election night party, leaving a brother in attendance; through Mum's later life as the asthma worsened Giles and Ally and I worked as a team. It was understood that the Duty Sibling was responsible, stayed with Mum at all costs, did whatever was necessary and informed the other two afterwards, and through all the ups and downs of three lives we stuck to this routine. I counted myself fortunate; there are many examples in literature of only daughters having to give up everything for ageing parents but my brothers' honest-to-goodness reliable practical help and presence was cheering and comforting for Mum.

The BBC gives a party for the great and the good on election night and includes all the Governors. The host team were chewing their fingernails when I arrived; in 1992 the BBC's exit polls had suggested a narrow victory for Labour which had instantly been announced on all BBC news media, leaving everyone with egg on their faces as it became clear that wasn't going to happen. This time the exit polls were giving Labour a huge victory. Senior Management vanished from the party for the next hour, leaving Governors dealing with puzzled but courteous ambassadors and other grandees. Management reappeared about 11.30, having authorised News to declare the likelihood of a sizeable Labour victory and by 2 a.m. I found myself standing between John Birt and Tony Hall, then Head of News, looking at the big screens carrying projections close to the actual majority, which was to be 187.

'I am a lifelong member of the Labour Party and my bank's political guru, and I forecast an overall majority of twenty,' I said, raising one of the many glasses raised that evening.

'I am the Director General of the BBC,' John said, entering into the spirit of things, 'and I forecast an overall majority of forty.'

205

'And I am the head of BBC News, finger on every political pulse, and I forecast an overall majority of seventy,' Tony Hall admitted, downing his champagne.

You cannot, it turns out, predict a landslide. I got into my Charterhouse office late the next morning to discover six bottles of champagne on my desk; I had got second prize in the City lottery even with a prediction of twenty, nowhere near the mark, so reluctant was the City to believe in a Labour government. (The first prize went to a young trader who had bet on a majority of 200, reckoning correctly that we were in unknown territory where anything could happen.)

I heard reports of the sensational election night party at Party HQ from some of the worker bees (candidates do not get to this party until very late if at all because they are all in their constituencies biting their nails). The air was rent with cries of 'We've won *where*?' and 'Who?' as the election turned parts of the map red which had been blue for generations, and startled men and women appeared blinking and ecstatic on television screens and workers frenziedly hunted through constituency lists to find out who the hell *that* was.

It was amazing, being in government, it really was. It was also all new; we had only two people who had served as Ministers, Jack Cunningham and Michael Meacher. Some of our true ministerial stars – Roy Jenkins, Bill Rodgers, Shirley Williams and David Owen – were active in the SDP but unforgiven for their contribution to our nineteen years of Opposition. So virtually every Secretary of State, Minister and Party Secretary was new. There were lots of women – nearly 20 per cent, most of *them* new too. Sadly one good friend was missing; Jenny Jeger, niece and daughter of Labour MPs, co-founder of Gifford Jeger Weekes, had expected to be a Minister in the Lords but was dying of pancreatic cancer as a Labour victory was announced. Ed Balls and Ed Miliband were advising in the Treasury, though neither was yet an MP. Peter Mandelson was at DTI, my old Department, who loved him from the off, recognising his raw ability, his lightning grasp of any situation and his reassuring competence in dealing with senior businessmen. Mo Mowlam got Northern Ireland, and the Press belatedly told us all about the brain tumour threatening her life and her political career. She had dropped out of sight during the election campaign, as I had been too busy to notice, but it was a shock to see her again, a couple of stone heavier, bright hair lank and thinning. My best friend in politics, George Robertson, got Defence; all had assumed he was to be Secretary of State for Scotland if we won but in the run up to the election, Tony Blair, worried about a wholesale commitment to a Scottish Parliament *now*, sent George and others to try and row back. George, ever dutiful, had done his best, but his attempts had been received with fury and devolution hastily reinstated as a policy, but George himself was temporarily unacceptable in Scotland.

We knew shortly after the election that Jim's father had a very limited time span, a verdict which he accepted with his customary composure. 'Better news would not have come amiss,' he said, memorably, to our Richard, discussing his plans for the summer, 'but I shall still be here when you get back in September, old boy.' He called all the children, including Isobel, 'old boy'.

Richard, as we understood only years later, had barely seen UCL. He got himself out of London and away to our cottage in Wales with two friends who were in a similar bind. Jim, assuming this was a brief holiday, lent him his car, but the time stretched out with a variety of improbable excuses, like the absolute necessity of waiting until the local shop had succeeded in ordering a pedal bin for the bathroom. We realised that this nonsense was hiding the unlikely truth that Richard, the highest IQ of our three, had finally got into gear and was working very hard. He got a 2:2, just missing a 2:1, miles below his ability but, as he said to me, if he had taken the exam two months earlier it would have been a pass degree at best. He spent the summer after his final exams at the boys' summer camp in the USA where he had worked before; he had no idea what he wanted to do next and it must have looked like a safe haven.

Isobel struck a blow to my heart. She loved Bedales but said she wanted to go to dance school, not university. I tried to believe that this would only be a Gap Year and a passing fancy but our experience with Henry was ominous. I found I minded more about my daughter than I had about our eldest son. Isobel is a true little swotty like me, who always wants to know more things, and I took her refusal hard. She was armoured against my disapproval by her relaxed Bedales contemporaries, who imitated, ruthlessly, me displaying all the symptoms of frustrated middle-class mother. She did predictably well at A-level and, as the icing on the cake, turned out to have come equal first in the prestigious Oxford and Cambridge Board exams for German, thereby ensuring that she could walk into Oxford or Cambridge. She held out, supported by Jim, who reminded me that we had snatched this child from the jaws of a potentially fatal illness and the fact that she was still alive and well and planning her own future was all we could ask.

She started in September 1997 at the London Studio Centre, on a three-year course. The obvious solution was to have her share the Chalcot Road flat, not far from the school, with Richard, who had decided to go to SOAS and learn Japanese, which cheered me; for a moment there I saw our second son in a merchant bank. Isobel on the other hand was working with young men and women in a lawless part of King's Cross, where men in cars would crawl along propositioning the teenage girls as they came out of class. I felt she was utterly misplaced; all students were required to bring in their GCSE certificates to the office on entry to the course and it became clear that the norm was five very average GCSEs. Isobel's glittering collection caused a stir and, as she said, did not add to her popularity. She was having a hard time keeping up; her confrères had sung and danced and acted pretty much exclusively since they were six. I could have wept; she understood the doctrine of comparative advantage but like our Henry she simply did not want a career in any field in which her natural advantage lay.

The other unhappiness of 1997 came out of a clear sky. My brother Alexander, then fifty-two, had married for the fourth time, in 1996, a well-off American woman with whom he had been going out for nearly three years. He had recovered, again, from being bust in 1993 and had done an architectural job for an old friend in Ireland. He had put his fee into buying a plumbing business from another Irish friend, and it looked like a successful new enterprise for him. Jim had always viewed the plumbing venture with concern on the basis that Alexander's expertise lay in middle-class consumer businesses, like restaurants and the video rental business he had invented and run for several years. I thought a plumbing business in central London could be categorised as a middle-class consumer business, and the success of Pimlico Plumbers proves my case.

The marriage – and the promised enduring love – lasted three months. The plumbing business – which indeed Alexander had not understood – started to collapse slowly and even running it for cash he found he could not pay the huge mortgage on his house in Fulham. The accumulation of disaster was too much for my gifted, creative brother; as my mother said, a spring broke in his personality. The house had to go and he had to move in with us for six months, right through Mum's operation, Dick's bad news and the General Election.

In the end, we used our credit to buy a small flat in Fulham, where Alexander still wanted to be, in joint names. We hoped then that, with a small flat and a much lower mortgage burden, he would get a job and pay his share. He was only 53 and able, but he never got started again; he was of course less than well, although medicated reasonably successfully for bi-polar disease. But he had lost his support system and his real reason for living and he effectively never worked again, Unlike Giles, he had no loving wife to take him back and it all proved too much for him to deal with.

During this time I had a short run on the board of the London and Manchester Group (L & M), and was also on the board of United Assurance (UA). Life company accounts are arcane but it was clear that the business model of both companies was broken. Both operated by sending an agent to collect the premiums from the principal earner on the day he or she was paid, usually Thursday, an expensive collection method rendered unviable at a stroke by new legislation which limited the amount of selling costs on any life or savings product. Many weekly-paid small savers with modest life insurance ceased either to save or to assure their lives as an unintended consequence of this well-meaning legislation.

The only thing to be done was to sell both companies to Mutual Life Funds which could use locked-up assets. London and Manchester however, in common with much of the pensions industry, was struggling with actions brought against them for mis-selling pensions. People who had been immaculately and correctly advised saw an opportunity. L & M was not one of the larger companies but they had had a special unit of hundreds of assessors working through claims for four years, and it was, inevitably, easier to settle some blatantly opportunistic claims rather than go on disputing with a determined pensioner who had nothing else to do. The other problem was that L & M had been selling some pensions which guaranteed return up to 8 per cent – and it was already becoming obvious that this was too high to be sustained. It was a very small part of the L & M business and did not impede that sale so I at least failed to see its longer-term consequences.

At this time however a former civil service colleague, the immensely able Jenny Page, was on the board of Equitable Life, a high-prestige job of great interest, which I envied. But real disaster lay in wait for Equitable Life, its pensioners and all its directors and senior managers. For years Equitable had offered annuities on a commission-free basis to its middle-class customers which would guarantee them an income of around 8 per cent on the amount invested for as long as they lived, a promise which depended on inflation staying at about 6 per cent. The inflation rate dropped sharply in the 1990s and Equitable could no longer find enough investments that enabled them to pay out at the promised levels. The Board decided to reduce the designated fund – the pension pot – so the pension was still payable at 8 per cent but on a lesser overall sum. It was intended to be a fair solution to a joint problem but their pensioners did not see it that way. It is just about possible to interfere with people's incomes while they are of working age and can adjust, but retired people's incomes are inflexible and tightly budgeted and they will fight like tigers to protect them. Non-executive, as well as executive, directors, had their careers destroyed and lived under threat of personal bankruptcy for years. The Directors and Officers Liability Policy, in which all Directors anywhere put their faith, was exhausted early, leaving the Equitable pensioners to go after the Government, who offered only limited compensation.

The whole episode brought into sharp relief the issue of provision for old age in an era where businesses can no longer afford guaranteed benefit schemes for their employees and where no one will offer anything other than short-term guaranteed returns. My family are long-lived, as are Jim's, and we have always understood that if longevity in the general population rises in the way that it has, no financial promises, by Government or private companies, to sustain us in our old age can be kept. Equitable Life was the bellwether, high-profile casualty that meant no private company would ever again sell financial products that offered security in old age. Our solution is to keep on working as long as we can and put not our faith in Government. This is the only nugget of personal Financial Advice I can confidently offer together with the advisability of paying off the mortgage.

Chapter 14

TRANSITION 1998–2000

Dick died on January 8 1998 at home, having been confined to his bedroom for the last three months of 1997. Characteristically, he made the best of his last months; we had taken him to Glyndebourne that summer, where he and Margaret had been founder members and to the Proms, with his much-loved niece Lucy Ismail, in the best seats in the house (I was still a Governor of the BBC and was allowed priority booking). He visited old friends and old friends poured in to see him. Susi Dell, widow of Edmund Dell who had been in Wilson's cabinet, invented reasons for being in Cambridge almost every week and came to lunch. His next-door neighbours, the Dicks, were similarly considerate and provided lunch and entertainment regularly, particularly important on the days I had to be in London. His great-nephew Tim Aitman, then Professor at Hammersmith and the star medic in the next generation of Cohens, also came regularly; they would discuss Dick's symptoms and the progress of the disease before settling to long rambling discussions of almost anything else. We persuaded Ruth, the German-born nurse who had eased Jim's mother's passing, to leave her baby with her own mother-in-law and to come to us twice a week so Dick could get a bath. Ruth weighed about 8 stone at that point but could whisk him, a tall man of 14 stone, in and out of a bath without apparent effort. Devine Merry, their long-standing daily help, moved her schedule to do a lunch shift every week. Henry came every other weekend and in the last weeks every weekend. And dear Louis, our American lodger, was in every day to say hello. Connie Sattler and Marianne Livant, who had come to the Cohens on the Kindertransport from Germany, visited from the USA, as they had done in Margaret's final illness.

Between them all not only did Dick get much-needed variety but I was able to keep a career going while dealing with the logistics of feeding and watering the Cambridge household until October 1997 when I abandoned the London house and moved to Cambridge. That Christmas stretched our organisational capacity; my mother and Ally were coming and all three children were expected, as well as Dick's elder brother Harold, called 'Uncle' by all of us. He was devastated by the illness of his much-loved younger brother, but uncomprehending because he himself had reached ninety-five with barely a sick day in his life. He was a heavy pipe-smoker, a convert from cigarettes, and had never quite mastered the new technique; he would set match to pipe and a smoky bonfire would erupt in front of his face, scattering onlookers. I set up two living rooms, one in each side of the house, one non-smoking for Mum and one smoke-filled cavern for Uncle and those brave enough to join him, and concentrated on Beds. Louis had gone off to Stonor to stay with his grand Camoys friends, leaving us his room to dispose, so it was just possible to find eight bedrooms although the pressure on two and a half bathrooms was intense. Then Richard confessed that he had invited two American friends from his camp in the USA and they had nowhere else to go for Christmas. I put them into the Holiday Inn in central Cambridge, suppressing a pang of envy at the thought of their big quiet room and a swimming pool at hand.

Dick ate his Christmas lunch with Henry in his bedroom while Jim and I presided over lunch for ten downstairs. Richard's American friends, wide-eyed at this scene of English family life, usefully diluted and cheered what would have been a gloomy family party.

The aconites which he so loved were just getting their heads up when Dick died. Jim had come back from a meeting in London to be met by the nurse who had warned him that his father was near the end but when it came she would call him. Dick died very peacefully just after midnight with Jim in the room. Nurses who see a lot of deaths say that the dying wait to see their loved ones before letting go.

Dick and I had built an affectionate relationship in the eighteen months when he was a widower. When Margaret was here, Dick's life revolved round her; she was his most important concern and he stood between her and anything or anybody she found difficult, like me. I admired her, she gave me a lot of help and gave the children the most loving and imaginative nurturing, but we found

212

each other difficult. She disliked me working, feeling with some justice that I was neglecting the children. Extremely able herself, she had come away from Edinburgh University with the top First in English and then done a PhD at Cambridge, but life had knocked her about and ruined her confidence. Her eldest child, a girl, was stillborn and she herself was treated with the customary harshness of the medical profession in 1938. The scramble to save the baby had left her physically damaged and the baby's death had caused unalleviated emotional damage. She had been a confident capable woman who addressed difficult meetings in the Liberal interest before this happened, but afterwards she could never be persuaded into teaching, at which she was brilliant, or indeed into going out much into society. My father-in-law did not mind, except on her behalf, he loved her, she looked after him superbly and loved him back, and they were always happy just with each other. But, free of that responsibility, he was an optimistic, cheerful, deeply social being. No party turned down, no sight unvisited, as a friend of his youth observed, and that is what he did for his last nine months, including his own ninetieth birthday party, celebrated in the Cambridge garden under a huge marquee with over a hundred people. With the common sense of the good doctor he sought and accepted physical help easily and knew its limitations. He stumbled as I helped him to the lavatory in late November and I managed to stop him falling. 'You're very strong,' he said approvingly, and I went off to get lunch. Dick however rang Dr Owens, his GP, who came round that afternoon and confirmed, as Dick had understood at once, that the muscles no longer supported him and that he could not walk without risking a serious fall. I tried to commiserate but he brushed it off. 'That's what happens, at this stage, Janet. I was very lucky you were able to stop me falling.' A fall would indeed have immobilised him, in pain, in a geriatric ward, but his instant understanding that he had moved a further step down and that he must not endanger himself or cause distress to his attendants was deeply impressive.

He left me £3000 in his Will, one of a small number of legacies, with a graceful note of thanks for the care and delicacy with which I had looked after him. 'Delicacy?' my brothers said, doubtful but affectionate, all too clearly not recognising it as one of my attributes. The point I think is that with Dick I was able to be direct so that he too could be straightforward about what he needed, so perhaps that amounted to delicacy.

We held the funeral a week later, with the same undertakers and at the same crematorium chapel as eighteen months earlier for Margaret. She had wanted her ashes scattered in the heart of the Scottish Borders and Dick wanted the same so Jim and Henry went off together to do that. The children all read poems at the funeral; Dick had chosen a long one by Housman which struck me as difficult to read so I persuaded the twenty-two-year-old Richard down to the bottom of the garden to practise. Richard did not at that stage read books and conversed entirely in an argot which combined Jamaican slang with the shortage of consonants characteristic of North London. He looked at the poem, opened his mouth, and out came purest BBC Received, without hesitation or faltering. We looked at each other, he perceptibly smug and I moved to tears and hoping that wherever *that* had come from would go on being accessible.

After the funeral Henry rushed back to Germany. Silke's mother, only my own age, was critically ill in hospital with a combination of bladder and lung cancer, and was being operated on and generally over-treated when she should have been let go gently. She died in February with Henry, who she had come to love, at her side as well as Silke. Jim and I joined them for the funeral, on an unremittingly wet day. It was a truly desolate occasion; Silke's father had died when she was three, her mother's only sibling had died recently and she was left with only one living relation in Germany, an estranged half-brother who was sulking at the rear. Henry's suit was dark with rain and plastered to him but he held the umbrella steadfastly over his dear Silke for the committal ceremony. Jim and I were wearing raincoats and sheltered by umbrellas but we were soaked through and still damp when we flew home hours later.

Henry persuaded Silke to marry him in short order. She was unwilling at first, feeling that she could not marry in the same year as her beloved mother died because her wedding anniversary would always carry the mark of that untimely death. Henry, a very fine negotiator, countered with the suggestion that they should marry on her birthday, always an important celebration in Germany. Henry sensibly left her to do all the preparations so it was a lovely wedding, held with the full Catholic marriage service. Henry, a principled atheist, had refused to convert but Silke had paid the church tax – a survival of the tithes paid in

England until 1879 – so the Catholic Church had to marry them, whatever Henry's views or religious status, as their cheerful local priest explained. At the wedding we prayed, in German, that Henry might grow in his understanding of the Catholic faith. Isobel and I, watching Jim through our fingers, could only hope that the stubborn orthodoxy of the Church of Scotland as well as his own convinced atheism was not going to cause him to rise in wrath.

It was followed by a dinner party for over a hundred people held in a local barn, which went on for hours and hours and was full of country rituals. A horse made of straw and filled with coins was presented (Isobel and I unpicked it for about three hours the day afterwards), games were played and presents handed over in person and unwrapped on the spot. Jim and Richard, neither of whom has German, were a bit lost and my German enabled me to do only a bit better, but Isobel, just 19, was a raging success, in four-inch heels, speaking beautiful German and dancing with all comers. It was clear that Henry had found his country; watching him work the room, with Silke on his arm, stopping to sit at every table, we could see that he was at home.

It was a period of transition for Richard and Isobel as well. Richard had done a course in Japanese at SOAS and met a fellow student, Indy Priestman, and decided to move in with her and out of the Chalcot Road flat. We all liked Indy, an immensely capable Scot, small, pretty and determined, who had persuaded SOAS to let her complete her degree in two years on the basis that she was already a fluent Japanese speaker and had spent a lot of time there with family friends. Richard's departure left a gap in the Chalcot Road flat, so I suggested my adopted godson Ruaidhri Donnelly, who had finished his degree at Nottingham and was working in London, poorly housed. He was still on the shy side of quiet at that stage but had grown into a capable twenty-three-year-old, with a mop of dark curly hair dyed a spectacular white blond as befitted his part-time membership of a rock band. Underneath the hair he was as steady as his father Gerry, old friend of my youth, with a proper day job. He made a generous flatmate for Isobel, he tidied her up and put up with having to wait for the flat's only bathroom when he was trying to get to work and she was intent on putting on enough slap to keep up with her contemporaries at stage school. In return she introduced him to more of London's artistic life and lots of girls and they lived in perfect amity for the next two years.

We had decided to trade down from our big house to a flat in London and also to buy in the other half of the Cambridge house against our retirement. We got the timing wrong, selling the London house before we had a flat to move into, so we lived in two different rented flats for eighteen months while we found, and converted, a mansion flat in Victoria. A poor decision financially and a terrible decision operationally. I felt like a refugee and was miserable for eighteen months. I drew some comfort from the fact that our contemporaries, coming up to sixty, were making equally misguided decisions about where and how they lived, some buying houses in parts of the country they had visited a few times and where they had no friends and a forty-mile drive to the nearest good hospital, others buying palaces on impulse in France or Spain, ignoring the realities of long awkward journeys to get there and the language difficulties of becoming a resident. 'At least we haven't done *that*,' I would mutter as I shifted furniture – again – and packed things into plastic boxes for the third time. Retirement *is* difficult and the people who weather it best seem to be those who stay serenely in places they have always lived, with the friends they are used to. We knew that we wanted to retire away from London but we did at least understand that two people who had lived and worked in London all their lives would need to retire to a city in their old age with the amenities Londoners take for granted like first-class teaching hospitals, accessible world-class museums and theatres and cinemas and at least a starter collection of like-minded friends, and Cambridge fitted the bill.

We were both working, Jim full-time, and I was doing four days a week, so that was the immediate issue for us in 1998. BICC, a great name in British engineering, had suffered disaster as the market for cables dropped away, compounded by a couple of mistimed investments, but Balfour Beatty, their less fashionable but very large construction subsidiary, had continued to flourish, and Jim with it. He and his team had made several profitable PFI investments in roads and were getting into schools and hospitals; he had taken over the rail business and was making it pay, and the rest of Balfour Beatty was doing very well too. The result was inevitable but striking to observe; BICC shareholders and management finally had to accept that the cable business was dead; so BICC people retired or left and Balfour Beatty people were speedily added to the Board to join Peter Mason and his later successor Mike Welton. Jim was invited onto the Board not long afterwards, in recognition of the fact that he was running two major divisions, in Rail and PFI.

My career at the Yorkshire Building Society ended in 1998 after eight years, four as Vice Chairman, and I would expire, as the phrase was, as a BBC Governor early in 1999. I was on the Board of BPP and employed on a very part-time basis by Charterhouse but I wondered whether anyone was going to offer me more employment. I had written two more books: *A Time to Die* (published in 1998), which used my experience of setting up Café Pelican in St Martin's Lane back in the 1980s, and *O Gentle Death*, published in 2000, which is about Bedales and the last in the Francesca Wilson series. Constable were still glad to publish me and the books went into paperback but sales were gently declining, and writing, while essential to me, had never made me a living wage.

My friend George Robertson had been conducting an urgently needed Strategic Defence Review at the Ministry of Defence, which he had initiated shortly after the 1997 election. In the summer of 1998 when I was still adjusting my life after Dick's death I got a formal letter from George inviting me to be one of an informal panel, unpaid naturally, 'to critique the emerging conclusions of the Strategic Defence Review (SDR)'. I admired George and understood what he was doing. The Ministry of Defence, like the Home Office, has a tendency to talk only among themselves, and the emerging conclusions of any review might easily have been revealed as barking mad when exposed to the light of common day. So George had decided to try them quietly and privately on fourteen sensible people, experts in different parts of the subject, leavened with a few generalists like me.

We all met on a bright morning at the MOD, and two things were at once clear to a civil service trained eye; neither the unarmed nor the armed wing of the MOD wanted us there, and there was no way the fourteen of us could be usefully welded into a group. We agreed on the second of these conclusions and all of us selected the bits of the monumental piece of work where we felt best able to contribute. We were eleven men and three women and I asked George afterwards how we had been selected. He said his Private Office had produced a list of twelve men, all of them sensible choices. He had pointed out that this wasn't very New Labour and what about members of the opposite sex. The MOD had triumphantly denied knowledge of any suitable women, so George had had to find his own; he invited Lady (Janet) Morgan, a strategic policy specialist, and me and then the MOD remembered that there was a senior female person in Geneva with responsibility for regulating nuclear disarmament. The MOD referred to the group dismissively as the Luncheon Club, a massive canard since we met only once as a group and nobody ever bought us lunch.

I decided that as a banker I should follow the money, which, apart from pay and rations for the armed forces, was then, as now, being spent on procurement and logistics. The MOD budget was then £20bn odd and it was accepted that it could not go up much; as George said, we had other priorities and it was difficult not to see three primary schools flying overhead as you listened to the RAF's latest demands. For that £20bn the nation got a standing Army (and Navy and Air Force) and the Trooping of the Colour. When and as we needed to go to war, extra money was (and is) provided from the public purse through the mechanism of Urgent Operational Requirements (UOR) put in to the Treasury by the MOD.

I attached myself to Richard Lapthorne, then Chairman of BAE and a contemporary whom I knew slightly, and a senior logistics man from BT, Alan, to look at Procurement. 'The MOD,' Richard said, addressing a group of us, 'does not put out properly specified contracts to us to bid on, it outlines a vision which we are charged with realising. And then they wonder why this vision costs more than they had vaguely assumed.' Cue angry disagreement but he was right. I was married to a contractor and had listened to accounts of dealing with clients who wanted a railway which would both carry commuters to and fro at high speed *and* bring the whole banana crop down *and* all the products of an emerging mining industry, and then wanted to change their mind about the gauge and extend it by thirty miles mid-contract. The MOD equivalent request would be something like a fighter aeroplane which could also carry a couple of tanks and be used for the Tattoo.

I decided to leave Richard and the senior BT man to fight this battle and to have a look at Logistics, which no one else seemed to want, but years with Unipart had taught me a lot. The Accounts showed stocks of £20bn, equal to the Annual Defence Budget and I knew that stocks of that size were bound to be 'unbalanced', meaning that there would be too many of things that were obsolete or of which we used very few and too little of things we needed. Bernard Gray, at that point George's Special Adviser and who years later under a Conservative-led coalition government was to be Chief of Defence Procurement, encouraged me so I went to look.

At Donnington, one of the biggest of the Army warehouses, I found the problem mercilessly illustrated. After five minutes in a massive new and air-conditioned shed I asked what a particular steel object did. My escort consulted and announced that it was a sand filter for a tank. For desert warfare. I asked, idly, which tank. There was a long pause, with much consultation and quick phone calls. When the answer emerged I said, genuinely puzzled, that I thought that particular tank was obsolete. It was, and despite my escort's acute and obvious misery I had to ask how long these sand filters had been in store. A further expedition was detached to find out and the senior chap they had left with me, sweating slightly, explained that the thing was, you see, Ma'am, that they were a Warehouse. They stored things consigned to them. I asked, unhopefully, whether there was a system for asking the consignor whether he still wanted the stuff. Oh yes, he replied, cheering up, we do that every year, and just then another bit of the escort returned to confirm that the sand filters had been with them since the early 1980s, but the consignor had confirmed every year that they still needed them. 'You don't charge for storage,' I said, suddenly understanding what I had not seen when the MOD had briefed us on the new system of accounting – RAB – then being installed with the assistance of most of Price Waterhouse. In future units *would* become accountable for all their costs including costs of storage, and this particular problem would very slowly disappear. I was on familiar ground; Jim's grandfather had put the contents of a nine-bedroom London house into store in 1939 and there they had stayed until he died in 1952. Margaret, charged with sorting it out, said for thirteen years' storage fees you could have paid for everything in there. I could see it would be the same story in all the other MOD warehouses, and that to wait for the operation of RAB to squeeze out their contents was not going to get the savings hoped for any time soon. The problem got worse the more you looked; each of the three Services had dedicated warehouses because each of them organised their own logistics. All three Services stored batteries (typically the same brand of batteries), and the big new Navy warehouses were also storing things like lavatory paper and light bulbs, counting them in and counting them out expensively, rather than having them delivered straight from contractors to ships.

I discarded, reluctantly, the option of demanding my own platoon and going round the country clearing out the sheds. A larger and faster revolution was going to be necessary to take these huge costs out of the system. The MOD was going to need modern logistics systems, with goods they needed delivered when they needed them directly by contractors, never touching a warehouse, freeing up shed space for large objects which could not be ordered off the shelf like tanks (and indeed matching sand filters) and awkward specialist nuts and bolts. And it needed *one* logistics system for all three Services in order to realise savings. The logic also extended to putting logistics and major procurement together. It did and does; if you order a ship, you will also need to maintain it in service for many years with all its attendant spare parts, but the two processes were then run by two completely separate organisations.

The final run through the Strategic Defence Review ground on and one day reached Logistics. Five Ministers, George, his two Ministers of State and two Parliamentary Secretaries sat through presentations with an audience of about fifty senior MOD people who were spending their days in the big gloomy MOD main conference room. When Logistics came up I was invited to join the meeting and summoned to sit next to George, with John Reid MP on my other side. George's cheerful easy delivery of the idea of combining all three Services' logistics fell into a stony silence, and I watched, appalled, as any questions asked of the audience by any of the four junior Ministers and even George himself were greeted by long dragging silences, the audience contemplating fixedly the pieces of paper in front of them.

'Janet,' George said, heavily, at the end of twenty minutes of this. I had been thinking furiously. George had not warned me of the level of opposition to our proposals for change. He was not, I was sure, going to put up with this behaviour and would find a way of dealing with it but I was not at his right hand for decoration, I was there for a purpose and I would do my best even if I was then defenestrated. I abandoned my original script, which had thanked everyone for their kindness and flexibility, and went for the provocative statement.

'I have here, Secretary of State, the introductory paragraph of a

Cabinet Paper. It goes: "Prime Minister, the MOD carries stocks of £20bn, hopelessly unbalanced, substantially obsolete and worth £5bn if that. This situation is exacerbated by the fact that all three Services make their own logistics arrangements and all of them fall well short of the best modern logistics system. And no change is proposed in the Review. " Were I the PM I think I would ask why.'

No one moved; the beating heart of that room was well and truly stilled. Then the Permanent Secretary, Richard Mottram, slapped his papers together: 'Because we're idiots, that's why'. I could not believe my ears; George patted my hand and Richard dispatched me and a clutch of senior military persons to set up a small impromptu group to tackle (or in the Services' case, try to derail) the whole logistics issue.

'Why would no one answer questions from your own Ministers?' I asked the embryo group as we emerged blinking. Looking miserable they said they had all been told not to (by the Service Chiefs presumably, all of whom were in the front row). They did answer a few of my questions but they were, all too clearly, still looking over their shoulders to an invisible senior person who would ruin their careers. But George never let go of a point once he had grasped it and the Treasury had the bit between its teeth, so at the eleventh hour he took a paper to Cabinet supported by Treasury which meant that Army, Navy and RAF logistics would be combined under one full General, who would be a four-star to ensure that he ranked equally with the three Service Chiefs. George decided however against trying to combine logistics and procurement, on the basis that the amount of change thereby generated risked collapsing both organisations, and there was, as always, a war on.

Just before the Expert Panel was disbanded, we were offered the chance to see a bit of the MOD in which we were particularly interested and I asked to see a submarine on manoeuvres. A submarine represents the ultimate logistical challenge because they can be at sea for six months and have to carry everything they need; a diplomatic incident or a small war could follow if you have to pop up out of the sea in some far flung port to do a bit of shopping. At that stage no woman had ever spent a night on board a submarine because there were no separate facilities for them. But the Navy, as ever on its home ground, was hospitable, courteous and innovative; the First Officer of HMS *Talent* moved out of his cabin to enable me and my chaperone, a senior woman from MOD personnel, to sleep the night, and I was briefed to bring almost nothing with me, particularly not night clothes, because there was no room. My fellow groupie Alan from BT was also with us, and had displaced another of the sub's officers; there are no spare rooms on a submarine, and the officers we displaced – as they did not tell us – spent the night in hammocks slung between the sub's torpedoes.

HMS *Talent* was (and is) an ordinary submarine; like all the submarine fleet she is powered by a small nuclear reactor; anything else is too noisy and can be readily detected underwater. She was on sound trials off the West Coast of Scotland, in the Sound of Raasay between Skye and the mainland, and as the dinghy splashed over the usual sullen heaving West Coast sea I realised I had failed to ask a key question.

'No one's ever been seasick on a submarine, have they?'

My escort considered the point. 'Not when the sub's below periscope depth, no.'

'And sound trials are conducted ...?'

'At periscope depth, yes.'

Worrying about that usefully distracted me from the business of getting into a submarine. There it was, suddenly, a massive black tower rising from smooth, slippery, heaving curved steel sides.

'You jump, Mrs Cohen, and the sailors will catch you.' A frieze of sailors were arranged round the base of the tower. I am fifty-eight years old, I thought, contemplating this prospect, and if I miss my jump I will be crushed between the sub and this sick-making little boat. I looked across at the sailors, locked to each other with one arm and the other extended to me, jumped as instructed, and was hauled in through a very small door to the relative safety of a steel ladder leading down into the sub, where all was calm, hot, stuffy and full of men going about their business in small cramped spaces.

We were given a second breakfast which I approached cautiously until I understood that the distant gentle motion of the sea, thirty feet down, wasn't going to upset me, then I ate everything offered in the relief of having got there. The food was excellent, they showed us the kitchens; active twenty-four hours a day because a submarine runs on shifts and there are always people working. They baked their own bread and rolls twice a day and were always ready to feed the crew and you could have eaten anything off the shining steel surfaces. There didn't seem to be any fat sailors although three months of food like the four meals we ate on board (delicious scones for tea) would have put 10lbs on me in the time. 'There are exercise facilities of course,' the Captain said when I put the point to him, and so there were, a tiny gym, entirely full of men. There is a technique to living in very small spaces. Twenty men in the petty officers' mess, sitting close on benches, their elbows to their sides, kept their attention on what they are doing, reading, writing letters, drinking coffee. It was not unfriendly but it did not look like the ordinary canteen where people sprawl and chatter. Unsurprisingly the life does not suit everyone, and the submarine service is self-selecting; people are offered a trial voyage and no one thinks the worse if they have to opt out.

We were invited to have a go on the simulator at torpedoing targets. I was comically hopeless; had it not been a simulation I would have cost the taxpayer several million pounds and left six rusting torpedoes somewhere on the ocean bed. Alan, a man of my own age, hit the target every time. I felt a little better when I recalled that men are proportionately much much better than women at spatial relationships, which is what trying to line up your vessel, the vessel you are attacking and your torpedo is about.

We gazed respectfully at a young rating confined uncomfortably in a pressure suit which would enable him to be pushed out of the submarine and get to the surface in an emergency, and Alan asked, in a jocular way, whether they had suits for us. The First Officer, beaming, produced two packages from a shelf, labelled for us, which silenced us both.

The day ended with a third superb meal and a whist drive. I was paired with a chief petty officer, an older man, as submariners often are, dour and sardonic. We did rather well; whist is only partly a game of skill and we had the run of the cards and we were ahead at the last game when I made a stupid lead. Contrite, I apologised to my partner after the game, saying I should of course have known where the Jack was. A great smile broke out, a different man showed through, and he said no, I was all right, and at least it wasn't a Jack of trumps I had failed to place. As we all relaxed with a late-night cup of tea (submarines are for obvious reasons alcohol-free zones) I understood what a strain it must have been for the sub to have to deal with us, feared emissaries of the Secretary of State, when if anything went wrong the reverberations would reach all the way up to the Chiefs and boomerang back again. News travels instantly by some process of osmosis on a sub and men who had been on duty in the farthest corner of the boat popped up to commiserate with me on the whist and shyly tease me about the torpedoes.

As we chugged to the shore in the tender the next morning, debriefed, breakfasted and just not embraced, I found a set of papers I had picked up accidentally with my own. The whole of the two days before our visit had been occupied, not only in driving the sub slowly up and down a fixed course, but in rehearsing every step of our programme; *there* was the young rating, thirty minutes before we were due to pass, being told to get himself into his escape suit (he must have been much too hot), and *here* the kitchens, ready for our visit an hour ahead, and there the whist drive: had I not seen the packs of cards being unsealed and shuffled I would have been prepared to believe all *that* had been fixed too, and that, but for my forgetting where a Jack was, my partner and I would have triumphed. It's how you win wars, we agreed, soberly.

In 1999 my time at the BBC was coming to an end and so was John Birt's. Christopher Bland, the current Chairman, had caused a long list of possible successors to be produced but many-tongued rumour had it that Greg Dyke, lurking low down on this list, was the only man Christopher wanted for the job. I was opposed to his proposed appointment; I could not see that the man who had given us Roland Rat was going to be interested in the intensely high-profile and difficult part of the Director General's job, which is to ensure News and Current Affairs present a balanced view. Baroness (Barbara) Young, who was by then Deputy Chairman, agreed, but I was close to Expiring that summer and there was not much support for our view. Barbara did her best by going to see Greg to tell him that at the first sign of a skateboarding duck on the BBC News she would resign.

Greg turned out to be a brilliant success with programmers and producers; immensely popular, he revitalised BBC1, cut out administrators in favour of programme makers, and raised morale everywhere. But, just as Barbara and I had feared, he was never closely concerned enough with News and Current Affairs and he had also decided, on arrival, to do without a Deputy Chief

Executive, the vastly experienced BBC lifer Mark Byford who would I think immediately have sorted out an offending and unbalanced interview rather than leaving it to fester for three weeks and prove Greg's untimely undoing.

As my time with the BBC ended, a brisk phone call as I sat at my desk in Charterhouse announced that the Chief of Defence Logistics, General Sir Sam Cowan, would like to come and see me, now.

General Sir Sam Cowan, Chief of Defence logistics Organisation 1999–2004.

'I'll come and see him,' I suggested, feeling that the unknown General's time must be more committed than mine, but the caller insisted and an hour later I was in a Charterhouse conference room with a chunky man of my own age with bright blue eyes and a Northern Ireland accent, disappointingly in a suit rather than uniform. We weighed each other up while I fussed hospitably with coffee and congratulated him on his appointment.

'The Treasury say I have to appoint a non-executive director,' he said, drinking the coffee in one gulp. 'To teach my new board how a board should operate.'

'And you want me to recommend someone?'

'No, I want you to do it. I need some help with this job.'

'If you are asking me because I am close to George Robertson, don't do it. I am, I am a friend of George but in six months' time he could be gone somewhere else and your Secretary of State could be someone I've never met.'

He promised me that it was not my friendship with George – useful though that was; I had been recommended by several people whose opinions he respected. And by the Treasury, he added.

Immensely flattered, I asked half-heartedly whether the job paid (answer not so as you would notice) and whether he had advertised it and did he envisage appointing more NEDs since a single one – as I had been for years for BPP – was of limited use. Sam said he had special consent to hire me without going through a formal process, on the grounds of my experience of the SDR and the urgency of the appointment; the job was here, now, and yes he had agreement to hire more NEDs.

Duty called loud and clear; Sam's very existence in this job was partly my doing, and besides, the whole thing was irresistible; Sam, who by then felt like another brother, had the task of putting together the three logistics streams and welding them into one efficient cost-effective body, just as George and Bernard and I had envisioned.

Within a week the full difficulty of Sam's job stood revealed. The management structure was a nightmare. The Chiefs (I should have known) had managed to fight a rearguard action which left Sam keeping the three Services' logistics separate for a transitional year, thereby postponing any meaningful reform and giving both Sam and the 'legacy' three-star generals a miserable time; they didn't want to have to nurse their erstwhile commands for a year before handing them over, any more than Sam wanted to wait to get on with his job. I asked George how he had allowed this to happen; the answer was as always that there was a war on, this time in Bosnia.

The first Board meeting left me very thoughtful. It wasn't a board as we in the private sector know them; sitting at Sam's left hand, I was the only NED to fourteen executives. There were the three-star heads of the three shadow service logistics operations, then all the two-star deputy heads of the single service operations, then all the two-star service people who represented our customers at Land Command, Naval Command and the Air Force plus a civilian finance director and a few specialists. The three 'legacy' generals, despite being dispossessed and shunted into a dead end, behaved with grace and made real efforts to consider the interests of all the armed services, and the finance director did so too because he knew that was his job. The others were there to ensure their own Service did not lose out; they would only be in the DLO for a year or two before returning to their units and their career would not depend on whatever they had done while they were with us unless they had let some key point of advantage slip. The finance director was totally enmeshed in the coils of the RAB accounting system which all hoped would be wonderful when fully installed but as it stood was a quagmire. Every last one of them was reading from a brief, as opposed to listening to their colleagues or their Chairman. The result was a dialogue of the deaf; a series of points logged and refuted with no meeting of minds.

What did I think, Sam asked after the meeting and I told him, well within the hearing of several hangers-on, that the board might work better if we had the people who had written the briefs at the top table rather than the people reading them. At the next meeting no one read from a brief; even if they had memorised them before they came in, their heads stayed up and they had to look at colleagues, and that behavioural change made a small but useful difference.

I believe that the men (at that stage there was no woman above one-star rank in any of the services) did not mean to be obstructive and uncooperative but the structure of their career paths was desperately unhelpful. And there was a war on, which was used as an excuse for falling back on old expensive ways of doing things. All armed services know in their DNA that civilians are unreliable and take away any cash or savings the military make at the slightest opportunity, so they hide old tanks and jeeps away round the back of the Mess because they know their day will come. They hide people away too, often from the most honourable of motives. All services try and keep their wounded in jobs somewhere in their establishments. The Air Force hoards engineers because they may never get those again and the Navy hides seamen for the same reason even if their ships have gone, never to be replaced. An MOD-wide survey done around this time revealed moreover that 22 per cent of our fighting forces were not medically fit for active service. Some of course were only temporarily disabled, having broken ankles or legs in training, but many had been unfit for years, deployed in what were fundamentally civilian jobs on military pay rates. It was difficult to know where to start and I understood from the beginning that the task could be beyond all of us, but whatever the problems I really liked the services and wanted to help, so I settled down to do my best.

Chapter 15

2000–2001 In the House and 9/11

In December 1999 we moved into our mansion flat in Morpeth Mansions, looking out on Westminster Cathedral with its two attendant schools, the Choir School and a small, crowded, sought-after Catholic primary school. I had fallen in love with the block when an old friend, Christopher Campbell, then retired from a distinguished business career, had us to dinner. We had been looking for a flat in St John's Wood but we told each other that *this* flat was convenient for the MOD where I was spending a lot of time and a sensible choice for Jim because the main Balfour Beatty management offices were in Croydon, only readily accessible from Victoria Station. All the flats in the block have three magnificent rooms but because they assume the presence of living-in staff the kitchens are all in the wrong place, one side is a rabbit warren of small rooms, and there is only one decent bathroom. With the help of the architect David Ashton-Hill, who had done our last house in St John's Wood, we moved the kitchen and took a bite out of a bedroom to enlarge the tiny en suite bathroom into something where two of us could wash at the same time, reordered the spaces at the back and put in built-in cupboards everywhere. The Salmons, a small building firm from Cambridge who had done work for my parents-in-law, then us, since the 1980s, lived and worked in the flat for months, sleeping on mattresses. They were relieved to get the job finished. Aside from domestic disruption they were worried about losing Cambridge clients, but Mick and Matt Salmon (father and son), who take pride in and responsibility for every job, were not short of work for long.

Unlike many a decision made for love not logic this one turned out brilliantly. Within a year, I was in the House of Lords, twenty minutes' walk away, and Jim was only five minutes from his office. The Balfour Beatty board had deliberated long and hard about where to put the new combined office; its members' homes were distributed round the M25 and we feared Jim might have to drive over an hour every day. Finally however, banning Jim from participation in the vote because they all knew where he lived, they decided to move to the old BAA office, half a block away from Victoria and the trains to Croydon and a block away from us. Both of us, then aged 58 and 60 respectively, were able to walk to work for the first time in our lives, and it enabled Jim to carry on for a further seven years to 65 with Balfour Beatty and me to manage with the Lords and a lot of other work.

Janet as Peeress on admission to the House of Lords June 2000.

I am often asked – many of us are – just how we got into the House of Lords. I am a lifelong Labour supporter in emulation of my father and I have been an active member for much of my life. I voted, just once, Conservative, in 1979, and abstained in 1983 but returned to active support once the gifted, persistent Neil Kinnock started the fightback against the hard left. I know a good deal about British industry, and had twenty years in the City, and in the Labour party there were not that many of us with those qualifications who were also able to put in the time. I had long experience of both public and private sectors, and I am usefully Female. The combined efforts of all parties in the Lords had managed to raise the percentage of women to just over 20 per cent. Despite all-female selection lists the Commons had even fewer, more like 15 per cent. None of my qualifications however might have been sufficient had the House not been in a period of massive transition; the legislation removing most of the 600-odd hereditary peers had received Royal Assent in 1999 and my party, which had struggled for years against a huge inbuilt Conservative majority, wanted to ensure that its legislation got through. In 2000 the House of Lords had 92 hereditary peers, most of whom took the Conservative whip, plus another 100-odd Conservative Life Peers, 150 cross-benchers, most of whom we believed (wrongly as it turns out) to be closet Conservatives, and 80 superbly disciplined Liberal Democrat Life Peers. With 150, we were heavily outnumbered and Tony Blair, as PM, took the opportunity to appoint Labour peers while he could. The List which announced my own appointment in May 2000 contained thirty-five names, twenty-five of them Labour, and it followed another List containing a substantial number of Labour peers in 1999.

You are not allowed to tell people until the day before the List is published so only Jim and my trusted PA Margot knew. On the designated day I told Mum and the children, Paul Baines, by now head of corporate finance at Charterhouse, Sam at the MOD and Richard and Charlie at BPP. Paul was simply pleased for me, but Sam was overjoyed, rose from his chair, seized me by the waist and danced me round the room. He and I needed a boost; as I had warned, my friend and supporter George Robertson had gone, with honour, to be Secretary General of NATO and been replaced by Geoff Hoon whom I had never even met. Mum's congratulations were more nuanced; as always totally supportive of me, she noted that she would have some explaining to do because she was an active member of the Brent Conservative party. Conservatives were thin on the ground in Brent, and the ladies' committee which my mother joined were mostly in their mid to late eighties; indeed Mum claimed that all meetings started with a minute's silence for the latest of the fallen. After a bit of thought however she decided that she would give a Tea for colleagues at which I would be guest of honour, saying privately to them that though Janny was in the wrong party it was still an honour for her to get into the Lords, a position acceptable to all sensible women with daughters. Our Margot, herself a natural Conservative but also mother to two clever daughters, did a brilliant job on the Tea.

Richard and Charlie's reaction was straightforward; they bought me a champagne lunch in their favourite posh restaurant and pleaded with me not to abandon them or BPP. I was able to reassure them; the House of Lords is not a full-time occupation for most Members. It also isn't salaried, I needed an income and I had been appointed to the House on the basis that I was still involved in the world of work. And I loved them and BPP for heaven's sake. We finished lunch around teatime, an unusual event for all three of us. It was a happy day.

You have to be introduced into the House, which means getting two of your fellow peers to dress up in ermine and support you through the swearing-in ceremony. Mary Goudie and Swraj Paul, both of whom I had known since the 1970s, were my supporters, and we hosted a large lunch attended by Mum, Jim, all the children and Black Rod and Garter King of Arms, who also had to get into costume to swear me in. Henry, who had come from Germany, refused the traditional privilege available to the Eldest Son of sitting on the steps of the throne, preferring to sit in the gallery with his wife and his sister. Richard was in Japan but Isobel tore herself from a jazz class in King's Cross and arrived out of breath and wearing an exiguous skirt.

We trooped in preceded by Black Rod and Garter, I took the oath then we all marched out again to the heart-warming traditional noise of colleagues on all sides thumping the benches and murmuring a welcome. The family reaction was mixed; our German daughter-in-law Silke and Henry dined out for years afterwards in Germany on her description of the experience, received in heavy-duty Westphalian business and horse-riding circles with the same incredulity as if I had been introduced at a ceremony involving semi-naked dancing priests. Isobel's jazz class was similarly astounded. Margot and Mum were thrilled. Jim went back to work to be received with much merriment from Balfour Beatty colleagues who, finding that he did not get an honorary title (husbands don't, unlike wives, who get to be called Lady), referred to him for months afterwards as Dame Jim.

Later that year we had to say goodbye to Isobel who had decided to go to the Alvin Ailey school in New York. They ran a course for dancers who weren't going to be suitable for their justly renowned mostly black company but it was a good course and it was New York and adventure. We had arranged for her to stay in a hostel for the first four days while she found somewhere to live, and the whole project seemed reasonably under control, but right at the end as she was staying with us in London I could see her courage fail her. She was only 21 and as she packed the final bits in her suitcase, hair still wet from the shower and face covered with the spots that still tended to affect her under stress, I wished I had arranged to go with her to settle her in.

The hostel turned out to be grim and unwelcoming, and finding somewhere to live in crowded New York on a student budget seemed impossible. News from the front became more and more worrying; somehow, in despair, she had moved onto the sofa of a young man she had met in the subway but it was fine, Mum, really, he works for Morgan Stanley and he is never there. Then she was turned down for a couple of places she had liked, then saw a series of impossible rooms in impossible places. I was about to get on a plane and house her, by use of the credit card, in some grossly expensive little apartment, just as she had specifically not wanted, when she found a room in an irreproachably respectable family apartment in uptown Manhattan. Jim and I, lifelong Londoners, had not understood about the problems of accommodation for the young in big cities and Isobel had never had to find her own place either. We were grateful she had come to no harm and vowed to be more careful in future.

She loved New York, and quickly found a kind young man, a resting actor and musician called Michael. He was film star good looking, very dark, with Cherokee blood in his background, but endearingly unconscious of his looks. One of my lasting memories is of him in the Guggenheim Museum, inspecting pictures at close range (he was short-sighted), with a group of beautiful teenage girls following him, vainly trying to attract his attention.

We went to New York when we could and it was clear that Isobel was privileged among her colleagues in that she had a whole room to herself to live in and enough money to eat. She told her dancer friends that her parents wanted to buy everyone dinner when they came and we presided over a table of polite but starving foreign-born young dancers, all ordering the cheapest dishes on the menu. We announced hastily that we were both having steak, and would everyone else like that too, and had the pleasure of seeing them all devour their first protein-heavy meal in months. Several of them were not only going hungry but sleeping on floors or sofas in other people's apartments in order to dance so we always fed her classmates when we were there. New York is a hard place for students and foreigners in other ways; Isobel could not find a bank in which to deposit her limited funds so I asked my then employer HSBC on her behalf. They did not cater for poor transient students either but as a favour to me they opened a VIP account for her so that, clad in shorts and sandals and smelling of sweat as dancers do, she would wade through thick red carpet to cash a cheque for $50.

My working life had changed again. Eighteen years at Charterhouse ended abruptly; in the summer of 2000 the mighty HSBC bought our immediate owner, Crédit Commercial de France. Charterhouse was a very small fish in this deal and presented a problem rather than an asset to HSBC, who knew exactly what they wanted to do with Crédit Commercial and its multiple retail branches covering an area where HSBC was weak. They sensibly offered us all jobs and waited to see what happened. Of my particular friends, Tom Bartram was long gone, relishing the success of his mezzanine lending business, and Sandy Muirhead had gone more recently to be a partner in Phoenix, a venture capitalist. Mike Higgins had gone to a partnership at KPMG.

Another particular friend, Mark Sebba, had left well before the takeover. Mark had been brought in by Victor Blank in the early nineties but in the event they did not work well together and Mark had gone off to work as a specialist in media investment. In about 1991 I had found myself at a health farm, following a bad case of flu, with Mark and his talented wife Anne, a well-respected biographer. I was trying to write the semi-autobiographical *Children of a Harsh Winter* at the time and Anne and I had a lot in common. I was listening idly to Mark telling an anecdote about his Deaf Cousin Ernest when I realised I had heard this one before, from husband Jim about his Deaf Cousin Ernest. Mark and I settled down to draw family trees and established that he and Jim were fourth cousins (all Scots families like mine and Jewish families like Jim's and Mark's work out this sort of thing).

I was sorry when Mark left us but he was to go on to greater things. He took a job as adviser to a start-up, Net-a-Porter, who asked him to be finance director and then CEO in 2002. He did me the honour of asking me whether I thought he ought to go down this route. At that stage I spent good money on clothes, but I didn't believe in the business model. I was clothed by a shop where I bought mostly Italian imports which were altered to fit as necessary, and had real difficulty with the idea that women would be prepared to buy expensive clothes from a picture on a computer and go through the hassle of packing them up and sending them back if they did not work. I did understand career trajectory, however, and told Mark that he was far too young (seven years my junior) to settle into a non-executive career and should take this big job forthwith. He was to be CEO from 2002 to 2014, his last day in the office there famously commemorated with affection and dancing and singing employees on videos full of love from every part of the Net-a-Porter empire, all of which embarrassed him but pleased him immensely.

Paul Baines arranged, immediately, to go to Hawkpoint. He offered to take me too but I felt that I had more than enough to do and I didn't want him to have to look after me while he made his way in a new organisation; so I joined the exodus to HSBC.

So I had a day a week with HSBC, the House of Lords, BPP, the Defence Logistics Organisation and a small media consultancy, Informed Sources. Olswang, the media lawyers, had set this company up under the leadership of one of their partners but the venture had not gone well, the shareholders were arguing with each other, and I had been hired on a vague brief to sort out the relationship back in 1998. In 1999 I was sitting opposite an Olswang partner trying to knock out a shareholders' agreement, when I saw, as if a neon sigh had been switched on above the Olswang partner's head, that he was totally fed up with the discussion and wanted only to get back to his real work.

'This isn't working, is it?' I had said across the table. 'Would you like to sell your shares to us? For about sixpence halfpenny?'

Yes, he said, sitting up, yes, yes. For a fair price, he added, proper lawyerly caution coming belatedly over the hills, but the deal was done and the managers and staff had become the company's owners. It didn't function that much better; two of the four principals were married to each other and wanted to be in New York setting up an office there, and one of the others wanted to work only three days a week, leaving us seriously short of experienced leadership in the UK and losing money in the US. By 2001 we had to conclude that our gifted but difficult personnel would be better housed in a bigger organisation and we sold the company to the Mercer group who were in the consultancy business but had no media specialists.

I was trying to communicate with the HSBC internal system, late in the autumn of 2000, when I got a call from Whitehead Mann. They reminded me that I had been invited to apply for a place on the London Stock Exchange Board back in 1999. Was I still interested? It was like being asked if I was still interested in winning the lottery but I tried for a mature response and said I was, yes. A weary voice said well, it had all taken longer than expected but could I be available for interview tomorrow. I assumed that I was trying to get onto the long list of twenty or so possible candidates that clients usually want but it turned out that matters were well past that stage, the client had seen the long list and reduced it to a list of four of us to fill four NED vacancies. Overnight however I had belatedly recalled that I had two Charterhouse colleagues whose careers had been damaged by working for the Exchange, so I talked both to my contemporary Stewart Douglas Mann and to Richard Kilsby, who had been put in as Finance Director. The Exchange in the 1980s and 1990s had carried on two businesses, that of trading securities, done electronically since the late 1980s, and had been pioneers in abandoning the time-honoured 'open outcry' consigning the scenes with which we were all familiar, of men shouting at each other, to backward places like the New York Stock Exchange and the newly developed LIFFE, the futures exchange. The computer system supporting our market however went on falling apart, shredding reputations with it. The Exchange had also had responsibility for the complex, lucrative business of clearing and settlement, essential for executing the trades and had tried to move this business too onto an electronic system, 'Taurus'. This had been an even more spectacular failure, and the Bank of

England had removed the business from the Exchange and set up the London Clearing House under separate management.

So what I would be joining was a pure electronic market whose systems were apparently now stable, owned by the members (banks and stockbrokers) who used it. The plan, as explained by the then Chairman Don Cruickshank, was to move the Exchange from a Mutual owned by its members to a public company, put it onto the market and make it into an efficient competitor, able to grow rather than being a Gentleman's Club. To this end, four new directors, all independent of any of the big users of the market, would be appointed: Nigel Stapleton, who had been CFO of Reid Elsevier, Rob Webb, corporate counsel to BAA, because of his expertise in a regulated industry, Oscar Fanjul, a distinguished banker from Madrid, to add a bit of European clout, and me, as the all-purpose female with sound public sector experience and a reassuring background in a small City bank and in the Mutual sector with the Yorkshire Building Society. We four were appointed in February 2001 alongside a new and untried woman, Clara Furse, whose first CEO job this would be.

We had been appointed to demutualise so that is what we did. I knew from my time with the building society movement that once you were a company, with a share price, you could no longer control your destiny, but I reminded myself that Cassandra had been murdered by exasperated colleagues, shut up about the potential problems of hostile takeovers, and luxuriated in the simple pleasure of being in the citadel of the financial industry. I was only just mature enough not to stand on the steps shouting 'Nyah, nyah ne nyah nyah' to the City grandees who had so thoroughly patronised me and all my fellow women.

The rest of 2000 was distinctly mixed. I had a bad year physically. I got a cold in about July and still had it in October, when it turned into an ear infection. I did something to my right foot so that I arrived in the House of Lords limping so badly that I began to wonder whether aged 60 I was going to be on a Zimmer frame. The full appalling difficulty of the job Sam was having to do at the Defence Logistics Agency was becoming clear; nothing was settling down and there was, as ever in the affairs of the MOD, a major financial crisis, compounded by a ministerial demand for a 10 per cent cut to the Defence budget. Sam also had the cold and suffered even worse than I did. At a strategy conference in Bristol he turned up hardly able to speak and coughing continuously;

the all-male group eyed him uneasily while I, weighing the balance between undermining my boss and ordinary common sense, took him aside and told him he must go home, at once, that was bronchitis at the very least he had and likely to be pneumonia if he went on. He yielded and his young Military Assistant thanked me, respectfully, as they took him away. Sam struggled for months afterwards, with the cold and associated infections never quite leaving him, worn by the stress of pulling together the DLO.

In a commercial organisation, you look at the cash you can generate and work out what you can spend it on, abandoning things and people you can't afford. The MOD looks at the cash it has, then looks at the (invariably) large numbers of programmes for which there is no money, and decides that just the same they want the programmes. So they describe them as being 'at risk', a total misnomer. I used to feel like the protagonist in the famous dead parrot sketch: this is an ex-programme, I heard myself say, it is lost, it has Gone Before. It is Dead. The MOD troops would look at me, boot-faced, because they knew better. Long experience – probably starting well before the battle of Waterloo – told them that if you just kept the programme going, after a bit it got too expensive to cancel and it would, grudgingly and late, get done. I briefed Geoff Hoon, the new Secretary of State for Defence, an ex-barrister with the good, quick, incisive mind that goes with that trade, and he got the point at once but he couldn't do anything effective about it any more than any of his predecessors could. Right now projects for which there is no funding will be growing mushroom-like in the dark of the MOD accounts, even if Ministers think they have hit them on the head.

It was frustrating and I felt we were going backwards, despite the small initiatives we did manage to introduce, like an Audit Committee, the key governance tool of the private sector. It wasn't an Audit Committee as we know them, consisting as it did entirely of executive directors chaired by me, whereas the private sector equivalent consists entirely of non-executive directors. I discovered however that various sub groups in the DLO had non-executive directors dotted about, imposed on them by the Treasury, so I found a dozen good men who were more than willing to help and formed half of them into an Audit Committee. The other half were openly disappointed not to be included, so we set up a DLO Non-Executive group who met quarterly, usually in our big Victorian flat which had a table that could take fourteen.

These meetings, which took place over soup and sandwiches, were immensely popular and were regularly attended by the whole group. Men took to arriving earlier and earlier, and sitting in the kitchen having coffee with Margot and chatting while I would rush back from wherever I was and break up the party by doing business over lunch. I did know about informal networks but this was a very striking example and it decreased the sense of isolation we all suffered.

A disaster happened much closer to home in October 2000 and was to affect us for years. A train was derailed at Hatfield causing the death of four people, and it happened on a stretch of rail maintained by Balfour Beatty Rail, of which Jim was managing director. He was greatly helped by the collegiate nature of Balfour Beatty; no colleague reproached him and all treated it as a communal problem. The accident happened on a stretch of track that should have been replaced in May that year; the now defunct contractor Jarvis had failed to finish but were due to complete it the week after the crash. Balfour Beatty could have insisted on a slow speed limit until the track repairs could be completed but both they and Railtrack, the owner, believed that the track, while in need of repair, would hold up, and no one wanted to increase journey times. Several senior executives including Jim were interviewed under caution after the tragedy and warned that they would be prosecuted and Jim had to wait until 2003 to be told by a kindly policeman that he would not be charged. The Balfour Beatty people who *were* charged were acquitted immediately. The company pleaded guilty to the lesser HSE charges and was ultimately heavily fined. The track which had failed at Hatfield was, as a Railtrack man unguardedly said, no worse than lots of other places and the failure had been catastrophic and unforeseeable. Railtrack's reaction in 2000 was illuminating; they imposed speed limits everywhere on the East Coast line, totally disrupting the overcrowded train schedule, and deployed every crew they could get from the private sector to repair track hitherto tolerated as safe enough. It was a painful period which Jim endured with his usual stoicism and moral force, reminding colleagues that there were four dead and that an enquiry and court case were inevitable and would have to be lived through without attempting to blame others.

2001 was also not an easy year. For a start it was the year of the builder. Henry bought a solid German house and had moved into it as it stood but Richard and Isobel have both inherited the Neel gene which cannot see a building without wanting to tear it apart. We had handed over the Chalcot Road flat and its mortgage to Richard and as soon as Isobel and Ruaidhri were gone he sold it for a huge profit and found a twenty-two room nineteenth-century mansion in East Dulwich, in need of a complete refurbishment. I am the archetypal North Londoner and suffer deep anxieties about crossing the Thames, but since it was clear that we would have to guarantee a substantial mortgage to make this project work, I had to go and look at it. I am ashamed to recall that I petrolled up the car, set the satellite, checked my mobile, took a thermos with me and allowed one and a quarter hours to meet Richard in East Dulwich for a journey that in the event took twenty minutes from Victoria. I did at least have time to walk the area of wide pleasant streets, with good houses half the price of the North London equivalent and terrific parks.

Richard and I went round the huge semi-detached house together and the full extent of his ambitions revealed themselves; he intended 'just' to dig out the basement and make a wonderful house with a two-bedroom flat underneath it that would finance the mortgage. No one had done anything to the house since about 1920 and the outside walls looked a bit dodgy but, hey, £100,000 would see it all done, Mum, and the asking price was only £185,000. In London the pressure of demand always meant that good houses went at or above the asking price even in a mini-recession such as we had in 2001. I told Richard I thought he needed to make a slam dunk offer of £200,000, reminding him that we had had to bid over the asking price for his flat in 1995. Gulping nervously he made the offer and got the house and, in those far off days, took £200,000 on a mortgage guaranteed by us. The project was to swallow all the mortgage, a legacy from his great-uncle Harold Cohen and five years of his life, and there were many times when we felt we should have counselled our son against behaving like us. But he managed to extract a two-bedroom flat from the ground floor and let it, and over another two years to produce another little two-bedroom flat at the top where he housed girlfriend Indy's brother and his family, and a five-bedroom house in the middle which housed him and Indy and a floating cast of lodgers.

Isobel also had money from her great-uncle so she decided to buy a flat in London and let it to finance herself in New York.

She came home on a flying visit in the summer of 2001 and spurned anything ready to move into in favour of a flat consisting of two floors of a house in a quiet street just north of Camden Square which had been poorly and cheaply converted but had huge rooms. When she started to wave her arms to conjure second bathrooms and larger bedrooms out of the air and to move staircases, I settled resignedly to buy it with her and arrange the conversion while she did her year of work experience (aka dancing for no money) in New York.

Somewhere in the summer of 2001, while driving myself mad trying to get both these property purchases financed and completed, I realised – pushed by Jim – that I would have to do something about my physical self. I was limping on both legs; a duff left knee and an acutely painful right foot were still threatening my ability to walk anywhere. I had an MRI scan which revealed that I had somehow stubbed the second toe on my right foot, and the bone was broken and eroding. In late July, after the House rose, I had an operation to sort out the toe – which was sufficiently unstable to need a pin through it – and to deal with a bunion on that foot. Trevor Prior, the young podiatrist who had taken me on, urged me to let him do both operations, saying endearingly that having your feet operated on was so horrible that I would never be willing to let him take a second cut. I spent a happy and peaceful August in Cambridge convalescing while trying to sort out the house and garden, with Mum and Margot staying with me, sometimes together, sometimes taking turns, while my foot healed and the pin was removed.

I got to the old War Office on September 11 2001 in order to spend the day interviewing for a head of operations for the DLO. The MOD operated an interview board where the candidates were put forward for consideration on the basis of age, rank and Buggins' turn, and the interview was intended as an affirmation, not part of a process. Sam and I were engaged in breaking that mould by seeing people whose turn it wasn't but who we thought had the necessary qualifications to do the near impossible job for which we were recruiting.

We started the second interview at about 2.30 in the afternoon but Sam's Military Assistant summoned him from the room, leaving me to ask our agreed list of questions. Sam came back after twenty minutes very pale and the Military Assistant indicated, urgently, that I was to come with him. I was beginning

241

to think the Secretary of State or Permanent Secretary had resigned on the grounds of some hitherto unimagined misdemeanour, but I found him, all his Ministers, two full generals and a supporting cast spilling out of his private office staring at a TV showing the staggering sight of one of the Twin Towers in New York aflame, fire running down the sides, and a hole where the other one – the one I had been up in March that year – had once been. As I watched, open-mouthed, the burning tower crumpled on itself and a cloud obscured the picture.

'Lady Cohen, we know – well, you have a daughter in New York?'

'She isn't anywhere near there,' I said, and everyone's faces cleared.

My mobile was ringing and I scrabbled in my handbag to find a message from the London Stock Exchange assuring me, as a director of the organisation, that the Stock Exchange had gone into terrorism alert, the Tower had been evacuated and was under guard and our duplicate market was operating smoothly, a couple of miles away. Where I was, the Secretary of State, three junior Ministers and almost the whole of the top of the MOD, both armed and civilian wings, were standing on the first floor of a Victorian building in the heart of London.

'The Stock Exchange have just told me they are on full terrorism alert,' I said cautiously. 'I wonder if perhaps the whole of our Defence Establishment should be stood here?'

Military men bent disapproving stares on me but the Private Secretary assured me that there would be a meeting of COBRA in half an hour in the bunker rooms under the Cabinet Office. Others grudgingly acknowledged that I might have a point and drifted off. I went to fish Sam out of the interview to send him underground as well because Defence Logistics would be needed. The Stock Exchange and other parts of the city did not engage in thought, they activated the procedure required if people rain death from the skies on us or our closest ally. I could only wonder then as now why the top management of the MOD had not planned to do the same.

The phone was ringing as I got home and it was Kate, one of Isobel's closest friends, to assure me that she had spoken to Isobel in the last hour. I thanked her warmly, not having been anxious at all, and got a terrible shock when Isobel herself somehow managed to get through late that night. She had been on her way an hour later than she had intended down to a dance studio in Canal Street, half a block from the Towers, when all the subway trains going downtown were stopped at 34th Street and passengers summarily decanted. Had she got up when she had intended she would have been in Canal Street and at best covered by the thick white compound of building materials and organic matter that billowed round those streets. As it was she had walked fifty blocks back uptown into Michael's arms. I pleaded with her to hole up, stay indoors and avoid gangs of looters, remembering my own experience in Boston in a major power cut in 1965. It wasn't like that, she said; people were all on the streets talking to each other and offering shelter and help and checking on elderly neighbours. She and Michael had gone to a hospital to offer blood. Michael had been accepted as a donor but she had been refused, brusquely, on the grounds that British blood was unsafe because we were all likely to be infected with either CJD or foot and mouth disease, but by then it was clear that blood, British or American, was not going to be needed because the thousands who died had been killed or vaporised immediately. She was allowed to help in the end: she and fellow dancers put on a show to rally New York pride and resistance, in which she appeared as a lead dancer wearing an exiguous bikini made from the British flag. It sounded like a riot of good taste and I wish I had gone over for it.

The rest of 2001 didn't go much better; I was anxious that Isobel had become so settled in New York after 9/11 that she would never come home but this worry was quickly overtaken by two more immediate problems. There were two Black Days in one week, the first when the acquisition of LIFFE, the futures trades business with which the newly demutualised LSE had planned its future, collapsed because the directors of LIFFE decided to sell the group to Euronext, the major French exchange. At one blow LSE's ability to branch out from trading cash equities into the vastly larger and more profitable business of trading derivatives contracts vanished, a setback from which the Group was not to recover for many years. It was a disaster for the Group and, worse, exposed us immediately to bids from other exchanges who coveted our solid cash equity business because then as now trading in 50 per cent of all European cash equities took place on the London Stock Exchange. The second Black Day involved my friend Andrew Skynner at HSBC, who had to break it to me that the organisation had decided to dispense with my services as well as those of two other ex-Charterhouse part-timers. I had not found a way of being really useful in eighteen months with HSBC and I should have known that I wasn't going to make enough impact on a place where I wasn't known and had no formal role working only a day a week but I was very disconcerted. Andrew, a sensitive man, utterly loyal to HSBC, was to suffer a fatal heart attack in the train in the middle of the grim process of making substantial numbers of his friends in mid-career redundant. I wept at his packed funeral in St Bartholomew's; it was a very poor reward for having the fatal flaw of imagination and a kind heart allied to a loyal and conscientious devotion to an institution.

Chapter 16

2002–2003 WAR AND DEATH

We started 2002 with a holiday in Tobago. Henry and Silke joined us from Germany, Richard came but without Indy because she would not leave her own close-knit family over the New Year and Isobel came with Michael. Three weeks before they were due to fly Michael had cautiously enquired of Isobel just where in the United States Tobago was. Michael, like eighty per cent of all American citizens, had never been outside the USA and not only was he hazy about Tobago but he did not have a passport, and it was a scramble to get him properly equipped.

It was an excellent holiday; Tobago is Trinidad's safer quieter cousin and the word goes that if you are insufficiently sharp to make your living in Trinidad you move to Tobago, which means that even the local drug and nightclub scene is laidback and unthreatening. We had a lovely villa and a good time was had by all.

I came back to be Chairman of BPP, working with my old colleague Charlie Prior. Charlie is a big, capable, clever man, nephew to the late Jim Prior, one of Mrs Thatcher's cabinet. He attempted a career in politics, as a Conservative naturally, but I had spent much of my working career with people who did not vote Labour. Charlie is superficially the standard right-winger, opposed to social security and the European Common Market, any reduction in Defence spending and probably the Old Age Pension. He is also a superb teacher, and believes that everyone can have a successful career if they are properly trained, regardless of social origin. When I worked with him, it was never easy to change his mind about anything but once he decided on a course of action nothing would stop him. Richard Price had been a full-time executive chairman with the office next door to his; I was non-executive, and did not have an office in the building because of the pressure on space and it took time to persuade him to treat me as a real Chairman, but we achieved a successful way of working. We would meet for lunch at an attractive little Italian restaurant round the corner from BPP's Shepherd's Bush head office and teaching block. Both of us would declare our intention to lunch off a lettuce leaf accompanied by a glass of water since we were both permanently in the position of needing to lose ten pounds before our next holiday. Three hours, several courses, and a bottle of wine later we would still be there, having worked through all the issues that the business threw up and decided which of us would do what. Charlie always said it was my judgement of people he valued most; but, infinitely loyal as he was to anyone who worked for him, he didn't necessarily act on it. He inspired loyalty in return, so what he lost on the swings of employing some misplaced or less competent people he gained, emphatically, on the roundabouts of commitment and teamwork. We were and are very fond of each other and we worked well together; it was with Charlie that I developed of necessity a technique of starting my more trenchant and urgent suggestions with the words 'I wonder if...?' before filling in with words like 'whether it would be wise to close that bit of the company before it loses any more cash and destroys next year's forecast?'

There were other pleasant surprises in other parts of my life. A good Labour colleague in the House, Geoff Filkin, and a cross-party set of colleagues had managed to start the Parliament Choir which meets weekly in the ravishing medieval chapel which sits tucked in beneath a corner of Westminster Hall. I had sung in the London Girls' Schools and Board of Trade choirs on the basis of being a second alto, pitched very low, rare and thus useful. I had not sung for years, my voice is only moderate but I was still a second alto and I could read music. There were no auditions and no voice tests; it would not be easy in an institution like the Houses of Parliament to tell a Member of either House that they just weren't good enough.

In order to get it started, the Choir was constituted as an All Party Parliamentary Group, officered by people from all three major parties in both Houses and sponsored by British Telecom, old friends and erstwhile employers of Geoff's. In return for their generous sponsorship BT got free seats for forty guests at two big concerts a year and the Choir sang at an annual private party for them. They were a tactful and undemanding sponsor, they never lobbied any of us to do anything, and they loved the parties.

Uniquely the choir is open to all staff of the Palace of Westminster, without whom indeed it would be a sadly unbalanced group. For us Members the effect was to open up the Palace so that the organisation became explicable and familiar and friendly rather than respectful and polite. I hope and believe staff feel the same, but the act of working to produce a performance is a very powerful exercise in bonding, and singing alongside the head librarian, the head of IT, the head of Banqueting, several researchers, and members of Black Rod's staff changed the place for me and made me feel I belonged there.

The Founding Fathers of the choir had also been uniquely fortunate in finding a leader to take on this enterprise. Simon Over, a big friendly capable ex-rugby player, had been Director of Music at St Margaret's, the parliamentary church which sits quietly next to Westminster Abbey. It has first-class music and an excellent boys' choir of its own, and is part of the musical gang which is responsible for the Abbey. Simon has been conducting choirs since he was fourteen, in Coventry, and trained as a pianist and organist and read music at Oxford. Musically he knows exactly what he is doing, just as well because he is required to turn up to a hundred people into a choir, many of whom cannot read music. Worse, given the exigencies of a parliamentary timetable, Members run in and out of rehearsals regularly interrupted by shouts of 'Vote in the Commons' (signal for a small posse of tenors and sopranos to push their way out) or 'Vote in the Lords' which results in a rather slower exodus of several altos and basses.

There are a few voices of rare quality among the Members not yet reduced by the pressures of office or the ravages of time. Bernard Jenkin MP, who was with us from the start, is, like his late father Patrick a wonderful bass and indeed considered doing it professionally. We were joined after the 2005 election by Sarah Teather MP, a Minister in the Coalition Government of 2010, and a soprano of real talent. Lord (William) Wallace is a convincing bass who sang as a treble at the Coronation in 1953. Lord (Martin) Thomas and Baroness (Joan) Walmsley (confusingly husband and wife) are both well-trained church singers with a wide repertoire who also sing in other choirs and Geoff Filkin and Patricia Hollis have long experience and good strong voices.

The Choir developed very quickly under Simon's strong leadership, the more credit to him since at the same time he was engaged in starting up Southbank Sinfonia. He had long been concerned that promising young musicians were lost to the profession because they could not make a living after their university or conservatoire training. His target was the good musician who could make a career in an orchestra, or in small groups, as a conductor, or even as an impresario or a producer, rather than the soloists. Supported by Michael Berman, a successful businessman who is also a high-quality musician, he started a training orchestra which plays together for a year under a selection of conductors for practice, and is taught how to handle themselves in the professional world. Several of us in the Choir helped with cash and contacts. For years Jim and I sponsored a trumpeter, then, as our income diminished, half a trumpeter; while Martin Thomas, as befits his Welsh blood, sponsored a harpist, and others joined in. In a flash of taste I squashed the idea of a T shirt for the players naming their sponsor; not that any musician would have minded; they were all practical people who would have played in bathing suits if need be.

A lot of small physical things were going wrong with me at this time. My knee, my foot, my hip, my back were giving out on me or preventing me sleeping or both. I had to find time for a minor operation on my left knee. I had jumped off a fence when walking with Jim in 1987 and had suffered pain for years afterwards. Like many well-educated, apparently sane middle-class women I never went near doctors. These days I have no choice, but it was always stupid to try; armies of people trained to fix or alleviate physical problems awaited me, courtesy of the NHS, but unless something was obviously broken or I couldn't breathe I never went to my good GP. My behaviour would have been just about understandable if any of the things that ailed me were embarrassing like piles or impetigo.

I did one thing to help myself. I started in a Pilates class, six of us, on mats in the upper room of a mews house in South Kensington. Lawrence Petersen, the strong young man who was teaching the class, kept me back and suggested that I had a few private lessons with him because I wasn't keeping up with the class, and he feared I would get discouraged and give up. Half German, half English, brought up in Germany, he had come to England to dance, but had crippled his back in the course of his training. He had turned to Pilates to fix it and become so interested in the whole process – and found the ability to earn enough to eat and pay the rent so seductive – that he had trained as a teacher and set up his own practice. He was tired of teaching fit young dancers, he said, and would welcome the challenge represented by my good self. I knew a potential saviour when I saw one so we started on the basis that I would have one private lesson a week, two if I could get there, and exercise by myself three days a week at home. That, and lifts in my shoes, worked; I could walk, straight and for long periods, and I have not had a cross word from my back since 2003. Lawrence remained patient, confident in his own skill and clear about the value of the strong patient/healer relationship which he developed with the people he helped, until he decided in 2008 to go back to Germany and cash in his very high pass at the Abitur to train as a doctor.

I was however still limping in 2002 when I went with Jim to New York to see Isobel, who was truly happy there and had decided she wanted to stay. Death in my heart, I said of course I would help to keep my treasured only daughter three thousand miles away, perhaps for ever, and went back again by myself to help to get her a visa. We started with a legal firm recommended by Linklaters; a deeply discouraging interview in which they explained that the options for securing the sought-after Green Card which would enable her to live and work in the USA were very limited, and all involved her being classified as a person of outstanding artistic ability. It seemed a tall order and Isobel burst into tears as we went down the stairs but I recognised that the orthodox advice we were getting did not reflect what was happening on the ground, where the young of every country were finding a way of staying where they needed to be. After that we found no shortage of lawyers who would, for a hefty fee, guide Isobel through to a Green Card. They tended to be based in North Carolina or Tennessee and Isobel would be required to state as fact things that were, at best, partially true. She was still considering what to do when early in August she woke in the night and looked at her J2 visa to find that it expired in three days. The advice from the respectable and the less than orthodox lawyers alike was unanimous; she had to leave the USA within three days or she would become an Overstayer and risk never getting a visa of any sort for the USA ever again. Impressively she got herself out in forty-eight hours, undergoing tearful farewells, giving away ruthlessly the really bulky stuff and piling the rest of two years' possessions into two enormous cases. She never did try for a

Green Card, deciding that her inability to lie her way through the procedure was telling her something important about her bone-deep preference for Europe as a place to live, and her dependence on family.

She had come back from the USA a much improved and much stronger dancer and was regularly getting to the last five or six out of over 100 aspirants at the huge auditions that are one of the demoralising aspects of a dancer's life but she wasn't getting into any of the companies so she decided to train as a Pilates instructor to carry herself through lean periods. Obviously my Lawrence was the man to advise, so I took her with me one morning and started to introduce them but they threw themselves into each other's arms, babbling. It turned out that they had been in the same class at the London Studio Centre and good friends, so he saw her through the training. To have my daughter back cheered me immeasurably.

While I was in New York I had been to see the senior people at NASDAQ who were seeking an alliance with the Stock Exchange and found them complacent posh boys, very much like some of the less effective City men I knew at home. I relayed this conclusion to my fellow Board members; much to the pleasure of Clara Furse the CEO who agreed with me. In the event, as Rob Webb and I had always warned was likely, the American regulators, the SEC, refused, very late in the process, to accept our proposed structure for a merger. Nothing, the SEC said, that did not put NASDAQ in control of the joint venture would be acceptable, while we and the UK regulators were united in agreeing that placing control of our Stock Exchange in the hands of the Americans would be unacceptable in the UK so the deal was off.

At this point with the loss of LIFFE and our way to the USA barred it was clear that a serious rethink would be required and Don decided he was not going to lead it. He had tried and failed to achieve three new settlements for the Exchange, a three-way merger between us, Deutsche Börse and NASDAQ in 2000, a merger with LIFFE in 2001, and a merger without Deutsche Börse but with NASDAQ in 2002. Time for someone else to have a go, he said, so early in 2003 the Nominations Committee which comprised all the four independent NEDs set out to find a successor.

The competition for Chairman came down in the end to two people: Dr Chris Gibson Smith, recently retired from the main

Board of BP, and a City hard man, coming to the end of a full-time career. I wanted the City man; Clara was still finding her feet and had not proved able to bring off the admittedly difficult but crucial deal with LIFFE; we were likely to face predators and I thought she needed heavy-duty City-experienced support. My colleague Nigel Stapleton felt the same but Clara herself, supported by her deputy Martin Wheatley (who went on later to be head of the new Financial Conduct Authority), and the other two NEDs wanted Chris. I agreed that Chris was a real businessman of deep experience and we would learn a lot from him, but I worried privately that he would take the business apart, with the BP-trained capacity for thorough analysis, and that we could not in our fragile and vulnerable state afford him.

An NED does not lightly vote against the executive, or not when their preferred candidate is so obviously a sound businessman, and Nigel and I both said that we would support the choice of Chris. I allowed myself one final grumble, saying to the Committee and our advisers that the trouble with senior oilmen was that they were used to raising their right arm and watching the Red Sea part and it just wasn't like that in the Exchange business. Anna Mann, leading the process for Whitehead Mann, defended her candidate on the basis that life wasn't like that at the National Air Traffic Service, which Chris then chaired, and Chris wasn't like that either, and well beyond time I shut up.

I assumed Chris would be told that I had preferred another so I asked to see him immediately after his formal appointment. We met grandly at the Ritz for coffee and I opened the bidding by saying that he had not been my preferred candidate but that I would like both to welcome him and to explain why I had taken this view. They didn't tell me about you, he said, but they did tell me about Nigel Stapleton. He chairs the Remuneration Committee, I said crossly, losing my script, and is thus in the business of frustrating their wilder financial ambitions, that's why. He is a cracking good finance director who really understands the various bonus schemes, and I believe him to be right. I noticed that Chris behind an impassive mask was laughing so I was able to share with him my concern that a well-trained businessman who habitually turned over any stone he met would present a problem to our organisation at this stage. He thanked me warmly for coming to see him and for the gypsy's warning, so

I told him about the oilmen and the Red Sea before anyone else did. Somehow that settled it for Chris and me; that was 2003, and ten hard and eventful years later we were both still on the Board, allies and friends through it all.

In and among all of this was the build-up to the Second Gulf War, of which I had a privileged but partial view. The Defence Logistics Board was frequently consulted in 2002 about the feasibility – rather than the desirability – of joining the Americans in an attack on Saddam Hussein. We replied to the initial questions in the affirmative and made our plans accordingly; yes, we could kit up 15,000 assorted troops and get them and all their stuff to the battlefield. Suddenly the questions got more difficult; three weeks later we were asked to raise the number to 25,000, which caused a bit of tooth-sucking from our suppliers, and plaintive observations from those who were being asked to supply the tropical uniforms that they only had smallish factories, guv, and it would most certainly be an extra. At this point a Quartermaster appeared and explained coyly that he had in his warehouses some 7,000 sets of tropical uniform, stored since the *first* Gulf War. The Board were disposed to treat him as a hero but I was furious; the cost of storing all that for ten years would have bought them all new with probably a couple of rockets thrown in, and I had campaigned against just this sort of thing apparently to no avail. We could however only be grateful when, within two weeks of the first missile being launched, the total number of people needing kit rose to 42,500 in order to make the UK contribution a better match for the 140,000-odd that the Americans were sending. Massive supply problems were being encountered all round the DLO over every commodity from ammunition to field rations and in some areas we didn't get away with it. Newscasts featured our people sweating in hot military green clothing rather than the cool desert camouflage suits. Six months later in October I was visiting a British Forces Post Office in Hertfordshire and was greeted by a double file of soldiery all wearing desert kit, which had just arrived, and I bet *that* has now been stored somewhere at hideous expense, probably by the same QM.

I was a supporter of the war and, like many of us who were, have spent the intervening years wondering what possessed me. Having read a lot more military history than I had then, I understand why I voted as I did, but I do not seek to excuse it.

The media coverage in 2002 and early 2003 was full of Received Nonsense; the invasion would not work; we and the Americans would be repelled by mystery weapons, the heat and the Republican Guard. You didn't have to know much about defence to understand there was no way that the armed forces of a medium-sized Middle-Eastern country can stand up to the American fighting machine in the short term. The US superiority in weapons and manpower dwarfed most countries, including the UK, and enabled them at that time anyway to deliver a resounding slap (think shock and awe) to any smaller nation. It is difficult to resist, the pleasure of clouting a hated enemy; it was the same emotion which drove the Japanese high command in 1941 to launch the attack on Pearl Harbor which they knew would bring the mighty USA into the war against them. But in 2003 it was unforgiveable to forget that a population's hatred of the enemy and thus their resolve is only strengthened by being mercilessly bombed, as has been accepted since the Second World War, and it was also insanity of the first order not to have a plan for post-war Iraq. We in the UK were very much the junior partner but it should have been made part of the deal for our co-operation. When the degree of chaos became clear General Tim Cross, who had been briefly on the DLO Board, was asked, by several of us, why the UK hadn't insisted on a plan. No one, he said, believed the US neocons didn't have one, and when they found they didn't it was too late. I thought then and think now that the leading proponent of the resounding slap, Lady Thatcher, would have made sure that the Americans had a plan for the aftermath.

2003 ended in sadness. In the summer I had taken Mum, aged 89, for a week at our cottage in Wales and she had been well and had a good time, paddling in the sea, sitting in the little railway that goes up the long valley from Porth Madog to Blaenau Ffestiniog. Towards the end of September we had had another holiday; I had read about the Eden Project, the three great domes built in a disused china clay pit by Tim Smit, the entrepreneur who had found and opened up the magnificent Lost Gardens of Heligan. Mum loved the Eden Project; the distances to the bottom of the pit and the three Biomes were too great for her to walk so we acquired a wheelchair and found that I was allowed in free as a carer, a small gesture of civilised kindness that I found entrancing. The wheelchair, and Mum, were bolted onto a flatbed attached to a little steam engine which chuntered its way up and down to the pit and I was allowed a seat in the little carriage in my capacity as carer. We saw everything there and when we tired, Mum and her wheelchair were once more bolted on by many kind hands and up we went to the car park and back to our B & B and our dinner. We had three days there on top of four days in other places and could hardly tear ourselves away. Both of us were thrilled by the sheer inventiveness of the project: you start with a blighted place with lots of huge, dead, empty china clay pits and unemployed people. So in a giant leap of imagination you turn them into a lovely place to visit by putting giant greenhouses at the bottom of them and filling them with exotic plants from all over the world, and in a few years you have a million visitors and are employing hundreds of locals, all year round.

Mum, Mary Neel in 2002.

254

We got home on the train, I put Mum and her luggage into a taxi, she, as always, telling me she did not need help reinstalling herself in her own house and I plunged back to work. She was due to come for the weekend two weeks later when I had a key meeting of the Defence Logistics Organisation on the Friday in Bath, so I arranged for her to be picked up from her flat and I got a series of trains across country to get to Cambridge, arriving late and exhausted to find her ill, apologetic and frightened. She was a bit better on the Saturday but she had a poor night and we called out CAMDOC, an admirable institution staffed by Cambridge GPs on a roster. A pleasant capable Croatian doctor came round, did a few tests and made a phone call and we were told to take Mum forthwith to Medical Admissions at Addenbrooke's, where she was welcomed in with reassuring speed and preparedness and Jim and I were told to go away and come back later. We were sitting limply eating lunch when we were called back; Mum had collapsed quite suddenly and stopped breathing but they had resuscitated her and she was lying quietly in a corner of Medical Admissions on a bed with bars at the sides. I ran to her but Jim saw two consultants holding up X-rays and went to talk to them. 'I take it your mother-in-law has spent a lot of time in hospital', one said, disconcerted by the fact that at that stage Jim had to take off his thick glasses and hold any document very close to his face and look at it sideways if he needed to see anything small and unfamiliar. Jim explained that Mum had only been in for one week in each of the last two years, in London, and the consultants were more than surprised to hear that she lived on her own and drove herself everywhere within a ten-mile range. I sat by Mum remembering her insisting on seeing everything a mere three weeks ago and saw that I had not understood what was happening. Her asthma was always worse some days than others, but sitting beside her bed I saw how she fought to breathe and realised that this was not just asthma, it was failing lungs and an overstretched heart.

Her eyes opened after a bit and you could see she didn't like what she saw, consultants, nurses, and me, white with anxiety. Addenbrooke's, true to their excellent training and careful systems, had pulled her back from the edge so all of us, but above all Mum, would have to cope.

It was a dreadful time. I got Alexander, unwell as he already was, to come up for a few days to visit Mum and to give me enough time to do one urgent meeting in London. I had Devine Merry, the rock on which my parents-in-law's household was founded, to help me on the spot and I got Margot who filled the same role for us in London to come up later and join us because I was out of my depth. Mum had rallied, briefly, after the first three days and rejoiced with me in feeling much better. I believed then that yet again we were going to take her back home and all would be well. I shared this view with her consultant – we were closeted in a cupboard because there isn't much space in the big wards – and he looked horrified. 'Lady Cohen, she is not going to be able to go on living by herself. It's going to be a question of a good nursing home.' You don't know my mother, I thought, forgetting momentarily that she was 89 and the chest X-rays had been truly dreadful and that she had nearly died in Medical Admissions. It was not until late into the second week, when Mum was regularly starting to rave by the afternoon because she could not get enough oxygen to her brain, that I understood the battle was lost, agreed to palliative care, summoned brother Giles, and rang my mother's sisters to say, hopelessly, that I was sorry not to have kept them better informed or left time for them to say goodbye.

Giles did get to see her before she died. I had just been called to the hospital when he came up from his office in Hackney, driving like the wind. We ran into heavy traffic. Giles, without hesitation, drove up a bus lane, pointing out that this was the ultimate emergency and he needed to say goodbye to his mother. I would have sat and fumed and wept and apologised in the traffic queue and I thought sadly that it still took a man to cut through all that.

Mum was sedated and no longer struggling. Ward routine dictated that although not really conscious she was being bathed, kindly, by a couple of male orderlies, then we were let in. Giles secured agreement that the sedation be not renewed since if she woke he wanted to say goodbye, and sent me home to the Cambridge house, where I fell stone asleep for three hours on the living room sofa, woken only by his phone call. Mum had died, he said, weeping, without waking, while he was outside having a quick cigarette. It was the second time it had happened to him; he had sat all night by the bedside of his mother-in-law a few years before, and she had died early in the morning when he was just down the corridor having a much-needed comfort break.

Giles took charge of the funeral and burial arrangements. It was held in London and, in accordance with Mum's wishes, done by the Co-op. By agreement I as the eldest spoke the funeral oration, which appears as an Annex to this chapter. Giles wept his way through a poem in her honour, and because Alexander, though present, did not feel able to speak, his son Matthew spoke, with love, for himself, starting bluntly with the statement that his father's life had meant all the grandchildren spent a lot of time with their grandmother, and being extremely, affectionately funny about being taken for Improving Trips. Giles' stepdaughter Sophie, also in tears, spoke and our Isobel recited 'Fear no more the heat of the sun', as she had for Jim's parents, wobbling on the last lines.

We all cheered up as we arrived at the big Irish pub for the funeral tea which Mum had decreed. It had taken us two weeks after she died to get her back to London and a place booked at the West London Crematorium, which did mean we were able to assemble a substantial attendance of family, ex-colleagues, aged neighbours and, to represent the Brent Ladies Conservative Committee, one member even older than Mum and the Constituency Chairman. We didn't know quite what to do with him but at some stage I looked over a table to find him staring fixedly at me. 'Janet,' he said, 'if I may. How did Mary come to have a Labour Peer for a daughter?' A substantial audience craned to hear me explain that my lady mother had been a Labour voter for years but without my father's moral authority to guide her she had returned to her natural political orientation. Affectionate laughter all round and as we spilled out into the darkening evening Giles and I were able to feel we had given her the send off she wanted.

I had not thought I would be knocked over by Mum's death; we loved each other, she had made 89 and she had always said she didn't want to be 90, being terrified of losing her driving licence. But I was, utterly, flattened and I think everyone who loves and gets on with a parent is similarly affected. The Chief Whip at the time, Bruce Grocott, a big capable hardened politico of my own age, told me, tears in his eyes, that it had taken him two years to get over his mother's death. Only Margot, who had nursed her own loved mother in the years before her death, offered comfort that I could accept. 'At least, Janet,' she said gently, as I found myself unable to go on with writing a letter about Mum's Disabled

Badge, 'neither you nor I have to cope with sad little voices ringing us up from nursing homes beseeching us to come and get them out.' Indeed, and I got my head up sufficiently to push on with the work of sorting out the estate, indeed *that* would have been unbearable.

Her Will was straightforward, leaving two legacies to her godchildren, son and daughter of her sister Jane who had died forty years before, and the residue between the three of us, with Alexander's share to be held in trust. Selling the flat wasn't difficult either, once Giles and I had realised the first agent we appointed was in the pay of a developer – I am told this is standard form in an executor's sale – and appointed someone disinterested who got us a proper price. Clearing the flat was awful; it was only a two-bedroom flat but crammed with possessions, all much treasured and all painfully reminiscent of the touch of a vanished hand. I invited everyone in the family to choose one thing and then allocated the rest. There were a lot of her paintings – she was a more than capable amateur – which she had told me were to be burnt or recycled if no one wanted them. I think every member of the extended family has one; I have five and it took me six years to recycle the rest, and then only under the pressure of converting our own house and needing to clear the attics. Anything else left over we slid into a nearby skip, free of guilt because in Kilburn people are not well off and most of it got recycled immediately. I downed tools indeed to help a small Indian man who collected all Mum's kitchen china, much of which did not match, for the restaurant he was setting up.

There was one comforting sequel. I sent a copy of the Funeral Oration to my mother's college, Somerville, who invited me to their annual commemoration service which featured at that stage a brilliant speech composed by their Librarian celebrating the alumnae who had died in the year. I sat, deeply comforted by the references to my Mum, in the college she had loved. She had refused to leave any legacies, except to her godchildren, citing a long-held view in her Scots family that legacies weakened an estate, so I gave a donation to Somerville for her, feeling the need to explain why she herself hadn't left them anything, and getting an amused and sympathetic letter in response. She had wanted me to follow her there but never once suggested she had been disappointed by my preference for Cambridge.

EULOGY FOR MARY ISABEL NEEL, BORN SEPTEMBER 1 1914, DIED OCTOBER 31 2003

Mum was born Mary Isabel Budge on September 1 1914, at the outbreak of the First World War, the second of four daughters born to two Scots who were living in South Wales where our grandfather's work as a mining engineer had taken him. Her elder sister Jane Martin died nearly forty years ago, but the two younger sisters, Grizel Watts and Hope Rixson, are here today. Mum was educated at St George's, Edinburgh, and Malvern Girls' College, and she went up to Oxford in 1933 to read French and German, where she had a wonderful time and did very little work. To the end of her life she used to wake sweating from a nightmare in which she was doing her Finals again, but in fact she managed a respectable Second in the end.

She worked as a secretary for three years, then in September 1939, at the outbreak of the Second World War, she married George Edric Neel, an architect, whom she had met on a trip over to Cambridge to see her sister Jane. With his assistance she produced me, Giles and Alexander in pretty short order between 1940 and 1944, but three weeks after Alexander was born she was back in hospital with a mystery virus and was extremely ill for six months. She recovered and we all spent the war in Hampstead, together, because Dad having been refused for military service on health grounds was working in London. And it was good that they had that time together, denied by war to many couples of their age, because Dad died in 1952, aged 37, from cancer, in the middle of a very successful career, leaving her with three children of 11, 9 and 7.

It was a hard row to hoe; of course there was not enough money but she was always resourceful, hard working and uncomplaining and we grew up thinking ourselves privileged to live with three lodgers and have a mother who had a job. In the midst of all this she did A-level Russian and went twice to Russia in the 1950s when it was both uncomfortable and occasionally dangerous to do so. And we children had much better and more interesting holidays than our contemporaries, being taken on cycling and holidays in Scotland and Brittany, staying in youth hostels – then very mixed in quality – and on camp sites. It was, despite the loss of Dad, a very happy time for us, and it is a tribute to her that she rose above her own sadness and loss to make it so.

Ultimately – and she did once say that it had seemed a very long time – she got us all out of the house and launched herself on a new life. She joined the Women's Council which worked with women all over South East Asia, and she went on a long trip there. She took a Master's Degree in Social Administration at the London School of Economics which she very much enjoyed. She was academically very capable and always curious about new things and ideas. She had for long worked as a volunteer, most notably for the Children's Moral Welfare organisation, a voluntary group which took on the families that had defeated the official social services.

After her degree she worked for many years as a Truant Officer for the Greater London Council, but she always refused to be taken away from what she knew was the real work of getting children promptly back into education. She said she wasn't particularly good at children but she was wonderful with the depressed mothers that are so often behind a truanting child. She had a deeply practical approach to problems and no interest in promotion, recognition or official praise. She was the living example of Edith Cavell's dictum that you could achieve anything you wanted provided you did not care who got the credit.

Her practicality went bone deep – faced with the problem of getting enough volunteers to sell flags for Children's Day, she pressed into service the children for whose benefit the flags were being sold. I can still see a plump fourteen-year-old, in a very short skirt and tights more ladder than fabric, shaking a collecting tin seductively at shrinking passers-by, chanting 'Children's Moral Welfare – help children in danger'.

The families she helped became very fond of her, and some of them kept in touch long, long after the GLC had retired her, protesting, at 68 years old.

By then she had moved from the family house in Oakhill Avenue to her house in Cavendish Road, given up taking lodgers, and organised her life so that she lived in the ground floor flat. She found herself bored in retirement, and decided to have a stall in a street market on Saturdays, selling second-hand clothing and household goods. This proved a source of great pleasure to her, introducing her to a world of back street cash and carries which provided some of the stock, and to the camaraderie of fellow stall holders. Many of her clients from her social work days found time to visit her there, seek her advice and buy something from the stall.

It is the more remarkable that she managed all this because at age 62 she had developed severe asthma, which at one point threatened to cripple her entirely and against which she always had to struggle. She was resolute in face of the restrictions it imposed on her. 'Small pause', she would say, apologetically, after fifty yards which was all she could walk without a rest, and after a minute or two she would go resolutely on. She was over 80 before we persuaded her to apply for a Disabled Parking Permit though she used it with relish once she had one.

She must have been 80 when she gave up the stall and concentrated her efforts on her garden, which always gave her great pleasure, and on her art. She was the only one of us who could draw a line, and her pictures decorate our houses. She also joined the Conservative Ladies Committee for Brent East, which made for some interesting moments when I was appointed to the House of Lords as a Labour Peer, but the Ladies were very nice about it, taking the line that everyone had trouble with their children.

She often came on holiday with us, with increasingly large and noisy grandchildren, and in the last fifteen years she and I had many a good holiday together. Her curiosity about how things worked – she particularly loved large complicated machinery – and her determination to see all that was to be seen made her a wonderful holiday companion. Once a year the destination was her choice which meant that I have been to places I might never have gone to, such as the Eden Project and the Lost Gardens of Heligan, where we were together only six weeks ago.

She lived on her own, with only limited domestic help, and drove her car until two weeks before she died.

If she had written her own epitaph she would have said that

she tried to be reliable, and she tried to cheer people up. Well, she was and she did. She did what she saw needed doing and did it cheerfully. She rejoiced generously in my professional career, never grudging me the opportunities she had not had. She was much loved and her advice was relied on and respected in the wider family – I have had letters from several cousins paying tribute to her wisdom at difficult moments in their lives. She had a gift for friendship, as the presence of so many attests, and very unusually the capacity for making new friends as she grew older.

She did not do this without cost. She was sometimes sad and lonely and anxious, but she believed that these emotions were universal and had to be lived through rather than counselled away or spilled over friends and children. She was a brave woman, and I miss her very much.

I would like to finish with a quotation from St Paul's Epistle to the Philippians, which she used to cheer herself on bad days.

'Finally, brethren, whatsoever things are true, whatsoever things are honest, whatsoever things are just, whatsoever things are pure, whatsoever things are lovely, whatsoever things are of good report, if there be any virtue and if there be any praise, think on these things.'

Chapter 17

2004–2006 FAMILY TRANSITION

After Mum's death my family of origin disintegrated. Giles had always agreed with Elisabeth that they would retire to the South of France in 2002 when he was 60 but he had postponed his departure until 2005, by which time he had done all that a good son could for his mother and his mother's estate. But he had hoped for another few years living in Kensington, earning money, and he found moving, even to a country he knew well and with his treasured wife, acutely painful. They went off early in the year to their little flat in Deauville, putting all their possessions in store. I felt for them both. I didn't want to lose Giles; we had strengthened our relationship in the aftermath of Mum's death, and if he went there was no one else of our generation to help with Alexander.

Our brother wasn't well physically or emotionally and he had gone downhill to the point where a few hours a week volunteering for a charity was no longer possible. He was hospitalised with serious thyroid trouble in 2004, while his eldest son Matthew and I, supported as always by Margot, converged on his flat and got rid of an unsatisfactory lodger and his barely house-trained dog. We threw away bedding and clothes and decluttered the flat, including a trunk full of school clothes that the younger son Luke had deposited some seven years before. It took us a further weary year and another long spell in hospital for the local authority and the NHS to install reliable carers who would at least ensure that he took his pills.

In those years I was engaged with four major groups, the Stock Exchange, BPP, Management Consulting Group and the Ministry of Defence, all of which needed attention. The Exchange was under siege from a predator, blessedly one who did not in the end offer enough cash to tempt our shareholders, but it seemed to me that I started every day at the Exchange with a special

Board meeting. At BPP, we were considering linking up with another group and Charlie and I were starkly divided; he wanted to do it, I didn't, so none of that was easy either.

The DLO was also difficult; Sam had retired at the end of 2003 to be succeeded by Air Vice Marshal Sir Malcolm Pledger, a clever man whom I liked and who invited me to stay on to help. We were all still struggling with the Iraq war and it is impossible to make changes to military support in the middle of operations. Malcolm despaired first and offered his resignation after eighteen months and because I didn't think I was making a difference either I went at the same time rather than stay on to assist Malcolm's successor.

I gave my leaving party from the DLO at the House of Lords early in January 2005 and a very popular occasion it turned out to be. The military are good at getting the most out of any new experience, and they loved the House of Lords and everything about it and were delighted to be fed champagne (like my mother I feel no party complete without it) and it was altogether a success. The Permanent Secretary, Sir Kevin Tebbit, who started his career as a diplomat, gave the speech of thanks which moved me to tears, and I floated out of the House clasping bouquets and walking on air.

The military have wonderful venues up their sleeves for leaving parties so it was nice to provide another. Somewhere in 2004 we had dined out Jonathon Band – who was to end his career as First Sea Lord – on HMS *Victory*. This was Nelson's ship, immaculately preserved and unbelievably small. Nelson himself had a spacious day cabin which would have been comfortable until up to a dozen officers came in for meetings, but his bed is in an alcove and is tiny. The spaces allocated for hundreds of men to hang their hammocks to sleep below decks are ridiculous. Moreover if you stood up straight at Nelson's dinner table you would crack your head on a beam, whence cometh the naval tradition of drinking the Sovereign's health from a sitting position. You could easily have had to go into battle with half your officers concussed had this sensible rule not been introduced.

Management Consulting Group was (and is) the quoted holding company for a group of management consultants with operations ranging from the USA, through Europe and out to the Far East and Australia. I had been invited to apply by the Chairman, Dr Rolf Stomberg, another senior retired BP man, whom I had met at the Königswinter Conference in 2003 when I had been asked, at about two minutes' notice, to propose a toast to thank the German CBI for the excellent lunch we were eating, since Digby Jones (now Lord Digby Jones), the expected speaker, had not arrived. I had a couple of glasses of wine in an empty stomach and not much in my brain after a hard morning so I rose and explained earnestly that *I* was *really* Digby Jones. The party, equally well away, fell about and repeated this very simple joke to each other while I waited for the opportunity to render the proper thanks. As I sat down I found Dr Stomberg, who had chaired the discussion group in the morning, gazing at me fixedly. He got back to London, rang up a couple of colleagues and the next thing I knew I was being interviewed by the Board and offered the job.

Arguably no person of sense would have looked for more work and more trouble, not with the family and business load I was carrying. But the Aztecs believed that if their priests ever stopped holding up the sky with prayer and sacrifices it would collapse, taking all life with it, and I have always understood their position. I took on MCG, lobbied hard for a committee chairmanship at the Lords, and agreed to be the next Chairman of the Parliament Choir as well as spending a lot of time in Cambridge seeking to get a Head of House job and/or a place on the University Council.

It wasn't all gloom and hard work in 2004 and 2005, however. My literary agent, Anthony Goff, much grander than my writing career has merited, rang me in September. He had been trying to sell my book *Ticket to Ride*, rewritten in its entirety under the beady supervision of Prudence Fay who had edited all the Janet Neel thrillers. 'You are not going to be rich,' he said, breaking the news of an advance of a quarter of the last one, 'but you *are* going to be published again.' I had never, even in my heyday, made more than the average NED salary from writing, so I didn't mind about the money, but it was very cheering to find that people still wanted what I wrote.

There was also the wedding of Giles and Elisabeth's daughter Olivia in a castle near Lyons in 2005. This was a somewhat mixed pleasure. It was good to meet Olivia's steady prospective husband, Eric Lamare, a Breton rising rapidly in Air France, whose family, as he cheerfully confirmed, were fully as difficult as anything we could produce. It was nice to see again other members of Elisabeth's mixed Irish/French family, like Yves Coueslant who had been her uncle Desmond's partner and was the successful founder and proprietor of Diptyque, the scented candle manufacturer, which he had just sold very well. On the debit side we had Isobel with us who had just split up with her American boyfriend Michael and dissolved in tears whenever she thought about him, and Giles was still fighting the serious depression brought on by leaving England.

Giles and family: Elisabeth Neel, Eric Lamare,
Olivia Lamare (nee Neel), Giles, 2005.

It was a beautiful wedding, for which Giles, in a flash of mordant humour, observed his wife and daughter had been preparing since said daughter was three years old. It had its eccentricities. The civil ceremony took place in the morning and for the religious ceremony we were all seated in the garden in rows. The bride's side drew the chairs on which the sun beat down so all our make-up ran, which did at least render inconspicuous the tears that Isobel was trying not to shed. The ceremony went on a bit; they had found the only Anglican priest in that predominantly Catholic area to perform the ceremony and he took a rare opportunity to give a very long sermon while our carefully applied faces fell off in the sun. The evening party went on all night. We had the room above the swimming pool and at about 6 am the next day after a

266

very noisy night I decided to lean out and wonder, courteously and in French, whether people might consider making a little less noise. The words died in my throat; the bride still in her exquisite wedding dress was perched on a wall below us smoking, drinking, high as a kite and shrieking to her colleagues. The stamina – you could only be impressed. We got up and had breakfast, hollow-eyed, before a final lunch, and farewell to the bride's parents.

I had been only just well enough to get to that wedding. Early in 2005 we were due to fly to Cuba accompanied by all three children and their partners. I had woken up three days before covered with a rash, feeling exhausted, but it was the key strategic Awayday for BPP so I got up, put make-up on and chaired it, feeling, as always, better for being in action. That evening Jim, looking doubtfully at the rash, sent me to our GP, who thought it was probably just a viral thing, but conscientiously did a blood test. The next morning brought an alarmed phone call bidding me get myself forthwith to the Chelsea and Westminster Hospital. I realised in the taxi that I knew what it was: a recurrence of the disease I had had as a child of 12 and again as a young woman of 25. After a few tests the consultant confirmed that it was the old enemy, now called ITP, an auto-immune disease in which the body turns on itself and destroys the platelets which are the very structure of the blood. I felt well enough to reassure my husband and Isobel and Richard and an anxious Henry ringing from Germany. None of them had been around in 1965 when this had last happened so all of them had feared it was leukaemia, and I was surrounded by family weeping with relief. It was still a narrow escape. My platelet count on admission was 6 and it took two weeks to get it up to 40, at which point you can walk around without risking your life. Had Jim not insisted I had the rash checked I would have been on a plane at very high risk of an internal bleed, probably in the brain.

We had to send the children off by themselves, loosely under the charge of Henry. They were hardly children at 32, 30 and 26 but they had been looking forward to a holiday with us under the cover of the parental credit cards, and now they were on their own, and poor Jim – also exhausted – wasn't going to get his holiday either or have the time with the children he had wanted. It was a very bad moment and one I had brought upon myself by stupid amounts of overwork.

My 65th year however improved from this low point. I was forced to recognise that I had been ill, that I probably wasn't going to get any more paying jobs and that Jim's executive career was reaching its natural end. He was 63, when the normal retirement age for executive directors of Balfour Beatty was 62, and the end in some sense *must* be nigh. We were both going to retire, or rather *be* retired and I might as well accept it with what limited grace I could muster.

Except that it didn't happen. My four-year term as Chairman of BPP came to an end but I was co-opted onto the Academic Council which we had set up to steer us through an application for Degree Awarding Powers. A Labour government had decided to extend substantially the number and type of institutions of higher education who could issue their own degrees. At BPP we already trained the brightest and the best graduates to work as lawyers, splitting the market principally with the College of Law, and Charlie realised at once that we needed to be able to offer these gilded students both the professional training qualification and a Master's degree. It was just a question of whether we could get there before the College of Law, politically much better placed than we were because they were a Charitable Trust. BPP, as a profitable commercial organisation, is always a living breathing target for attacks from all quarters of the Education Establishment.

Changing BPP into a university was fascinating, demanding work. There were very difficult political issues and at times it seemed that the higher education lobby would stymie us. I was reminded of my efforts to wrest Unipart from British Leyland in 1986 or Allied Steel and Wire from British Steel in 1987, when it was official government policy that Unipart and ASW should be sold but every man's hand was against me. Getting BPP through felt much the same but this time it was a Labour government and I was in a position to remind people personally that it *was* their policy, wasn't it, and where was it written that if you made a profit from being top dog in the field you would not be eligible? BPP was finally to get Degree Awarding Powers in 2007, a tribute to the unassailable quality of our teaching.

We had had to make huge changes; we had to detach the Law School from BPP plc and arrange that all services were provided to the new entity on an arm's length basis, but we slowly got there, thanks to our CEO Carl Lygo's personal and organisational qualities, to Peter Crisp as Head of the Law School, to Professor

David Murray, lately of the Open University, who combined a very clear view of how a university should run with a wealth of experience of academic skulduggery, and to Martyn Jones, who came to join us as the Head of the Academic Council. Even so we were not allowed the full University title so we had to trade as BPP University College of which I was President from 2007 until 2013, when we were granted the full title of BPP University (and me Chancellor of same). An irony given the very low quality and performance of many other establishments who were then and still are entitled to call themselves universities.

2005 was also my 65th birthday. The Parliament Choir sang 'Happy Birthday' for me in four parts at our rehearsal the day before, conducted by Simon, which again moved me to tears. I combined my birthday party with the launch of *Ticket to Ride*. My publishers, as usual welcoming all efforts by an author to sell books, had no money for the sort of party I was prepared to give, the one with champagne, plenty to eat and added entertainment. I had help this time; earlier in the year I had found my lost friend and fellow author Mike Ripley at a party in the Commons to help publicise Public Lending Right, an institution so valuable that all authors rally to the cause. Mike told me he had had a stroke (he was 50 at the time) so I got him to show me then and there what he could do, like not stand on one foot. The ice thoroughly broken he asked me how long I had had to queue to get through security. I said bewildered that I had come from next door, at which point he realised I had a House of Lords badge round my neck. When he had stopped laughing he told me he had a book coming out that year with Allison and Busby, the same publishers as mine. Mindful of Mike's wide network of friends and acquaintances, his long track record with the 'Angel' series and his connections with publishing, I asked him would he consider doing the legwork if I did the money for a joint launch. Mike, always one for a party, agreed instantly, so what would have been a major chore became easy. It was a lovely evening, like the parties I had given in the late 80s and 90s for earlier books. We held it at the Mall Galleries, who were very good to us; lots of Mike's crime-writing and publishing associates came and again I had the pleasure of watching people from the various companies I worked for getting on splendidly with crime writers, agents and PR girls. In a moment of inspiration I introduced another part of my life and employed a string quartet, recruited at 24 hours' notice from the ranks of that year's Southbank Sinfonia. They played, beautifully, throughout the party, ignoring the fact that most people, while making the odd appreciative comment, went right on talking. I thanked them, somewhat embarrassed, and pressed on them the fee I had agreed with Simon Over, who had negotiated me up from my initial bid like the professional all-rounder he had become. They laughed and assured me they had enjoyed playing even if no one was listening. I had forgotten that professional musicians are happy, for a decent fee, to play in odd places, at 24 hours' notice, and wearing a white wig and baggy velvet britches if need be.

On the family front Isobel was still struggling to make a career in dance. I tried to be encouraging but Jim was far more convincing than I because he genuinely believes that people must follow their passion however grudgingly said passion is reciprocated. All I could see was a gifted much-loved 26-year-old daughter breaking her head against a stony wall in a business which, at best, struggles. Classical ballet attracts large audiences, musical theatre works brilliantly and is the mainstay of the huge London theatre trade, whereas Contemporary Dance seemed to be forever condemned to tiny theatres and other venues only a grade above church halls. She was managing to keep going because she owned her own London flat and had my godson Ruaidhri as a lodger, and she has always looked carefully at every pound before she spends it. She was also an excellent dancer, but she never got into one of the main companies. She was and is very practical, as all who make their living precariously in the arts must be, and so she decided to audition for the Covent Garden production of *1984*. This time she got one of the eight coveted places along with many of the best contemporary dancers of her generation. We were delighted for her, and the more so when it turned out that Covent Garden treated their people properly; rehearsal time was paid, Isobel's costumes were made for her and she had a shared dresser, unbelievably luxurious after working in a field which characteristically features hard-pressed dancers zipping each other into home-made costumes in draughty corridors.

Artistically the experience was mixed. This was Lorin Maazel's first production and much of the projected dance, intended as an integral part of the production, got cut because audience attention is distracted from solo singers by other people moving on stage. Given that any of the soloists came at a price in excess of the wages of all the dancers put together, when a soloist sang the dancers had to stand still, so that eight excellent contemporary dancers were ultimately employed as human scenery. Isobel didn't mind that much, they all got extra cash per performance because they were deployed at over 2 metres from the stage (arranged on scaffolding mostly) and Isobel herself got an extra £45 per performance as a body double. The lead female singer sensibly did not wish to be hoisted up into a notional helicopter, for fear of injury or looking like a sack of potatoes, but being strapped into a harness and flown is easy for a strong dancer. The night we went I could see that there was a delay before Isobel rose into the air elegantly braced and pointing at the sky. She confirmed afterwards that it had proved inordinately difficult to attach the harness that night. Were it Contemporary Dance rather than Covent Garden, I thought darkly, they would have sent her up with whatever bit it was missing.

She was to do three more operas, gratifyingly without being asked to audition, so I knew that it was not just a mother's delusion that she was a really good dancer. She was also a choreographer financing her own productions and, learning from her Covent Garden experience and I hope from her parents' example, she always paid everyone properly, rather than asking if they would do it for free as was the practice in Contemporary Dance. She never departed from the principle that you have to pay your people properly, not just because the labourer is worthy of his hire but because you have not got the basis of a viable business unless it gives all participants a proper wage.

Even though I could not feel that Isobel's chosen way of life was yet viable, I was at least less anxious about her. Richard, on the other hand, we were both worried about on several grounds. He had no job, although in fairness his last three years had been spent on the major work of reconstructing his large house and doing a degree in sculpture, but his long-standing relationship with his girlfriend Indy was degenerating, slowly but measurably, and it was plain that he had no idea what he wanted to do about any of it. By his own confession years later he was using enough cannabis that for much of the time he simply wasn't in this world.

I offered him a 'Mummy Day'. The rules are simple; I attend for eight hours and do any practical chore that I am asked without comment or cavil. Richard wanted to tackle the accounts for his house conversion but confessed that there was very little to work on. He had employed an architect and a builder to do the rough and difficult work involved in digging out the basement and there were proper bills for this work. After that he had operated as the Main Man (or Principal Contractor as I primly re-defined it) and there were hardly any receipts and such as he had were of doubtful value. He pleaded in mitigation that this *was* his principal house and as such any gain made would be exempt from tax but he wanted to know for his own self. I saw this as a good sign that he was taking responsibility for his own life and, literally, putting his accounts in order, so I was particularly willing to help.

We started with what slender documentary evidence he had and then turned to the solid proof provided by his bank statements for the last two years. One Mummy Day stretched into two, and the list of amounts identifiable only as Miscellaneous got longer and longer, and Richard put his head on the desk in despair. I sought to cheer him up by pointing out that a good large house in South London was always going to show a profit, and that his father and I had routinely overspent on every conversion we had done and had always made good money when we sold. It fell to the hard-nosed Henry, who visited us a few days later, to ask what we had allowed for Richard's living costs in those two years. Richard and I realised simultaneously that we had made ourselves unnecessarily miserable and that once you made a reasonable allowance for his living expenses the real cost of the conversion, while high, was a good deal lower than we had feared.

Henry was in the UK because he applied for the vacant finance director job in his company in Germany and was turned down, regretfully because they valued him, on the grounds that he had no formal qualifications other than an apprenticeship ten years earlier. Jim and I sided with his German employers; both of us had had experience of people who thought they could be finance directors without the formal qualifications, like ex-merchant bankers, and we knew it didn't work. Henry, audibly grinding his teeth, had decided to do an MBA and a formal accountancy qualification alongside it. He knew he would have to do it outside Germany because he had tried a part-time course in Germany and found it mind-numbingly dull, entirely theoretical and taught from long poorly written books, so he was looking at business schools in the UK and elsewhere in Europe.

We pointed him at the Judge Business School in Cambridge where I thought he would at least be interviewed given his track record. They saw him, and after forty minutes offered him a place, and he became one of the only two people accepted (the other was a gifted New Zealander) who did not have an undergraduate degree.

We emptied the other half of the Cambridge house so he could persuade his wife to come with him. Silke brought the treasured cat Cleopatra, whom they had taken on as a kitten when they first set up house together ten years before, and her much-loved stallion, Pharos, then getting on for twenty years old and a member of the family. The cat wasn't a problem but Pharos needed a proper stable and a field and people to look after him, so we looked around with increasing urgency, finally finding a place with the assistance of Elisabeth Pickard, with whom Henry had started lessons as a small five-year-old. I took Henry to look at the place and, out of my comfort zone as always when dealing with the Horse, followed a few steps behind him. His bleak gaze took in an unlatched gate which he fiddled with until he got it to close, and then turned on a teenage girl and a horse in the middle of the yard, the horse stamping and fretting and pawing the ground in the way they so tiresomely do, and the girl, increasingly desperate, trying to get it to lift up a foot for inspection. Henry watched for a few seconds, walked quietly into the middle of the yard, took the bridle and had a word with the horse, who stopped fidgeting and kicking at once, laid its head on his shoulder, then raised, meekly, the off right foot to allow him to remove with one sharp jerk whatever had been worrying it. For good measure the creature then offered him all the other feet as well. I was transported back many years to watching Miss Pickard with just that same bleak eye advance on a fretting pony and an anxious child; the pony at once stood on all four feet, a model of docility, and the child sat bolt upright in the orthodox style.

'Not very well run,' Henry said to me quietly and I braced myself to point out that this place was new and perhaps not quite as we would wish but it *was* registered and it *was* only fifteen miles from Cambridge, and his father and I had looked everywhere else. It wasn't necessary; Henry was pounced on by one of the partners who had observed the whole scene and was being led off on an inspection of the facilities and promised whatever he wanted for Pharos and Silke, and very possibly a partnership in the stable. Someone who knows what they are doing is irresistible in any field.

It all turned out very well. Henry was one of the oldest and certainly one of the most experienced on the MBA course but was clear that he was filling useful gaps in his knowledge. He and Silke made friends instantly, with the New Zealander and his wife, and with an American, Tyler Dennis, who had come from running part of the PGA Tour, a golf franchise which runs major tournaments, and his very good-looking wife Anna, who had been a State Champion in pole vaulting. Tyler does not look like an athlete; he is only my height and a little plump, but he can do any sport he sets his hand to. An excellent golfer who had given up his plans for a competitive career because Tiger Woods was an exact contemporary, he was also a fine skier and a first-class tennis player. He is also both clever and physically gifted; when he murmured that he had been on a scholarship at Stanford I assumed stupidly it had been a sports scholarship, but no, it had been a music scholarship, he said, sounding surprised.

Henry flourished; he has always been one to learn things only when he needed them and he took much that he needed at the Judge and also from the CIMA course that he did on a part-time basis with BPP. He had of course learned early to form and lead teams and to present in both English and German, which put him ahead of many of the rest of the student body.

I got an accidental sidelight on his progress. I went to the Norfolk Dinner at St Edmund's College, who had kindly made me an Honorary Fellow in 2000 when I was appointed to the House of Lords. There I met a real Fellow, a gifted Chinese marketing specialist who disclosed he was teaching at the Judge. I said I hardly expected him to know all the students but my son Henry was doing an MBA. He looked again at my name tag, took half a step back and said, doubtfully, 'You're Henry *Cohen*'s mother', and I was back on what I thought was familiar ground dealing with the people trying to teach my brothers or my sons anything, so I said oh dear, had he not settled down, braced for accounts of any amount of unfortunate behaviour. Still looking dazed, my new friend said no, no, Henry was immensely capable and doing brilliantly. Just as the bell went for dinner he leant urgently towards me and asked what Henry's father did for a living and I explained he was a main Board director of Balfour Beatty and my new friend nodded, lips pursed. When I went home I found the lights in Henry and Silke's side of the house were still on so I popped in to enquire of Henry why this nice man had seemed so surprised that I was his mother. My son slowly turned crimson – I have rarely seen him embarrassed.

'Ah well you see,' he said, 'I have told everyone that I am this poor boy from a German stableyard.'

'But darling,' I said, horrified, 'do they not know … where do you tell people you are living? In a hovel by the station I assume rather than just over the fence from St Edmund's in a big house? Do you *have* parents, may I ask?'

He laughed, still embarrassed. I retreated, warning him that his cover was blown. The facts leaked out of course as Henry invited his teams and then the whole of his year to parties in the garden and introduced them to us; but by then he had made his point: people had to take him for who he was, not for his background or his parents.

Silke had a good time too, as soon as we had managed to persuade her to abandon the achingly boring business of doing a German MBA by correspondence. She read me an extract of one of the papers and I felt my eyes closing after a couple of minutes just as hers did. No case studies, no anecdotes, nothing to lighten pages and pages of clumsily stated theory, and this came from one of the most admired schools in Germany. She gave up, reluctantly because she is an academically capable persistent woman, with a double degree in pharmacy and highly rated in her field, but she could bear it no longer. After that she had a happy time, with more of Henry's company than she had had for years, new friends, and her horse Pharos to see every day. She even liked the English weather; she said to me at the end of their fourteen months here that if she could take the English climate back to Münster she would, pointing out that in North Germany it can rain or snow for weeks at a time, whereas in England, always, there is an interval in every day when you can go for a quiet, dry walk.

It helped, of course, that Pharos had settled well. In North Germany the horses are kept in stables in the winter; here Pharos was turned out, suitably rugged up, into the fields every day, where he could run and talk to his friends, and he loved it. He made new friends too; one day I met Henry sitting in the garden mending a horse cloth.

'Pharos took his blanket off,' he reported, cursing as he missed the stitch and got his finger instead.

'How?' I asked, reasoning while it is true that horses can lift one leg up with which to kick you I didn't think they could get one up to neck level and tear a blanket off.

'Oh he had help,' Henry said irritably. 'His best friend is a pony, and he used his teeth.' He held up the cloth with its ragged hole to show me and I realised that a good time was being had by all.

We mourned when Henry and Silke decided to go back to Germany where they had the life they wanted, living in the country, their horses stabled twenty minutes away and both of them only a twenty-minute drive from work. None of it would have been possible in the South of England, so my half-formed plan of luring them to live near us died, this time permanently.

Chapter 18

JOURNEY TO RETIREMENT
2006–2007

By late 2006 I had absorbed what the world was telling me by then; there were no more corporate jobs coming my way. Most companies wanted to be able to appoint an NED for two three-year terms, and I would be 72 if I served six years. I was fortunate still to have paid employment at BPP, the Stock Exchange and Management Consulting Group. I had also managed to get a political role, chairing a Committee in the House of Lords, a sub-committee of the House of Lords European Union Committee. The EU Committee considers all legislation and legislative proposals coming from the European Union. The United Kingdom was obliged by various treaties to take into our own legislation anything that the European Parliament agreed. The Committee examined everything that would have to become part of UK law. They had a huge task; 6.8 per cent of statute law, 14.1 per cent of secondary legislation and perhaps as much as 30 per cent of regulation originates in the EU. The Lords EU Committee considered not only the legislation but the initial discussion documents and proposals that precede legislation and all the regulatory proposals. It is the sort of patient high-quality scrutiny that the House of Lords is equipped to do and does well; in 2006 there were seventy-nine of us deployed on seven sub-committees and the main Committee. Now, post the Brexit vote, the Lords are producing detailed analyses of changes that will come about as and when we formally leave the EU, which no one on either side of the debate has elucidated.

In 2006 I had expected to chair Sub-committee B which covered Industry, Transport and Energy. In the haggling that goes on among the Usual Channels however it had been agreed that the next Chairman of that Committee had to come from the Conservative side of the House. Sub-committee A, covering the

EU Budget, Wholesale Finance and Trade, on the other hand, it was agreed could go to a Labour peer provided one could be found with the right experience. I was a good candidate for the job, being a lawyer, a banker for twenty years, on the Board of the London Stock Exchange, and acceptable to the Chairman of the main Committee, Julian Grenfell.

When the House returned in October 2006 I met my Clerk, Simon Blackburn, who was, disconcertingly, as new to the job as I was. It is not given to everyone to enjoy life as a Clerk; they are mostly male, all clever, patient, tactful and able to cope with the eccentricities of the Members. They are a remarkably capable and resilient lot; Simon was moved on after two years, to the accompaniment of wails of despair from me, to be replaced by Rob Whiteway, only 21 but as competent and equally fearless, who saw me through the second two years.

Chairing a House of Lords Committee is a unique experience. At various points my Sub-committee included an ex-head of the Foreign Office, John Kerr, who was involved from the beginning of our membership of the EU, Claus Moser, the infinitely distinguished retired head of Government statistics, David Trimble, newly arrived after his bruising career in Northern Ireland, John Browne, fresh from managing BP, and any number of others laden with years and honour.

The Sub-committee's first duty is to inspect the various proposals, progress notes and bits of legislation referred to it by the Chairman of the main Committee, and to write to the relevant domestic Minister to urge them into action if it seems necessary. To this end the Clerk produces a note for the Chairman on each item plus, if need be, a recommendation for action and a draft letter to the Minister. In my time in the Civil Service I had been the equivalent of the Clerk, doing all the work, then presenting the conclusions neatly wrapped to Ministers. Now I seemed to be the Minister and I did my best to read and think about what was being recommended, remembering how we had hated Ministers who did neither.

The second duty, and much more fun, was to conduct Enquiries into anything the Sub-committee thought useful (cue the Clerk producing a well-organised list of topics for the Chairman). The Sub-committee, assisted by a Special Adviser, an under-remunerated expert in the subject under discussion, would then take evidence from expert witnesses. The Clerk of course wrote the questions and the Committee would produce a Report (yes, the Clerk writes that). These Reports were and are well received, not only by fellow Members, but also more widely in the European Union, as models of style and clarity.

It was never possible to keep the Sub-committee in place for more than two hours every week, so I had to move smartly through the business. At a party in the House not long after my appointment, David Trimble and Claus Moser bowed low to me as I arrived, with cries of 'here comes our honoured Chairman, *now* we'll have to behave' and I feared I might have been too brisk. I managed over time to get Ken Woolmer, another Labour peer, and Bill Jordan, an admired trades union colleague from my days as a BBC Governor, into vacant Labour places. Ken would take the chair when I couldn't, and Bill has always been invaluable with his wide knowledge of European institutional behaviour after years in the ILO job in Geneva.

I chaired from 2006 to 2010 right through the worst of the near-collapse of the financial system, for which our European colleagues had no hesitation in blaming, publicly, the Anglo-Saxon world in general and the United Kingdom in particular. It was galling to have to sit through abuse from the French and German financial establishments when we knew that beneath the stolidly self-righteous German front lay a mess of Landesbanken carrying bad loans and having to be quietly supported by the Bundesbank. The French were even more annoying and it was impossible not to engage in schadenfreude when their big banks, starting with Paribas, fell over their collective feet and were revealed, publicly, to be in as poor shape as any of the UK banks. Revenge was a

Janet chairing Sub-Committee A of the EU Committee of the House of Lords, taking evidence for the Ten Years of the Euro enquiry in 2008.

dish that had to be eaten cold; our European colleagues took years to acknowledge the problems in their banking systems whereas our accounting rules require us to come clean about bad debts or over-valued assets on an annual basis.

In 2006, before the crisis, we had decided to hold an Enquiry into the first ten years of the Eurozone. It was difficult to frame; the Conservative Members of the Sub-committee would have liked to agree that the Eurozone was going to fail at any moment, whereas the pro-European Liberal Democrats and my own Party hoped to be able to conclude that it had been an economic success for its members.

My own position was then and remains now as an advocate of the European Union, a Remainer to the core, but an opponent of the single currency. The sterling crisis in 1992 had told me that a trading country, on the outskirts of dominant economies like France and Germany, would be ill advised to try and conform to their economic patterns and their currency. I did think however that after ten years of the Eurozone the European financial market, complete with Eurobonds and European securities was *there*, and of increasing financial importance in the world. It was John Kerr, drawing on his years in Brussels and Washington taking totally divergent views and packaging them so that they looked like a Way Forward, who suggested a possible framework. We agreed that we would list and consider all the advantages the proponents of the Euro had put forward when it became a new currency, and then list and consider the disadvantages that opponents of its foundation had adduced, and decide with magisterial detachment what had actually happened. For the supporters' side it was clear that the hoped-for growth of European bonds and securities had indeed taken place. The worst consequences envisaged by the opponents were not however, in 2006 and 2007, in evidence. The southern European countries ('the Club Med group'), despite their weaker economies, did not seem to be damaged by membership of the single currency; quite the contrary, they were feeling prosperous, there were new jobs and they were selling massive amounts of property to the citizens of the northern states. The process had indeed caused inflation in the Club Med countries but overall I would have been ready to conclude that the single currency had brought prosperity to its members and had enabled the development of a thriving financial market. The difficulty lay in getting agreement to that conclusion from my four Conservative Members. The invaluable John Kerr suggested my view was too definitive; might we not be better to conclude that the Euro had been a success in many respects and that none of the dire warnings about a split between North and South had come to pass BUT on the other hand there had been no major financial shock like the oil crisis and the world economic situation had been benign. Would it not be wiser to conclude that we didn't really know?

I thought that this was a pusillanimous way to go but I could see the sense of it. If it had come to a vote my Conservative colleagues could have been outvoted but these Sub-committees, by tradition, do not vote except in extremis and any chairman who manages to reach that point is felt to have failed. So I accepted John's suggestion and our Report has stood the test of time. We did not suffer the embarrassment of having produced a widely circulated Report which concluded that the single currency was a Good Thing and all was well in the Eurozone only a year before the banking crisis revealed mercilessly its structural weaknesses.

The Sub-committee also had responsibility for Trade, and a second massive round of negotiations to reduce tariffs on trade even further than had been achieved in the last General Agreement on Tariffs and Trade was in progress. We decided that these talks were a proper subject for an Enquiry so we summoned witnesses and headed over to Brussels to take evidence from our very own EU Commissioner, Peter Mandelson. I had known Peter since the 1980s; a gifted politician who had been integral to New Labour both in policy formation and in holding together the personalities involved, but I had never seen him doing a Real Job like trying to get 161 countries to agree on tariff reductions. On the day we met him he was so tired that he couldn't stop talking; the last round, the last hope for these talks was a few days after our visit and he told us all about it in great political detail. It was with difficulty that I stemmed the flow long enough for committee colleagues to ask their questions but it was a fascinating session and it was above and beyond the call of duty for him to have given us as much time as he did. We missed a train, I had to ignore the Clerk's disqualifying eye, but it was worth it. As all know – and Peter probably knew at the time – the talks failed, narrowly, and weary and frustrated people all over the world got their first night's sleep in weeks.

I had also been trying to find something to do in Cambridge. We were planning to retire there so I asked one of our Cambridge friends, Nigel Brown, for help. He had set up and run a substantial business in Cambridge and over a long career had a finger in most pies. A lover of music, he had set up the Stradivari Trust, a scheme whereby people invest in good instruments for promising young musicians to play – and indeed to buy if their careers go well enough. He is also a motor cycle aficionado, and at the time was on the University Council and was to become High Sheriff of Cambridgeshire in 2011. I asked him if he knew an organisation who might find me useful and he suggested I might take over from him as Chairman of the Cambridge Arts Theatre. I was astounded; I had not set my sights so high. The Cambridge Arts Theatre had been the institution to which all the undergraduate actors of my generation aspired, and my distinguished friend Johnny Lynn, co-author of *Yes Minister*, had cut his teeth as Artistic Director there in the 1970s.

The theatre was founded by John Maynard Keynes in 1925, partly as a showcase for his Russian dancer wife. He was then First Bursar of King's College, immensely successful in making money for them by investing their assets, and, in gratitude, they gave him a large oddly-shaped roughly triangular piece of land across the road from the college. He built and paid for the theatre, which he gifted to King's, and, knowing enough about the arts to doubt the theatre's ability to pay for itself, also endowed it handsomely.

The Keynes endowment had run out sometime in the 1950s and the theatre – always well respected artistically – continued to lose money but was kept going by a set of distinguished Artistic Directors, charitable donations and money from the Arts Council. It was and is an important and much-loved regional theatre, as evidenced by the support for the urgently needed refurbishment of the whole building in the mid 1990s when the theatre was dark for two years. I had subscribed modestly to that refurbishment and recalled that the building contained a restaurant which had been confidently expected to support the theatre from its profits. Not so, Nigel told me, the theatre was bust again, the restaurant lost money, and the theatre had a £150,000 overdraft limit against which they regularly bumped. There were months, indeed, when it seemed possible that the Trustees would have to sign personal cheques for the staff wages.

Carole Todd and Dave Murphy at rehearsals for the most successful Cambridge Arts Theatre panto ever (Aladdin) in 2018.

There were two bright spots: Nigel had found a successful businessman, Dave Murphy, in his early forties, who was seeking a career change and was working for the Trustees as a part-time CEO and Artistic Director and was succeeding in cost-cutting and revenue-raising. He had been going to see everything he could in any theatre since his teens and thought he knew how to provide audiences with the right stuff. And the Arts Council had initially offered a rescue grant, the only problem being that the Arts Council for the East was seeking to block the award until an Artistic Director with a background in the arts was appointed to the job businessman Dave was doing.

I met Dave the next day and recognised him, whatever else he might be, as the archetypal company doctor, the hard man who stems losses by cutting costs to the bone, but carefully, and looks for every possible increase in revenue, so that, slowly, a dying business rises from the ashes, pays its debts and trades on. Dave years later said that he recognised in me a gift from the heavens, a Baroness with an interest in theatre, powerful friends, a sound grasp of finance, and some restaurant experience. It was love at first sight.

I was invited on to the Board as Chairman designate and we managed to persuade the Arts Council to disgorge the promised

Rescue Grant over the protesting body of the local head of Arts East who was still trying to dislodge Dave. The Board, well before I got there, had refused to consider losing Dave, which would indeed have been an appalling decision. We were and remain grateful for the Arts Council rescue package which paid off the theatre overdraft and enabled us to do some well overdue maintenance but it is Dave who has turned the theatre into one of the very few regional theatres (count them on the fingers of one hand) which consistently make a surplus while offering a superb programme.

The Arts, like the bulk of regional arts theatres, is a Receiving Theatre. It receives other people's productions, and (typically) gives up two-thirds of the ticket price to the production company. The theatre lives on a combination of the other one-third, a booking fee, typically £2–£4 for a ticket, and on selling drinks and ice cream to the audience. None of this would enable the theatre to make a surplus so our hopes – as at most regional theatres – revolve round the Pantomime, produced by the theatre itself and running two or three performances a day for a blessed six to seven weeks, and where all the ticket money stays with us.

Despite the panto and support from the Arts Council and the local authority the Cambridge Arts Theatre had lost money for the first seventy years of its existence but a year after Dave arrived it returned a tiny surplus which has increased steadily every year and now hovers between £100,000 and £200,000 annually. This is still not enough to make it possible to undertake major capital expenditure – for that the theatre relies on grants and gifts – but it is enough to enable it to manage without a revenue subsidy from any institution. And just as well; the theatre lost the Arts East's subsidy and the City Council grant in the recession, which in combination would have tipped any less tightly run organisation into deficit.

Dave's methods were, and are, old-fashioned and simple. When he arrived – eighteen months before I did – the theatre had productions in it for thirty to thirty-five weeks a year. Dave, observing that if the shop isn't open you can't take any money, programmes as close as he can get to forty-four to forty-five weeks a year, pretty much the maximum, given the need to repaint, rewire, re-carpet and let the staff go away on holiday. He then took out any unnecessary cost he saw and after eighteen months the theatre was just in surplus.

It sounds easy but it wasn't then and isn't now. The key to the income side is getting hold of the productions that people want to pay good money to come and see, while providing a judicious mix of more difficult plays, plus some opera and music. Programming is an art but Dave very quickly knew everyone in the business and was able to manage the complicated process of scheduling the right mix and, critically, making the right financial deal. He is risk-averse, as all the best company doctors are, and tries never to guarantee a minimum level of payment to any visiting company, arranging instead a judicious split of the proceeds which does not leave the theatre at risk of loss. Production companies put up with him because he is straight and because our theatre has a deserved reputation for the basic business of marketing and selling tickets, so that there is always money to share.

Dave also colonised the Pantomime. He took over as producer, hiring all the actors, writing the script and commissioning the sets and costumes. There are really only four basic pantomimes, Cinderella, Aladdin, Dick Whittington and Jack and the Beanstalk, and all involve (at least with us) six really good singers/dancers, and at least eight Babes. These are children of 8 to about 12, who cannot legally be asked to work for two or three shows a day, so we recruit two teams of ten children to cover the six-week season. My first year as Chairman I attended the open audition for the Babes; 150 children, mostly girls, all accompanied by at least one parent, which went on all day. At the audition, the dance captain for the show teaches group after group a very simple routine. Some of the candidates have no idea, gazing out bewildered from our big stage, and finally being gently jollied off into the arms of their mothers, while the stage and dance school children are terrifyingly proficient, all dressed in identical leotards and pick up the routine at once. And there are never enough boys.

At some stage in a very long Saturday I asked Dave, sat rocklike in the third row, what we paid a Babe for the season and got an incredulous look. Children fight to be allowed to do it for free, every year, for the glamour of the show and the costumes and the experience and indeed it is a fitting introduction to the hard lives they are mostly going to lead as dancers or actors.

I had agreed with Jim that we would go away on his retirement from Balfour Beatty on his 65th birthday in February 2007. He had already stayed on an extra three years past the normal retirement age of 62 in order to settle, finally, the aftermath of the Hatfield rail disaster, and to make sure his legacy of a decent rail business in Europe and the Far East and the wildly successful Private Finance Initiative work was in place. He knew he would be miserable if he had to wean himself, cold turkey, from a routine of ten-hour days running a company and we therefore planned to leave, the day after he retired, for a seven-week trip to see our friends Francis and Dianne Small in New Zealand and to tour around with them.

We had two stops on the way out, the first in Dubai at the desert hotel, the Al Maha, where we had three nights of ridiculous luxury, with an air-conditioned tent and our own plunge pool. Most of our holidays had been in damp cottages in beautiful places, and while we agreed that we could move a little closer to the 7-star experience it was never going to be anything we actually needed. I was reminded of brother Giles, at one of his frequent periods of financial pressure, saying he could give up any day of the week the steam yacht or the private aeroplane, should he own either.

Then a stop in traffic-ridden Bangkok with a personal guide, a luxury I continue to think worth paying for, particularly in very poor countries, and, as with Mum in Morocco, the guide enabled us to get to places and see things without being exhausted or hassled. He was interesting, if prone to lapse into loud worshipful adoration of the King of Thailand as being the country's saviour and beloved of Buddha, which alerted us at once to the tensions in the country.

We were met by Francis in Auckland, wearing the shorts in which male New Zealanders spend their summers. We picked up a cheap rental car, an old Japanese four-seater van with endless space behind us for the mountains of luggage we had managed to bring. I am an anxious traveller who has difficulty leaving anything behind and Jim, who has travelled everywhere on business with hand luggage only, had brought a lot of comfort objects with him like five changes of underwear. We drove with Francis through dazzlingly beautiful virginal forest up to the North coast and the Bay of Islands, the sub-tropical bit of New Zealand, where we had a couple of cabins round a shared swimming pool and shops to hand and perfect weather, and the washing machine with which the poorest hotel or b & b in New Zealand is always equipped. More robust travellers than we could readily go round both islands with one change of clothes and a good jacket in the summer.

We drove south from there with the weather confusingly

becoming less balmy and more like home as we approached Wellington via a detour to Rotorua, the part of North Island composed of still active volcanic material. The whole of New Zealand sits on a fault, where the plates on which the land sits grind into each other continuously, occasionally releasing some of the molten metal which burns at the centre of the earth. The part round Rotorua is still gently active; there are warm springs, hot enough to enable the cooking of raw food by putting it in a dish and burying it, and you don't get cold at night. The Maoris who colonised New Zealand in the seventeenth century must have thought they had found utopia because the ingredients of any meal were easy to come by as well as easy to cook. The now extinct moa, a huge flightless bird, a not-very-fast-walking ton of protein covered with feathers like a fat ostrich, were everywhere and the Maori hunted them to extinction in about a hundred years. People from the old world of Europe, the UK and Ireland would have done the same, I am sure, if they had got there first; in a hard settler life an easy to catch creature that would keep a family through weeks of winter must have been irresistible.

The current New Zealanders however are acutely conscious of the need to preserve the trees, the pure rivers and the wildlife of their environment, perhaps because so much could be lost at any moment by an earthquake of the intensity that destroyed San Francisco in 1906. Our trusty hiking boots were steam-washed as we landed at Auckland in order to prevent us spreading foreign germs in the soil and it was no good claiming we had already done that, as directed in all the tourist literature; wet boots had to be parked by the swimming pool to dry off in the gentle warmth of the Bay of Islands. Every path in the country is marked with stern injunctions not to stray off it for fear of damaging the ecosystems on each side, and leaving rubbish of any sort, even the biodegradable varieties like sandwiches, is strictly interdicted. It seemed a bit repressive to us, used to walking out of our damp cottages onto the hill and going wherever we want and by whatever route, but the purity of the air and the freshness of the countryside in New Zealand are worth preserving. The wildlife isn't *that* interesting; the birds are few and far between and endangered by a rash importation of possums from Australia between the two World Wars. Possum fur is peculiarly warm while being very light in texture, making a winning combination with heavier denser sheep wool, but the possums themselves remain

287

a major problem because they escaped and are everywhere and live off birds and their eggs.

Jim had wanted for many years to walk the Tongariro crossing, a high pass between two substantial volcanoes, one quiet and the other quiescent, though with a habit of erupting a substantial stream of molten lava unforeseen by all and devastating everything in its way. We had been joined by then by Dianne, Francis' wife; she and Francis had done the crossing before, but Parkinson's disease had taken its toll and a very long walk featuring a hard climb and a hard descent was beyond him. I am slower than Jim and I wanted him to enjoy a walk he had dreamed of for years undisturbed by responsibility for me. Dianne and I decided we would fly over the route in the very small plane parked in a field beside the car park. Francis refused, having inspected the plane, on the basis that he didn't fly in single-engine planes as a matter of policy. It was not until Dianne and I were peering out of the windows as the plane banked to get us a better view of the wonderfully coloured rocks and the toiling ants working their way up that I thought to wonder how Francis could cheerfully wave off much-loved wife and respected visitor friend in a mode of conveyance he did not consider safe. It hadn't occurred to Dianne either – New Zealanders don't let much get in the way of a good outing.

We did a few more walks in North Island, one well-known tramp (the New Zealand word for walk) around a beautiful mountain. None of us saw it, rain poured down for a solid five hours while we toiled on, assuring our hosts truthfully that it was exactly like walking in Scotland, no worries. Francis came with us this time, buoyed up with pills and a steady supply of sandwiches. I walked at that stage, with proper sticks, on a combination of Ibuprofen and frequent sandwiches, so Francis and I were on a similar level. We also did the lovely walk up a disused railway line originally built in the 1890s to bring cattle from the hills down to the rapidly growing capital city of Wellington. Francis, who had been the Chief Executive of New Zealand rail and had spent all his working life in the business, had had the task of closing this line but had been able to convert it into a spectacular walk which wound its way uphill with the reasonably gentle gradients manageable by a freight train full of cattle with engines at both ends.

We had a few rest days with them in Wellington in their house perched on the hill with magnificent views of Wellington harbour. They had bought the house when they knew that Francis' future and activities would be compromised and arranged it in a way I envy and would gladly emulate if I could bend a listed house in Cambridge to my will. They live on the ground floor with only one small set of steps down to the big living room and guests are accommodated in two bedrooms and a bathroom on the upper floor, so everybody has some privacy and only the fully able-bodied need ever go upstairs.

Their youngest son Warwick had joined us up in Auckland for dinner. We had taught Francis, the well-brought-up only son of a conventional family, to share out the pudding course, raiding each other's plates. Francis contributed his own spin on it; if you are unwilling to share the particular dish you place your elbow on the table next to it and growl 'get your own'. Years of patient upbringing vanished, as Warwick said, promptly adopting the same practice. Cameron, the eldest son, 6'4", bright red hair, with all his parents' calm, working as a paramedic for the hospital service, appeared in Wellington to say hello and I could only think how wonderfully reassuring it would be to have this gentle and skilled giant appear if you were lying on the road after an accident.

We headed south from there, with the weather getting colder because we were going towards the snows of the Antarctic. New Zealand is a long thin island and you get sub-tropical climate at one end and huge snowfalls lasting through five months of the winter at the other. We were making for the Otago track, another railway built originally to shift cattle. It had also been closed by Francis, who had arranged for it to be turned into a cycle way traversable in four days at a gentle tourist pace on hefty bicycles hired on the spot. Small townships to house railway employees and small hotels had grown up to service the railway, and Francis had feared that closure of the railway would bring desolation and tumbleweed blowing in the streets. The cycle tourists, however, who stay in the little hotels and eat at the stalls and restaurants that have grown up along the line, have provided a life-giving trickle of money, now grown to a stream, which has enabled people to stay in their homes and make a living.

Days one and two were hard work and everyone including Francis did better than me. Day three we rode into an Eden, grapes growing everywhere and deer farms and small trees. Otago, which is high, dry and with poor soil, has the perfect combination for the grapes that go into Pinot Noir and the wines of Otago are famous, even in a country which makes a lot of wine, partly for fun and partly to diversify away from the 90 per cent dominance of sheep and cattle rearing in the economy. New Zealand could no longer sell much meat or dairy products to their historic, protected markets in the UK but do sell huge amounts to Japan and the newly rich countries of the Far East.

Day three provided two other treats. We were getting our ears bent by a young farmer who lived on the Trail and felt the government's electricity supply policy did not take account of his needs and those of others like him. Familiar political ground, but Francis, listening with folded arms and a defensive scowl, was then Chairman of Meridien, the New Zealand power company which had responsibility for precisely the ill that was being complained of. To his credit – and that of New Zealand's democratic policy and behaviour – he disclosed his interest and suggested the man come and visit a minion in Wellington.

That night, after dinner, we walked out to go back to our hotel into a darkness illuminated only by the most dazzling sky I ever hope to see. In the clear unpolluted air of the Otago hills we saw stars clustered everywhere in every corner and the thick white of the Milky Way arced right across the centre of the sky. We stayed and looked for a long time, craning our aching middle-aged necks to see more, silenced by the realisation that all this glory was always there, every night, if we could but see it.

Jim and I also walked the Milford Trail, one of the famous walks into the interior of the West Coast of South Island. The coast is deeply indented and mountainous, rather like Norway, and much of it is not readily accessible by sea. Captain Cook looked at one of the bigger sounds (New Zealand for fjords) and recorded that if he got the ship in he was doubtful about getting it out again and Doubtful Sound it remains to this day. The New Zealand tourist authorities have opened up a walk from the interior over a high pass through to the next-door Milford Sound; numbers are limited, you are counted in and counted out, you must carry out all that you carry in, and stick to the paths. The regimentation is necessary; that coast has an average rainfall of ten times the West Coast of Scotland and floods and rock falls frequently block the paths. Even on the Guided Walk for wimps and oldies, on which we were, where you have only to carry food and toiletries plus enough clothes to cope with anything from 25° heat to flood and tempest, much can go wrong. The guided party a week ahead of ours had had to be helicoptered across a swollen river because a two-day wait for it to subside would have left them without shelter, wet and hungry. Our group however walked in sunshine, defying the odds. We were a group of about forty with three guides – two strong young New Zealanders and one Japanese, always included on major tourist trips because of the increasing numbers of Japanese tourists attracted to New Zealand by the space and the freshness. One guide led, one guide jollied along the middle section and one brought up the rear, this mostly being me and an older couple. On the longest day, where you do 3000 feet to the top of the pass, then 4000 feet down to the next site via a path strewn with boulders and eroded by constant flooding, Jim, who has walked from childhood in the high hills of the Scottish West Coast and was going easily, stayed at the back with me. He reported that the guide behind us would go to sleep on a comfortable rock for half an hour at a time, then wake and run down boulders and streams to catch up with his labouring charges. That guide was 27, a veteran of the New Zealand equivalent of the SAS, and could obviously have carried not only my rucksack, to which I stubbornly clung, but me if need be. It was a hard, hard day – I am better going up than down and by the time I got to the bottom I could do no more than lie resentfully, with every muscle jumping, under layers of blankets while Jim and the young of the group and the guide trotted off to see a famous waterfall at an hour's distance.

We wept when we left New Zealand and Dianne and Francis. It had turned out as I suspected all along that if we had lived in the same country, or even the same hemisphere and not 6000 miles away from each other, we would have been among each other's closest friends. We are all of Northern or Scottish ancestry and there is a symmetry between the couples which helps; Dianne and I are both capable, bossy, eldest children, with no sisters but each with two younger brothers close in age who have had difficult lives. Jim and Francis are both treasured only children, both highly intelligent, immensely hardworking men, both leaders in their fields. Dianne and I agreed that like must have called to like at some level but that the unusual thing was that all four of us liked each other as people. Jim and I would have liked to have either or both of them as a sibling.

We flew home via Sydney and had three nights there in a good hotel with great views of the opera house and the Bridge on the basis that we might not pass this way again, and it was worth paying for. Sydney is a beautiful and rich city but we were immediately brought up against the radical difference between Australia and New Zealand which lies in the way they treat their native populations. In New Zealand the occupying forces signed the Treaty of Waitangi in 1837 which affirmed the rights of the Maori population. The Europeans more or less stuck to it and, critically, Maori and Europeans intermarried to the point that it is now acknowledged that there are no full-blood Maoris in New Zealand, and the newspapers are full of names like Hamish Mantingua, Ti Pepe Farquharson, to name but two, underneath pictures of heavy-duty Scottish faces, hair and skin no darker than one sees any day in the Highlands. The settler population was largely drawn from the younger sons of Protestant Scotland and the north of England; indeed Francis' parents came from Yorkshire as did Dianne's. In Australia by contrast the native population was always treated with contempt and with total disregard for their rights by the immigrant Europeans, particularly the Irish who came escaping the Famine to run the prison camps and, later, to dig the mines. There is an ugly history of murder and enslavement of both the transported prisoners and the native population and the result is a deeply depressed native society, largely cut off from the majority European and Asian groupings and the subject of guilt-ridden and patronising relief work and a half-hearted adherence to the doctrine of equality. In New Zealand more rights have been yielded to the Maoris whenever they have complained that the Treaty was being breached legally or in spirit. Segregation in New Zealand has gone completely; its last vestige being the creation of a separate Maori brigade, who fought magnificently at Cassino and were taken to their hearts by the Italians. Segregation renders Australia the poorer as a society; they managed to overcome much of the hostile and divisive white Australian policy towards immigration that dogged the years after World War II, but have not managed to reach out to the people who have always lived there. You feel it even though the native population is nigh-on invisible, it is a less relaxed and comfortable place than New Zealand, where a man is a man for a' that. The Government attitude to refugees – anyone who arrives in the little boats is put into camps in the Pacific islands and their appeals for asylum processed with glacial speed – also makes both visitors and many Australians uncomfortable.

Chapter 19

INTERMISSION 2007–2008

While I was in New Zealand the Exchange was engaged in stately negotiations to merge with the Italian stock exchange. The Borsa Italiana was then a private company owned by its members, as we at the LSEG had been back in 2001 when I joined, so there was no need for the untidy and often panic-stricken processes involved in putting together two public companies with two share prices and two sets of shareholders.

A merger with another exchange was well recognised as a vital step for LSEG. We were hardened veterans of takeover battles, having fought off bids from Euronext, Macquarie, the Australian investment bank, and the mighty Deutsche Börse, then four times our size. All of these could have paid a premium price at which our shareholders, despite their declarations of love and loyalty, would have sold us out, but in the event our would-be predators offered prices barely above our share price, so we were able to see them off, and Deutsche Börse had lost a CEO and a Chairman in the fallout.

Chris Gibson-Smith had put a lot of patient work into stabilising our shareholding and had persuaded the sovereign funds of Qatar and Dubai to invest, so Qatar owned 15 per cent and Dubai 20 per cent, both of whom proved over the years to be supportive shareholders. He and the team had also worked to increase our reach and to bulk up the business; journeying to Russia and its old mineral-rich satellites like Kazakhstan so that those companies, as well as the newly rich, rapidly growing Chinese companies, came to our market rather than to New York. Despite all this hard work however in 2006 we were still a small company, trapped in a corner with no place to go. Having failed to buy LIFFE we were unable to break into derivative trading, where the growth was and remains. Nor could we find a way back into Clearing and Settlement, the lucrative back office processing of sales and purchases on the market.

In 2006 the first intimations reached us that a merger with the Borsa Italiana, driven by the Italian Ministry of Finance, might be possible. We were inclined to snatch this offer with both hands; the Borsa had only a small European cash equity business but we had over 50 per cent of that market. They had two key businesses we did not have: a well regarded, flourishing, fixed interest business, based on Italian government debt, and the most efficient clearing and settlement business in Europe, this last a necessity because they held at any one time most of the value in the Italian banking system.

We inspected this gift horse from every angle. I joined in in 2007 when I got back and met my delightful Italian colleagues, observing at a key meeting, with furrowed brow, if the Italian government limited their borrowing, the fixed interest business would be threatened. There was a pause while the Italian colleagues looked at each other, then all burst out laughing and assured me that that eventuality could be discounted; their government had been living beyond its means for years and wasn't about to stop. I compressed my lips like Mrs Thatcher for a moment before recalling that my own Labour government was also in the business of borrowing, albeit to fund the NHS and social security, and wasn't going to stop doing *that* any time soon either. I often think of this conversation as the governments of both countries struggle with imposing austerity on their citizenry.

Janet as Vice-Chairman of BorsaItaliana; *Professor Angelo Tantazzi,* BorsaItaliana *Chairman; Giorgio Napolitano, President of Italy (2006–2015).*

The Borsa while smaller than us was in the same size bracket so a merger was possible. They coveted our powerful cash equity business but also the Alternative Investment Market (AIM), which we had set up and regulated to provide a trading market for smaller companies on their way up. Northern Italy is full of clever small family-owned companies who do not grow beyond the capacity of the family to finance or manage them because Italians (unlike the Italian state) do not like to borrow money. The Italian Finance Ministry hoped that these companies would see their way to growth via equity and would also see the virtue of monetising their tightly-held shareholdings.

We edged slowly towards a deal, the English side startled and worried by the three-year staff contracts and ironclad union rules which were going to make rationalisation of our joint staff and cutting costs in Italy slow and expensive. The Italians were worried about all sorts of things but like us they were in a corner, small, successful, but unable to break into new markets. They too were much sought after and their Finance Ministry had staved off a bid from Deutsche Börse, who would have swallowed them whole. The French/American group, NYSE/Euronext, getting wind of our negotiations, indeed sought to derail the process at the eleventh hour by a direct offer to the Borsa executives in an attempt to bypass the Italian Treasury.

Valuations of the two companies were slowly agreed, on the basis of how many shares in the new company would be issued to the two participants, giving us about 55 per cent and the Borsa 45 per cent of the Group. As always, the social issues – who goes and who stays and who has which jobs where – were the problem. The new group enlarged its board to twelve and there was an agreement that for at least the first five years five members would be Italian citizens and seven UK citizens or UK residents. That meant that LSE acquired the Borsa's CEO, Massimo Capuano, and the Borsa Chairman, Dr Angelo Tantazzi, plus three new independent directors, all distinguished representatives of Italian business and Italian banking: Paolo Scaroni, who had held most senior business jobs in Italy including CEO of ENI, the company which owns all Italy's energy and energy distribution assets; Sergio Ermotti, then high in the ranks of Unicredito, Italy's biggest bank, who is now CEO of UBS; and Andrea Munari, then equally well placed in Intesa Sao Paolo, another key bit of the Italian banking system. Superbly trained and infinitely stylish they added brio and sophisticated intelligence to our equally capable but more stolid gang. Two of the longest-standing members of our Board, Peter Meinertzhagen and Michael Marks, had already left, and the committees were reorganised so Nigel Stapleton went back to chairing the Audit Committee and Rob Webb took over Remuneration, always a difficult committee because its duty is to stand between the cash and the executive. Rob always said he didn't really *do* numbers but that a long working career in the divorce courts had left him very good at difficult money issues. This gross over-simplification seeks to conceal Rob's first-class mind, his years as British Airways corporate counsel, and the barrister's ability to absorb a complex brief at high speed, which, combined with a cheerfully thuggish approach, makes him effective in any situation.

I was posted to the Board of the Borsa Italiana to be the sole non-executive representative of the main Board, along with two of our senior executives, and was courteously invited to be Vice Chairman. I was delighted, albeit anxious; the Borsa Board considers and decides on amendments of their market rules, the sort of detail which the LSEG Board never sees. I always made sure my LSE executive colleague had seen the papers, to ensure that I did not agree out of ignorance to some new way of assisting insider trading.

We learned quickly that Italy is painfully bureaucratic and lawyer driven. I wrote Chris a note after my second meeting to tell him that these were not meetings, or not as we knew them. The executive members had heard it all before, having prepared the papers, and all members, including the Italian non-executives, chatted throughout to each other throughout. If their phones rang they would answer them and only if the conversation became animated or personal would they retire to a corner of the room. An Italian chairman was expected to plough on, reading from a prepared script, with me and the other two Brits plus the mandatory Italian outside lawyer the only people listening in attentive silence. Even our three 'international' Italians were initially prone to take phone calls or chat to each other during meetings of the Group Board but slowly Chris persuaded them to stick to boring staid Anglo-Saxon rules. I think of those days as I watch an Italian congregation chatter through Mass in Milan Cathedral, breaking off to bend the knee or make the sign of the cross. It is a different style.

I have little Italian but took great pleasure in being able to say in Italian 'I am Vice Chairman of the Borsa Italiana and where is my car?' instead of as in beginner's German classes to ask how best I might arrive at the railway station. The language of the Borsa had been English for several years and they all spoke well. One of the excuses for the monoglot Brits is that the whole of Europe speaks better English than most of us will ever speak French, German or Italian. Jim was able to acquire and run a big German rail company for Balfour Beatty without a word of German because everyone spoke English, and this is a common experience.

I like Milan and went as often as possible though I can never look at its Cathedral without remembering that Isobel, on encountering its endlessly repeating rows of columns, had suggested it had been digitally remastered. I would sit in the square having coffee and looking at its stylishly dressed people and visit its elegant shops though none of the lovely clothes are available in much over a size 10. Even as a student I was a size 12 but I have friends of model elegance who can't buy in Milan either.

I had also agreed to take on the Chair at three small private UK companies. I knew my days in public companies were numbered and I was glad to be invited to work with old friends, the first being Anderson Cheng who I had met when I was doing Defence. He had put substantial funds into Inviseo, a small company that sold advertising on the back of the tray tables in aeroplanes. I was so charmed by the idea that I failed to do proper due diligence, so I found myself chairing a seriously loss-making company with a majority of disgruntled Swiss German investors and a very difficult business model. We had one contract with Germanwings, a successful small airline, which brought in some cash. We did have – and this looked very promising and indeed had enabled Anderson to refinance the company – a contract with Ryanair to equip the entire fleet with our tray tables.

The plan was that we would fit the trays into the planes at Ryanair's main hubs and we set ourselves up accordingly. It turned out that Ryanair replanned its schedules on a daily basis so that the aeroplanes we were waiting to fit were routinely diverted to pick up 300 travellers in Eastern Europe or Inverness or Spain or Germany. Our arrangements were completely disrupted and we could fit only about a fifth of the fleet over time. Companies that we had managed to persuade to advertise on these trays naturally pulled out, and the whole thing, despite Herculean efforts by our people, fell apart over two years. Our other sales efforts bore little fruit except, finally and too late, a decent contract with Flybe. The NEDs took no salaries to ensure that the executives got paid, but the business model simply didn't work. It was a waste of talent; all our executives were capable, innovative, hard-working people who were re-employed readily after we had to let them go.

Some of this failure can be blamed on the recession. I did not take proper account of the economic situation in 2007, but businesses depending on advertising revenues were the first to catch the cold blast.

One other factor was deeply unhelpful although I didn't see it at the time. Mike Kirkham, an experienced businessman who had worked with my old friend Liz Nelson at the firm she had founded, and I went together in 2009 to Zurich to talk to our Swiss German shareholders about a modest refinancing for the company. A boot-faced audience gazed at me and reacted not at all while I set out our stall, such as it was, and took questions along the lines of 'why should we put another Swiss Franc in the hands of such a hopelessly incompetent English management'. I closed off the meeting after twenty minutes of trying to get discussion going with a request that they would all please think whether they would prefer to put in a relatively moderate amount of cash or for us to close down the company. Mike, knowing I had an urgent meeting in London, said quietly, go, Janet, he would stay and see what he could do. So I went, shaking reluctant hands in the correct German manner learned from son Henry. I glanced back through the door as I left to see the audience clustered round Mike, and it was obvious from the body language that he was getting through where I had failed. We agreed in a full and frank discussion afterwards that the representatives of the Zurich financial community there assembled had not heard a word I said largely because I was female. Mike managed to come away with reluctant agreement to putting up a bit more cash but the whole episode brought back times I thought had gone for ever with the 1970s. One day Swiss women will sort out their men but news from that front suggests there is much work to be done.

I agreed to chair another private company, Trillium. This was started by an ex-colleague from my days in the HSBC corporate finance department, Stephen Routledge, with another friend, Philip Mastriforte, also from banking. They were both refugees from the chaos they could see coming in the big banks, both highly competent men in their early forties who wanted to advise small and medium size media firms. The Charterhouse corporate finance department had been built on advising that size of company. In 2007 as a smaller company advised by Rothschilds or Lazards you would be lucky to see the team leader after the day you had signed up, whereas at Charterhouse the man you saw when you signed was always available, and I liked the idea of chairing another group that would do that.

We all knew that a two-principal firm was sub-optimal, and Philip and Stephen had secured finance from a small long-established group of investors in order to grow. We started up in business just as the full force of the recession hit in 2008. The companies we had hoped to advise ran for cover, abandoned plans to expand, hoarded their cash, and went on doing so for the next five or six years. We missed all our targets; we couldn't recruit extra people and it became clear over eighteen months that we were not going to be able to pay our creditors or remunerate our principal investors, so we put the company into administration, a new and distressing experience for me. As Directors we put up enough money to buy the assets out of administration and enable the executive directors to complete one deal which meant that they could start again, with everyone taking heavy reductions in salary or continuing in post unpaid. The reconstituted company survived the recession but was unable to expand or grow until very recently.

To complete a trio of disasters, I also became Chairman designate of Freshwater, a small Welsh PR company. I was invited by one of my Labour Party friends who was a director and his Welsh CEO, with the intent of floating the company on AIM. I cleared the appointment with Chris Gibson-Smith, as I was required to, and we both agreed it would be interesting and useful to have a main board director of LSEG get firsthand experience of what it was like to exist in the secondary market. This company too was a casualty of the recession – Public Relations turns out to be another service that companies in difficulty decide they can do without. After eighteen months I stood down as Chairman in favour of a fellow NED, but in the end the company had to be taken over by another.

On the home front 2007 was a better year. Son Richard, then 32, approached Jim and me to help him by jointly becoming his Executive Coaches. He had done a degree in sculpture but was finding he could not follow his intended career as an artist. We refused initially, feeling that parents should not be Executive Coaches any more than they should be therapists, but Richard pointed out we knew him very well and had matchless contacts in every business field between us. So we conducted formal meetings with the dear son, during which we established that he needed to find employment within a group of people and in a field with a strong artistic content. We jointly arrived at a spectrum of possibilities from theatrical set designer at one end to architect at the other, via interior decorator and commissioner for arts festivals in the middle.

Set design was easy; we knew nothing at all about it but there was my friend and colleague Dave Murphy at the Cambridge Arts Theatre. Richard came away from two hours with Dave knowing that a life where you worked – if at all – as a freelance, much of it by yourself, and which involved continual travel in the UK and Europe, was not for him. Indeed he was so horrified that he turned down a good job at the theatre, Dave having correctly identified the capable all-rounder sat before him.

Neither of us knew any interior decorators at that stage, but we did know a London architect, Elsie Owusu, a contact of Jim's and also one of the senior women of the Links gang. We Links routinely tried to help with each other's children, so I approached her to ask could her firm provide work experience for our son to enable him to decide where best to use his talents. 'Of course, Janet, any child of yours', she said warmly. 'How old is he?' 'Er, well, 32', I said feebly, and eyeing me uneasily Elsie told me it was the practice at Feilden+Mawson, her firm, to take Work Experience graduate trainees for a maximum of three months, paying them very little, at the end of which they either employed them or asked them to leave. I said that seemed very fair and I hoped and believed that our Richard would be useful, adding that I thought he was a project manager apart from his other talents. Richard joined them and within four weeks had become indispensable and was on the payroll. He is very capable, as we knew, and turned out to be able to put together bids for large contracts and indeed, in the case of the contract to furnish the new Supreme Court, to run one as well. He found full-time employment a huge relief after a freelance poorly paid existence, and flourished there.

His employment also had a directly useful effect for us. We had begun to realise that it was unrealistic to expect our friend and architectural adviser of many years, David Ashton-Hill, to complete the design and supervise the massive contract involved in reuniting the two halves of our house in Cambridge and in bringing it up to date from its 1911 origins, which would involve re-roofing, re-wiring, re-plumbing and re-doing virtually everything else. David had moved to Lincolnshire to build a house for himself and his second wife on a family-owned plot, it was two and a half hours' hard driving to get to us, and he was a one-man practice, with no one to do the drawings and specifications for him. Regretfully, early in 2008 we agreed that we would have to say goodbye and that the job of finishing the design, writing the spec, finding a builder and supervising them would have to be undertaken by a Cambridge firm with several people in it who could be deployed to manage.

The Cambridge branch of Feilden+Mawson accepted the challenge. An efficient, brisk Chinese woman, one of the senior partners in Cambridge, and an older man appeared to see me (Jim was elsewhere but had insisted we must Get On). I handed over all the drawings we had and explained why we were having to change the principal architect. The woman partner gazed at the drawings with the expression of one faced with a pile of mediaeval manuscripts. 'But these are hand drawn,' she said, with barely concealed incredulity, and explained kindly that computerised drawings which could be quickly amended were needed for every part of the process. I felt overtaken by Life; we were used to hand-done sketches, and, sister and daughter of architects, I really wanted someone who could draw.

Richard must have explained about his desperately old-fashioned parents because the older man, David Yandell, gently took over the meeting and explained that he was not much younger than us, on the verge of retirement, and would be very glad of a large project in Cambridge and yes, he had all the resources of the Cambridge office at his back, and yes, of course he could draw, indeed the sketch was his preferred medium of communication. He had been trained in the School of Architecture in Cambridge, narrowly not overlapping with brother Alexander, and he liked and spoke admiringly of the other David his predecessor's designs. He started as soon as he could to organise us and get all the other advisers in place and above all to get planning consent.

The house was designed by one of the foremost Arts and Crafts designers of the late nineteenth and early twentieth centuries, Charles Baillie Scott. It is Grade 2 listed, which means going through several layers of planning consent to get anything done. It is additionally complicated by the fact that, although we own the freehold, St John's College has substantial planning control over what takes place, given to them as a concession in the Leasehold Reform Act of 1976. There were days when reconciling St John's College's desire not to let any improvement take place that would render it more difficult to exercise their putative right to buy it at market price from us for Educational Purposes, the demands of English Heritage and the Cambridge City planners' requirements with the task of turning two crudely divided parts of the same draughty cold house, offering between them seven bedrooms and two bathrooms, into a warm and comfortable five-bedroom, four-bathroom establishment looked impossible. David Yandell got there by perseverance and because of his deep knowledge of and respect for conservation, which meant everybody involved felt that this conversion was in safe hands. Even St John's College yielded in the end and we came to an amicable deal where we gave them money and they agreed to the proposed modern extension, a design masterpiece built over a slippery courtyard. I felt, throughout, like the man who, asking his way to Brighton, was advised not to start from there. Left to myself I would have started again somewhere else but Jim, who had known and stayed on and off in the house from childhood, pointed out that there were few good houses from which you could walk to the centre of the city because the University or its colleges own much of the centre and guard it jealously. I caved in when he started wondering aloud about a house in one of the surrounding villages. I have lived in central London since I was a week old and was already a bit uncertain about Cambridge but I knew village life would be beyond me.

In 2007 the Management Consulting Board was in difficulty. We had bought a large French consultancy, Ineum, to add weight to an unbalanced stable of consultancies. We had nothing much in Europe, but we did have the long-established, profitable and enduring Proudfoot in the USA, a smaller consultancy in London, and operations in Australia and South Africa to exploit Proudfoot's historic mining experience.

The recession however was starting to take its toll; companies also give up management consultants in a slowdown. The purchase of Ineum had proved an instant disaster because, already locked in internecine dissent, their Board extended the war to Kevin Parry, our CEO, our Board and the other consultancies. Rolf and Kevin were increasingly unpopular with investors who objected to the heavy load of debt caused by the Ineum purchase, our wavering profit record, our falling share price, and what they saw as the unreasonably large salary we paid Kevin and the size of the main Board.

I had indicated to Rolf Stomberg my intention of leaving the Board at the 2008 Annual General Meeting in May. I was the Senior Independent Director (SID), a controversial piece of corporate governance which requires all quoted companies to appoint a director as an alternative channel for shareholders who feel they are failing to get through to the Chairman. In 2004, I had been the only choice available; our long-standing NED, JP, a distinguished Boston consultant, was based in the USA, and the other NED was not getting on with Rolf and was to leave a year later. The Board had however since been strengthened with the recruitment of three heavy-duty NEDs, Steve Ferriss, English-born, who had worked all his life in Latin American banking; Andrew Simon, a trilingual graduate of all sorts of British businesses, who was doing a brilliant job, in perfect French, on mediating the issues with Ineum; and Alan Barber, lately senior worldwide partner of KPMG and an old acquaintance of mine, so I thought it would be acceptable for me to abandon ship. The Board agreed that we would sell Ineum to the managers, and with a reduced Board trade on as a smaller group, mostly consisting of Proudfoot, as it had back in 2004. It was a retreat but it was at least a plan.

It foundered immediately. The day after the Board meeting in February 2008, the Ineum directors made common cause with our principal shareholder, Gartmore – who had opposed the last pay rise for Kevin and had never been happy with Rolf – and demanded their resignation and the reconstitution of the Board. Rolf called an emergency Board meeting to deal with the crisis but the only members of the Board physically present in London were Rolf himself, Kevin, me and a very newly appointed finance director, Craig Smith. I came in to find our merchant bank advisory team Rothschilds installed in force. They had assembled our top adviser, no mean feat in itself, as well as the rest of the team, in a conference room and got the four absent NEDs attached to telephones in Boston (JP), California (Steve), Geneva (Andrew) and Tokyo (Alan), all at the same time. Rolf opened the meeting by announcing that he and Kevin were going to resign and nobody could stop them. Long experience enabled me to thank them both gracefully for their service, accept their resignations, and to ask our advisers to offer us an update and their views on the situation generally. Rothschilds had by then talked to Gartmore and a couple of other shareholders and relayed their views that the company had to be stabilised under the leadership of an Executive Chairman who would run the company while searching urgently for a new CEO. Normally of course, as Rothschilds observed, it would be the SID who would undertake this role.

I realised that I was staring down the barrel of a gun; I knew, absolutely, that I could not manage to be Executive Chairman for any length of time, requiring as it would travel continuously round New York, Miami, London and Paris to re-organise groups of warring men. Rothschilds added that they knew I had intended to step down at the AGM and if this was still my intention I would have to go now. Tempting though this option was, it wouldn't do and I knew it, I had taken the money for three years and the only proper course of action was to stay and do my best.

I reminded the meeting that I was 67 and heavily committed elsewhere, but would take on the job if I were the only candidate we could find on the Board. Addressing myself to the black triangle on the table, through which my fellow directors in several different time zones were able to communicate, I asked formally all four of the other non-executive directors to see if we could do any better than me. The black triangle crackled and JP refused on the unassailable grounds that he was even older than I, resident in the USA, and this was a company quoted in London. Steve managed an equally prompt refusal on the basis that he spent much of his year in the USA, and Andrew also turned down this dubious honour on grounds of age and other commitments. I said a short prayer before calling on Alan, much our best candidate given his previous experience, who said, wearily because it was some ungodly hour in Tokyo, that he would consider the role but would have to think very carefully about the terms. It was clear I needed to talk to him privately so Rothschilds found me a room and a phone. Craig, our new FD, followed me out of the room to tell me that he would like to resign too. I absolutely understand, I said warmly, but could you hang on while I do this phone call.

Alan is a clever man with years and years of experience of managing temperamental people. We agreed a decent salary straight away and that he should fly first class on long haul because he would be doing a lot of that and his back was failing. I agreed to stay on in the interests of stability. Alan persuaded Craig to stay on and help for a limited time, so I was able to report to the meeting that we had an Executive Chairman and a Finance Director and to receive congratulations from a much relieved Rothschilds and my Board colleagues. We then settled to the work of producing a Press Notice that would convince any reader that this had been an orderly process and that the ship was under control, and there at last I was on home ground, removing all adverbs and most of the adjectives from the Rothschilds draft to produce the spare Civil Service bone-dry drafting that can render everything, including the outbreak of war, everyday and unexciting.

Talking to other colleagues I was able to think I was not so stupidly unprepared for a crisis as I had felt; all sorts of enterprises go along nicely until a concatenation of troubles – a perfect storm in the current phrase – catches everyone unawares. At that point nothing will save you except a lot of luck or good colleagues and I had both, but it was a dreadful moment. Alan, steadily, found an experienced CEO, some new money and new shareholders. We all persuaded Ineum to settle down and be the high-quality colleagues we all hoped for, and I was still on the Board for another three years.

After the events at Management Consulting I was relieved to be only a spectator while the BPP Group, under a new Chairman, was sold to a large American corporate, the Apollo Group, owner of the University of Phoenix. Charlie Prior had always thought it likely that once BPP had degree awarding powers it would attract suitors, and so it proved; both the Apollo Group and the Pearson Group bid for us but the Americans bid £2 per share over the Pearson offer. It quickly became clear that there was little synergy between BPP and its new owners. The University of Phoenix was and is a huge organisation teaching entirely on line while BPP was and is very much smaller, heavily regulated, and teaches face to face. The deal however worked well for both parties. Once the Americans had realised that we really were not equipped to take over a 48,000- strong business university in India or make a useful contribution to an art college in Chile but if left to ourselves would go on producing steady profits without running foul of our regulators, they did leave us to get on with it and we outlasted and proved much more profitable than many of their more ambitious investments.

Professor David Holmes, Janet and Professor Martyn Jones at BPP University Graduation Ceremony 2017.

Chapter 20

THE GREAT CRASH 2008–2009

I was in a position to understand the reality of the financial disaster looming over us from early in 2007, as a Chairman of the Sub-committee on European Wholesale Finance and Trade, a director of two publicly quoted companies, three private companies and a substantial regional theatre as well as President of a new university, but I did not get the recession in focus or accept how serious it was until September 2008. At the domestic level Jim and I were still earning a lot of money and could afford to pay our bills, support our younger children and plan an expensive conversion to a house in Cambridge. I suppose we were both far too busy to allow any time for sustained concentration on the economic front, but I hope we reacted sensibly when the recession finally appeared in 2008, like the Big Bad Wolf, to try and blow our house down.

This was the year when it became clear that brother Alexander needed more help than he was getting, and that his kitchen – in which he spent most of his waking hours rather than in a small but well-organised living room – needed complete refurbishing to encompass a separate washing machine and tumble dryer and a dishwasher, so that the carers could cope without leaving him surrounded by damp washing. It also needed a new boiler and an electric rather than a gas stove for safety's sake. The whole process, intended to take ten days, stretched to four weeks, while he stayed with us in Cambridge. I managed with help from Devine and everyone else whom I could pressgang into service to ensure he took his pills and ate on the days when I had to be in London, but it stretched us all to the limits. Giles offered to come and take over for a week so Jim and I could go on a long-planned holiday in Anghiari to cheer on Southbank Sinfonia who were then and remain the resident orchestra and lynchpin of the Anghiari Festival, but three days before he was due to fly to our side, his wife Elisabeth tripped and fell on the stairs down to her kitchen, breaking an ankle and smashing three teeth, so Giles was needed where he was. We cobbled together a Plan C, calling in every favour I was owed so that Al would be safe and fed and Jim could have what turned out to be an urgent emergency operation for a slipped disc, while Isobel and I got to Anghiari. It was a neat illustration of the assets and liabilities of having family; one member gets sick or old and puts weight on the rest but if there are enough of you the strain can be shared out.

By October 2008 we were worrying about Isobel and Nick Bailey, her then fiancé. Nick, a Cambridge-trained engineer, had been introduced to Isobel at one of her dance shows and they had got together immediately and had bought a small house ten minutes away from us in Cambridge. Nick was running a small boatbuilding business but he had managed to convince a mortgage company to lend him cash, and Isobel had cash in the bank from the sale of her London flat. The house was certainly in need of repair and renewal but all they seemed to do was to knock down walls, and there was no sign of Nick displaying his advertised skills as a handyman.

We were also much occupied with finalising the design and getting planning consent for putting our Cambridge house into shape. Thanks to the untiring help of David Yandell who kept us and a huge programme of work at Keble College, Oxford, both moving forward, we had reached a specification and were biting our fingernails over four bids for the work on our house, wondering whether we should stay in our half of an increasingly decrepit house and continue to let the other side of it to people hardy and competent enough to manage with a creaking heating system, questionable wiring and old rickety furnishings. In the end we decided to go ahead with the conversion and also that it would be worth renting a flat for ourselves in Cambridge in order to be able to keep an eye on the work.

My diary records that Jim and I did have one sensible discussion about the recession, on our way to the Faenol (pronounced Vinyl) Festival. This was only its second year; it took place about 30 miles away from our cottage in Wales, in a field near Caernarfon. It was fronted by Bryn Terfel, and there were 7000 of us in the field and a lot of BBC people, who were there to record enough material for one *Songs of Praise* and another separate programme for S4C. The singers were in a tent, the great Bryn, Katherine

Jenkins, and Aled Jones. It also featured a Welsh conductor who knew, absolutely, that he could get 7000 of us to sing hymns, led by Bryn, in four parts and in Welsh, and the strength of his conviction was such that his audience, taken out of themselves, joined in, all of them, including the tone deaf and the monoglot English speakers.

We went home from this peaceful and uplifting entertainment to the financial crisis made manifest. On September 22 Lehman Brothers went into Chapter 11, which gave them shelter from their creditors, but it was clear that only a bailout from the US Government could keep them in being; so interdependent was the US banking system that if Lehman's were to continue not paying their creditors in other financial institutions, then those too would be in danger. Against precedent – and against advice from many sources – the US Government decided not to save Lehman's and the financial crisis ran abruptly out of control. The newspapers were once more full of alarming headlines when, over a weekend, the Bank of England and the Treasury had to put together a deal to underpin our tottering banks. This was, finally, we understood, the other shoe dropping after the run on Northern Rock which had happened almost twelve months before. I had been shopping in Cambridge when I was arrested by the sight of long queues of people outside the local branch of the Northern Rock. I had stopped and stared; but my distinguished economist colleague, John Eatwell, Master of Queens' College, had crossed the road, introduced himself to the queue and asked its members how much they had on deposit with the bank. The answers varied from amounts like £7,000, representing a vital piece of saving, to investment sums of £200,000 plus, all attracted by Northern Rock's offer of relatively high interest rates. This was not just Northern Rock running into well-deserved – and containable – trouble but the first blast of the storm which was going to threaten the whole financial system. I assumed that the regulators would insist on combining them with some better-run and more conservative organisation, as would have happened in the early1990s, when we were regulated by the Building Societies Commission under my distinguished friend Rosalind Gilmore. Northern Rock, which had formed itself into a bank, was however now under the much less competent and detailed supervision of the FSA. Had the Bank of England and the FSA not been asleep at the wheel it would have been perfectly possible to prop up

Northern Rock and put in new management or get one of the bigger banks to absorb them. Nothing – or nothing that the regulators could have done by September 2008 – could have averted the storm unleashed in the USA, but it could all have been better controlled. The authorities in the USA also handled the crisis badly; they were on the wrong foot; it was an election year and the last gasp of the George W. Bush administration. The American political classes, entirely fixated either on getting Barack Obama elected or on keeping him out, had delegated the task of dealing with the worst financial crisis since 1929 to the Treasury and Alan Greenspan. The decision to let Lehman's go was Alan Greenspan's, and we know, because he told everyone, that he was driven by considerations of Moral Hazard, the doctrine which holds that lax and corrupt bankers should have to bear the full consequences of their behaviour. This consideration reportedly had also kept Mervyn King, Governor of the Bank of England, from doing anything sensible about Northern Rock. The problem is that by 2008 sinners and saints, rich and poor, all lived in an interlinked financial world. Punishing the careless bankers of Northern Rock or Lehman Brothers by letting their institutions go into bankruptcy threatened other financial institutions, to the point where the only groups that could support the whole organism were governments, with their access to taxpayer bases. By the time the US Treasury understood this it was too late, Lehman's was gone, and the backlash threatened the entire financial system of the USA and Europe. Over the following weekend in September Gordon Brown, as Prime Minister, had had to lead a team of Treasury Ministers plus the Governor of the Bank of England and officials from both to shore up the system so that people in the UK would be able to draw cash from their accounts on the Monday morning. It was that close; a year later I went to a conference at Ditchley Park, at which I met an old acquaintance, Sir John Gieve. John, just retired as Permanent Secretary at the Treasury, told a group of us about that September weekend in vivid detail. They had believed we had an understanding with our American colleagues which, as so often with the Special Relationship, turned out not to be the case. At least we in the UK had a stable political structure and a Prime Minister in Gordon Brown who understood the banking system and who did not need to deal with an election any time soon, unlike the Americans, and we weathered the storm. The

Americans, terrified by how close they had come to disaster, managed to agree – just, and only at the second time of asking, in October 2008 – to pass the TARP legislation which put the plug back in the dam in the USA.

In 2008 I stared at the News and the headlines in the papers like a rabbit looking at a snake, then went back to parochial concerns, raising my head only to rejoice unconditionally at the election of Barack Obama in November to be President of the USA. He arrived at a dreadful time, economically and politically, but there he was, a black man in the highest office. I remembered the people, black and white, who had died in the 1960s challenging the law on registering black voters, and the still segregated barracks in Fort Gordon, Georgia, in 1966, less than fifty years before, and my heart lifted. The News featured black people in the USA, as incredulous as I was, weeping with joy. It was a series of great moments.

A week or so after the crisis had passed I went to a hastily convened all-party meeting at the House of Lords. It was intended to brief us all on the financial crisis and featured a panel of Terry Burns, ex-Treasury, my colleague John Eatwell and Robert Skidelsky, the economic historian. Robert, I recorded at the time, warned us against complacency, saying that the history of the 1930s depression was one of many false dawns when recovery seemed at hand. This current crisis was likely to be the same, and would be likely to endure 'for some time'. We all listened gloomily but I don't think anyone took from the meeting the perception that it would be 2014 before the dawn light looked reasonably secure.

At the LSEG our new issues business had shrunk to nothing and trading had slumped. We had a doom-filled November Board in which we were also collectively worrying about whether our low share price would tempt NYSE/Euronext or another known predator to bid for us. The debate was totally changed by Paolo Scaroni, who, exasperated, called on us all to stop worrying about this issue.

'These are terrible times, Chris,' he said, crossly. 'No one is going to bid for us, they are all huddled against the storm. And we should be looking to our balance sheet and our cash.' Truth sat in the room and we did as he said. I said later to Chris, so must a mediaeval Chancellor have warned his King and his associates that this was not the time to think about war with

France, could we please check the stores and repair the walls on all our castles.

Gordon Brown was also in the business of repairing breaches and getting all his people into the same castle and he recruited Peter Mandelson to the colours, appointing him to the Lords and returning him as Secretary of State for Business to his old department. It was not just members of the Blairite wing of the Labour Party who were delighted to see Peter back; the civil servants of the Department of Business and Industry crowded into the lobby of 1 Victoria Street, spilling over onto the pavement outside, to clap him in on his first day, a scene unprecedented in my adult lifetime. The PM found him both popular and useful in many roles as the autumn wore on; as the sardonic Tom Strathclyde, leader of the Conservative Party in the Lords, observed, Peter quickly became not only a Secretary of State but Minister for Practically Everything Else.

Early in 2009 it became clear that Isobel's life was in crisis. The house continued to be in such disarray that I could hardly stand to go there, mess, plaster, tools everywhere and no discernible progress being made with any of it. In the spring of 2009, I offered her a Mummy Day – the one where without comment or criticism I do or assist with every chore I am asked. We did the best we could with tidying the house. We threw away old papers and a stack load of expensive flyers for her last production. We found a dry cleaner and gave them the bag in the back of her car which had been there for the last three months. I was truly worried; this was depression looking at me and I couldn't see what to do about it. I made us coffee having washed all the cups first and we sat down at the newly cleared table by the French window, my eye distracted by a pile of miscellaneous junk and rubble just outside in the ragged garden.

'I can't go on with dancing', she said, swallowing a too-hot mouthful of coffee. 'I have to do something else, I have to get a degree, only I'm not going to spend three years doing it.'

I managed to keep my head and wonder aloud, and reasonably casually, whether it would be worth a chat with the Admissions Tutor at the Lucy Cavendish College, the college for mature women next door to our house. I was an Honorary Fellow and it happened that I had the phone number on me, I added. She made the call and went off to be interviewed, leaving me to clean the rest of the kitchen, then appeared back, beaming, to report that they had said they would be happy to offer her a place that September to read English provided she did an Open University course to get her back into essay writing. And of course it would be a three-year course; Cambridge University was not going to recognise a Diploma from the London Studio Centre.

I was there and provided the contact and the phone number but it turned out that she had been struggling with this decision for some time and that it was Dave at the Cambridge Arts Theatre she had consulted first. He had again found time in a day when there was none to do Career Guidance for one of our children. His take on a liberal arts education (he had done accountancy at university) was as always worth having; he had listened for a long time while she bemoaned the parlous state of Contemporary Dance and her own difficulty in getting her work to an audience but she could not bear to give up. Surely, he said, she could keep up a dance career while reading a few books and writing a few essays, couldn't she? This reductionist view had got straight through to our daughter, who had never had any trouble with academic work. She would not have taken it from Jim or me and in return we do both try to receive other people's children at horribly inconvenient times to wear us out while they feverishly seek Guidance.

We hoped that with Isobel's future at the Lucy Cavendish settled, things would settle down, but she and Nick were quarrelling all the time, and the house was a slum despite all our best efforts and Devine going up to clean for them. Isobel was wretched although looking forward to doing a degree and taking pleasure in doing the reading. Finally a great truth dawned on us all; Nick's boatbuilding business was not just struggling, it was bust and he had not been able to admit it to anyone. He had no money; in a last desperate throw he had put the cash Isobel had put up to equalise up her share of the house into the business, but it was all gone. Jim put aside other concerns to help him reach a way forward, out of the mess, and persuaded him to apply for a Creditors' Voluntary Liquidation and put in a professional liquidator. It was now clear why the house was such a mess – Nick had had neither the time nor the cash to do anything about any of it, and he had never brought himself to reveal the problem to our capable and business-like daughter. The company was duly wound up, and Nick went straight out and got a good job in one of the small growing engineering consultancies which flourish in Cambridge. We were truly pleased for them both and hoped that as the house became habitable the relationship would be alright.

Freed from those concerns, we were spending any spare moments struggling to get rid of Stuff; we had never cleared the house properly after the death of Jim's parents in the late 1990s and the sale of our London house in 1999, postponing all difficult decisions by hiding furniture, books, papers and pictures away in the huge Cambridge attics.

It was the attics that brought my downfall. Ten days before the contractors were due to start, late on a Sunday afternoon in March 2009 Jim discovered some *more* Stuff half-hidden at the far end of the attics. So, once again, I climbed up the steep awkward loft ladder and wearily received yet one more unwieldy bundle. I had it clasped to my chest with one hand, using the other to hold onto the wobbly hand rail, when the bundle fell apart, I tried to catch it and fell down the last four feet of the ladder, backwards, landing painfully against the wall opposite the foot of the ladder.

At the time it seemed as if I had got away with it; I took a couple of pills and went round for a drink with our immediate neighbours, then got myself off to our London flat the next day. The week was full of things I wanted to do, including the first graduation ceremony for BPP University College. I was due to award an Honorary Doctorate to Charlie Prior, my old colleague and co-founder of the accountancy training business, onlie begetter and tireless supporter of the BPP Law School, and the man with the vision to insist on combining the two in a university. The other Honorary Doctor – a coup for the new group – was David Neuberger, another friend of many years' standing who was later to become President of the Supreme Court. I had to cancel – I could have done it with a temperature of 100+° but not with the accompanying tummy bug. I left the decision as late as I possibly could knowing that Martyn Jones, the head of the Academic Council, could take over for me effortlessly, while I lay at home in bed, weeping with disappointment. I got myself back to Cambridge at the end of the week, worrying about a rash that I seemed to be developing, and trying to prepare in order to lead a session at Newnham College the next day. I woke to find that Isobel was with us, having arrived, in tears, at 2 a.m. and just managed to wake Jim by throwing stones at the window. She had left Nick, she told us, and loyally we consoled her and unpacked linen we had tidily packed away so she could be comfortable and promised her the spare room in our Cambridge flat. Devoted as I am to her, no visitation could have been less welcome; our house was still not clear of Stuff with the removal men due on Monday.

I was also hiding from the realisation that the rash and the fever and the livid bruise on my back were the symptoms of the ITP which had felled me in 2005 and ruined a holiday in Cuba. I got through the talk at Newnham but the next day the rash was worse and I had blood in my urine. We didn't then have a GP in Cambridge, and it was Sunday morning, but the NHS rose to the occasion; the GP-staffed night and weekend service CAMDOC sent me to Medical Admissions at Addenbrooke's, where blood was taken and an MRI scan of The Bruise because they feared kidney damage, to which I had given no thought. I came out of the scan to find two doctors showing each other the blood tests with every sign of interest and pleasure. Most people have a platelet count of between 100 and 200; at this point I had 2 and, as they said warmly, Haematology was looking forward to having me. And the kidneys looked alright but in the fall I had chipped off the ends of several vertebrae so my back probably did hurt, yes. And I had done all this a week ago and had not thought to seek medical help? I was given a room to myself in Haematology, which worried me. My father-in-law Dick had always said that if you were seriously ill the only place to be was in a bed next to the nursing station where if you turned blue or fell out of bed you would be visible to all. Jim had to leave me, desperate to get back and clear the remaining bits of the house.

I had time, unwelcome amounts of it, to think. I had been felled by serious illness, again. This time I had not ruined a family holiday but I was about to leave several organisations and my exhausted husband well and truly in the lurch and, again, you could only say that I had brought it on myself. I was in my 69th year; did I think I was immortal; I tossed and turned, remembering the look on the admitting doctor's face, until I took the offered sleeping pill.

The next day I woke, and my diary records that by 11 a.m. I had made ten phone calls to my various associates. Mike Kirkham agreed to chair the Inviseo meeting, Jim told me to go away because he was surrounded by Removal Men but was relieved to be told I was in no need of visitors. Rob Whiteway, my clerk at the Lords, reeled at the news that I might be out of commission for weeks when we were in the middle of re-drafting a Report, but another phone call rallied my good colleague Ken Woolmer to agree to take over for me once more.

I rang Dave Murphy who was alarmed by the prospect of having his Chairman incapacitated but matter of factly agreed to arrive bringing with him two nighties from Marks and Spencer. I was not short of visitors. Jim arrived briefly every day to bring me up to date on his struggle to get us finally out of the big house and into our little flat, involving several different vans moving in different directions. He would then fall asleep in a chair on one side of the bed, leaving the other chair for a weeping Isobel or a distressed Nick. Dave arrived the next day bearing nighties as requested, chocolates, and the news that he had managed to reach a deal whereby he would close the theatre restaurant on the fourth floor, and redirect the theatre audience to the Chop House on King's Parade, large and well-run enough to feed all our customers pre-theatre, in exchange for them buying advertising in our brochures. I threw the traditional theatrical tantrum (how could you *do* this to me, close our treasured restaurant, when I am flat on my back in hospital), but my heart was not in it. The rules of catering are inexorable and running a restaurant on the fourth floor where no one can see it as they pass cannot work unless you can somehow make it an expensive Destination Restaurant, and a theatre audience in Cambridge doesn't want that, they want a decent meal, quickly served, before the show. Dave, professionally unmoved by tantrums even from his Chairman, reminded me that we were trading on the patience of the Charity Commissioners who are correctly opposed to charities supported by the taxpayer losing money on peripheral activities, and went back to sort out a hole in the programme.

The day after this I was moved out into the main ward; I wasn't much better but I was not as ill as the next incomer; most Haematology patients are there because they have cancer, or leukaemia or an imbalance of the blood often associated with chemotherapy, and I was much better off than most. On this thought the phone rang and it was old friend and ex-lodger Louis McCagg, who did have cancer, asking to come and see me. I demurred, feebly; I had been tired by the move, but Louis said he was only downstairs, in Oncology, and it would only be for a few minutes. We had all got into the way of thinking that Louis,

316

diagnosed four years before with cancer and given a year to live, had either been misdiagnosed or had, by grace of the NHS and the existence of sheer will power, dispelled the cancer. Not so, of course, and as Louis lowered his skinny 6' 5" into a small hospital chair I saw that he had bad news.

'They say I can't go to Wyoming', he said, without asking how I was, shaken out of his natural courtesy. 'They say 7000 feet is too high and I won't be able to breathe.'

We were both silenced by this disaster; Louis treasured the four months he spent every summer in his log cabin in Wyoming and it provided a vital respite from his small flat in Cambridge. And the cancer must be getting the upper hand; no one had suggested that altitude was a danger before. Louis was eleven years older than I but I felt a cold warning for myself as I looked at him and saw that he was even thinner and that he was wheezing even in a warm ward. I thought of my mother, fighting for breath in an asthma attack, and holding his hand told Louis that it was too frightening not to be able to get breath into the lungs and that he would have to accept the doctor's verdict. We would give him a holiday in the UK somewhere, as would others, where he would not be breathless or frightened and would have the mighty Addenbrooke's to fall back on rather than being dependent on the local hospital in Sheridan, Wyoming, a town of only 26,000 souls. Characteristically, by the next day Louis had talked to family and friends and resigned himself and was making other plans. I think that my father-in-law would have said the same as I did; he believed that idle optimism was a waste of time, and the truth, gently but clearly delivered, is the only thing that works for the seriously ill.

Then I had to consider whether I too had joined the ranks of those who were suffering a life-threatening illness. This particular attack of ITP took many long weeks to settle but my platelets slowly restored themselves and it became clear that this was not a chronic problem meaning that I would have to accept crippling restrictions on my activities, but instead a warning, an episode which was telling me to consider my life and my future.

So I resigned from the three small companies I had taken on in 2007, all of which needed a chairman in good health to give them a chance of survival. My friend Ken Woolmer took over Sub-committee A for the eight weeks of the Summer term. Four chairmen said they assumed I would recover and they would give me time, and I managed, just, to get to Board meetings with the papers read. I gathered Alexander's sons Matthew and Luke and told them that I would have to give up trying to share responsibility for their father. In 1999 I had felt it impossible to load the full responsibility on young men of 19 and 29 with their way to make, but ten years later they and I felt they could cope, and of course they have. And I settled down to write these Memoirs.

Chapter 21

2010–2015 RETIREMENT AND GRANDCHILDREN

After being hospitalised with ITP in 2009 I was still well below par in August 2010. I was struggling with breathlessness which all assumed to be asthma, like my mother and grandmother before me. After six months on inhalers which had no discernible effect, an ECG revealed I had atrial flutter, where a patch of cells in the heart causes one piece to beat at anything up to 300 per minute (my normal heartbeat is 65), which will stop you in your tracks gasping, at best, and at worst can cause heart failure or stroke. I was immediately put on Warfarin, sent off to the Royal Brompton Hospital and interdicted from flying, running and bicycling or in any way exerting myself until I could have an Ablation early in 2011. This procedure is high tech, involving putting a wire with a soldering iron on the end of it up from the groin and destroying the rogue cells in the heart. It took less than an hour and Jim was thrilled to receive a wife back with normal pink colouring, entirely different from the white-faced, blue-round-the-lips woman to whom he had said goodbye that morning. Another triumph for modern medicine and another reason to be thankful that I was born in 1940, not 1840 or even 1920. Tony Blair, as PM, had had the same operation over a weekend in the same hospital in about 2001.

I had decided to retire and tried to do so in 2010 before anything else could happen. At LSEG we were considering a merger with the Canadian Stock Exchange, and if it had come off either Rob Webb or I as the two longest serving NEDs would have had to stand down, along with Chris. I volunteered; Rob is eight years younger than I, likes flying, as befits an ex-General Counsel of British Airways, and, critically, would have chaired the Remuneration Committee. I was opposed to the deal; I had been sent off with Rob to interview the Canadian chairman who would have headed up the joint company and been unimpressed, regarding him as a poor exchange for Chris. The merger would have involved huge overstretch with our people trying to manage in places between eight and fifteen hours' flight time away from base. In the event to my relief a consortium of Canadian banks decided they did not want their home Exchange controlled from overseas and outbid us.

Immediately after that deal collapsed our CEO Xavier Rolet went into the delicate task of acquiring 60 per cent of the London Clearing House, which was, unlike the Canadian deal, critical to our strategy. The French authorities did not want a British-owned Exchange to have a majority shareholding and LCH directors would have preferred independence. It took the clever, tireless, and above all *French*, Xavier to reassure all parties and get the deal done, and it was to be another three years before all was finally completed.

In the event I stayed on the Board till July 2013 when I was 73 and the LCH deal done, and was still Vice Chairman of the Borsa Italiana until the end of my seven-year term in June 2014. I was succeeded on the LSEG Board by three female NEDs in 2013 so it is possible to feel that I have not lived in vain. The Borsa Italiana also made huge progress during the time that I was on the Board, although that is down to Management. By 2011 we had managed to improve the basic business and to lose a few of its bureaucratic layers, but we had achieved little to advance the AIM market in Italy, on which the Italian Finance Ministry had set such store. Recession and the Italian distaste for paying taxes remained a problem but everything changed with the appointment of Massimo Tononi as Chairman and Raffaele Jerusalmi as CEO in 2011 and the increasing inability of the Italian banks to lend anyone money. Rafi and Massimo designed the ELITE programme, a shelter and training ground for smaller companies who are cautiously considering exposing their business to the open market, weighing up the advantages of getting cash into the business and monetising their assets against the horrors of having to produce proper accounts and pay tax on their profits. A steady trickle, rapidly becoming a stream, of excellent craft-led Italian companies is being floated on AIM ITALIA, and the ELITE programme is now launched in the UK, a fine example of an improvement made abroad being re-imported back to the mother ship.

And I was there and pushing hard for the deal in 2013 when we succeeded in buying the other half of the FTSE index, which was owned equally between us and Pearsons. In 2012 Pearsons sold us their half for what the City described demurely as a full price; at a key moment in anxious discussions about whether it was Too Much to Pay I made an impassioned and influential case for the deal on the basis that the potential benefit from having the whole company meant it didn't much matter what we paid. I did not foresee quite what a dazzling success this purchase would turn out to be; it brought us an immensely able manager from Pearsons who, liberated from having to deal with two owners, got us to fund the purchase of several index companies in the USA, which successfully expanded the group far far beyond its original base, and nearly doubled its size.

My term at Management Consulting ended in 2011. I had had to miss two Board meetings in 2010 because they involved flying to our HQ in the USA, impossible for me before the ablation fixed my heart condition. My chairman, Alan, was good enough to say that I was still very important to him and the group but neither of us thought I was irreplaceable, so we agreed that I should leave at the 2011 AGM, just before my seventy-first birthday.

I assumed, after being apparently seriously ill in both 2009 and 2010 and being rescued by the NHS in both cases, that good luck would always attend me, but that turned out not to be true. One icy day in January 2013 I was running late so I set off on the bicycle rather than on my feet. I hopped to get on as I have always done since my father taught me to ride a bike when I was 6, but there was ice on the sole of my left boot, which slipped across the pedal and toppled me and the bike backwards. I fell like a sack of potatoes with the bike on top of me, shattering my left hip so badly that it had to be replaced in its entirety.

I had injured myself on a Friday afternoon at the same time as a nasty collision on the notorious A14, so I had to wait 48 hours for the necessary operation; it turns out that even major hospitals like Addenbrooke's do not have surgeons who can replace whole hips on duty at weekends. By Saturday night my temperature and blood pressure were both soaring and I was diagnosed with a full-scale pulmonary embolism. The operation went ahead on Monday but because of the embolism my kidneys had to be protected, which meant inserting a wire through the groin, attached to a wire umbrella which would catch and break up any wandering blood clots. Neither procedure, the surgeon explained, was without risk of blood poisoning, bacterial infection, further embolism, or Death.

The operation itself was uneventful. The wire protecting the kidneys was removed equally routinely through my neck a week later, clutching a blood clot in its wire paws just to show it had been working. I did the exercises and was soon walking again, but my right hip, already afflicted with osteoarthritis, started to hurt, and my left knee, injured many years before but kept quiescent by careful exercise, joined in.

Eleven weeks after the fall, I went to Mrs Thatcher's funeral. I got myself to St Paul's Cathedral via the Stock Exchange for a cup of coffee and a rest and finally joined a small huddle of Opposition politicians in the North Transept, sitting between (Baroness) Helene Hayman, the first Speaker of the House of Lords, and an old friend, (Lord) Paddy Ashdown, erstwhile leader of the Liberal Democrats. The Conservative part of the audience – naturally most of it – had settled in some time before and were catching up with friends and not just having a picnic lunch, though I did think I heard the rustle of sandwich paper. The tribute by the Bishop of London (Richard Chartres) was memorable; he reminded us all that Lady Thatcher came by her iconoclast ideas partly from her lifelong adherence to the Methodist Church, which throughout the nineteenth and much of the twentieth centuries had campaigned against slavery, child labour and exploitation of the working class, all of which the Church of England had accepted as the natural order of things.

I went because I had wanted to acknowledge a remarkable woman, and at the reception I found George Robertson huddled together with a handful of Labour colleagues. We all ran into flak later from fellow Party members, which seemed to me churlish, though it was ever thus. I remember contemporaries of my grandfather refusing on political grounds to go to Winston Churchill's funeral in 1963.

I struggled through the rest of 2013, still trying to get back to normal, but my diary for Christmas Day 2013, which we spent in Antigua with all the family, records that I was in pain in several different places, and suffering from night sweats and sleeping badly. An operation for carpal tunnel syndrome early in 2014 fixed the severe pain in my right hand and Jim and I went off to the

USA to see our friends Anne and Chris Widnell, partly to get a holiday by ourselves and partly because Anne had had another setback. The pain got steadily worse and spread itself all over and when we got back I ran for medical help. I tested negative for everything but in the end all agreed that it was a version of arthritis and I was put on low doses of steroids and an immuno-suppressant, Methotrexate.

In the same year I had my left knee replaced. It had been giving trouble for years and it turned out on X-ray that I had no cartilage left. The knee is still swollen and while logically I cannot have arthritis in an artificial joint, it feels as if I do, but it is stable. I was just getting myself back into shape in 2015 when, walking on flat ground by myself near our Welsh cottage while Jim was walking in the high hills in September, I fell on to a rock, breaking my right femur. I was greatly fortunate; a young couple were near enough to hear me scream, the land ambulance arrived quickly and their people kept me warm and fed me morphine until the Air/Sea rescue helicopter arrived to pick me up and deposit me and Jim at Bangor hospital, both of us in what we stood up in plus in Jim's case a mobile phone and a credit card.

It was a fascinating experience. The nursing staff at Bangor were local women, mostly living in Caernarvon. The clinical staff were almost entirely Indian, either born in the UK or resident here ever since they had finished their clinical training in the sub-continent. The NHS could not manage without them but their own country must feel their absence. I also understood how varied the experience in different parts of the UK must be; the Bangor clinicians assumed that in Cambridge we were well funded with lots of space in our hospitals, and I had to explain when they tried to send me back to Addenbrooke's that there would not be a bed, and to get myself dispatched to a private hospital. We paid to get me back in the tiny helicopter which normally collects casualties from the Welsh roads.

Getting a roof over our heads in Cambridge also proved difficult. By August 2010 we realised that work on the conversion of our Cambridge house had inexplicably slowed down. The long-standing Cambridge builder whom we had chosen for their experience in conservation work went into administration, dragged there by a property venture in Gibraltar. An awkward choice faced us; the conversion was less than half-way through, but a national contractor had bought the firm out of administration and offered to complete the job. Our architect David Yandell offered to try and complete the contract by taking on the sub-contractors and using the resources of Feilden+Mawson. We should have asked him to do that, but decided not to. Jim was still heavily deployed as executive chairman of Empower, NED of Implenia, the largest Swiss contractor, and NED of Office2Office, which constituted full-time employment and I was ill, so neither of us could have been Assistant Project Manager. The new contractor discovered that they could not complete the works at a profit and refused to pay the existing sub-contractors the full amount they were owed, with the predictable result that the work was either finished grudgingly or not at all. The contract ran six months late, the contractor sued for a huge sum in Extras for poorly completed works, and matters reached the point where I thought I would have to prise Jim's hands from the neck of the regional manager. I was being pusillanimous but no lawyer wants to go to court. We have spent a lot of the intervening years since we got back in the house late in 2010 getting in our long-standing small builder, M.J.Salmon, to fix things; old friends as they are, they look just perceptibly smug as they tidy up yet another piece of careless workmanship.

Isobel provided a welcome bright spot. Despite counselling she and Nick had decided in 2009 that they could not marry and she had sold her share of the house to him. She joined the Lucy Cavendish College in October 2009 and lived in college, next to the building site that was our house, until September 2010 when she arrived as the first occupant of the barely completed student flat we had carved out as part of the conversion.

Francis and Dianne Small in 2007.

We had gone again to New Zealand to see Dianne and Francis Small in 2010 and in 2011 they came to Europe, to join us on a Baltic cruise. Francis, who had held out against the onset of Parkinson's for many years, was becoming less mobile and had decided to try a cruise. It worked well; it was a small ship and Dianne had taught Jim and me how to help Francis up. (You must not just tug or you risk dislocating a shoulder so the trick is to stand facing on either side of the person you are helping to rise, hook an arm under each of theirs and stand up. Works every time.) The cruise was terrific and the sightseeing a lot of fun. Francis mostly walked but if he tired Jim would move him in the wheelchair.

We met again a couple of weeks later in Orkney. It was a bit late in the season but they were charmed by Orkney. This group of islands was settled with people in little houses growing crops and trading with their neighbours by the fifth century BC. The climate was better then and the northern trading routes were of key importance. William the Conqueror's armies reached Orkney not long after the battle of Hastings and twenty years after that William Rufus built the red sandstone St Magnus cathedral to stamp their imprint on the place. Mary Queen of Scots' half-brother Robert was given the earldom of Orkney together with its castle nearly 500 years later. Visitors stare at these substantial buildings, wondering what they are doing so far from the world, but Orkney was an important place for a long time. My mother's Budge family comes from there, the name appears all over the islands and somewhere in the early nineteenth century some of them travelled down to Caithness; an entry in the parish records for 1848 shows five Budge brothers in the county town, all called by the names still used in the family: Jock, Douglas, Wheems, Eric (the Viking influence is strong in the islands) and Alistair and George.

Isobel got a First in her Prelims in 2010 while doing a lot of other things including the movement and choreography for the Marlowe Society's *As You Like It*. She also choreographed and produced one of the two dances commissioned by the University as part of its 800 years celebration. There she met Ewan Campbell, charged with composing the music for the other dance, who had a First from King's, London, in music, a Masters from King's, Cambridge, and was working for his PhD at King's, London, and, warily, she agreed to lunch with him. Weeks later, without having been allowed to meet him, we realised this might be serious. Isobel persuaded him to get a part-time teaching job, and we were confirmed in our view when he arrived from London early in 2011 with most of his possessions, explaining that he had come to see Isobel through the revision for her Part I exams. We opened up and furnished the big attic room as a sitting room for them but in practice they lived with us downstairs and Ewan worked for his PhD in a centrally heated, carpeted garret with en suite bathroom and view of garden.

Isobel did indeed get a First in Part I in 2011 at the same time as she was planning and choreographing a new mixed media dance/drama show for the Edinburgh Festival and writing and directing a play which won the University prize. She has always fitted a lot in but her third and final year was nearly to undo her. She found she was pregnant, with the baby due on the first day of her final exams. She and Ewan decided that however dreadful the timing the baby took precedence over all else, and in February 2012 they married and on May 23 2012 the much-treasured Beatrice Silke Eriskay, the first grandchild in both the Cohen and the Campbell families, was born in Addenbrooke's two days before her mother's final exams. Isobel got her First in Finals, doing two exams in hospital and the Chaucer paper still suffering from acute pain from one misplaced stitch, from college, lying on her side on a chaise longue while we and a maternity nurse waited next door with the baby. With the enthusiastic assistance of the Lucy Cavendish she set out to get maximum publicity for this staggering feat and she and Beatrice were heavily featured in national newspapers and magazines as well as local radio and TV.

The new family lived with us for the next seven months while their house ten minutes away was being taken apart, extended by 12 feet and put together again in the usual Cohen style. They managed to get into it two days before Christmas 2012, fractionally ahead of Ewan's immediate family and their partners coming to stay in both houses. Shortly afterwards, Ewan's PhD thesis was, unusually, accepted without alteration, so he is Dr Campbell.

Isobel had one more shot at keeping her career as a contemporary choreographer and dancer alive; in May 2013 when Bea was a year old she revived her dance drama about the Stasi era – a truly original and convincing piece of work – and took it with the assistance of Arts Council cash to the Recklinghausen festival. We made the usual parental contribution whereby we housed the cast and production team for four weeks, and put in a bit of cash to ensure that Isobel could have a German dancer to replace herself rather than being Producer and Director as well as lead dancer. We went out there with the production. It didn't attract the audience in Recklinghausen that it should have, although, as in Edinburgh in 2011, people wept and came to thank Isobel afterwards.

She decided however that at least for the moment a career in the arts was not sufficiently rewarding, either emotionally or financially, and got a job in recruiting for all four of the Cambridge colleges that take undergraduates aged twenty-one and over, a big part of the University's diversity agenda. She was very successful; I had feared that her privately-educated background would be a handicap but she has the gift of empathy and was able to help and guide people who might never have considered applying to Cambridge through the admission procedures. It is a job which calls for sound judgement; there is no point encouraging people to apply who will struggle with their selected course, because either they will be discouraged by failing to get in or, even worse, fail to keep up if they are admitted.

She then spent eighteen months working for Nigel Brown as the administrator and fund-raiser for his Stradivari Trust. In the end this suited neither of them and they parted, so in 2015 she applied for Deputy Development Director for Fitzwilliam College, of which my brother Alexander was an early graduate. There were candidates with more direct and relevant experience and she did not expect to get it and her expectations were further diminished by the day of the interview when she knew that she was just pregnant again. To Fitzwilliam's lasting credit they overcame their worries and gave her the job. Their courage was rewarded. Isobel was instantly successful, finding herself able to get a key part of the funding to start to redo and restore seven staircases of student rooms designed by the late Denys Lasdun, friend of my father and godfather to her Uncle Giles. She is very good at fund-raising, clever, innovative and persistent, using all her, and our, networks to rally Fitzwilliam alumni who have not yet contributed as well as those who have and might do more. She is even better at sorting out the Department's IT system and, as one of her colleagues said wonderingly after she had been there a year, no one could remember a time when she was not there. The baby, our much loved grandson, Arran Henry, was born in October 2015 without incident but turned out to have inherited the infantile eczema which runs in both families, and his diet has been challenging because he is allergic to milk and eggs, but he is a lively, cheerful little boy, adored by all.

Ewan, with his PhD safely under his belt, gave up his part-time teaching job to try to combine composing with working as a music director and general musical entrepreneur. In 2015 he did a very well-received gig at the Wilderness Festival, recruiting a 45-piece orchestra to play his own adaptations of the Radiohead hits. It attracted an audience of 5,000, in refreshing contrast to the contemporary dance or contemporary music concert which gets around 50 people on a good night.

Jim continued to work about four days a week until 2013 and then found himself working six days a week when he took over the Chair at Office2Office, the small quoted company where he had been an NED since 2006. David Callear, the Chairman, had had to give up because his wife Pat, diagnosed with motor neurone disease a few months earlier, was going downhill fast and needed her husband at home. The company was in difficulty; the share price was in the pits and its shareholders wanted out. Jim managed over ten months' unremittingly hard work, on top of his existing commitments, to keep the company on the road and achieved a sale at 190 per cent of the share price. Tough, equable and very experienced as he is, he found that age was taking its toll and he found stressful negotiations which he could have done without breaking sweat in his early sixties exhausted and worried him in his early seventies.

He survived the experience, though it was almost a year before he felt fully well again. He took a job chairing Green Africa Power, a government company charged with spending £100 million plus on helping entrepreneurs and governments develop environmentally friendly power supplies in sub-Saharan Africa, interesting, difficult work involving judgements about putting in enough subsidy to persuade a promoter to build a hydro-electric or wind-powered substation rather than the ubiquitous polluting gas equivalent. He did the same, though as a Board member rather than Chairman, for the German government fund GETFIT, restricted to Kenya and Uganda. He was hired as an adviser to DIFF, a Dutch infrastructure investment fund, in 2010, and is still there, advising on their latest new fund, in 2018.

Henry continued in his chosen way of life as a very successful one-man management consultancy. It is a very good mind; an email received from him in English contains no superfluous word and he is never short of work. Our daughter-in-law Silke continued to work as a supervising pharmacist for a sizeable drug production company; she is immensely experienced and conscientious and she kept – and continues to keep – her employer from the kind of errors common in production. She looks after three of the family horses, including the beloved and now retired Pharos, and a lively dog called Ellie acquired from a rescue charity, part Labrador, part dachshund and with terrier ears. Pharos and Ellie are still with them, as are two different horses.

Richard, who had decided to be called Dickie, went back to his first love, organising music festivals. He liked Feilden+Mawson but did not want to be their business manager and chief salesman. It might have been different if he were an architect but it is a long training and he did not want to be a student again in his mid-30s. He had been spending his holidays helping at festivals and parlayed that experience, his project-managing skills and his gifts as a salesman into a full-time job in 2010. He became part of the company that ran the Wilderness Festival near Oxford which they grew to 30,000 people in 2015. He married in 2015, not long after his 40th birthday, a lovely young woman Jessica Ince, who runs her own successful corporate events company. If you want a really good party for 300 sales representatives in a new and interesting place, Jess is the girl to do it for you.

I was still Chairman of the Cambridge Arts Theatre until the summer of 2015. The theatre flourished; a jewel among regional theatres for its programming and its much increased audience. We had hoped to raise enough money to turn ourselves into a major arts centre, with a studio theatre as well, but the recession put paid to those plans and in 2013 Dave decided we could wait no longer to refurbish the bar facilities and came up with a plan to open up the wasted space on the ground and first floors (involving propping up two mediaeval buildings and shifting a staircase over to the side) and to replace all the bars so that we could sell drinks at a speed which would, finally, enable the audience to have a drink *and* visit the loos in the interval. Dave himself got a small works grant from the Arts Council. King's College, as our landlords rightly impressed by Dave's capability, which had turned a worrying loss-making responsibility into a free-standing source of pride, agreed to put up the bulk of the rest in return for an increased rent, and Jim and I led a list of personal donors to make up the balance.

The refurbishment required initially a ten-week closure during the slack summer period in 2013. It overran by several weeks, inevitably, and the dinner party on stage in September 2013 to celebrate the re-opening did not go entirely to plan. The distinguished audience was escorted onto the stage by theatre staff armed with torches and the promised tour involved guests being led up scaffolding and shown several different building sites, floodlit for the occasion. We only just managed to avert the Health and Safety requirement for all of us to be clad in safety boots, helmets and high-vis jackets on top of our evening dress. Mine and Dave's speeches of welcome and thanks necessarily radiated confidence; our staff, who had put up with three months' worth of noise and dust in the offices and knew full well there was more to come, loyally kept their faces straight. The Globe touring theatre opened four days later with all three parts of *Henry VI*, fortunately with a cast of only nine rather than the twenty-five required in the play. The Globe does not use three actors where it can manage with one with a change of doublet or a new frock over the lot, so the fact that the paint in the Green Room was still wet was less of a concern than it might have been. The refurbishment finished under budget *and* despite the summer closure we made a surplus of £140,000 that year.

We held a strategy conference in January 2014 after the refurbishment, facilitated by (Baroness) Genista McIntosh, who had been deputy Chief Executive of the National Theatre and of Covent Garden in her years of full-time employment and is one of the most valued opinions on any point of running an arts organisation. She had been at the dinner and peered at the floodlit building site and was suitably impressed by the finished product. But she led us to agree that we could not rest on our considerable laurels; opening up the building to the light and installing new bars had revealed that the auditorium, restored in the mid-1990s, was looking tired, to put it kindly. The sound and the lighting equipment are even more in need of attention; any breakdown in the sound deck finds us advertising on eBay for 1990s computers which we can cannibalise, and the archaic lighting systems have been saved from failure only by a generous anonymous donation.

At BPP, we passed our six-year inspection in 2013 with flying colours, we gained the right to use the full university title, and I became Chancellor rather than President with two Deputy Chancellors, my old friend Martyn Jones, who was also Head of the Academic Council, and (Lord) Chris Holmes, the blind ex-Paralympian swimmer and part-architect of the 2012 Paralympic Games, who was trained and taught at BPP.

This period also saw three major losses. Margot, my right hand from 1993 to 2010, died late in 2013 after a long battle with bowel cancer. She was one of the nicest women I ever met and competent at everything but her upbringing had left her with very little self-confidence. She came when I was 53 and she 54 and stayed until I was 70 and she 71 and too ill to continue. She only told me she was a year older than I when I told her we must start a pension scheme for her and she had to confess to her age. She had never told me because she feared I might think her too old to be working for me. I was incredulous but did I hope convince her that she was the mainstay of the household, and I the envy of my contemporaries for having her.

Margot Morris.

331

In a house containing two people with demanding jobs a lot of help is needed just to maintain the basic amenities of life, like shopping, cooking, cleaning and laundry. It might have been possible to find someone to do all that, but Margot also did all the human tasks like receiving the teenage Isobel and Richard back from school with cups of tea and a warm welcome, and also acting as a PA and general support for me. I recognised some of her contribution by paying her properly, providing holiday and sick pay and paying tax and National Insurance for her when we started to employ her for longer hours, which she valued not least because she would have found it very difficult to *ask* for these basics of employment.

She became part of me: she coped from time to time with my brothers when their lives fell apart. Alexander lived with us for six months in 1997 when his last marriage and last business collapsed and it was Margot who often cheered him up with cups of tea and a good lunch while I was off working. Giles lived with us in 1993, the first summer Margot was working for us, and she was one of the people who saw him through the breakdown that in the end restored his marriage.

She took on the care of my mother as well. Mum was rational in all things except when it came to getting proper help and life changed for her when Margot offered to be her daily help; Mum loved her and relied on her and Margot was able with great delicacy to tell me what she thought I ought to know, like the fact that the flat was slowly silting up with old newspapers or that the fridge was working only intermittently or that the neighbour's tom was beating up Mum's treasured cat. Margot was the last person to visit Mum in hospital, with me.

In 2015 Isobel and I went to the funeral of my much-loved and missed executive coach, Mike Milan, who had collapsed in September 2014 actually on the way to an appointment with Isobel, who he was also coaching. It was a brain tumour, which finally killed him early in 2015. He had advised and counselled me from 1994 until 2014. We had just decided his work was done as I retired from my principal jobs but for the rest of our lives (he was six months younger than I) we planned to lunch together twice a year because neither of us wanted the relationship to end. He was a wonderful man, all 6'5" of him, of mixed Central European descent but English to the bone, who sailed small boats as a recreation and did good to all who were counselled by him. My world is narrower without him.

In January 2015 came the third loss. Chris Widnell, friend of my youth, Cambridge contemporary and husband of Anne, one of my best Cambridge friends, died of a stomach aneurysm. I had difficulty in absorbing the news when Anne rang me. She had been ill in 2014 when we had gone out to see them in South Carolina, got better, then contracted septicaemia over that Christmas. But it was Chris, not Anne, who had died; Chris who took trouble to keep himself fit because he was Anne's carer and lifeline, and who was wont to bully me about having the kind of checkups and tests that Professors of Biochemistry in the USA have and we in the UK regard as a fuss. We went out for the Memorial to Chris in April 2015 and were as useful as we could manage to be to Anne, but it was a terrible loss to her and to their children.

*The Cohen family at Janet's 70th birthday party
at the House of Lords, 2010.*

Chapter 22

2016 to 2018

Like my mother I always want to know what happened to the various people in the stories I have been telling so I shall assume anyone reading this is the same.

I am finally retired in this my 79th year. I have made a good recovery from the various physical problems I had, but it is still painful to walk despite the painkillers. It requires careful stretch exercises to keep mobile and once again a really good Pilates teacher is coming to my rescue. And I had another scare in 2017 when I started to suffer with dizzy fits. Finally it was established that it was heart trouble (again) and I have had a pacemaker installed. None of this is life-threatening and it seems likely I shall live into my nineties.

We are however having to adjust our lives earlier than we had planned; with me mostly confined to ladylike deadheading, the garden threatens to overwhelm us. The house is too big, but we have not found anywhere else we want to be and so are managing, mostly by spending money. Once we had accepted that my hill-walking days were over we sold our much-loved but dilapidated Welsh cottage, and handed over our share in the Scottish cottage to Isobel. The old family friends to whom we sold in Wales turned it into a wonderfully comfortable modern holiday cottage where we can still stay, so that too has ended well.

After eleven years as Chancellor of BPP University I have handed over to my friend and colleague (Lord) Chris Holmes. The organisation has changed in other ways. My loved ex-colleague, Martyn Jones, still chairs the Academic Council and has been able, with the assistance of experienced colleagues like David Holmes, to ensure that the regulators were happy to award the full university title in 2013 and that the place remains a model of professional education, with a widespread reputation among senior business people and politicians, which stood me in good stead when working on the Higher Education Bill in 2017. Carl Lygo, our distinguished CEO, who has moved on after nearly twenty years with the Group, sits on the board of the regulator as well as doing his new day job. Peter Crisp, Head of the Law School, has also moved on. Both have been replaced by internal appointments and Tim Stewart is now CEO of the University, which continues to flourish. We have 20,000 students, 6,000 of them undergraduates, and we get stunning results. I do the odd Graduation ceremony and advise and help where I can. We are leading players in the growth of degree-level apprenticeships and I was heavily involved in the debate and scrutiny of both the Higher Education Bill 2017 and the Technical and Further Education Act 2017. I am our first and only Honorary Patron.

I retired in 2013 from LSEG and in 2014 from the Borsa Italiana. The group, which when I joined in 2001 had been about a quarter the size of the mighty Deutsche Börse, had grown to the point where it was able to negotiate a merger in April 2016, with LSEG taking 44 per cent of the merged group. The deal never happened, derailed by the Brexit vote and, I am told, by the French (as always) pushing their luck by trying to detach the Italian clearing and settlement business, the very core of the Italian banking system. The LSEG is an important national infrastructure asset and if I were PM I would legislate for a Golden Share which would prevent ownership ever going outside the UK.

I am also, following my retirement in 2015, Honorary President of the Cambridge Arts Theatre. Just as there is no such thing as a free lunch, there is no such thing as an Honorary President; one works for the title and I am to be involved in raising the £5m odd we need for the Auditorium Project. I am also on the Board of a multi-academy trust here in Cambridge. The trust has taken over one of the university technical colleges set up by old colleagues – the Lords Baker and Dearing – and I am Deputy Chair of that too.

And I am the one at the end of the bench, as my aunt and godmother Grizel, who died in 2017 aged 95, used to say. She was the only survivor of my parents' generation and I am the oldest of the current crop of Neel and Budge grandchildren.

Giles has the same seronegative arthritis and is on the same medication as I am, and he has just had to have his left knee done. He remains in the south of France, surrounded by loving family, and I wish we lived nearer to each other.

My brother Alexander died unexpectedly on September 30 2018. He had been suffering from vascular dementia probably since 2002 though none of us realised that until 2005 when a young doctor at Charing Cross Hospital, assuming I knew already, mentioned it casually. He was never well after about 2001 but lasted, with carers, in his little flat until 2015, when Charing Cross, looking at the amount of time he was spending with them, insisted he go into a nursing home. He was content there. I could not bear to take the flat back under the terms of our agreement without knowing that he would not need it. It fell to my niece-in-law Victoria, a neurosurgical registrar, to ask him if he missed the flat. Goodness no, he said, looking startled, while nephew Luke, who had not realised his wife was going to ask this radical question, tried to escape from the room.

In the later years none of us – me, Matthew, Luke – felt we had done more than the minimum of care or visiting. Ally always knew us but forgot instantly that we had been there. All of us including brother Giles were unexpectedly knocked sideways; it had been, we confessed to each other, our worst nightmare that he would live on in the home till his nineties like my grandfather, but we were still devastated, remembering the gifted, endlessly energetic star he had once been. We assembled as many of his old friends as we could find and the funeral and party afterwards were both poignant but soothing and we were able to bring back, at the end, something of the brilliant man he had been.

His sons were a pleasure to him; Matthew Neel has used years of experience in catering to start a wildly successful enterprise near Tufnell Park in North London, the Bear + Wolf café, decor by talented wife Juliette, cunningly set up as a haven for middle-class parents and children, with a playroom at the back, and designed with the help of their lovely eight-year-old daughter Lorelei. It gives me particular pleasure because it is a version of the success Matthew's father and I had in the 1970s, only this time Matthew, a careful man, is going to capitalise on it and make it endure. Luke Neel, who is a partner in a small company, is making a good living, has a house in South London, a doctor wife Victoria and two children.

Jim is also retiring; Green Africa Power was folded into a larger group but he remains on a subsidiary Board. He continues to do

336

the investment committee for a major Dutch infrastructure group. We are both conscious that we are lucky to have each other and no life-threatening diseases, and we are removing the commitments that cut down our leisure time.

Henry and Silke continue in their chosen paths and we spent time with them last summer as well as several weekends – Henry drove us round East Germany, which was fascinating. The East remains quite underpopulated and depressed, reflected in its support for the far-right party Alternative für Deutschland.

Dickie is now an international consultant adviser on where to site or how to structure a festival as a holiday place, and is working on a new career in property development, while Jess continues in her career of organising corporate events. Sadly they lost their first baby, taking the brave decision to terminate a pregnancy in 2015, and we will remember the lost Arlo Swift Lionel Cohen on August 11. There is a happier ending; Cecelie Rae Sirocco Ince-Cohen was born on December 15 2017, received with joy by all of us.

Isobel, now 39, says she has enough children and has taken a new job, raising funds for the major conservation charities attached to the University, which is where she found she meant to be, although she was sad to say goodbye to the good colleagues at Fitzwilliam College. Ewan won the 2017 competition to write a ten-minute piece for the LSO and it formed part of a concert this year where it was very well received. He has now done three successful gigs for Wilderness, playing his own arrangements with a 43-piece orchestra, and three well-paid gigs organised by Jess for corporate events with a somewhat smaller orchestra. And he has just got the sort of job he has always wanted, the Director of Music for Churchill and Murray Edwards Colleges, and acquired a brass band and a chapel choir as part of his empire.

Of our other friends and family, the shadows are closing around our loved friend Francis Small who has staved off Parkinson's disease for fifteen years. We went out to see him and Dianne early in 2016, taking a long time in travelling to accommodate me, my broken leg and the arthritis, and it was wonderful to see him. He is more crippled than I but from the moment we fell into each other's arms at Wellington airport none of it mattered. We had a good time, going out every day for lunch, but it was all too clearly an effort for Francis and, as Dianne had feared, he is now in long-term care. Characteristically that strong couple had understood that Dianne was risking her own health and have found a good nursing home for him close to home.

Connie Sattler too is gone; she died earlier last year, having effectively been Jim's sister since her arrival as a Kindertransport child in 1939, so she was there to greet him when he was born in 1942. We went to her Memorial in Connecticut and had her daughter Val and husband Wolfie to stay last year.

A very unexpected blow came with the death of Mark Sebba. He had an immensely successful career as CEO of Net-a-Porter. I had last seen him in 2013 when he came to Cambridge and I urged him to retire, which he did and collected an enviable set of part-time directorships. I felt – and told him so – that he had done it all right, but he died, untimely and much mourned, this year, aged 69.

I am 78, and when you look at the statistics which suggest that the average life expectancy is rocketing up into the 80s, rattling governments and insurance companies alike, I do wonder if they are correct. In the last three years Jim and I have lost my brother and three close friends and many acquaintances and friends of our own age who are part of the architecture of our life, in their late sixties to mid-seventies, all people who have looked after themselves and benefited from modern medicine. Of the four of us who came up to Newnham in 1959, Heather is dead these fifteen years, Anne is more crippled than I and without Chris has had to move into an assisted living facility in Washington, where we visited her last summer. Jenny died in February 2019 after ten years of devoted support from her partner Edward Mayhew. They had meant to marry but a series of mini-strokes took her. Perhaps it is that all of us have lived much harder lives than our parents but from where I sit there is something in the Biblical view that our lifespan is threescore years and ten and after that you are struggling.

Writing this has helped me to draw some conclusions about how I have arrived at where I am. I had a privileged education, and Cambridge furnished me with a network of good friends in politics, banking and the law. But I always knew I needed a career and chose my path accordingly. I am the daughter of a widow and unwilling to depend on anyone but myself. I was nearly deflected from this course by my first marriage to a man who was going to earn enough to keep me and a family and who would always have wanted my full attention. But he left me, and I was back on course.

I have been kept there by the continuing and ungrudging support of my much-loved husband Jim whose life and career have had to change to accommodate my needs; he gave up international commercial negotiations in 1982, much to his employer GEC's regret, and, offered the MD job he so much wanted outside of London in 1988, he turned it down because I could not move from London, and there are plenty of other examples.

My mother always cheered me on and was of practical help when all was chaos in the early child-rearing years; the nanny sick, the cleaner away, Jim abroad and me with a meeting to go to, she would appear, tell me to go to work, now, and we would improvise from there. This kind of steady unquestioning support from the generation above is of immense importance; it validates what working mothers are trying to do.

My brothers made a vital contribution too. Burdened by mental illness, neither of them ever grudged me my success or been less than supportive. I learned from them how to work in the male-dominated workplaces that those of us born in the War inherited. Alexander was the one to see the point first, watching me deal with the restaurant accountants: he observed that I treated all men as if they were him and Giles and that meant that working men could treat me as a sister. He is right; a close relationship with supportive, intelligent and generous brothers is a very good template for sound working relationships in a male world.

If I had to do it again, however, I might do it differently. Rather than knocking myself out – and giving the children less of me than we all wanted – I would have worked part-time or perhaps have started my own business as clever women do these days. But the children are kind enough to say they would not have had me do otherwise, and it has been an interesting and privileged working life. And I fear I was always too anxious about money to have been able to accept the huge risks involved in starting a business.

I am often asked what were the key decisions that have enabled me to lead the life I have. At risk of sounding like Polonius (I have always believed that Hamlet stabbed him in order to avoid ever having to sit through 'Neither a borrower nor a lender be ...' again) the advice I always give is to get a professional qualification. It sounds old-fashioned in days where seventeen-year-olds can set up a multimillion internet business from their mother's spare room but it worked for me, and I believe it is particularly important for women. I have never worked formally as a solicitor nor held a practising certificate but time after time the qualification has enabled me to branch into a new life. I had the best job in the rescue squad in the Department of Industry because I knew about receivership and debt. I know that when I was headhunted into a bank, my sponsor's colleagues wondered aloud about what to *do* with me if it wasn't a success. Stewart told me years later that he had reminded them that I was a solicitor, and all the worried faces cleared as they realised (correctly) that I could be deployed on someone else's deals if I could find none of my own to do. Similarly, anyone in those benighted days who might have wondered whether a female person would be able to deal with the statutory obligations attaching to a director of a public company closed their mouths on that question because I was, and am, a Solicitor of the Supreme Court of Justice. So get a qualification, particularly if you are female; it is the way through to major careers and to good part-time jobs if that is what you need. I am sure accountancy training would have worked as well, but it has to be the full professional qualification. No one is particularly impressed by a degree; everyone is impressed by a full qualification, and so I tell young women and their anxious parents whenever asked. In these days I would also recommend Engineering; everyone wants engineers, particularly female engineers. And all of us should follow the advice given by my late loved friend and executive coach, Mike Milan, that you must always look after the horse – namely your health and sanity – first, because, like the heavily armoured crusader knight who was useless without something to carry him into battle, you are no use without these essential props.

The next generation: (back row) Janet, Jim, Silke, Henry, Cecilie and Jess,
Ewan; (front row) Isobel, Beatrice, Rudi (the whippet), Dickie, Arran.

CPSIA information can be obtained
at www.ICGtesting.com
Printed in the USA
BVHW081043040919
557540BV00021B/999/P